ARISTOTELIAN LOGIC

ARISTOTELIAN LOGIC

William T. Parry
and
Edward A. Hacker

State University of New York Press

Published by
State University of New York Press, Albany

© 1991 State University of New York

All rights reserved

Printed in the United States of America

No part of this book may be used or reproduced
in any manner whatsoever without written permission
except in the case of brief quotations embodied in
critical articles and reviews.

For information, address State University of New York
Press, State University Plaza, Albany, N.Y., 12246

Library of Congress Cataloging-in-Publication Data

Parry, William T. (William Thomas), 1917–
    Aristotelian logic / William T. Parry and Edward A. Hacker.
      p. cm.
    Includes index.
    ISBN 0-7914-0689-X (alk. paper).—ISBN 0-7914-0690-3 (pbk. :
alk. paper)
    1. Logic.   I. Hacker, Edward A., 1930– . II. Title.
BC71.P377 1991
160—dc20   90-44126
                                                                             CIP

10 9 8 7 6 5 4 3 2 1

This book is dedicated to the memory of the senior author, William T. Parry. Perfection was his standard and truth his goal.

Contents

Preface ix

I. Basic Concepts of Logic

1. Arguments and Validity 3
2. Propositions 23
3. Logical Form and Counterexamples 37
4. Terms 51
5. Definition 79
6. Division and Classification 129

II. Basic Concepts of Aristotelian Logic

7. Standard Categorical Propositions 145
8. The Traditional Square of Opposition 155
9. Existential Presuppositions of Aristotelian Logic 179
10. Distribution of Terms in Categorical Propositions 189
11. Conversion 205

III. Immediate Inferences Not Needed for Standard Syllogism

12. Negative Terms 215
13. Obversion 227

14.	Contraposition	233
15.	Inversion and Partial Inversion	239
16.	Tables of Immediate Inferences	245
17.	Relations	249
18.	Reversible and Non-Reversible Inferences	261

IV. Aristotelian Logic: Mediated Inferences

19.	The Standard Syllogism: Definitions	265
20.	A Deductive System of the Standard Syllogism	271
21.	Rules of the Standard Syllogism	291
22.	Chain Arguments Including Sorites	309
23.	Reducing the Number of Terms in Arguments	319
24.	Singular Propositions	329
25.	Standardizing Categorical Propositions	339
26.	The Enthymeme	359
27.	The Antilogism for N-Pair Arguments	367
28.	The Hypothetical Syllogism	373
29.	The Disjunctive Syllogism	383
30.	The Dilemma	395

V. Informal Fallacies

31.	Proof and Fallacies	409
32.	Linguistic Fallacies	423
33.	Contextual Fallacies	443
34.	Illicit Appeals	463

VI. Transition to Symbolic Logic

35.	From Aristotelian to Symbolic Logic	491
Index		537

Preface

This text is designed for a one-semester course in traditional logic, but it may also be used in conjunction with a text on symbolic logic.

Modern logic texts tend to minimize traditional logic and many omit it entirely. The authors think that this is a mistake, that traditional logic contains many topics of value to the student, and that these topics are the theory of terms, the theory of definition, and the informal fallacies. We have taken care in this text to treat these topics in some detail.

From the theory of terms, the student learns techniques that are helpful in solving semantic problems; that is, problems caused by confusing the various meanings and usages of terms. From the theory of definition, students learn the different kinds of definitions and the criteria by which each is judged. They also learn that definitions are like tools in that some are better suited for particular tasks than others.

Four chapters in the text are devoted to informal fallacies, which reflect the authors' opinion that the informal fallacies should be an integral part of a course in introductory logic. In this section on informal fallacies a concept of proof is presented, without which some of the traditional informal fallacies cannot be adequately explained. This section also contains a classification of the informal fallacies, more thorough than usually found in a textbook.

The concept of logical form and use of counterexamples as a test for invalidity is presented early in the text. The deductive system of the standard syllogism is given as well as rules for testing the syllogism for validity. These rules also proved a test for sorites. A short chapter treats singular propositions and a chapter is devoted to ordinary language.

Due to the untimely death of the senior author, William T. Parry, this book was prepared for publication by the junior author, Edward A. Hacker.

The junior author also takes responsibility for chapter 15, chapters 26 through 30 inclusive, and chapter 35.

EDWARD A. HACKER

I

Basic Concepts of Logic

1

Arguments and Validity

1A LOGIC AS THE STUDY OF ARGUMENTS

This book is an introduction to deductive logic. The scientific study of logic began with Aristotle in the fourth century B.C. His impressive work, combined with other influences, is the foundation of a long tradition of logic that still continues. This tradition has taken diverse forms, but typically emphasizes the formal analysis of reasoning. Its technical language is the language of common discourse with certain modifications. This type of logic may be called "formal" logic; it is now more often called "Aristotelian logic" or "traditional logic".

Out of Aristotelian logic, and under the influence of mathematics, there developed a logic, even more formal, with special symbolism like that of mathematics. This is called "symbolic logic" or "mathematical logic". Since the creative work of De Morgan and Boole in the mid-nineteenth century, symbolic logic has flourished vigorously.

The first three chapters of this book are a general introduction, presenting concepts common to traditional and symbolic logic (without use of the special symbols of symbolic logic). With chapter 4, we follow mainly the line of traditional logic and continue that emphasis to chapter 35, (the last chapter) where we cross the bridge "From Aristotelian to Symbolic Logic".

1A1 Some Basic Concepts. Logic has sometimes been defined as "the science of reasoning". But this definition is too broad. Some psychologists study reasoning scientifically, investigating such subjects as the development of reasoning in the child, individual differences in reasoning ability, conditions favorable or unfavorable to reasoning, and so on. These studies are important, but are not in the province of logic. Logic is concerned rather with the evaluation of reasoning as it is expressed, particularly in arguments. In another way, the proposed definition of logic is too narrow (as we use the term). In application to concrete argument in ordinary discourse, logical judgments may lack scientific precision, so that logic in practice is an art rather than a science, just as the practice of medicine is an art though based upon medical science. A more complicated definition will serve better as our starting point, though it will require clarification here and in later chapters.

> **Def. 1. Logic*** is the science (and art) of evaluating and constructing arguments and systems of reasoning and studying their components, making use of such concepts as those of sentences, propositions, definitions, terms, etc.

For the present, we define just two of the terms in this definition: *proposition* and *argument*.

> **Def. 2.** A **proposition** is a sentence (or a clause that may be used as one) that, as taken with a specific meaning, is true or false.[1]

That every proposition is true or false is one formulation of the **law of excluded middle**. That no proposition is both true and false is the **law of contradiction**.

The sentence "If he is not at home, he is on his way home", as used in a given context, is a proposition to a person who understands English. It contains two clauses; with "if" deleted, each of these clauses is also a proposition. Any change in wording makes a different sentence and a different proposition. A change in meaning without change in wording makes a different proposition with the same sentence. Thus we have a different proposition if "he" means Hosiah Q. Terwilliger than if it means his brother Zachary. The one proposition might be true and the other false.

To a person who understands English, the following sentences would be propositions:

> (a) "George Washington was the first president of the United States".
>
> (b) "Abraham Lincoln was the second president of the United States".
>
> (c) "Some people are fond of cats and some people are fond of dogs".

---

*The key word in a definition is emphasized by boldfacing.

(d) "Exactly at noon (E.S.T.), 1 January 1940, there were exactly one trillion cockroaches on the planet Earth".

To a person who does not understand English or to a young child who does not know the meaning of all or some of the words in the above sentences, these sentences would not be propositions. It should be noted that it is not necessary to *know* that a sentence is true or to *know* that it is false in order to determine that the sentence is a proposition. All one has to know is that it is *either* true or false. Hence, sentence (d) above is a proposition, since the sentence is either true or false.

Sentences that function as questions, commands, or exclamations are not propositions, since they are neither true nor false. The following sentences are *not* propositions:

(e) "What is your name?"

(f) "Please shut the door."

(g) "Great balls of fire!"

Sentences that are propositions are generally declaratives, but not all declaratives are propositions. A declarative sentence that is not understood by a person is not a proposition to that person. Such declarative sentences may not be understood by a person because they are in a language not known by that person or because some word or words in the sentence are not understood. Also the declarative sentence may not be understood because the sentence literally has no meaning. Such nonsense sentences are not propositions, since they are neither true nor false.

Examples of declarative sentences that are neither true nor false, due to lack of meaning, are:

(h) "The square root of minus one snores redly."

(i) "Square curves float singingly sideward."

In this chapter we focus our attention on arguments. We need a definition such as the following:

Def. 3. An **argument** is a sequence of propositions that offers one or more propositions in the sequence as grounds or evidence for another proposition in the sequence.

An argument may or may not claim to give conclusive evidence for its conclusion. (See section 1B below).

An argument may also be considered as the verbal expression of a process of reasoning. An argument may be one compound proposition, for example, "I had $25 and spent just $2.50, so I have $22.50 left."

An argument is not one simple proposition. It contains two or more propositions, but not any set or sequence of propositions constitutes an argument. Nor does "an argument" in logic means a dispute between two people. Of course it is correct English—even if it is gossip—to say: "Mr. Jones had an argument with his wife". But this is not the way the word "argument" is used by a logician.

An argument is also not a sequence of propositions that recounts a series of events (narration), such as "The airplane skidded past the end of the runway. It hit a tree and exploded in a ball of orange flame. There were no survivors".

An argument is not a sequence of propositions that explains the nature of an idea or an object (exposition), such as "A dictionary is a book that explains the words of a given language. The words are listed alphabetically. The pronunciation, etymology, and grammatical usage of each word is also given".

Also an argument has to be distinguished from propositions that picture a setting, scene, object, or person (description), such as "The UFO was saucer shaped and about twenty feet in diameter. It was surrounded by a pulsating soft, white glow. Around its circumference were a row of portholes that emitted from its interior a dull red light".

An argument is often called an "inference", the latter term emphasizing the process of thought by which a conclusion is reached (i.e., inferred). The term "inference" is also applied to the conclusion of an argument, thought of as the result of the process.

>**Def. 4.** A **conclusion** of an argument is a proposition that is inferred from one or more propositions.

The other propositions in the argument, the propositions that are supposed to serve as evidence for the truth of the conclusion, are called "premisses".[2]

>**Def. 5.** A **premiss** of an argument is a proposition offered as grounds or evidence for the conclusion.

Every argument has a conclusion and at least one premiss. An argument may have any finite number of premisses. Some examples of arguments, though not necessarily good arguments, are:

(a) "Only if a solution is acid will blue litmus paper turn red when immersed in it. This piece of blue litmus paper turned red when I dipped it in this liquid. Therefore, this liquid is acid."

(b) "Jones and Smith are the only people who could have committed the murder; but Green testified that he and Smith were at the movies at the time of the murder, and Black testified that he was with Jones at the race track at the time of the murder. So either Green or Black is lying."

(c) "My girlfriend is redheaded and bad tempered; therefore all redheaded girls are bad tempered."

1A2 Identifying Conclusion and Premiss. One must identify the conclusion in an argument. This is absolutely necessary in order to analyze an argument. The conclusion is what the argument is trying to prove, so that if one does not identify the conclusion as such he misses the whole "point of the argument". The conclusions of the above arguments are, respectively:

(a) This liquid is an acid.

(b) Either Green or Black is lying.

(c) All redheaded girls are bad tempered.

Finding the conclusion is not a matter of luck. The English language often makes use of certain words and phrases to indicate to the reader or listener that a conclusion immediately follows. The following list gives some of the more common words and phrases that may introduce a conclusion:

Therefore . . .	This entails that . . .
So . . .	This proves that . . .
Consequently . . .	I conclude that . . .
Hence . . .	I deduce that . . .
It follows that . . .	I infer that . . .
This implies that . . .	One may infer that . . .

The presence of one of the expressions above does not guarantee that there is an argument. In "He liked the book, so he bought it", the second clause does not state an inference from the first. It narrates an event, of which the first clause gives a psychological explanation.

Once the conclusion of an argument is identified, the rest of the sentences are either premisses or material that has no logical relevance to the conclusion. The task of identifying the premisses may be aid by the following words and phrases which may immediately precede them, (three stars indicate premisses, three dots the conclusion):

    . . . , for ***
    . . . , because ***
    Since ***, . . .
    . . . , since ***
    . . . . The evidence is that ***
    . . . . I deduce this from the fact that ***
    . . . . I infer this from the fact that ***

Again the individual words do not guarantee existence of an argument, but if there *is* an argument, they introduce premisses.

Sometimes the conclusion can only be determined after the premisses are located. For example:

(d) "Charles is not at home, since he did not answer the phone when I called, and he never fails to answer the phone when he is at home".

In this example, the words "since" and "and" each precede a premiss. The pattern is: ". . . , since *(premiss)*, and *(premiss)*." Therefore the first clause, "Charles is not at home", must be the conclusion. Note that the conclusion of an argument may be in any position. It may be the first or last sentence of the argument or it may be somewhere in the middle.

1A3 Distinguishing Arguments from Causal Explanation. The word "because" generally occurs in a causal explanation rather than an argument. Examples in which "because" occurs in an argument and is used to indicate a premiss are:

(a) "Bill is taller than Harry, because Bill is taller than John and John is taller than Harry".

(b) "We are in an economic recession, because unemployment has steadily been increasing, the stock market has been declining, and business is very sluggish".

The following are examples in which "because" occurs in an explanation and does not indicate a premiss:

(c) "Mr. Smith is absent from class today because he is ill."

(d) "Hitler did not listen to the advice of his Generals, but opened a second front in Russia. Also, the Nazi's production of war materials was significantly less than that of the Allies. Consequently, the Nazis lost the war".

(e) "Bertrand Russell opposed the first World War since he was a pacifist".

These are causal explanations, not arguments, so they have neither premisses nor conclusions. Such explanations attempt to give the cause or causes of an event, not evidence for the truth of a proposition. Causes may be physical, psychological, social, economic, etc.

The word "Consequently" in (d) does not indicate a conclusion, and "since" in (e) does not indicate a premise. In an explanation the aim is not to prove a proposition true, but to explain why some event did or did not take place. Thus example (c) is not intended to give evidence of Mr. Smith's absence, but to explain it.

The expression "because of" *never* immediately precedes a premise, because it requires a noun, noun-phrase, or pronoun as object. Almost invariably the presence of the expression "because of" indicates that an explanation is being given. The following two examples are explanations:

(f) "Because of the death of his parents, Howard missed two weeks of school".

(g) "The center of the hurricane struck the island with its full fury, because of it thousands died".

Statements of causal relations and causal explanations as such are not arguments, but like other proposition, they are either true or false. It is possible for an explanation or causal statement to be a premiss or conclusion in an argument. For example, in the following argument evidence is given for an explanation, which is the conclusion of the argument.

(h) "Mr. Smith's wife called me this morning and informed me that he is in the hospital with the flu. Therefore, Mr. Smith is absent from class today because he is ill".

It is important to note that a description of an argument (or explanation) is a *description* only, not an argument (or explanation). Consider the following examples:

(i) "When Frank Murdock was charged with the murder of Harry Smith, he argued that he was innocent. He claimed that he had no motive for the killing and that he was having dinner with Smith's wife at the time of the murder".

(j) "The book explained that General Custard was defeated because he was a vain, glory-seeking person, who could not conceive of being defeated by a few thousand Indians".

Examples (i) and (j) are descriptions. Example (i) is a description (or report) of an argument. Example (j) is a description (or report) of an explanation.

1B DEDUCTIVE—INDUCTIVE; VALID—INVALID

The main concern of logic is to distinguish between correct and incorrect reasoning. Correct reasoning consists of arguments in which the conclusion follows in some sense from the premisses.

The correctness of reasoning is judged by different standards of strictness. Logicians have commonly divided arguments into two kinds (which may not be exhaustive): deductive and inductive.[3] A deductive argument is judged in the strictest possible way, that is, by the standard of validity. Inductive arguments are judged in less strict ways.

Def. 6. A **valid argument** is an argument whose conclusion follows necessarily from its premisses.[4]

An example of a valid argument is:

"There are over seventy students in this classroom; therefore, there are over ten students in this classroom".

Definition 6 is met since the truth of the proposition "there are over ten students in this classroom" follows by necessity from the truth of the proposition "there are over seventy students in this classroom".

Def. 7. An **invalid** (in-VAL-id) **argument** is an argument that is not valid, i.e., an argument whose conclusion does not follow necessarily from its premisses.

Here are some alternative ways to say that an argument is valid:

(i) A valid argument is an argument such that if its premisses are true, then its conclusion must be true.

(ii) The conclusion follows necessarily from the premisses.

(iii) The conclusion validity follows from the premisses.

(iv) The conclusion is validity inferred (from the premisses).

(v) The premisses gives conclusive evidence for the conclusion.

(vi) The premisses together entail the conclusion.

(vii) The premisses logically imply the conclusion.

(viii) The premisses would, if true, prove the conclusion.

Def. 8a. A **deductive argument** is an argument which its maker is claiming to be valid.

Def. 8b. (Short form of def. 8a). A **deductive argument** is an argument that claims to be valid.

Def. 9. Deduction is inference from premisses to conclusion in a deductive argument.

Def. 10. Deductive logic is the branch of logic concerned with deductive arguments and auxiliary matters such as definition.

A person arguing deductively claims that if certain premisses are true, the conclusion must be true. He also asserts or at least supposes that the premisses (and hence the conclusion) are true.

A principle task of deductive logic is the development of methods (rules, etc.) for evaluating claims of validity.

A valid argument is almost always a deductive argument, that is, an argument that claims to be valid. But any argument may be evaluated as if it were deductive. If a person claims that the conclusion of his argument follows necessarily from the premisses, it is a deductive argument. If in fact this claim is correct, then it is a valid argument, regardless of the truth of the premisses or conclusion.

If this claim is not correct, the argument is still a deductive argument, though invalid. Validity is an objective matter, but being deductive is a subjective matter, depending upon the intention of the maker of the argument.

In respect to validity all arguments are either "good" (valid) or "bad" (invalid). That is to say, the conclusion follows necessarily from the premisses or it does not. From the standpoint of inductive reasoning, however, arguments are not claimed to be valid.

Def. 11a. An **inductive argument** is an argument for which its maker merely claims that if the premisses are true, the truth of the conclusion is sufficiently likely for the purpose at hand.

Def. 11b. (Short form of def. 11a). If a person claims that the truth of the conclusion is made likely enough (for a certain purpose) by the premisses, the argument is **inductive.**

An inductive argument claims that its premisses serves as evidence giving the conclusion a certain degree of probability, or raising it to some level of probability, perhaps not quantified. Inductive arguments differ in the degree or kind of likelihood they assert, as well as in the extent to which their claims are justified.

It might happen that an argument asserted as inductive has a conclusion that follows necessarily from the premises. Such an argument, though inductive because of what its maker claims, would be in fact valid, and could be called a "valid inductive argument" by someone who recognized both aspects.

Any argument, regardless of its claims, may be judged from the deductive standpoint, and is then valid or invalid. But to evaluate an inductive argument as invalid is not to evaluate it from its own standpoint. From the inductive standpoint an argument is judged as good or bad according to whether or not the premises give evidence for the conclusion sufficient for the purpose at hand. There are different criteria for judging inductive arguments, depending on circumstances and purposes. For example, a jury should decide that A owes B money if the evidence makes it more probable than not. On the other hand, a jury should not convict a person of a crime unless there is proof "beyond reasonable doubt".

Since this book treats deductive logic primarily, it will usually be assumed that the arguments considered are intended to be valid; hence, they are deductive arguments. In the treatment of informal fallacies, later in this book, the line between deductive and inductive arguments may not be sharply drawn.

A very common but false distinction between deductive and inductive arguments is that a deductive argument has general premises and a specific conclusion, and an inductive argument has specific premises and a general conclusion. This distinction is false and has no merit whatsoever. The distinction between deductive and inductive argument has nothing to do with the kinds of propositions in the argument. The distinction between deductive and inductive arguments is based on what is claimed for the argument. If one claims that the conclusion must be true, if the premisses are true, then the argument is deductive. If one claims that the truth of the conclusion is likely enough for the purpose at hand, based on the truth of the premisses, then the argument is inductive.

A deductive argument may have general premises and a specific conclusion, general premises and a general conclusion, specific premises and a specific conclusion, or specific premises and a general conclusion. An inductive argument may also have all of the above combinations.

Example (k) is a deductive argument having general premises and a specific conclusion. Example (l) has the same premises and conclusion as (k) but it is an inductive argument.

> (k) "Most tigers are dangerous animals; therefore it follows by necessity that this tiger is a dangerous animal".
>
> (l) "Most tigers are dangerous animals; therefore it is likely that this tiger is a dangerous animal".

Table 1.1: Classification of Arguments

ARGUMENT	**Deductive Argument** (*claims validity*)	**Inductive Argument** (*claims probability*)
Valid (i.e., conclusion follows necessarily)	Valid Deductive Argument	Valid Inductive Argument (exceptional case)
Invalid (i.e., not valid)	Invalid Deductive Argument	Invalid Inductive Argument (good or bad as conclusion is more or less probable).

(1) (= def. 6) A **valid** argument is an argument whose conclusion follows necessarily from its premises.

(2) A **valid** argument is an argument such that *if* its premises are true, then its conclusion *must* be true.

(3) (cf. def. 8a) If a person claims that the truth of the conclusion is *made necessary* by the premises, the argument is **deductive.**

(4) (= def. 11b) If a person claims that the truth of the conclusion is made *likely enough* (for a certain purpose) by the premises, the argument is **inductive.**

(5) In rare instances an inductive argument may happen to be valid.

(6) Inductive arguments are properly judged from the inductive point of view, that is, by the sufficiency of evidence relative to the purpose at hand.

1C THE RELATIONSHIP BETWEEN VALIDITY AND TRUTH

1C1 Principles of Validity. A valid argument is one in which the truth of the conclusion follows necessarily from the truth of the premises. For an argument to be valid, it is not necessary that the premises be true or that the conclusion be true.

For example, consider the argument: The floor of my study is a rectangle twenty feet long and ten feet wide; therefore it has two hundred square feet of floor space. This is a valid argument; that is, if the premises are true, then the conclusion must be true. However, the correctness of the multiplication does not guarantee the truth of the premises or conclusion.

From the definition of a valid argument (def. 6) follows the principle:

a. If an argument is valid, it is logically impossible that the premises be true without the conclusion being true.[5]

From principle *a* three useful principles follow:

b. If an argument is valid and the premisses are true, then the conclusion must be true.

c. If an argument is valid and the conclusion is false, then at least one of the premisses must be false.

d. If the premisses of an argument are true and the conclusion is false, then the argument must be invalid.

1C2 Combinations of Truth-Value and Validity.

Def. 12. The **truth-value** of a proposition is truth if it is true, or falsity if it is false.

Combining mechanically the possibilities of validity or invalidity of an argument with truth or falsity of premise and truth or falsity of conclusion, we obtain eight combinations. (For the sake of simplicity, we show argument as having only one premiss. But a conjunction of premisses may be taken as a single premiss.)

COMBINATION	1	2	3	4	5	6	7	8
Argument	Valid Arguments				Invalid Arguments			
Premiss	True	(True)	False	False	True	True	False	False
Conclusion	True	(False)	True	False	True	False	True	False

Important: Of these eight combinations, only number 2 is impossible. This follows from 1C1, principle *a*, or from the definition of a "valid argument". If the truth of the conclusion follows necessarily from the truth of the premiss, the conclusion of a valid argument must be true, if the premiss is true. However, it is possible to find examples of the seven other combinations. Examples will be given of numbers 1, 3, 4, and 5.

(a) Example of combination 1 (Valid argument, true premiss, and true conclusion):

                                         Valid Argument
True Premiss: *More than 500 living humans are males.*
                                          Therefore
True Conclusion: *More than 400 living humans are males.*

(b) Example of combination 3 (Valid argument, false premiss, and true conclusion):

	Valid Argument
False Premiss:	*All living humans are males.*
	Therefore
True Conclusion:	*At least one living human is a male.*

(c) Example of combination 4 (Valid argument, false premiss, and false conclusion):

	Valid Argument
False Premiss:	*Less than six living humans are males.*
	Therefore
False Conclusion:	*Less than ten living humans are males.*

(d) Example of combination 5 (Invalid argument, true premiss, and true conclusion):

	Invalid Argument
True Premiss:	*More than ten living humans are males.*
	Therefore
True Conclusion:	*More than fifty living humans are males.*

Exercises for Chapter 1

EX 1A, I (for Subsections, 1A1, 1A2). Write the letter for the most appropriate answer.

_____ 1. According to the authors, logic is: (a) just an art. (b) just a science. (c) a science and an art. (d) neither a science nor an art.

_____ 2. A proposition is a (an): (a) sentence that starts with a capital letter and ends with a period. (b) interrogative sentence. (c) sentence, taken with a specific meaning, that is true or false. (d) imperative or interrogative sentence.

_____ 3. Every argument has: (a) at least two premisses and a conclusion. (b) at least two conclusions and a premiss. (c) exactly one premiss and exactly one conclusion. (d) one conclusion and at least one premiss.

_____ 4. A proposition in an argument that is offered as grounds or evidence for the conclusion is called a (an): (a) declarative sentence. (b) inference. (c) premiss. (d) expository sentence.

_____ 5. In logic, an argument is often called a (an): (a) altercation. (b) a verbal controversy. (c) debate. (d) an inference.

_____ 6. An argument *cannot* be: (a) one simple proposition. (b) a sequence of propositions. (c) one compound proposition. (d) a set of proposition offered as a reason for believing in another proposition.

_____ 7. The word in the following list that is least likely to introduce a conclusion in an argument is: (a) *so*. (b) *hence*. (c) *since*. (d) *consequently*.

_____ 8. The word or phrase in the following list that is least likely to introduce a premiss in an argument is: (a) *since*. (b) *because*. (c) *hence*. (d) *the evidence is that*.

_____ 9. The conclusion of an argument: (a) is always the first sentence of the argument. (b) is always the last sentence of the argument. (c) must be a sentence that comes in the middle of the argument. (d) may occur anywhere in the argument.

_____ 10. In the sentence, "He refused military service because of his principles", the word "because" precedes: (a) a premiss. (b) a conclusion. (c) neither a premiss nor a conclusion. (d) a phrase that functions as a premiss and a conclusion.

EX 1A, II (for Subsections 1A1). Identify the propositions by writing "P" in the appropriate space.

_____ 1. The square root of 1,456 is 45.88.

_____ 2. Look out!

_____ 3. The proposition "There are fewer than ten anteaters in the world that weigh over 400 pounds" is false.

_____ 4. Meet me tonight at 8 P.M.

_____ 5. How many angels can dance on the head of a pin?

_____ 6. The last word that George Washington spoke was "country".

_____ 7. The month of April runs faster than purple Monday.

_____ 8. If the proposition "More than ten students are in this room" is true, then the proposition "More than fifty students are in this room" must be true.

_____ 9. There are only two living people in the world who have a last name of "Zilch".

_____ 10. Help me with my homework.

EX 1A, III (for Subsections 1A3). Only some of the following numbered passages are arguments. If the passage is an argument, write "A" in the blank, and place brackets "[ ]" around the conclusion and parentheses "( )" around each premiss. If it is not an argument write "No" in the blank.

_____ 1. The defendant is guilty of murder, since three witnesses testified that they saw him commit the crime; it was proved that he had an excellent motive for killing the victim; and finally, he freely confessed to the crime.

_____ 2. The District Attorney claimed that the defendant is guilty of murder. He pointed out that three witnesses have testified that they saw him commit the crime. He said that the defendant had an excellent motive for killing the victim. And he closed with the remark that the defendant had freely confessed to the crime.

18   *Exercises/Chapter 1*

_____ 3. When the earth is directly between the sun and the moon, then earth's shadow is thrown on the moon. The earth's shadow on the moon is curved; therefore the earth must be a sphere.

_____ 4. This liquid is an acid, because it turns blue litmus red and it reacts with zinc, liberating hydrogen gas.

_____ 5. In their trip around the sun, the Leonids approach the earth every thirty-three years. Good displays of meteoric showers were produced in 1833 and in 1866. Since then showers have been faint.

_____ 6. Before 1890 no starlings existed in North America. In 1890 sixty starlings were released in New York City and in 1891 forty more were released. Because of these two events, we now have thousands of starlings in North America.

_____ 7. Evergreens are divided into two groups, the conifers and the broadleave evergreens, so if an evergreen is not a conifer it must be a broadleave evergreen.

_____ 8. The frustration of the South, strong sectional interests, unscrupulous politicians trying to take advantage of the aftermath of the war—from all these things follows the assassination of President Lincoln.

_____ 9. A meteor in flight may look larger than it really is because of its intense glow.

_____ 10. It seems highly probable that the continents were once together in one large land mass, since it is possible to fit the continents together like the pieces of a jigsaw puzzle.

_____ 11. If the given torque is greater than the torque required by the device being driven, acceleration will take place until the motor torque and the load torque are equal. Conversely, if the torque required is greater than the given torque, the shaft will slow down until the required torque and the given torque are equal.
                    adapted from *Grolier Encyclopedia*,
                    Vol. 14, p. 190, 1960.

_____ 12. If the first switch is closed and the second switch is open the red light is on; but if the second switch closed, then regardless of whether the first switch is open or closed the red light is out. Also if both switches are open the red light is on. It follows that the second switch being open is a necessary but not a sufficient condition for the red light being on.

_____ 13. It looks like a duck, it waddles like a duck, it smells like a duck, and it quacks like a duck, so it's probably a duck.

_____ 14. We know that the argument is valid and we know that the conclusion is false, hence it must be the case that at least one of the premises in the argument is false.

_____ 15. It is very hot in this room since the air conditioner broke down.

_____ 16. The school janitor just informed me that the boiler is being repaired and will not be fixed until tomorrow. Hence, the school will have no hot water until tomorrow.

_____ 17. Mr. Slyfoot will make a good United States senator, since he is hardworking, highly patriotic, and almost completely honest.

_____ 18. Mr. Slyfoot stands a good chance of winning the election, since the popularity polls two months before the election show him leading his opponent 53 percent to 40 percent.

_____ 19. Mr. Slyfoot lost the election, because he was indicted for embezzlement one week before the election.

_____ 20. For want of a nail the shoe is lost, for want of a shoe the horse is lost, for want of a horse the rider is lost, for want of a rider the message is lost, for want of a message the battle is lost, for want of a battle the Kingdom is lost. So for want of a nail a Kingdom is lost.
(Cf. George Herbert, 1640)

EX 1B (for Section 1B). Place the appropriate letter in each blank. If "All of the above are correct" is true, no other answer is acceptable.

_____ 1. Which statement is true? (a) All deductive arguments are valid. (b) A deductive argument is one which claims to be valid. (c) All inductive arguments are invalid. (d) An inductive argument is an argument that claims to be invalid.

_____ 2. Which statement is false? (a) Any argument may be evaluated as if it were deductive. (b) From the standpoint of inductive reasoning arguments are not claimed to be valid. (c) An inductive argument is an argument with a conclusion that states that some event will probably not occur. (d) The main concern of logic is to distinguish between correct and incorrect reasoning.

_____ 3. Which statement is true? (a) All deductive arguments go from general premises to a specific conclusion. (b) All inductive

20 Exercises/Chapter 1

arguments go from specific premises to a general conclusion. (c) In deductive arguments the conclusion always comes last. (d) All of the above statements are false.

_____ 4. Which statement is false? (a) The same argument may be evaluated as deductie or inductive. (b) The same criterion is always used for evaluating inductive arguments, regardless of circumstances or purposes. (c) For an argument to be valid it is not sufficient that the premises make the conclusion highly probable. (d) A valid argument is almost always a deductive argument.

_____ 5. An alternative way of saying that an argument is valid is to say: (a) Its premises entail its conclusion. (b) The conclusion is a valid inference. (c) The premises logically imply the conclusion. (d) All of the above are correct.

_____ 6. A deductive argument is an argument: (a) that is valid. (b) in which its conclusion follows necessarily from the premises. (c) that its maker is claiming to be valid. (d) that infers a specific conclusion from general premises.

_____ 7. A valid argument is an argument: (a) that has a true conclusion. (b) that has true premises and a true conclusion. (c) whose conclusion follows necessarily from the premises. (d) that cannot have a false conclusion.

_____ 8. An inductive argument: (a) can never be valid. (b) quite frequently is valid. (c) is rarely valid (and then accidently). (d) is always valid.

_____ 9. An inductive argument is an argument: (a) in which the premisses make the truth of the premisses sufficiently likely. (b) which claims that if the premises are true then the truth of the conclusion is sufficiently likely for the purpose at hand. (c) where the conclusion does not follow from the premises. (d) which claims that the conclusion is possibly true.

_____ 10. A deductive argument is an argument that claims: (a) to be valid. (b) that its conclusion follows necessarily from its premisses. (c) that the premises entail the conclusion. (d) all of the above are correct.

EX IC, I (for Section IC). Place the most appropriate letter in each blank. If "Any of these" is true, no other answer is acceptable.

Exercises/Chapter 1   21

_____ 1. It is impossible for a valid argument to have: (a) a true conclusion and false premisses. (b) false premisses and a false conclusion. (c) true premisses and a false conclusion. (d) true premisses and true conclusion.

_____ 2. It is possible for an invalid argument with just one premiss to have: (a) a false premiss and a false conclusion. (b) a false premiss and a true conclusion. (c) a true premiss and a true conclusion. (d) Any of these.

_____ 3. If the conclusion of a valid argument is false, then the premiss (assuming that there is only one) must be: (a) true. (b) false. (c) neither true nor false. (d) meaningless.

_____ 4. Every valid argument has: (a) true premisses and a true conclusion. (b) at least one true premiss. (c) a true conclusion. (d) a true conclusion, if it has all true premisses.

_____ 5. If the premisses of a valid argument are true, then the conclusion: (a) must be true. (b) must be false. (c) may be either true or false. (d) is meaningless.

_____ 6. If a deductive argument has true premisses and a false conclusion, then the argument: (a) is valid. (b) is invalid. (c) may be either valid or invalid. (d) is meaningless.

_____ 7. From which of these conditions, if any, can the *invalidity* of an argument be inferred? (a) True premisses and a false conclusion. (b) True premisses and true conclusion. (c) False premisses and a false conclusion. (d) None of the above.

_____ 8. From which of these condition, if any, can the *validity* of an argument be inferred? (a) True premisses and a false conclusion. (b) True premisses and true conclusion. (c) false premisses and a false conclusion. (d) None of the above.

_____ 9. If an argument has true premisses and a true conclusion then the argument is: (a) deductive. (b) valid. (c) invalid. (d) valid or invalid.

_____ 10. It is impossible for an invalid argument to have: (a) true premisses and a false conclusion. (b) true premisses and true conclusion. (c) false premisses and a false conclusion. (d) None of the above is impossible.

EX 1C, II Problems. For each of the following arguments, judge whether the premiss is true or false, whether the conclusion is true or false, and whether the argument is valid or invalid. Write the appropriate letter in each blank: T = True, F = False, V = Valid, Inv = Invalid.

1. No reptiles are mammals, therefore no mammals are reptiles.
   _____Argument, _____Premiss, _____Conclusion.

2. Caesar crossed the Rubicon, since Lions are carnivorous.
   _____Argument, _____Premiss, _____Conclusion.

3. I have eight fingers on my left hand and six fingers on my right hand; therefore I have a total of fourteen fingers on two hands.
   _____Argument, _____Premiss, _____Conclusion.

4. Most Americans are over seventy years old, hence it follows that some Americans are over seventy years old.
   _____Argument, _____Premiss, _____Conclusion.

5. The word "love" has five letters, hence all five-letter words are expressions of love.
   _____Argument, _____Premiss, _____Conclusion.

6. The number 13 is a prime number, so it must be the case that no number less than 13 is prime.
   _____Argument, _____Premiss, _____Conclusion.

7. Some dogs do not weigh over forty pounds, since all house cats do weigh over forty pounds.
   _____Argument, _____Premiss, _____Conclusion.

2

Propositions

2A PROPOSITIONS AND THEIR KINDS

The following definition of *proposition* was given in chapter 1 (subsection 1A1) along with a brief explanation and examples.

> **Def. 1.** A **proposition** is a sentence (or a clause that may be used as one) that, as taken with a specific meaning, is true or false.

In this chapter the analysis of propositions is continued and a division of their kinds is given.

Propositions may be analyzed as having form and content (or form and matter). The form is presented by the form words or formal elements.

> **Def. 2. Form words** are certain abstract words that make up the logical form or structure of propositions, especially certain conjunctions, quantifying adjectives, and forms of the verb *to be*.[1]

In any given logical system, certain formal elements are taken as standard. In the basic system of Aristotelian logic developed in chapters 7 through 11 and 19 through 22, the principal form words are: "all", "no", "some", "are", "are not", "it is false that", "therefore", "since", and so on.

The content or matter of a proposition consists of its expressions other than form words. This includes most words in each grammatical category, except perhaps conjunctions.

In traditional logic, the matter appears as a term-expression.

Def. 3. A **term expression** is a substantival or adjectival expression—i.e., a noun, noun phrase, pronoun, adjective, or adjective phrase.

A division of the kinds of propositions follows:
1. Categorical: Subject-predicate propositions.
   a. Primary: Has no proposition as part of its subject or predicate.
   b. Secondary: Has a proposition as part of its subject or predicate. Includes entailment: "That . . . entails that _____".
2. Compound Propositions: Combines two or more propositions by connectives.
   a. Conditional (or hypothetical): "If . . . then _____".
   b. Biconditional: ". . . if an only if _____".
   c. Disjunctive (or alternative): "Either . . . or _____".
   d. Conjunctive (or copulative): "Both . . . and _____".
   Definitions of these kinds of proposition are given below.

Def. 4a. A **categorical proposition** is a proposition that affirms or denies a predicate of a subject, but is not an explicit combination of such propositions.[2]

Def. 4b. (Short form). A **categorical proposition** is a subject-predicate proposition.

Here are some examples of categorical propositions (the vertical line separates the grammatical subject from the grammatical predicate): "All women | are females". "Mr. Smith | is not lying". "Only the fool | is the knave". "Brutus | stabbed Caesar". "He | believes that all men are fools". "That all Latins are good lovers | is false". "That there are over twenty people in this room | entails that there are over fifteen people in this room".

Def. 5. A **primary proposition** is a categorical proposition that contains no other proposition as a part of its subject or its predicate.

Examples of primary propositions follow: "John is an electrician". "The stock market was unsteady last week". "New York and Atlantic City are south of Boston". "He is a liar and a fool". "Many professional actresses who worry about their figure diet regularly". The last sentence would be called "complex" in English grammar, the others, "simple".

Note that a simple sentence may have a compound subject (as in the third example, "New York and Atlantic City are south of Boston") or a compound predicate (as in the fourth example, "He is a liar and a fool").

Def. 6. A **secondary proposition** is a categorical proposition that contains at least one proposition as part of its subject or its predicate.[3]

These are examples of secondary propositions: "It is true that John is an electrician". "It is probable that John is an electrician". "That John is an electrician is generally unknown". "He believed that his brother was clever and his sister was wise". "All persons who believe that Mars is inhabited also believe that Mars has an atmosphere". "That all men are mortal entails that it is false that some men are not mortal".

The last example is a secondary proposition using the important logical relation entailment, which contains a proposition "all men are mortal" as part of its subject. The proposition contains the propositions "it is false that some men are not mortal" and "some men are not mortal" as parts of its predicate. The main verb introduces the important logical relation entailment. (Compare "alternative ways to say that an argument is valid" after 1B, def. 7).

Def. 7. A **compound proposition** is a proposition that consists of two or more propositions joined by connectives, i.e., what are called "conjunctions" or "conjunctives" in grammar.[4]

Because modern logicians use "conjunction" in the restricted sense of our definition 11 below, we use the term "connective" (as do symbolic logicians) for the general grammatical meaning of "conjunction".

The following are examples of compound propositions (with categorical propositions within them in italics): "If *there is inflation* then *prices will rise*". "Either *he is very clever* or *he is very stupid*". "*Man is the only animal that can laugh* and *man is the only animal that knows that he must die*". "If *John is promoted* or if *Bill is promoted*, then *David will resign*". In roman type are the form words—the connectives—that give the logical form of the compound proposition.

The last example of secondary proposition given above, "The fact that all men are mortal entails that it is false that some men are not mortal", is not a compound proposition, because it does *not* consist of "two or more propositions joined by connectives". It joins that name of a certain fact ("that all men are mortal") to the name of another fact ("that it is false that some men are mortals").

Def. 8. A **hypothetical** or **conditional proposition** is a compound proposition formed by connecting two propositions (categorical or compound) by the words "if . . . then _____" or equivalent expressions (e.g., ". . . only if _____"). The "then" clause is asserted to be true on the condition that the "if" clause is true.[5]

Here are some examples of hypotheticals: "If *there is frost tonight*, then *the crops will be damaged*". The proposition between the "if" and the "then"—in this case, "there is frost tonight"—is called the "antecedent". The proposition after "then" is called the "consequent". The most common forms of conditional propositions are the forms "if p then q" and "if p, q". In English grammar a conditional proposition is not called a "compound" proposition, but "complex". The "if" clause is said to be dependent.

Def. 9. A **biconditional** is a compound proposition formed by connecting two propositions (categorical or compound) by the words ". . . if and only if _____" or equivalent expressions. The biconditional form "p if and only if q" (abbreviated "p iffi q) is equivalent to "if p then q, and if q then p", a conjunction of two conditional forms.

Mathematicians and symbolic logicians have often used the abbreviation "iff" for "if and only if". It is hard to distinguish this from "if" in speech and hard to get copyreaders and typists to recognize that this is not just a misspelling of "if"; for these reasons we use "iffi" instead, pronounced like "iffy". Note that the last two letters reverse the first two, suggesting a symmetrical (i.e., reversible) relation. Recently mathematicians and logicians have adopted the expression "just in case", which avoids these problems and has only three syllables as opposed to the five of "if and only if".

Examples of biconditionals follow:

(a) "*He will pass the exam* if and only if *he studies for it*".

(b) "*A person is the Commander-in-Chief of the Armed Forces of the United States* if and only if *this person is the President of the United States*".

(c) "*A proposition is true* just in case *its contradictory is false*".

Biconditionals (and conditionals) differ in the kind of connection they assert. Example (a) above would be at best a prediction with some probability. Example (b) would be true as long as the present Constitution is observed in this respect. A biconditional used for a definition (as in 4A, def. 3a) establishes a necessary equivalence where that definition is accepted.

Def. 10. A **disjunction (alternation)** or **disjunctive proposition** is a compound proposition formed by connecting two propositions (categorical or compound) by the word "or".

These are examples of disjunctive propositions:

(d) *"Tomorrow I will go swimming* or *I will go boating"*.

(e) *"Either 2 is a prime number* or *I'm no logician"*.

Def. 11. A **conjunction** or **conjunctive proposition** is a compound proposition formed by connecting two propositions (categorical or compound) by the word "and" or a logically equivalent expression such as "but".

(In scholastic terminology, disjunctions are called "copulative propositions".)

The following are examples conjunctive propositions:

(f) *"John finished his dissertation* and *next week he will take his examination"*.

(g) *"All cows are animals,* but *not all animals are cows"*.

Other kinds of compound propositions (e.g., causal or temporal) not reducible to the four kinds defined above will not be dealt with.[6]

2B ARISTOTELIAN MODALITY

> *De Modalibus non gustabit asinus.*
> (*The ass will not like modals*).
> —Medieval saying.

Distinct from the division of propositions according to composition is their division according to *modality*. The doctrine of modality considers the use of certain words such as "necessary" and "possible", called *modal* (long "o") because they characterize the mode or manner in which things exist or events occur.

Modalities were much discussed by Aristotle, other ancients, and the scholastics. Though important in modern philosophy, they did not receive systematic treatment from modern logicians before H. MacColl and C. I. Lewis, who introduced them into symbolic logic.

There are many other kinds of modalities, for example, modes of obligation and permission: "This ought to be done", "It's permissible to park here". Symbolic logicians have recently begun to explore these modalities.

2B1 Aristotelian Modality

Def. 12. The (traditional) *Aristotelian modal adjectives* are "necessary", "possible", "contingent", and "impossible". The *Aristotelian modal nouns* are "necessity", "possibility", "contingency", and "impossibility". (Similarly for Aristotelian modal adverbs.)

While the modal words—or corresponding forms in other languages—have been constant, their meanings vary considerably.

"Necessity" may mean logical or physical necessity, absolute or relative necessity, and so on; likewise for the other modalities. The examples of this section (2B) may be interpreted in any appropriate way. Since this is a book of deductive logic, however, our references to "necessity", "possibility", and the rest in other chapters will mean *logical necessity, logical possibility,* and so on, unless otherwise specified.

Def. 13. A (logically) **necessary proposition** (or an **analytic proposition**) is a proposition that is true simply by virtue of the meaning of its words.

For example, the following must be true because of their meaning, regardless of the actual properties of the objects concerned: "If this object is completely red, it is not completely non-red." "If it is a trout, then it is a fish". (The first, but not the second, of these propositions is *formally* necessary; its truth can be known from its logical form alone.)

Def. 14. A (logically) **impossible proposition** (or a **self-contradictory proposition**) is a proposition that is false simply by virtue of the meaning of its words.

Examples: "This object is both completely red and completely non-red". "This is a trout but not a fish".

Def. 15. A (logically) **possible proposition** (or a **self-consistent proposition**) is a proposition that is not (logically) impossible.

Examples: "I caught a fish forty feet long". "If it is a trout, then it is a fish". "Contingent" (applied to a proposition) may mean (1) possible, (2) not necessary, or (3) possible but not necessary. The third meaning is now the most common and the one that we shall use.

Def. 16. A **contingent** (or **empirical** or **synthetic**) **proposition** is a proposition that is possible but not necessary.

Examples: "I caught a fish forty feet long". "Some dogs have fleas".

An exhaustive and exclusive division of propositions may be made by the three Aristotelian modal adjectives other than "possible" (as well as by the two adjectives "possible" and "impossible").

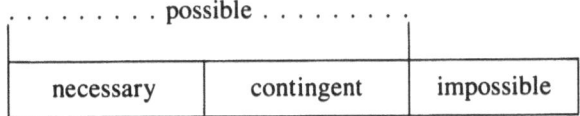

Def. 17. A (logically) **non-contingent** (or **a priori proposition**) is a proposition that is not contingent; that is, either a necessary or an impossible proposition.

According to definitions 13 through 16, definition 17 is equivalent to saying that a logically non-contingent proposition is one whose truth-value can be known from its meaning.

Def. 18. An **improper modal** adjective is either one of the adjectives "true" or "false".

"True" and "false" may be called improper modal adjectives, since typical (but not all) propositions in which they are predicated reduce to simpler non-modal propositions. Thus, "It is true that he is clever" is equivalent to "He is clever". We also say that "truth" and "falsity" are **improper modal nouns,** which stand for **improper modalities,** namely the abstractions truth and falsity. All other modal words occurring in this section are called "proper".

Contingent propositions are either true or false (though the logician as such does not know which). The modal terms "contingently true" and "contingently false", with "necessary" and "impossible", give an exhaustive and exclusive division of propositions. The following table groups these four terms according to the dichotomies of true versus false and contingent versus non-contingent.

Propositions	True	False
Non-contingent	necessarily true (possible)	impossible (necessarily false)
Contingent	contingently true (possible)	contingently false (possible)

For modalities of assertion see Appendix 2B.

Appendix 2B

2B MODALITIES OF ASSERTION

Inspection of the propositions in 2B1 offered as examples of necessary, possible, contingent, or impossible shows that none of them contains a modal adjective nor any distinctive expression that, by itself, determines which modal adjective applies to the proposition. In short, these propositions, considered from the standpoint of the mode or manner in which they make their assertions, are *non-modal* rather than modal. Thus, the proposition "This object is both completely red and completely non-red" is logically impossible but non-modal. The proposition "It is impossible that this is both red and non-red" is modal and true (in fact necessarily true). Modality as determined from this standpoint we call "modality of assertion" (or subjective modality). The best known list of modalities of assertion is that of Kant's *Critique of Pure Reason*.

Def. 1. A **modal proposition** is a proposition that contains a modal term, either as a term of objective (e.g., Aristotelian) or subjective (e.g., Kantian) modality.

Def. 2. An **assertoric proposition** is a proposition that simply states (or denies) that something was, is, or will be the case (without qualification as to its necessity or possibility).

An assertoric proposition may be necessary, possible, impossible, or contingent; but if a modality is not *asserted* by the proposition, then it is assertoric. Examples: "Some men are philosophers". "It will rain tomorrow". "John has finished his examination". "All prime numbers over 2 are odd numbers". "All men are mammals".

Def. 3. A **problematic proposition** is a proposition that asserts that a certain state of affairs is possible, contingent, unnecessary, or probable.

Examples: "John may have finished his examination". "Perhaps all swans are black". "It is possible that there is intelligent life on Mars".

Def. 4. An **apodictic** (ap-o-DIK-tik) **proposition** is a proposition that asserts something to be necessary or impossible.

"Apodictic" (also spelled "apodeictic") is commonly used as synonymous with "necessary" or "logically impossible". It seems useful, however, to distinguish them as we have done. We find precedent for our special usage of "apodictic" in the usage of Kant's *Critique of Pure Reason*.

These are examples of apodictic propositions: "All men are necessarily rational". "He cannot escape". "It is impossible to trisect an angle using only a straight edge and compass".

Exercises for Chapter 2

EX 2A, I. For each numbered term below, select from the key a label that applies to the same cases.

KEY

a. categorical proposition
b. primary proposition
c. secondary proposition
d. compound proposition

e. conditional proposition
f. disjunctive proposition
g. conjunctive proposition

_____ 1. Categorical proposition that contains no other propositions as a part of its subject or its predicate.

_____ 2. Compound proposition formed by connecting two propositions by the word "and".

_____ 3. Proposition that consists of two or more propositions joined by connectives.

_____ 4. Categorical proposition that contains at least one proposition as part of its subject or predicate.

_____ 5. Proposition that affirms or denies a predicate of a subject, but is not an explicit combination of such propositions.

_____ 6. Proposition formed by connecting two propositions by the words "if . . . then . . ." or equivalent expressions.

_____ 7. Proposition formed by connecting two propositions by the word "or".

_____ 8. Hypothetical proposition.

_____ 9. Subject-predicate proposition.

_____ 10. Proposition that is either primary or secondary.

EX 2A, II. Select from the key below the appropriate letters for each blank. Each blank will have just two letters.

KEY

a. categorical proposition
b. primary proposition

e. conditional proposition
f. disjunctive proposition

c. secondary proposition
d. compound proposition

g. conjunctive proposition

Examples:
d, e (i) If John takes the final exam in logic, then he will fail it.
Explanation: The form of this proposition is "if . . . then . . .", hence it is a conditional proposition and a compound proposition. The antecedent "John takes the final exam in logic" and the consequent "he will fail it" are categorical propositions, but the proposition as a whole is hypothetical.
d, g (ii) If Smith wins the first game or if Brown loses the second game, then Smith and Brown will be tied, and if Green wins the third game and he doesn't lose games after that, then he will win the match.
Explanation: this proposition has the form "(If p or q, then r) and (if s and t, then u)". The main connective is "and", hence the proposition is conjunctive and compound.
a, c (iii) It is certain that either John didn't take this logic exam or he took his logic exam.
Explanation: It is a categorical proposition since it is not a compound of propositions. The above proposition is not equivalent to "It is certain that John didn't take his logic exam or it is certain that he did take his logic exam". It is a secondary proposition since it contains at least one proposition (in this case two) as part of the subject.

_____ 1. If you pass the logic and French, then you will graduate.

_____ 2. I will meet you tonight only if you come alone, and I will give you the money only if you have the diamonds.

_____ 3. Categorical propositions are either primary or secondary, but if a proposition is conditional, then it is compound.

_____ 4. It is false that if you place a horsehair in rainwater then it will turn into a worm.

_____ 5. A proposition is either categorical or compound.

_____ 6. Either Humpty Dumpty sat on the wall and Humpty Dumpty had a great fall or the children's tale about Humpty Dumpty is false.

_____ 7. If lead can be turned into gold then the alchemists were right, but if the alchemists were wrong then it is false that lead can be turned into gold.

_____ 8. It is true that a proposition that is necessarily true is true.

_____ 9. Some logicians believe that it is not true that if p implies q then the falsity of q implies the falsity of p.

_____ 10. Either you are right or I am right, but in this case both cannot be right.

_____ 11. If you are right then I am wrong, and if I am not wrong then you are not right.

_____ 12. If a proposition is categorical then it is either primary or secondary.

_____ 13. It is true that both conditionals and disjunctives are compound propositions.

_____ 14. The American flag is red, white, and blue.

_____ 15. Love is an egoism of two.

EX 2B, I. From the key below select the letter for each blank indicating an equivalent expression.

KEY

a. non-contingent proposition
b. contingent proposition
c. impossible proposition
d. necessary proposition
e. possible proposition

The following table will be of use.

Propositions	True	False
Non-contingent	necessarily true (possible)	impossible (necessarily false)
Contingent	contingently true (possible)	contingently false (possible)

_____ 1. Proposition that is possible but not necessary.

_____ 2. Self-consistent proposition.

_____ 3. Proposition that is false simply by virtue of the meaning of its words.

_____ 4. Proposition that is either a necessary or an impossible proposition.

_____ 5. Synthetic proposition.

_____ 6. Self-contradictory proposition.

Exercises/Chapter 2   35

_____ 7. Proposition that is not impossible.

_____ 8. Proposition that is true simply by virtue of the meaning of its words.

_____ 9. Empirical proposition.

_____ 10. Analytic proposition.

EX 2B II. Complete the following, filling each blank with a single word.

1. The four Aristotelian model adjectives are _____, _____, _____, and _____.
2. Logicians now usually mean by "contingent" _____.
3. A synonym for "self-contradictory" is "logically _____".
4. A synonym for "self-consistency" is "logically _____".
5. A synonym for "analytic proposition" is "logically _____".
6. A synonym for "synthetic proposition" or "empirical proposition" is "_____ proposition".
7. From the standpoint of the way in which they are known, it is natural to divide propositions into a priori and _____.
8. An exhaustive (all-inclusive) and exclusive (non-overlapping) division of propositions into three kinds is made by the adjectives "necessary", "impossible", and "_____".
9. An exhaustive and exclusive division of propositions into two kinds is made by the adjectives "impossible" and "_____".
10. The "improper modal adjectives" are "_____" and "_____".

EX 2B, III. Select from the key below the appropriate letters for each blank. Each blank will have just two letters.

KEY

a. non-contingent proposition
b. contingent proposition
c. impossible proposition
d. necessary proposition
e. possible proposition

_____ 1. Some bachelors are married men.

_____ 2. Some bachelors are happy men.

_____ 3. A square is a rectangle having four equal sides.

_____ 4. A proposition is either contingent or non-contingent.

_____ 5. All green objects are colored objects.

_____ 6. Any number that is greater than four is a number that is less than two.

_____ 7. "I hear you perfectly"! shouted the deaf mute.

_____ 8. Some men have lived to be over six hundred years old.

_____ 9. It is logically impossible for a square to have five sides.

_____ 10. George Washington was really a woman.

3

Logical Form and Counterexamples

> "Then you should say what you mean," the March Hare went on.
> "I do," Alice hastily replied; "at least—at least I mean what I say—that's the same thing, you know."
> "Not the same thing a bit!" said the Hatter. "Why, you might just as well say that 'I see what I eat' is the same thing as 'I eat what I see'!"
> —Lewis Carroll, Alice's Adventures in Wonderland

3A LOGICAL FORM

3A1 Judging Validity. One of the principle functions of logic, Aristotelian as well as symbolic, is to distinguish valid arguments from invalid arguments. It is true that one does not have to be a logician to recognize that the following argument is invalid:

> *All women are men, since all women are human and all men are human.*

Many arguments, however, cannot be judged as easily as the above, and can be readily evaluated only by a person trained in logic. For example, this argument adapted from Lewis Carroll is harder to evaluate:[1]

> *No interesting poems are unpopular among people of real taste;*
> *No modern poetry is free from affectation;*

All your *poems are on the subject of soap-bubbles;*
No affected poetry is popular among people of real taste;
Only modern poems are on the subject of soap-bubbles.
Therefore, all your *poems are uninteresting.*

Most of the deductive arguments that are encountered in magazines, newspapers, political speeches, and ordinary conversation can be evaluated by a person trained in logic. The person knowledgeable in logic is able, not only to decide which of these arguments are valid or invalid, but also to explain how to tell the difference.

3A2 Formally and Semantic Validity. Consider the following argument:

$$\frac{\text{No camelopards are wombats.}}{\therefore \text{No wombats are camelopards.}}$$

The three-dot sign is used for "therefore". The line is a convention that separates the premisses (above) from the conclusion (below).

It makes no difference what we are talking about: camelopards, wombats, dogs, cats, gophers, sharks, ballpoint pens, and so on; it is the logical form of this argument that makes it valid.

$$\frac{\text{No } A \text{ are } B}{\therefore \text{ No } B \text{ are } A}$$

Now consider another argument:

$$\frac{\text{No camelopards are wombats.}}{\therefore \text{No giraffes are wombats.}}$$

In this second argument, if the premiss is true, the conclusion must necessarily be true, because "camelopards" is a synonym for "giraffes". But unless we know the meaning of "camelopards" we cannot tell whether the argument is valid or not. In Aristotelian and symbolic logic the logician judges validity by certain logical forms. He is not expected, as a logician, to know the meanings of most of the words of ordinary language. But he must know the meanings of such words as "no", "are", "if . . . then", "and", and so on, which we call "form words".[2] The second argument is not formally valid, but it is *semantically* valid.

Def. 1. A **formally valid argument** is an argument whose validity is determined solely by its form words and the pattern of its terms.

Def. 2. A **semantically valid argument** is an argument whose validity depends upon the meaning of its terms[3] (words other than form words), as well as its form words.

The validity of a semantically valid argument is not determined solely by its form words and the pattern of its terms; that is, it is not formally valid, since its validity depends also upon the meaning of its terms. In deductive logic we are primarily concerned with formal validity.

The relation of these kinds of arguments is shown in the following diagram:

Figure 3.1: Kinds of Arguments

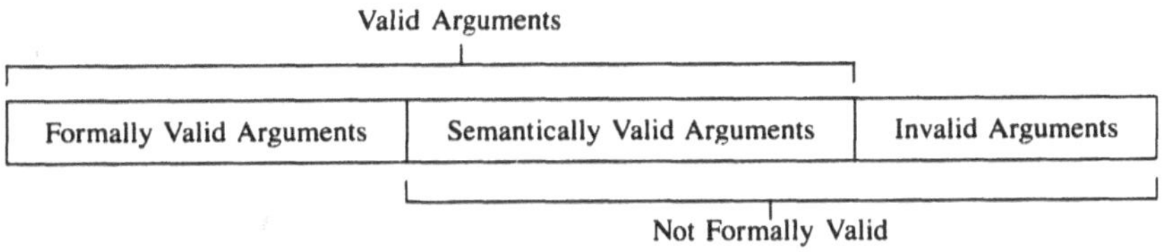

3A3 Forms of Propositions and Arguments. Every proposition has a plurality of propositional forms, which are formed by abstracting from certain expressions in the propositions. In term logic (the main part of Aristotelian logic), propositional forms are created by abstracting from the terms.

Def. 3. A **term** of a (subject-predicate) proposition is either the grammatical *subject* minus any form word such as "some" quantifying the whole subject, or the grammatical *predicate* minus "are", "is", "are not", or "is not", (if "are" or "is" is the main verb).

For example, the proposition "All train schedules are subject to change" contains the terms "train schedules" and "subject to change".

In term logic we can abstract the terms from all of the following propositions:

(a) *Socrates is wise*

(b) *Many Englishmen are coffee drinkers*

(c) *If rabbits are mammals, then rabbits are not snakes*

obtaining the following *pure* logical forms:

(a') _____ is . . .

(b') *Many* _____ *are* . . .

(c') *If* _____ *are* . . . , *then* _____ *are not* __ __ __.

Mixed proposition forms would result if we abstract from some term in each proposition but not from other terms. For example:

(a'') *Socrates is* . . .

(b'') *Many* _____ *are coffee drinkers*

(c'') *If rabbits are* . . . , *then rabbits are not* __ __ __

It is far more convenient to replace the dots or blanks with letters, which are called "variables". In the above examples "term-variables" would be used. Let us use a small letter in italic type as variable for proper name, and an italic capital as variable for a general term. Then (a'), (b'), (c') would become:

(a''') x is B

(b''') Many F are G

(c''') If B are C, then B are not D.

A proposition is an **instance** (or **example**) of a form if and only if the proposition can be recovered by correctly substituting values for the variables in that form. Variables may be of different kinds. In ordinary algebra the variables usually stand for numbers (of various kinds). In logic, the variables are usually propositional variables, term variables, or variables for other elements of propositions. For term variables only terms may be substituted, for propositional variables only propositions may be substituted, and so on. We shall limit ourselves in this chapter to forms containing term variables. Correct substitution for term variables means obeying the following Substitution Rules for obtaining an instance:

S1 For every occurrence of a given term variable the same term must be substituted.

S2 For distinct term variables, distinct terms or the same term may be substituted.

For example, by rule S1, from "All *B* are *B*" we may obtain by substitution "All sharks are sharks", or "All purple hats are purple hats", but not "All parrots are talkative creatures". By rule S2 from "No *B* are *C*" we may obtain by substitution "No wombats are mongooses" and also "No wombats are wombats". When making substitutions in a form, if one encounters a variable for which no term has yet been substituted, then any term may be substituted for it, even a term that was substituted for another variable.

Def. 4. A (**propositional**) **form** of a proposition is an expression obtained from it by replacing part or parts with a variable(s), in such a way that we may recover the proposition by correct substitution for each variable.

This definition covers both pure and mixed propositional forms. Examples a''', b''', and c''', above are pure propositional forms.

A pure propositional form consists only of variables and form words. Some form words are words that connect sentences (connectives) such as "and", "since", "therefore", "then", "because", and so on. Other form words in term logic are "are" or "is" as main verb, and words that quantify the whole subject, such as "no", "all", "some", "at least one", and so on.

We shall now give an explanation of argument form parallel to our explanation of propositional forms.

Def. 5. An **argument form** of an argument is an expression obtained from it by replacing at least one part with a variable, in such a way that we may recover the argument by correct substitution for each variable.

Some examples of argument forms follow:

(d) Some *B* are *C*, therefore some *C* are *B*.

(e) *Some woodpeckers are B, hence no B are woodpeckers.*

(f) All *D* are *F*
 All *F* are *H*
 ∴ All *D* are *H*

Examples given of argument forms are generally pure forms, that is, expressions containing only variables and form words. Form (e) is a mixed form.

3A4 Distinctive Forms of Propositions and Arguments. A more specific concept is that of a distinctive form of a proposition or argument.

Def. 6. In term logic, a **distinctive form** of a proposition or argument is a form made by replacing each distinct term by a distinct variable and all occurrences of the same term by the same variable.[4]

The result is a pure propositional form or pure argument form containing only form words and term variables.

The procedure for finding a distinctive form of a proposition or argument is given by two Replacement Rules.

R1 All occurrences of the same term are replaced by the same variable. Any capital letter may be used, except the vowels, A, E, I, and O, (which will be used for form words in chapter 7).

R2 Each distinct term is replaced by a distinct variable.

For each of the following propositions a distinctive form is given below it:

(a) Some logic students are philosophy majors.
(a')   Some B are C.

(b) If dogs are mammals, then dogs are warm-blooded animals.
(b')   If G are H, then G are J.

(c) Dogs are mammals; therefore, dogs are warm-blooded animals.
(c') G are H; therefore, G are J.

Note that (c) is an argument as well as a proposition.

The Replacement Rules that give a distinctive form of a proposition give a distinctive form of an argument. (This follows from the fact that an argument may be written as a compound proposition.)

For example, by the procedure given in the Replacement Rules above, (d') is a distinctive form of the argument (d):

(d)   All rabbits are vegetarians.
       <u>All vegetarians are peaceful creatures.</u>
       ∴ All rabbits are peaceful creatures.

(d')   All K are L
       <u>All L are M</u>
       ∴ All K are M

Another distinctive form of argument (d) is (f) in 3A3 above.

3A5 Validity of Argument Forms. A valid argument was defined in chapter 1, definition 6, as an argument whose conclusion follows necessarily from the premises. As we have seen in subsection 3A2, there are two kinds of validity, formal and semantic. In general throughout this text our concern will be with formal validity, that is, validity based upon form words, unless otherwise specified. Since it is possible to determine whether or not an argument is formally valid from a knowledge of its form alone, the study of argument forms is important.

We have not explained what is meant by "valid" as applied to argument forms.

> **Def. 7.** A **valid argument form** is an argument form of which every instance (example) is a valid argument.
>
> **Def. 8.** An **invalid argument form** is an argument form that is not valid, i.e., an argument form of which at least one instance (example) is invalid.

An invalid argument form usually does not make every argument that is an instance of that form invalid. For example, "All A are B, therefore all C are D" is an invalid argument form, but by substituting "cats" for all the term variables, the valid argument "All cats are cats, therefore all cats are cats" is obtained. This argument is also an instance of the valid argument form "All A are A, therefore all A are A". Consequently, a valid argument may be an instance of an invalid argument form as well as instance of a valid argument form.

An argument form of which every instance is invalid is: "All S are S, therefore at least one S is not S".

> **Def. 9.** A **formally valid argument form** is an argument form of which every instance (example) is a formally valid argument.

A formally valid argument form is:

(a) No S are P, therefore no P are S.

A valid argument form that is not formally valid is:

(b) Some S are red objects, therefore some S are colored objects.[5]

It follows from def. 9 that an argument form is *not formally valid* if and only if there is at least one possible instance of this form that is not formally valid.

Important relations of formal validity between arguments are argument forms are stated in the following principles:

(1) An argument is formally valid iffi some argument form of this argument is formally valid.

(2) An argument is not formally valid iffi no argument of this argument form is formally valid. (This follows from (1).)

(3) An argument *form* is formally valid iffi every argument of this form is formally valid. (By definition 9.)

The use of counterexample, which we study in the next section (3B), is justified by definition 8.

3B COUNTEREXAMPLE

3B1 Definition and Explanation.

Def. 10. A **counterexample** to an argument form is a concrete argument of that form in which every premiss (or *the* premiss) is true, but the conclusion is false.

A counterexample to an argument form is used to prove that the argument form is invalid.

For example:

ARGUMENT FORM	COUNTEREXAMPLE
All D are M	*All dogs are mammals.* (true premiss)
All C are M	*All cats are mammals.* (true premiss)
∴ All C are D	∴ *All cats are dogs* (false conclusion)

The argument form above is invalid because a concrete argument (the counterexample) of this form can be given having both premisses true and a false conclusion, and no valid argument can have all true premisses and a false conclusion.[6]

3B2 Procedure for Finding Counterexample.

Step 1. Replace the variables in the conclusion with concrete terms that will make the resulting proposition (the conclusion) false. (Sometimes it works as well to start by substituting terms in the premisses that will make the resulting propositions obviously true.)

ARGUMENT FORM   COUNTEREXAMPLE

All *B* are *C*   All *B* are *C*
No *B* are *D*   No *B* are *D*
∴ All *D* are *C*   ∴ *All mammals are fish.* (false)

Step 2. Substitute the selected terms for the appropriate variables in the premisses. Care should be taken to substitute identical terms for identical variables. Thus in the above example, since "mammals" was substituted for *"D"* in the conclusion it must be substituted for *"D"* in the premiss, and since "fish" was substituted for *"C"* in the conclusion it must be substituted for *"C"* in the premiss. We now have:

ARGUMENT FORM   COUNTEREXAMPLE

All *B* are *C*   *All B* are fish.
No *B* are *D*   *No B* are mammals.
∴ All *D* are *C*   ∴ *All mammals are fish.* (false)

Step 3. Now one must find a term such that when it is substituted for the remaining variable (*"B"* in the above example) it will make the premisses true (preferably, obviously true). Such a term is "sharks".

ARGUMENT FORM   COUNTEREXAMPLE

All *B* are *C*   *All sharks are fish.* (true)
No *B* are *D*   *No sharks are mammals.* (true)
∴ All *D* are *C*   ∴ *All mammals are fish.* (false)

We could also have substituted "fish" for *B*, though we have already used it for *C*. If we had done so we would have obtained a **degenerate** instance (example), that is, one in which the number of distinct terms is less than the number of distinct variables in the original form. It has true premisses, "All fish are fish" and "No fish are mammals", and a false conclusion.

Step 4. If we cannot complete step 3, then it is best to return to step 1, select a different pair of terms, and proceed as before. However, if a counterexample is not found after many attempts, three possibilities are left:

(a) There is a counterexample, though it has not been found; or

(b) The forms for premisses are inconsistent, that is, they cannot both be made true by correct substitution; or

(c) The argument form is valid, so there is no counterexample.

It is important to note that failure to find a counterexample does not prove the argument form valid.

Note also that an argument form cannot be proved valid by giving an instance (example) of this form with true premisses and a true conclusion, because it is possible for both valid and invalid arguments to have true premisses and a true conclusion.

Exercises for Chapter 3

EX 3A1–3A3. For numbers 1–6, place the most appropriate letter in each blank. If "All of the above are correct" is true, then no other answer is appropriate.

_____ 1. An argument that is not formally valid: (a) may not be semantically valid. (b) may be semantically valid. (c) is not valid by virtue of its form words and pattern of terms. (d) All of the above are correct.

_____ 2. A false proposition: (a) cannot have a form. (b) may have the same form as a true proposition. (c) has a form only if the proposition could be true at some future time. (c) None of the above is the correct answer.

_____ 3. Which of the following statements is true? (a) A propositional form has at least one term in it. (b) A pure propositional form has no form words in it. (c) A pure propositional form consists only of variables and form words. (d) A propositional form consists only of form words.

_____ 4. The "A" in the propositional form "All A are camelopards" is called: (a) term abbreviation. (b) form word. (c) term variable. (d) term.

_____ 5. An argument whose validity depends upon the meaning of its terms as well as its form words is called a: (a) semantically valid argument. (b) mixed form. (c) formally valid argument. (d) completely valid argument.

_____ 6. Which of the following is not a form of "Some pilots are not epileptics"? (a) Some A are not B. (b) Some C are not C. (c) Some B are not D. (d) Some P are not E.

By replacing the terms by variables, give a pure argument form for each of the following arguments (7–10):

7. All parrots are talkative birds; therefore some talkative birds are parrots.
8. No black holes are visible objects, hence some visible objects are not black holes.
9. Only birds are passerines and all bluejays are birds; therefore only passerines are bluejays.

10. No violets are roses, since all roses are red flowers and no violets are red flowers.

EX 3A4–3A6. Place the most appropriate letter in each blank.

_____ 1. A distinctive form of a proposition is: (a) a mixed form. (b) a pure form. (c) a form that has only form words in it. (d) a form that has only one variable in it.

_____ 2. If a proposition has only two distinct terms in it, then its distinctive form will have: (a) less than two distinct term variables in it. (b) exactly two distinct term variables in it. (c) more than two distinct term variables in it. (d) any number of distinct term variables in it.

_____ 3. Which of the following statements is true? (a) A proposition has exactly one distinctive form. (b) An argument may have two or more distinctive forms. (d) If a proposition has a distinctive form, then it has no other form. (d) a proposition has exactly two distinctive forms.

_____ 4. Which one of the following statements is true? (a) A formally valid argument has a distinctive form. (b) A distinctive form of an argument is always valid. (c) A formally valid argument may have an invalid distinctive form. (d) A formally valid argument and an argument not formally valid may have the same distinctive form.

_____ 5. Which one of the following argument is not an instance of the form "All A are B, hence some B are C"? (a) All cats are felines, hence some felines are tigers. (b) All felines are cats, hence some felines are tigers. (c) All cats are felines, hence some felines are felines. (d) All cats are cats, hence some cats are cats.

_____ 6. If every possible example of an argument form is formally valid, then the argument form is: (a) formally valid. (b) a mixed argument form. (c) semantically valid. (d) not formally valid.

_____ 7. An invalid argument form is an argument form of which: (a) all instances (examples) are invalid. (b) most instances are invalid. (c) some instances are invalid. (d) no instances are invalid.

_____ 8. A distinctive form of the proposition "If some logicians are Romantics, then some Romantics are logicians" is: (a) If some

B are *C*, then some *C* are *B*. (b) If some *B* are *C*, then some *B* are *C*. (c) If some *B* are *C*, then some *C* are *C*. (d) If some *B* are *C*, then some *D* are *F*.

_____ 9. If an argument is formally valid, then: (a) every form of this argument is valid. (b) its distinctive forms are the only valid forms of it. (c) its distinctive forms are valid. (d) only its forms that are not distinctive are valid.

_____ 10. Which of the following statements is false? (a) An argument form may have two examples: one that is formally valid and one that is invalid. (b) If a distinctive form of an argument is invalid, then the argument is not formally valid. (c) If an argument is formally valid, then all of its argument forms are valid. (d) It is possible for two different argument forms, one of which is valid and the other invalid, to have an instance in common.

EX 3B. Prove the following argument forms invalid by counterexample. (Numbers 9 and 10 are the most difficult.)

1. Some *A* are *B*; therefore, all *A* are *B*.
2. A few *S* are *P*; therefore, most *S* are *P*.
3. Only *C* are *D*, hence only *D* are *C*.
4. Some *P* are not *S*, hence some *S* are not *P*.
5. Every *D* is an *F*; therefore nothing that is not a *D* is an *F*.
6. No *C* are *B*, therefore nothing which is not a *C* is a thing which is not a *B*.
7. No *C* are *D* and no *D* are *E*, hence no *C* are *E*.
8. Every *A* is *B* and every *C* is *B*; therefore, every *A* is *C*.
9. Over half the *S*'s are *M*'s and over half the *M*'s are *P*'s; therefore, over half the *S*'s are *P*'s.
10. At least one *S* is *P*; therefore, at least one thing that is not an *S* is not a *P*.

Review of chapter 3. Answer "Y" for "Yes" or "N" for "No".

_____ 1. Does every proposition have more than one propositional form?

Exercises/Chapter 3

_____ 2. Does an argument form ever contain concrete terms?

_____ 3. If an argument form is valid, then are all arguments having this form formally valid?

_____ 4. If an argument form is invalid, then are all arguments having this form invalid?

_____ 5. Can all of the premisses of a valid argument be true and the conclusion false?

_____ 6. Can a counterexample be used to prove argument forms valid?

_____ 7. Does failure to find a counterexample for an argument form prove this argument form to be valid?

_____ 8. Is the argument "*All mothers are females; therefore, all females are mothers*" a counterexample to the argument form "All B are C; therefore, all C are D"?

_____ 9. Is the argument quoted in 8, above, a counterexample to the argument form "All A are B; therefore all C are D"?

_____ 10. Is it true that an argument has only one distinctive argument form?

4

Terms

In chapter 2 it was pointed out that propositions consist of form words and terms.[1] It is the purpose of this chapter to distinguish, define, and classify some of the common kinds and properties of terms.

4A BASIC DEFINITIONS

Def. 1. A **substantive** (SUB-stan-tive) is a noun, noun phrase, or pronoun (in nominative or objective case).

Examples: "John", "dog of ill repute", "he", "him"; also "HCl" (as symbol for "hydrogen chloride").

Def. 2. A **term expression** is a substantive or an adjectival expression.

Examples: "John", "dog of ill repute", "beautiful", "democratic", and "long and tiring".

A term expression is a symbolic pattern consisting of a word or words or certain other written or spoken symbols. In short, it is the words or symbols that constitute a substantive or an adjectival expression.

Def. 3. A **term** is a term expression, as taken with a specific meaning.[2]

Definition 3 is further clarified by definitions 3a and 3b. Definition 3 corresponds to one of the more general uses of "term" in logic. There is also the more special use in "term of a proposition" defined in 3A3, definition 3.[3]

Def. 3a. Terms are **the same** iffi they have both the same term expression and the same meaning.

Def. 3b. Terms are **distinct** iffi they differ in term expression or in meaning.

In this chapter—and throughout the book—the terms "word", "sentence", "expression", and "term" will ordinarily refer to a repeatable sensory pattern, rather than to a token (i.e., an individual physical mark or sound).[4] Thus in the second sentence of this chapter, there are two occurrences of the word "the", three occurrences of the word "of", and two occurrences of the word "and". Hence the sentence in question contains only seventeen words (that is, word types), though it has twenty-one running words (that is, word tokens).

Def. 4. Equivalent terms are terms that have the same meaning. (They may, but need not, have the same term expression).

Def. 5. A term is a **homograph** of another term iffi they have the same written term expression but differ in derivation and meaning.

Examples: "Socrates" and "SOCRATES" as terms are the same term if they mean the same person; they are also equivalent. "Woman-hater" and "misogynist" are distinct equivalent terms (or synonyms). There are two kinds of equivalent terms and also two kinds of non-equivalent terms. "Dog" and "mammal" are completely distinct, differing in homographs and meaning. "Plane" meaning *airplane* and "plane" in geometry are homographs.

Table 4.1: Relations Between Terms

Term Expression \ Meaning	A and B have the **same meaning**	A and B have **different meanings**
A and B have the **same term expression**	A and B are the *same terms*	A and B are *homonyms*
A and B have **different term expressions**	A and B are *distinct equivalent terms*	A and B are *completely distinct terms*

This table sums up four equivalences; for example, if A and B have the same term expression and the same meaning, then A and B are identical terms, and conversely.

4B GENERAL AND DISCRETE TERMS

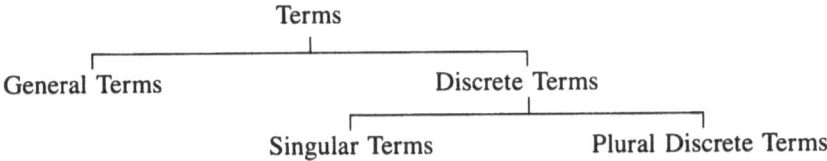

A basic distinction, going back to Aristotle, is that between a general (or common) term, which is predicable of each of many objects, and a singular (or individual) term, which is predicable of just one object.[5] Some clarification of these concepts is required. Also, we find there are terms that are neither general nor singular and introduce the expression "discrete term" to include those and singular terms.

A term is *predicable* of an object iffi it can be predicated with truth of the object.[6] To be predicated of an object is to be asserted as predicate of that object. To say that the term "dog" is predicable of Spot is to say that "dog" can be asserted truly as predicate of Spot—in short, that Spot is a dog. To say that the term "accident" is predicated of John's fall is to say that "accident" can be asserted truly of John's fall—in short, that John's fall was an accident. Note that for lack of a more general term in ordinary use that applies to all kinds of "things", we use "object" to mean physical and imaginary objects and events. We use "object" to mean "object of thought."

4B1 General Terms. The following definition of a general term is adapted from W. E. Johnson.[7] As distinguished from traditional definitions of a general term it makes use of what we call the No-Some Criterion.

> **Def. 6.** A **general term** S is either an adjectival term or a term that the quantifiers "no" and "some" can modify in grammatically correct sentences of the forms "No S is (are) P," "Some S is (are) P".[8]

It should be noted that in traditional grammar "all", "no", "some", "every", and other such quantifiers are called "adjectives" in certain uses, but they are form words, not terms. Hence these quantifiers cannot be general terms.

By "adjectival terms" we mean such terms as "red", "ugly", "absent from the exam", and "very clever" as used in the sentences "Roses are red", and "Gargoyles are ugly", "Some students are absent from the exam", and "John is very clever". Adjectival terms are not nouns, noun phrases, or pronouns; consequently they cannot be the logical subject of a proposition. Most of them by far can be truly predicted of two or more distinct things, which is sufficient to guarantee that they are general terms. In fact, they are all general terms.

The terms "cats", "logic student", and "integer between 3 and 5" are general terms, since each can meaningfully be prefixed by "no" or "some" in sentences of the form "No S is (are) P" and "Some S is (are) P". For example, the correctness of the sentence "No cat is purple" demonstrates that "cats" is a general term. Also sufficient to demonstrate this is the correctness of the sentence "Some cat is fat".

The terms "logic students" and "integer between 3 and 5" are proved to be general terms by the correctness, respectively, of the sentences "Some logic students are females" and "No integer between 3 and 5 is even". The latter sentence is grammatically correct even though false.

When a name such as "Hitler" is meaningfully prefixed by "no" or "some" in a sentence, the name becomes a general term. For example, "Hitler" is a general term in the sentence "No Hitler is wanted here". This sentence means the same as "No person like Adolph Hitler is wanted here".

Terms such as "these cats", "that student", "the oldest logic student" are not general terms, since they cannot meaningfully be prefixed by "no" or "some" in sentences of the form "No these cats are such-and-such",[9] "Some that student is such-and-such", "No the oldest logic student is such-and-such".

4B2 Discrete Terms,[10] Singular and Plural. The division of terms into general and singular poses a problem, because there are plural terms that are not general, but the expression "plural singular term" would seem self-contradictory. An example of a plural term that is not general is "the Smith brothers". If we say "Al and Ed are the Smith brothers" we are predicating the term of two objects, but we are not predicating the term of *each* of two objects. We cannot say "Al is the Smith brothers and Ed is the Smith brothers." Applying the No-Some Criterion for general terms, we find that "No the Smith brothers . . ." and "Some the Smith brothers . . ." are nonsense. Therefore we conclude that "the Smith brothers" is not a general term because it is not applied to each of the Smith brothers individually.[11] (It is assumed, of course, that the term "the Smith brothers" is being used consistently in a context to refer to a certain group of brothers, for example, Al and Ed Smith of 654 Apple Blossom Lane, South Toonerville.)

To avoid the awkwardness of calling "the Smith brothers" a "plural singular term", we use the term "discrete" for all terms that are not general. Hence "the Smith brothers" is a plural discrete term, and "Al Smith" is a singular discrete term or (simply) a singular term.[12]

An affirmative definition is generally preferable to a negative one, but the following definition is one of the cases in which simplicity and conciseness recommend making an exception to the rule.

Def. 7. A **discrete term** is a substantive that is not a general term.

Examples: (proper name) *Napoleon, the Alps;* (definite descriptions) *the wisest man, my parents;* (personal and demonstrative pronouns) *I, these.* We limit discrete terms to substantives because all adjectival terms are general terms.

As the above definition allows, a discrete term may name nothing. For example, the singular (discrete) term "Mrs. Smith's youngest child" might not apply to anything; but if the meaning of the words is fixed, we know from the nature of the superlative "youngest" that it cannot apply to more than one object even if *we* don't know which Mrs. Smith is meant.

Remember that by our definitions an expression is not the same term when used with a different meaning. I may call my dog "Socrates", but this is not the same term as the subject of the sentence *"Socrates died in 399 B.C."*.

Def. 8. A **definite description** is a noun phrase made by prefixing an individualizing modifier (e.g., *my, Napoleon's, this, these, that, the*) to a general term, the whole intended to refer to just one determined object or collection of objects.[13]

Discrete terms are divided into singular and plural, as our examples have indicated. The distinction usually agrees with the grammatical distinction of singular and plural in English. But, for example, a royal or editorial "we" is a singular term logically if it refers to just one person.

Def. 9. A **singular term** is a discrete term intended to name just one determinate object (which may be a collection taken as a unit).

Singular terms may be *abstract* or *concrete* (see 4E). Examples of abstract singular terms are: *triangularity, her beauty, the class of even integers.*

Concrete singular terms are of three kinds:

(i) Proper names: *Mr. Brown, Pegasus, Lake Erie,* etc.
(ii) Definite descriptions: *the oldest person here, that man,* etc.
(iii) Personal and demonstrative pronouns (standing for a determinate object): e.g., *He* in *"He is a clever man"* (but not in *"He who hesitates is lost"*).

Def. 10. A **plural discrete term** is a discrete term that names a collection of objects taken explicitly as plural.

Plural discrete terms may be abstract or concrete. An example of an abstract plural discrete term is: *The seven cardinal virtues.*
Concrete plural discrete terms are of three kinds:

(iv) Proper names: e.g., *the Seychelles, the Pyrenees, the Smiths,* etc.
(v) Definite descriptions: e.g., *the people who were swimming, the Smith brothers, these books.*
(vi) Personal and demonstrative pronouns (standing for a determinate plurality): e.g., *they, we, those.*

4C COLLECTIVE TERMS AND COLLECTIVE USE

Def. 11. A **collective term** is a term that names collections or a unique collection of similar individuals, rather than the individuals in the collection.

A **collection** here may be either: (a) an abstract entity, namely a class or set consisting of all objects having a certain attribute (or of certain enumerated objects), abstracted from their specific location and interrelations, (e.g., *the class of all bipeds*); or (b) a concrete or relatively concrete entity, not a mere class but an assemblage of objects, not only sharing a certain attribute but (naturally or artificially) brought or found together, localized in time and space (e.g., a *forest,* an *army,* a *stamp collection,* etc.).[14] The italicized expressions in the preceding sentence are all collective terms.

A plural common noun is usually not a collective term unless the singular form is collective. For example, "dog" is not a collective term, and "dogs" is the plural form of a non-collective noun. But in the sentence "Dogs are numerous here", "dogs" is being used collectively, as if the sentence read: *"The class of dogs here* is numerous". (See 4C1.)

Def. 12. A **non-collective term** is a term that is non-collective.

These are examples of non-collective terms: *trees, house, redheaded men.*

Both collective and non-collective terms may be general or discrete. Some examples are given:

COLLECTIVE TERMS		NON-COLLECTIVE TERMS	
General Terms	Discrete Terms	General Terms	Discrete Terms
regiment	the 23rd Regiment	soldier	that soldier
litter	my dog's litter	brown dog	Fido
mountain range	the Alps	mountains	Mont Blanc

4C1 Collection Use and Divisive Use. Terms in propositions may be used *divisively* (distributively) or *collectively.* A general term used collectively may or may not be a collective term.

Def. 13. A general (or collective) term is used **collectively** in a proposition iffi by its use the proposition asserts something of the objects to which the term applies *taken together* as a class, collection, or whole.

Examples of terms used collectively (such terms being underlined): "*Men* are numerous" and "*The Germans* are a nation".

Examples of singular collective terms used collectively: "*The Coldstream Guards* are *the only regiment representing the New Model Army*". (We exclude singular non-collective terms, for example, "Socrates", from the application of definition 13 to avoid artificial problems.)

Def. 14. A term is used **divisively** (or **distributively**) in a proposition iffi by its use the proposition asserts that something is true of at least one member or each member of a certain class, where the term applies either to each member of the class or to the class as such.[15]

Examples of terms used divisively (such terms being underlined): "Some *dogs* are *collies*", "All *dogs* are *collies*," "No *collies* are *terriers*", "Some *dogs* are not *collies*."

A general collective term is commonly used divisively while retaining its collective nature. "*Every regiment has a commanding officer*" predicates something of each individual regiment, without losing the collective character of "regiment".

Singular collective terms are most often used collectively, but are sometimes used divisively, that is, to assert something of individuals to which the term applies collectively. In Eaton's example (page 313), *"The 103rd regiment were all young men"*, the singular term "The 103rd regiment" is used divisively in this proposition, since the proposition asserts something of each member of a certain class, namely the 103rd regiment, and the term applies to the class (of which it is the name), though it does not apply "to each member of the class", that is, it is not true that each soldier in the regiment is the 103rd regiment. It may be thought of as an elliptical way of saying *"All members of the 103rd regiment were young men"*.

4D SUBTERMS AND SUPERTERMS

We now introduce the expressions "subterm" and "superterm", both of which apply only to general terms.

Def. 15. Term 'X' is a **subterm** of term 'Y' iffi every X is a Y or everything X is Y.

For example, subterms of "animal" are "land animal", "cat", "cold-blooded vertebrate", and "Australian rabbit". Also "animal" is itself a subterm of "animal", because every animal is an animal.

Def. 16. Term 'X' is a **superterm** of term 'Y' iffi every Y is an X or everything Y is X.

For example, superterms of "Persian cat" are "Persian cat", "cat", "feline", "animal", "quadruped", and "real object".

Note that if term X is a superterm of Y then Y is a subterm of X and, conversely, if Y is a subterm of X then X is a superterm of Y.

Parallel to the concept of "subterm" is the better known concept of *"subclass"*.

Def. 17. Class C_1 is a **subclass** of class C_2 iffi every member of C_1 is a member of C_2.

For example, subclasses of animals are land animals, cats, cold-blooded vertebrates, and Australian rabbits. Also the class of animals is itself a subclass of animals, because every member of the class of animals is a member of the class of animals.

Def. 18. Class C_1 is a **proper subclass** of class C_2 iffi C_1 is a subclass of C_2 and C_2 is not a subclass of C_1.

The difference between a proper subclass and a subclass is that no class can be a proper subclass of itself. The class of animals is a subclass of itself, but not a proper subclass of itself.

4E CONCRETE AND ABSTRACT TERMS

Though there are probably relatively few pages of a logic textbook that do not use both concrete and abstract terms, this division is taught less frequently in contemporary books than it used to be.

Def. 19. A **concrete term** is a term that can be meaningfully applied to a thing in time, a person, or an event, or to a group or collection of such things, persons, or events localized in time or space.[16]

The following are examples of concrete terms: *man, tree, sneeze, red, heavy, democratic, Mr. Smith, the tallest boy in the room, the Christian God, the Widner Library, the Washington Zoo, the 33rd Congress.*

Def. 20. An **abstract term** is a term intended to apply to an abstraction such as a property, relation, or class (distinguished from a concrete collection), and grammatically treating the abstraction as if it were a thing.

Examples of abstract terms are: *liberality, redness, color, heaviness, social equality, democracy in France, astronomy, the number 2, the class of all pairs, the class of animals.*

Note that positive, negative, and privative terms, as well as contradictory and contrary terms, will be covered in chapter 12, "Negative Terms."

4F THE MEANING OF TERMS: THREE MODES OF MEANING

The theory of meaning in traditional logic is largely based on Arnauld's *Port-Royal Logic (Art of Thinking)*, which distinguished "comprehension" and "extension" of terms (or "ideas"). This work contained a Cartesian revision of the scholastic doctrine of the properties of terms. We shall not attempt to present the historical background nor to explain the diverse modern theories of meaning. We aim simply to give a coherent account of one version of the modern doctrine of terms. In this doctrine we distinguish three principle modes of meaning of terms: intensional, extensional, and verbal.[17]

These modes of meaning are as important in everyday discourse as they are in logic. Effective communication depends upon the mutual understanding of the meaning of terms. The meaning of a term can be communicated in different ways. One can indicate a set of properties that the things the term applies to have in common: this is an *intension* of the term;[18] or one can give examples of things that the term applies to: such things are members of the term's *extension;* or one can give a word or phrase that means the same as the term in question: this is the *verbal meaning* of the term.

A term may apply to objects that are *actual,* like tables, dogs, and trees, or to objects that are *real* (but not actual), like numbers. Some terms do not apply to any real object, but apply to possible objects such as centaurs and chess-playing chipmunks.

The kind of object (actual, real, possible) that a term applies to has some bearing on the modes of its meaning; therefore, before we discuss each of these modes of meaning we will discuss the three kinds of objects a term may apply to or name.

4F1 Kinds of Objects. The kinds of intensional and extensional meaning that a term has are intrinsically related to the kinds of objects that the term names. Therefore, in order to present a systematic theory of the meaning of terms it is necessary to describe certain kinds of objects.

a *Possible Objects.* A **possible object** is an object that can be described or defined by a set of properties that is logically and semantically consistent. All physical objects (dogs, trees, tables, etc.) are possible objects, since each can be described by a consistent set of properties. Also imaginary objects such as unicorns are possible objects, since a unicorn can be defined by a consistent set of properties: an animal with the body and head of a horse, the hind legs of a stag, the tail of a lion, and a single long straight horn in the middle of its forehead. This definition may describe an animal whose existence is inconsistent with zoological knowledge, but the description is logically and semantically self-consistent.

Expression such as "round square", "four-sided triangle", and "married bachelor" do not name or describe any possible object, since these properties are inconsistent.

b *Real and Non-real Objects.* Possible objects are either real or non-real. Objects or possible objects are **real** if there are such things, **non-real**

if there are no such things. As logicians, we offer here no specific criterion of our own for distinguishing what is or is not. Most people, if asked whether there are such things as dogs, numbers, and dreams, would say "yes". And if asked whether there are such things as centaurs, a Santa Claus at the North Pole, and frictionless physical surfaces, they would say "no". Hence, we would say that these people regard dogs, numbers, and dreams as real objects (though not necessarily physical objects) and regard centaurs, Santa Claus, and so on as not real objects. If they are objects of thought, they are non-real objects. Of course people may disagree concerning what is and what is not. Examples of objects whose reality has been debated are God, human souls, and Unidentified Flying Objects (UFOs).

c *Actual and Non-actual Real Objects.* Real objects (objects that are) we divide into actual objects and non-actual objects. An **actual object** is a real object that exists in time and may or may not be in space. All physical objects such as dogs, trees, tables, and so on are actual objects as well as such mental objects as headaches and feelings. A feeling of unpleasantness exists in time, since it has duration, but it is difficult to locate it definitely in the space of the physical world or to give it precise boundaries. A **non-actual real object** is a real object that is not in time (which implies that it is also not in space). Examples of non-actual real objects are numbers, logical and mathematical relations (e.g., symmetry), and geometric figures (squares, cubes, trapezoids, etc.). These objects are real in the sense that there are such things, but they are not in real space or time. For example, numbers have neither spatial properties nor duration.

The division of possible objects may be summarized as follows:

Table 4.2: Possible Objects

	Real Objects (What is)	**Non-Real Objects** (What is not)
Actual Objects (Objects in time)	Dogs, trees, hats, headaches, feelings, emotions	(Actual, Non-Real Objects are Impossible Objects)
Non-Actual Objects (Objects not in time)	Numbers, logical relations, circles; non-temporal God (?)	Centaurs, frictionless surface; non-temporal God?

4F2 Kinds of Intensional Meaning. The meaning of the expression "applies to" as used in such sentences as "The term *dog* applies to Cocker Spaniels" is almost self-evident. Nevertheless, we formally define "applies to", since it is a basic term in our theory of terms and since it may be used in different senses.

Def. 21. The term *"Y"* **applies to** X iffi X is a Y.

For example, the term "dog" applies to Spot iffi Spot is a dog. The term "red" apples to my book iffi my book is red. the term "rich" applies to any person at whatever time that person is rich.

For substantive terms such as "dog", "little brown dog", "the number 2", we also say each names or is a name of whatever it applies to. For terms that apply to nothing real, as for example "unicorns", we interpret the sentence *"Unicorns applies to non-real objects only"* to mean: there aren't really any unicorns, but the term "unicorns" applies to certain imaginary objects.

We now give a definition of "intension" broad enough to cover the four kinds of intension of terms.

Def. 22. An **intension** of a term is a property or set of properties that the possible objects the term applies to have in common.[19]

The most important kind of intension is conventional intension.

Def. 23. A **conventional intension** of a term to a group of persons using the term is a property or set of properties of possible objects that the group accepts as necessary and jointly sufficient for the term to apply to such objects.

For example, a conventional intension of the term "triangle" to the vast majority of English-speaking people using this term is the property of being a three-sided rectilinear plane figure. An equivalent conventional intension of "triangle" is the set of properties consisting of being a rectilinear plane figure and being three-sided. If the object lacks either property it is not called a triangle (so each property is necessary); and if it has both properties it is correctly called a triangle; that is, the term "triangle" applies to it, so the properties are jointly sufficient.

A term expression may have different conventional intensions depending upon the different ways different groups of people use it. The intension of a term expression that the military accepts and uses as conventional may differ greatly from conventional intension in non-military use. Consequently, conventional intension of a term is not defined as the most widely accepted intension of the term or as the proper and socially correct intension of the term. Of course a conventional intension of a term accepted and used by a group of people that constitute a language-speaking group, such as the English, the French, or the Chinese, is generally more important than a conventional intension of this term to some subgroup, such as jazz musicians, Air Force pilots, or convicts.

To know a conventional intension of a term is to know the term's established usage for a certain group of people. And to report this establish usage is to give a correct lexical definition of the term as used by this group (see 5C1).

> **Def. 24.** A **subjective intension** of a term is a property or set of properties of possible objects the person accepts as necessary and jointly sufficient for the term to apply to such objects.

For example, the subjective intension of the term "dog" to a child might be the property of being a brown, friendly animal with a short stumpy tail. Logicians generally consider subjective intension the least important kind of intension.[20]

> **Def. 25.** The **analytic intension (comprehension)** of a term is the set of all properties entailed (formally or semantically) by a conventional intension of the term.[21]

Analytic intension includes conventional intension. The analytic intension of "triangle" in Euclidian geometry includes both "having three sides" and "having the sum of the interior angles equal to two right angles".

> **Def. 26.** The **total objective intension** of a term is the set of all properties (know or unknown) that the real objects that the term applies to have in common.[22]

For example, the total objective intension of the term "dog" is the set of all properties, known or unknown, that all dogs have in common. Some of these properties are the known properties of being a mammal, a vertebrate, a canine, and so on. There may be a minimal size, but this is presently unknown. The total objective intension of a term includes its analytic intension and its conventional intension.

In the absence of agreement among logicians as to the meaning of "connotation", we suggest adopting a literary usage, which, as Hospers says, is "the usual meaning of 'connotation' among users of English."[23]

> **Def. 27.** The **connotation** of a term to a person or group of persons is the class of thoughts, feelings, and emotions that the term elicits in the person or group by association.

4F3 Extension and Denotation. In 4F2 we discussed the kinds of intension of terms.[24] These were defined in terms of properties of possible objects. In this subsection we shift our attention from the properties of objects to the objects themselves, or from intension of terms to extension.

Def. 28. The **extension** of a term (relative to a given conventional intension) is the class of possible objects to which the term (as taken with that intension) applies.

Another way of putting it is to say that the extension of a term is a class of possible objects each of which has the properties included in the conventional intension of the term. The usual definitions of extension omit such references to intension as we include (bracketed) in our definition, thus obscuring the dependence of knowledge (or definition) of extension of a term upon knowledge of intension.

Def. 29. A **nominatum** (plural **nominata**) of a term is any possible object to which the term would apply.

For example, Pegasus is a nominatum of the term "winged horse". Bucephalus (Alexander's horse) and Whirlaway (triple-Crown-Turf Winner, 1941) are nominata of the term "horse". Simply put, the extension of a term is a specific class of possible objects, and a nominatum is a member of this class.

The term "denotes" is similar to "applies to", except that only a real object can be denoted.

Def. 30. Term T **denotes** an object X iffi T applies to X and X is real.

The term "horse" denotes Bucephalus, war-horse of Alexander the Great, and any other horse that ever was or will be. The term "Bucephalus" (as just used) denotes the aforesaid horse Bucephalus and nothing else. The term "Pegasus" applies to (and names) but does not denote a winged horse that sprang from the blood of Medusa, if we are correct in our belief that there never was any such animal.

The term "integer between 3 and 6" denotes the integers 4 and 5. The term "integer between 3 and 4" (exclusive sense) does not denote anything (also it does not apply to anything), since there is no such integer (and no possibility of such integer).

Adjectives may denote, as the term "green" denotes anything green.

Def. 31. The **denotation** (or **real extension**) of a term is the class of real objects that the term denotes.[25]

Def. 32. A **denotatum** (plural **denotata**) of a term is any real object denoted by that term.

The denotation of a term is a certain class of real objects. A denotatum is a member of this class. Hence every denotation is a subclass of an extension. Every denotatum (which must be a real object) is a nominatum (which is a possible object).

A singular term has either just one denotatum (e.g., "Bucephalus") or none (e.g., "Pegasus"). A general term may have no denotata (e.g., "centaur") or any number (e.g., "dog").

Def. 33. An **empty term** is a term that does not denote anything.[26]

An empty term has no denotatum, but it has a denotation, the empty class, that is, the class that has no members. An empty term may also be said to have zero denotation.

Since classes are considered identical if they have the same members, two terms have the same denotation iffi they denote the same objects. Thus, "the number of (running) words in definition 33 of this chapter" and "the integer between 10 and 12" have the same denotatum (namely, the number 11), and hence the same denotation (the class whose only member is the number 11).

4F4 The Relation Between Extension and Intension. The relation between denotation (or real extension) and (conventional) intension is expressed in a law precisely stated as follows:

Law of Inverse Variation of Denotation and Intension. If a series of terms is arranged in order of increasing intension, the denotation of the terms will either remain the same or diminish.[27]

(a) The following is an example of terms arranged in order of increasing intension:

   (i) cat
   (ii) white cat
   (iii) white Persian cat
   (iv) white Persian cat that dislikes milk
   (v) young white Persian cat that dislikes milk.

It is obvious that term (ii) has more intension than term (i)—that is, the intension of term (ii) could be expressed by adding a distinct property to the properties constituting the conventional intension of term (i)—and that term (iii) has more intension than term (ii), and so on. It is highly probable but not certain that each term in the series has less denotation than any term preceding it. It is certain that each term has no more denotation than any preceding term.

(b) Here is an example of terms arranged in order of increasing intension while denotation remains the same:

(i) man
(ii) mortal man
(iii) mortal man with ancestors
(iv) mortal man with ancestors that weigh less than four tons each

Here every term (we believe) has the same denotation as the first term "man". This is because all men are mortal and have ancestors who weighed less than four tons each.

(c) Another way of increasing intension and keeping denotation the same is to start with an empirically empty term.

(i) man with five hands
(ii) Australian man with five hands
(iii) Australian man over three years old with five hands

Term (i), "man with five hands", is an empty term. Its denotation is the empty class. Increasing the intension, in this case, cannot change the denotation; hence terms (ii) and (iii) are also empty terms.

4F5 The Verbal Meaning of Terms. A formal treatment of verbal meaning could be developed, but it would require a terminology rather formidable for an introductory text. Consequently, we give an informal and incomplete account of verbal meaning.

It is not uncommon, for example, when learning a foreign language, to regard a word or verbal expression as the meaning of a term. In other words, a term expression may be the meaning of a term (with a different term expression). For example, a student wishes to know how to translate the French word *bain*. The French-English dictionary indicates that it means "bath". Hence the word "bath" is a verbal meaning of the French *bain*.

Def. 34a. A **verbal meaning** of a term is a term expression claimed to apply to everything the term applies to.

Another example is a student who learns that the scientific Latin name for "walrus" is *Odobenus rosmarus*. To the student who knows little or no

Latin, these words are simply a verbal meaning to add to any other meanings of the term "walrus".

Another example is that of a child who wants to know what a moose is. He is told by a learned and unsympathetic adult that a moose is a herbivorous quadruped with very large palmate antlers. The adult has given a verbal meaning of the term "moose" to the child, since the child knows that this sequence of big words means "moose", even though he doesn't know the intensional or extensional meaning of these words.

Although there are different kinds of verbal meaning, parallel to the different kinds of intension and extension, we shall mention here only one, found in most verbal definitions, (see 5D3) namely, equivalential verbal meaning.

Def. 34b. An **equivalential verbal meaning** of a term is a term expression claimed to apply to everything the term applies to and to nothing else.

In the first two examples above, "bath" and *Odobenus rosmarus* are equivalent verbal meanings, respectively, of *bain* and "walrus" and would be such by virtue of the intention or claim even if not correct. In the third example, the long phrase, though correctly asserted of moose, is (we presume) not claimed to be equivalent to "moose", and so is not an equivalential verbal meaning.

A verbal meaning such as "bath" for *"bain"*, or *"Odobenus rosmarus"* for "walrus", when reasonably correct, is commonly called a synonym. Ordinary usage (which we follow) accepts words as synonyms—such as "big" and "large"—even if they are by no means interchangeable in every context. But a synonym is traditionally defined as a "word", meaning usually a single word (in the strict sense), though some standard combinations of words (probably including binomial names in Linnaean nomenclature, such as *Homo sapiens* or *Odobenus rosmarus*) are counted as single words.[28]

Exercises for Chapter 4

EX 4A. Place the most appropriate letter in the margin.

_____ 1. Two terms are semantically different if they: (a) have different meanings. (b) are spelled differently. (c) have different word orders. (d) have different words.

_____ 2. A noun, noun phrase, or pronoun (in nominative or objective case) is: (a) an adjectival expression. (b) a substantive. (c) a sentence. (d) a proposition.

_____ 3. A substantive or adjectival expression, taken with a certain meaning, is called a (a) term. (b) proposition. (c) propositional form. (d) sentence.

_____ 4. If two terms are identical, then they are: (a) equivalent. (b) distinct. (c) adjectival expressions. (d) substantives.

_____ 5. If two terms differ either as term expressions or in meaning, then they are: (a) identical. (b) equivalent. (c) distinct. (d) homonyms.

_____ 6. If two terms have different meanings and different term expressions, then they are: (a) completely distinct. (b) equivalent. (c) identical. (d) homonyms.

_____ 7. If two terms have the same meaning and the same term expression, then they are: (a) distinct. (b) identical (c) homonyms. (d) synonyms.

_____ 8. If two terms have the same meaning, but have different term expressions, then they are: (a) completely distinct terms. (b) distinct equivalent terms. (c) identical terms. (d) homonyms.

_____ 9. Two terms are distinct equivalent terms iffi they have: (a) the same meaning and the same term expression. (b) the same meaning but different term expressions. (c) different meanings but the same term expression. (d) different meanings and different term expressions.

_____ 10. Words that have different meanings but the same term expression are called: (a) substantives. (b) distinct equivalent terms. (c) homonyms. (d) adjectival expressions.

_____ 11. The terms "black crows" and "crows that are black" are: (a) occurrences of the same identical term. (b) distinct terms, but not equivalent. (c) equivalent but not distinct terms. (d) distinct equivalent terms.

_____ 12. The terms "dog house" and "house dog" are: (a) completely distinct terms. (b) equivalent terms. (c) identical terms. (d) neither identical nor distinct.

_____ 13. Which statement is true? (a) A term must be a substantive. (b) "Cat" and "feline" are identical terms. (c) "Wombat" and "dingbat" are completely distinct terms. (d) Adjectival expressions cannot be terms.

_____ 14. Which statement is true? (a) If *A* and *B* are identical terms, then they are distinct terms. (b) If *A* and *B* are distinct terms, then they have to be equivalent terms. (c) If *A* and *B* are equivalent terms, then they may be identical terms. (d) If *A* and *B* are equivalent terms, then they must be identical terms.

_____ 15. Which statement is false? (a) Synonyms are words that have the same meaning but different term expressions. (b) All homonyms are completely distinct terms. (c) If two terms are identical, then they are equivalent. (d) Synonyms are distinct terms.

EX 4B, I. Classify the following terms by placing the appropriate letter in the margin.

(a) general term (b) singular term (c) plural discrete term

_____ 1. men
_____ 2. bearded men
_____ 3. that bearded man
_____ 4. those bearded men
_____ 5. the bearded man
_____ 6. Joseph Zuckertort
_____ 7. the bearded men
_____ 8. Puerto Rico
_____ 9. these dastardly deeds
_____ 10. we
_____ 11. army
_____ 12. captain
_____ 13. leaping lizards
_____ 14. our children
_____ 15. my pet crocodile
_____ 16. your guess
_____ 17. Don Addis
_____ 18. your goldfish bowl
_____ 19. goldfish of yours
_____ 20. his goldclubs

_____ 21. unknown authors   _____ 22. violent headwinds
       _____ 23. bearded men carrying goldfish
       _____ 24. the student who had a perfect paper
       _____ 25. the officers of the 104th cavalry

EX 4B, II. Place the appropriate letter in each blank.

_____ 1. All terms are divided into: (a) singular and discrete terms. (b) singular and plural discrete terms. (c) general and discrete terms. (d) proper names and pronouns.

_____ 2. All terms that are not general are: (a) discrete terms. (b) singular terms. (c) plural discrete terms. (d) definite descriptions.

_____ 3. The individualizing modifier "this" prefixed to a general term results in a noun phrase that is called a: (a) general term. (b) personal pronoun. (c) plural discrete term. (d) definite description.

_____ 4. A term that names a collection of objects taken explicitly as plural is called a: (a) plural discrete term. (b) general term. (c) singular term. (d) class term.

_____ 5. Discrete terms are divided into: (a) general and singular terms. (b) general and plural discrete terms. (c) singular and plural discrete terms. (d) proper names and general terms.

_____ 6. The term "that man" is: (a) a definite description. (b) a proper name. (c) general. (d) a plural discrete term.

_____ 7. The term "Napoleon" is a: (a) singular term. (b) general term. (c) demonstrative pronoun. (d) definite description.

_____ 8. Which statement is true? (a) A singular term must be a proper name. (b) A proper name must be a discrete term. (c) A plural discrete term must be a singular term. (d) A definite description must be a singular term.

_____ 9. Which statement is true? (a) Only substantives are discrete terms. (b) Singular terms are general terms. (c) A definite description is intended to apply to an indefinite number of entities. (d) Singular terms are neither abstract nor concrete.

_____ 10. Which statement is false? (a) A singular term is a discrete term. (b) Proper names are discrete terms. (c) A definite description is a discrete term. (d) All adjectival expressions are discrete terms.

EX 4B, III. Classify the following terms by placing the appropriate letter in the margin.

(a) general term
(b) singular term: proper name
(c) singular term: definite description
(d) plural discrete term: proper name
(e) plural discrete term: definite description

_____ 1. Waldo Zilcrest
_____ 2. the clown in the orange suit
_____ 3. Matterhorn
_____ 4. his honesty
_____ 5. Florida Keys

_____ 6. fat, jovial monks
_____ 7. those red-breasted birds
_____ 8. pilgrims
_____ 9. Outer Hebrides
_____ 10. that camelopard

EX 4C1. Classify the following terms by placing the appropriate letter in the margin.

(a) general collective term
(b) general non-collective term
(c) discrete collective term
(d) discrete non-collective term

_____ 1. Harvard's class of 1909
_____ 2. flock
_____ 3. the man in the blue suit
_____ 4. that piece of pie
_____ 5. the nine o'clock logic class

_____ 6. herd
_____ 7. the 4th army
_____ 8. Florida Keys
_____ 9. Alexander the Great
_____ 10. mongooses

EX 4C2, I. Place the appropriate letter in the margin.

_____ 1. Which statement is true? (a) A collective term is a term that is used collectively. (b) The term "mice" is always used collectively. (c) A general term used collectively may or may not be a collective term. (d) All terms that are used collectively are collective terms.

_____ 2. Which statement is true? (a) Some general collective terms may be used divisively. (b) No general collective term can be used divisively. (c) All general collective terms are used divisively only. (d) All general collective terms must be used collectively.

_____ 3. Which statement is false? (a) Some general term may be a collective term. (b) Some discrete term may be a collective term. (c) Singular terms cannot be collective terms. (d) A non-collective term may be a singular term.

_____ 4. Which statement is true? (a) No general term can be used collectively. (b) All general terms must be used collectively. (c) It is possible for a singular collective term to be used collectively. (d) A singular collective term cannot be used divisively.

_____ 5. When a proposition affirms or denies something of some or each individual object to which a general term in this proposition applies, then this term must be: (a) used divisively. (b) used collectively. (c) a collective term. (d) a distributed term.

EX 4C2, II. Determine whether the subjects in the following propositions are used collectively or divisively. Place appropriate letter in margin.

(C) Subject used collectively.
(D) Subject used divisively.

_____ 1. Dogs are canines.

_____ 2. Dogs are numerous.

_____ 3. Some wombats are friendly marsupials.

_____ 4. Wombats are not common animals.

_____ 5. The choral group are expert singers.

_____ 6. The choral group are ten in number.

_____ 7. The choral group won the first prize.

_____ 8. One hundred soldiers are a company.

_____ 9. Robins are red-breasted birds.

_____ 10. Ten dimes are a dollar.

EX 4D, I. Place "T" for true or "F" for false in each of the following blanks.

_____ 1. Every term is a subterm to itself.

Exercises/Chapter 4   73

_____ 2. Every term is a superterm to itself.

_____ 3. A term "*Y*" is a subterm to a term "*X*" iffi every *X* is *Y*.

_____ 4. It is possible for two *completely distinct* terms to be subterms to one another.

_____ 5. Given two terms such that the first is a subterm to the second, then the second must be a superterm to the first.

_____ 6. The term "mammals" is a subterm to "dogs".

_____ 7. It is possible for a class to be a proper subclass to itself.

_____ 8. The class of fishes is a subclass to itself.

_____ 9. It is possible for a term to be a subterm to one term and a superterm to another.

_____ 10. It is possible for a term to have a plurality of subterms.

EX 4D, II. For each term listed below write three subterms and three superterms. If this is not possible explain why.

1. baseball player
2. submarine
3. logic textbook
4. thing identical with Socrates
5. everything identical with God
6. god
7. conceivable object
8. unicorns
9. physical thing
10. empty class

EX 4D, III. By writing letters in the margin, arrange the terms in each numbered group in a sequence so that each term is a subterm to its predecessors.

_____ 1. (a) food, (b) apple, (c) edible fruit.

_____ 2. (a) marine mammal, (b) dolphin, (c) warm-blooded animals.

_____ 3. (a) book, (b) means of communication, (c) written materials, (d) textbook, (e) logic textbook.

_____ 4. (a) lion, (b) feline, (c) organism, (d) vertebrate, (e) animal.

_____ 5. (a) vertebrate, (b) anthropoid, (c) mammal, (d) English waitress, (e) human female.

EX 4E. Classify the following terms by placing the appropriate letter in each blank.

(C) concrete term (A) abstract term

_____ 1. manliness
_____ 2. femininity
_____ 3. orange
_____ 4. France
_____ 5. philosophy
_____ 6. freedom
_____ 7. warrior
_____ 8. love
_____ 9. square root of minus one
_____ 10. brothers
_____ 11. brotherhood
_____ 12. cats
_____ 13. kindness
_____ 14. white mice
_____ 15. the most loving couple

EX 4A–4E. Place the appropriate letter in each blank.

Y = Yes   N = No

_____ 1. Can a proper name be a singular term and used collectively in a proposition?
_____ 2. Can a term not in a proposition be used collectively?
_____ 3. Are discrete terms divided into singular and plural?
_____ 4. Is every term either general or discrete?
_____ 5. Is it possible for an adjectival expression to be a discrete term?
_____ 6. Can a singular term be a general term?
_____ 7. Can a singular term be abstract?
_____ 8. Is it possible for a collective term to be used distributively?
_____ 9. Can a non-collective term be a general term?
_____ 10. Is a collective term always used collectively?
_____ 11. Can a singular term be a collective term?
_____ 12. Is the term "cheerfulness" an abstract term?
_____ 13. Are all plural nouns collective terms?
_____ 14. Is "unicorns" the plural form of a non-collective general noun?

_____ 15. Does a term have to be one word?

_____ 16. Is it possible for a general term to name only one actual object?

_____ 17. Are all form words terms?

_____ 18. Is it possible for a non-collective term to be collectively used?

_____ 19. Can a discrete term be an abstract term?

_____ 20. Can a definite description be a plural discrete term and used collectively in a proposition?

EX 4F1. Choose the most appropriate letter for each question.

_____ 1. All real objects are: (a) actual objects. (b) possible objects. (c) physical objects. (d) objects that have mass.

_____ 2. An actual object is defined as an object that is: (a) in time. (b) in space and time. (c) a physical object. (d) corporeal.

_____ 3. An object that can be described or defined by a set of properties that is logically and semantically consistent is called a(n): (a) actual object. (b) real object. (c) physical object. (d) possible object.

_____ 4. An actual object must also be a(n): (a) possible and physical object. (b) possible and real object. (c) object in space and time. (d) object that has mass.

_____ 5. Which statement is true? (a) All possible objects are real objects. (b) All real objects are actual objects. (c) All possible objects are actual objects. (d) All actual objects are real objects.

_____ 6. Which statement is false: (a) All actual objects are real objects. (b) All actual objects are possible objects. (c) All real objects are actual objects. (d) All real objects are possible objects.

_____ 7. Which statement is false? (a) An object that is not in time or space can be a real object. (b) An object that is not in time can be a possible object. (c) An object that is not in space can be an actual object. (d) No actual object can be a possible object.

_____ 8. Such things as pencils, flowers, buildings, etc. would be examples of: (a) actual objects. (b) non-actual objects. (c) non-real objects. (d) possible objects not in time.

_____ 9. Inconsistent expressions such as "circle with four corners" and "square with exactly three sides" are expressions that:

76 Exercises/Chapter 4

(a) apply only to possible objects. (b) do not apply to any possible object. (c) apply to inconsistent objects. (d) apply to imaginary objects.

_____ 10. Objects that are not in time are, by definition: (a) non-real objects. (b) non-actual objects. (c) non-possible objects. (d) physical objects.

EX 4F2–4F3. Place the appropriate letter in each blank.

_____ 1. The analytic intension of a term includes its: (a) conventional intension. (b) total objective intension. (c) subjective intension. (d) connotation.

_____ 2. The total objective intension of a term includes its: (a) connotation. (b) denotation. (c) extension. (d) analytic and conventional intension.

_____ 3. The extension of a general term cannot be determined without first knowing its: (a) connotation. (b) denotation. (c) spelling. (d) conventional intension.

_____ 4. The class of thoughts, feelings, and emotions that a term elicits in a person by association is called, in respect to this person, the term's: (a) conventional intension. (b) subjective intension. (c) total objective intension. (d) connotation.

_____ 5. A property or set of properties of possible objects that a person accepts as necessary and jointly sufficient for a term to apply to such objects is, for this person, the term's (a) conventional intension. (b) subjective intension. (c) total objective intension. (d) connotation.

_____ 6. Terms denote: (a) only physical objects. (b) only actual objects. (c) only real objects. (d) non-real objects.

_____ 7. A synonym for "real extension" is: (a) denotation. (b) connotation. (c) analytic intension. (d) denotata.

_____ 8. Any object denoted by a term is: (a) part of the intension of that term. (b) part of the total objective intension of that term. (c) the denotation of that term. (d) a denotatum of that term.

_____ 9. An empty term has: (a) no denotatum, but it has a denotation. (b) a denotatum, but no denotation. (c) neither denotatum nor denotation. (d) both denotatum and denotation.

_____ 10. Which statement is false? (a) Terms with different conventional intensions may have the same denotata. (b) The term "round square" has zero denotation. (c) Two terms can denote the same objects and yet have different denotations. (d) No non-real object can be denoted by any term.

EX 4F4. By placing the appropriate letters in each blank, arrange each group of terms in order of increasing intension from left to right.

_____ 1. (a) stringed, musical instrument, (b) musical instrument, (c) violin.
_____ 2. (a) evergreen, (b) plant, (c) yew.
_____ 3. (a) radio, (b) short wave radio, (c) communications instrument.
_____ 4. (a) whiskey, (b) Bourbon, (c) beverage.
_____ 5. (a) wine, (b) beverage, (c) Tokay, (d) aromatic wine.
_____ 6. (a) submachine gun, (b) weapon, (c) Tommy gun, (d) gun.
_____ 7. (a) snake, (b) anaconda, (c) animal, (d) reptile, (e) South American snake.
_____ 8. (a) vertebrate, (b) living creature, (c) carnivorous bird, (d) bird, (e) buzzard.
_____ 9. (a) hunting dog, (b) dog, (c) animal, (d) Setter, (e) mammal.
_____ 10. (a) lieutenant, (b) mammal, (c) army officer, (d) person, (e) soldier, (f) commissioned army officer.

EX 4F1–4F5. Discussion Questions on Chapter 4.

1. Explain why it is necessary to know the conventional intension of a term before one can know the extension of the term.
2. Select a term and describe a plausible event where one would request the intensional meaning of the term. Do the same for the extensional meaning of the term, and its verbal meaning.
3. Point out the ambiguities in the argument: "Centaurs do not exist; therefore the word 'centaur' has no meaning".
4. Try to find examples of terms of which the total objective intension is (or could be) known. If you do not think there are any such terms, explain why.

5

Definition

5A INTRODUCTION TO DEFINITION

5A1 The Place of Definition in Logic. Since every discipline from aesthetics to zoology makes use of definitions, a doctrine of definition is a necessary and important part of logic if it is to play its proper role in facilitating and evaluating the reasoning of such disciplines. Definitions are also important within the development and exposition of logic itself, as this book tries to make clear by its emphasis on definitions throughout.

The evaluation and construction of arguments (expressing reasoning) are primary functions of logic, and both processes depend heavily upon definition. Since different kinds of arguments are evaluated by different techniques, it is essential to distinguish these kinds of arguments by definition. And the techniques for evaluating arguments can only be used when certain factors of arguments are recognized and understood; for example: *term, distributed term, affirmative proposition, simple proposition, premiss, conclusion,* and so on. In order to understand these concepts and to recognize their occurrence in arguments, the exact meaning of each concept has to be known. Giving a definition is usually an important part of giving the exact meaning of a concept.

The three major purposes of definitions, as they occur in cognitive discourse, are: (i) to report an established meaning of a word or symbol, (ii) to stipulate what one means by a word or symbol, and (iii) to analyze or explicate a concept. In 5C, "Functional Types of Definition", these purposes are explained in detail. In 5D, "Ways of Defining", the various techniques of definition are explained. Finally, 5E codifies *rules* for definition, to aid in constructing and evaluating definitions.

While Plato made significant steps toward a theory of definition, the first systematic and extensive treatment of definition was given by Aristotle in the *Topics* and the *Posterior Analytics*. Aristotle recognized two kinds of definitions, one that gives the meaning of a word or phrase, and a second that gives the essential properties of some kind of existing object. Aristotle had a low estimation of the first kind of definition, and devoted his attention to the second kind, which he had in mind when he gave his definition of a definition:

> **Def. 1** (*Aristotle's Definition*). A **definition** is a phrase indicating the essence of something.[1]

The scholastics and most logicians of the nineteenth and early part of the twentieth century recognized the two kinds of definition in regard to what is defined. One kind (commonly called "nominal definition") defines a word or a phrase, and the other (called "real definition") defines a nonverbal entity. The statement "The word 'zebra' names horselike African mammals of the genus *Equus* with overall alternate dark and whitish stripes" defines the word "zebra." But the statement "The *zebra* is a horselike African mammal of the genus *Equus* with overall alternate dark and whitish stripes" may be understood as a real definition, that is, giving the distinctive properties of a kind of thing found in nature.

Some contemporary logicians take the position that all definitions are nominal definitions. They argue that a doctrine of 'real' definition presupposes an inacceptable Aristotelian metaphysics; that properly speaking one can define nothing but a name or verbal expression. Such a position, however, seems to ignore the fact that when a chemist defines water as a combination of hydrogen and oxygen with the molecular formula H_2O, he is not *intending* to inform others about the meaning of the word "water", but is giving an analysis of the physical compound water. Such definitions as these are generally intended to be real definitions, and for this reason we include in this chapter a modern version of real definition.

We do not attempt in this chapter to give a full account of modern doctrines of definition, nor to elaborate in detail a complete theory of definition. The aim is to present a fairly comprehensive doctrine of the definition of terms along lines indicated by some leading contemporary logicians, preserving what seems valuable in the tradition.[2]

5A2 Definiendum, Definiens, and Reality—Types of Definition. In Aristotelian usage, a 'definition' was a phrase by which one defines something in a certain way.[3] Contemporary logicians usually call such a phrase a *definiens*, and that which is defined they call a *definiendum*. The earliest authors in whom we have found these terms are Whitehead and Russell, who wrote in their classic work on mathematical logic: "We will give the name of *definiendum* and *definiens* respectively to that which is defined and to that which it is defined as meaning".[4]

The official theory of these authors, as of most contemporary logicians writing in English, was that only words or signs can be defined.[5] In this book, we take the Aristotelian view that things other than words—for example, concepts or properties—can be defined. This requires some modifications and elaborations of terminology.

a *Definiendum: 'Word' or 'Thing'*

Def. 2. A **definiendum** (plural **definienda**) is that which is (or is to be) defined.[6]

We distinguish two kinds of things that are defined: 'words' and things other than 'words'.

Def. 3. A **'word'** is a linguistic expression, i.e., a word, phrase, or conventional sign, written or spoken.

Def. 4. A **'thing'** is an object other than a 'word'.

Single quotes around an expression (as in definitions 3 and 4) are *scare-quotes*, warning the reader that we are using this expression with a special meaning, but not mentioning it. When a word is mentioned, as in this sentence we mention the word "thing", we use the double quotes of ordinary quotation (in American usage).

The principal purposes of definition (as stated in 5A1) are: (i) to *report* an established meaning of a 'word', (ii) to *stiplulate* what one means by a 'word', and (iii) to *analyze* or explicate a concept. For the first two purposes, the primary intention is to define a 'word', which is the definiendum. But the primary intention for the third purpose is to define a concept, which is not a 'word', but a thing other than a 'word', which we call a 'thing' for short.

Definitions defining 'things' (namely, concepts) were made at the time of Socrates. For example, the definition attributed to the sophist Thrasymachus in Plato's *Republic*, Book I—"Justice is the interest of the stronger"—is intended to *explain* the nature of justice, not to *report* the usual meaning of the word "justice", nor to *stipulate* an arbitrary new meaning for the word.

b *Definiens: 'Word' or 'Thing'*

Def. 5. The **definiens** (plural **definientia**) of a definition is that which a definiendum is defined to be or to mean.

A definiens, like a definiendum, may be a 'word' or a 'thing'. When both the definiendum and the definiens are 'things', the definiendum is said to be the definiens. For example.

(a) Yellow is the color of ripe lemons.

In this definition, the color yellow (a 'thing') is asserted to be the color of ripe lemons.

When the definiendum is a 'word', the definiendum is said to mean the definiens, or to mean the same as the definiens. Examples:

(b) By "yellow" is meant the color of ripe lemons.

(c) "Yellow" means the same as "the color of ripe lemons".

Definition (b) connects the word "yellow" with a non-verbal reality, a 'thing'. Such definitions give a 'meaning' of a 'word' by indicating a property that the 'word' designates or describes. Definition (c) connects two 'words' and asserts that one means the same as the other.

c *Reality Types of Definition: Nominal and Real Definitions.* We have divided reality into two kinds of objects, 'words' and 'things'. The definiendum may be a 'word' or a 'thing', and the definiens may be a 'word' or 'thing'. Hence there are four logical possible types of definition: word-word, word-thing, thing-thing, and thing-word. For simplicity we write these hyphenated expressions without single quotes. The table below serves as a definition of the four reality-types of definition

Table 5.1: Reality Types of Definition

Def. 6.	Reality Type of Definition	Definiendum is a:	Definiens is a:
	word-word	'word'	'word'
	word-thing	'word'	'thing'
	thing-thing	'thing'	'thing'
	thing-word	'thing'	'word'

The following are examples of reality types of definition. The definition statements in the following passages are underlined unless the whole passage is the definition.

Examples of word-word definitions:
(d) "P.n." is an abbreviation for "promissory note".
(e) "Cassel" is another form of "Kassel".
(f) The word "concupiscence" means the same as the expression "sexual desire".

Examples of word-thing definitions:
  (g) A definition of the word "capybara": *"Capybara" refers to a large, short-tailed, semiaquatic rodent of tropical South America.*
  (h) By a "tee" is meant a small peg with concave top for holding a golf ball.

Examples of thing-thing definitions:
  (i) Chemistry gives this definition of water: *Water is H_2O.*
  (j) He defined a scallion thus: "A scallion is a young onion."

The two examples below are intended as thing-word definitions. Such definitions are relatively rare, and it may be argued that they are of little or no importance, since their existence is scarcely acknowledged in contemporary theories of definition.

  (k) Aristotle indicates that thunder should be defined thus: *We explain what thunder is by the expression "Noise due to the extinguishing of fire in the clouds".* (Cf. *Post. An.* II, c. 10.)
  (l) I give the following definition of alcohol: *The chemical composition of alcohol is expressed by the formula "C_2H_5OH".*

Almost all logicians have been content with a twofold division of definitions: what is defined is either a 'word' or a 'thing'.

Def. 7 A **nominal definition** is a definition of a 'word' (that is, a definition whose definiendum is a 'word').

Nominal definitions are subdivided into word-word definitions and word-thing definitions; see examples (c) and (b) respectively above.

Def. 8. A **real definition** is a definition of a 'thing' (that is, a definition whose definiendum is a 'thing').[7]

Real definitions are naturally taken as thing-thing definitions. (See examples (i) and (j) above.) However, Aristotle's definition of a definition—"A definition is a phrase indicating the essence of something"—suggests he is thinking of thing-word definitions.[8]

Few logicians attribute great value to both nominal and real definitions, since most of them think either that nominal definitions are unimportant or that the notion of real definition is illegitimate. (The authors of this book are with the minority.)

As before, a 'word' is a word, phrase, or conventional sign, and a 'thing' is anything else. 'Things' include not only actual objects (i.e., objects in time, whether physical objects or not), but all real objects (as explained in 4F1) other than 'words'. For example, a concept (for us) is a 'thing', and so is an abstraction such as a species of animal or a number. However, most advocates of the importance of real definition have limited the definiendum to certain kinds of things: usually an abstract entity or a concept. Definition of concrete individual objects was excluded by Aristotle, and is allowed by few advocates of real definition.[9]

5A3 Formulating a Definition.

a *Definiendum Term and Defining Term.* Every definition has a definiendum and a definiens that are either expressions (usually 'words') or what the expressions mean. These expressions are now defined.

> **Def. 9.** The **definiendum term** of a definition is its definiendum in nominal definitions, the 'word' that stands for the definiendum in real definitions.

In nominal definitions the definiendum and the definiendum term are one and the same. For example, in the nominal definition

(m) The word "asteroid" means the same as the word "planetoid".

the word "asteroid" is the definiendum and the definiendum term. In real definitions, the definiendum is a 'thing', and the expression which stands for this 'thing' is the definiendum term. For example, in the real definition:

(n) Blue is the color of a clear sky.

the definiendum is the color blue, but the definiendum term is the word "blue", which stands for the definiendum.

> **Def. 10.** The **defining term** (or **defining expression**) of a definition is its definiens when this is a 'word', otherwise it is the expression standing for the definiens.

In word-word and thing-word definitions, the defining term and the definiens are one and the same. For example, in (m) above "planetoid" is the defining term and the definiens. In word-thing and thing-thing definitions, the definiens is a 'thing', and the defining term is the 'word' that stands for that 'thing'. For example, in definition (n) above, the definiens is a 'thing', namely, the color of a clear sky, but the defining term is a 'word', namely, the expression "the color of a clear sky".

Definition 85

b *Different Forms of Written Definition.* One may distinguish the reality types of definitions by writing them in different forms. The following list illustrates nine ways of writing a definition.

(o) Class C_1 is a **subclass** of class C_2 iffi every member of C_1 is a member of C_2.

(p) A **triangle** is a three-sided figure.

(q) We define a triangle as a three-sided figure.

(r) "Triangle" means the same as "three-sided figure".

(s) By "triangle" is meant a three-sided figure.

(t) By *triangle* is meant a three-sided figure.

(u) The word **triangle** means a three-sided figure.

(v) **tri' an-gle**, *n*, three-sided figure.

(w) triangle = df three-sided figure

Definitions (o) and (p) are thing-thing definitions, which illustrate the standard forms in which we usually write numbered definitions in this book. In a numbered definition, we boldface the expression whose meaning is what the definition is primarily intended to explain. We call this boldfaced expression the key word. In (q), we state what (p) does, or express a thing-thing definition without boldface.

Expressions with double quotes always refer to 'words', and our regular practice is to refer to 'words' in this way only (except that a sentence or other expression may be referred to by displaying it on a separate line). Definitions (r) and (s) respectively are word-word and word-thing definitions. It is possible to mention a 'word' by putting it in italics or boldface, as in word-thing definitions (t) and (u). These are alternative ways of writing (s), not ordinarily used in this book. The forms (t) and (u) are perfectly correct when used consistently; but the form "By triangle is meant a three-sided figure" would be regarded as incorrect by logicians and most contemporary writers of standard English.

Definition (v) will be recognized as in the style of a dictionary. Such a definition may be interpreted in more than one way. It is natural to regard it as a word-word definition; but it serves as a thing-thing definition if it is looked up in order to get a precise analysis of the concept of a triangle.

Definition (w) shows the sign "= df" often used by symbolic logicians, usually interpreted as indicating a word-word definition. Definition (w) may be taken to say that the word "triangle" is to mean the same as the expression "three-sided figure". This sign is more commonly used for defining logical and mathematical signs than for defining words of standard English.

5A4 Aristotle's Method of Definition. Aristotle recognized only one method of real definition, namely, the method of *genus and differentia*, applied to defining real things, not words. In Aristotle's version, the method of definition by genus and differentia is applicable only to a kind of things, to a species, not to an individual entity. Aristotle was interested in defining things like the human species, the oak tree, justice, and so on. He did not define Socrates, some particular tree, or a certain specific instance of justice.

Aristotle's method of definition by genus and differentia consists in analyzing the essential nature of a species by (1) putting the species in its genus, that is, abstracting its general type or plan; and (2) distinguishing or differentiating it from other species of the same genus by its differentia (or difference), that is, a predicate indicating the specific manner in which it realizes the general plan.

For example, in defining a triangle, one must look first for an appropriate noun or noun phrase to serve as genus. The most natural one would be "plane figure" (or "rectilinear plane figure"). "Figure" is too broad: Plane figures and solid figures are distinct general types. A plane figure has to have a certain number of sides; so we go on to specify the number of sides (or angles). In the case at hand, this specification is sufficient to differentiate our species from others of the same genus, and completes the definition.

A proposed definition is to be examined by various criteria: see 5E.

Here are some examples of definitions by genus and differentia:

SPECIES	DEFINITION	
	GENUS	DIFFERENTIA
Man	animal	rational
Bachelor	marriageable male	unmarried
Surgeon	medical doctor	practicing surgery
Triangle	plane figure	three-sided
Father	parent	male
Chair	piece of furniture	intended for sitting

5B CONTEMPORARY SENSES OF "DEFINITION"

We have dropped the Aristotelian use of "definition" for a definiens, but have not officially redefined "definition". In this section we define different senses of the word.

5B1 Broad and Narrow Senses of Definition. There is a distinction between a narrow or strict sense of "definition" on the one hand, and a broad or loose sense on the other. This distinction is not concerned with the actual correctness or incorrectness of a definition, but with whether or not the attempt at definition meets certain minimum requirements so that, abstracting from the specific facts, it is of such a form that it might conceivably be correct and complete.

For example, suppose someone asks, "What is a wombat?" and you reply:

(a) "A wombat is an Australian marsupial".

You are making a well-informed attempt to explain the meaning of the word; you are engaged in a defining process and have made a defining statement or definition (in the broad sense). However, you have not made—nor tried to make—a complete definition of "wombat", since your statement does not distinguish a wombat from a kangaroo.

Suppose, however, you give one or the other of the following answers:

(b) "A wombat is an Australian marsupial of the family *Vombatidae*".

(c) "A wombat is an Australian marsupial of the family *Macropodidae*".

Answer (b) is technically more exact than (a), and is intended to be a complete and exact definition, giving an expression theoretically interchangeable with "wombat". (If in fact all members of the family *Vombatidae* are wombats, it succeeds in giving an interchangeable expression.) In practice, it adds little to (a)—only the information that the wombat belongs to a family of which it is the typical (and perhaps the only) genus.[10]

Answer (c) has exactly the same form as (b), and may be taken to be an attempt to make a complete and exact definition. It is incorrect, however, because it mistakenly assigns wombats to the family of kangaroos.

Some logicians would say that (a) is not a definition at all, because it does not intend to assert that the subject and predicate are equivalent in meaning or coextensive in application.[11] Taking (b) and (c) as intended to assert equivalences, these same logicians would undoubtedly say that (b) and (c) are definitions, correct or incorrect.[12]

Other logicians would count (a)—in answer to the question "What is a wombat?"—as a definition, admittedly incomplete and inexact. The four textbooks cited in note 2 to 5A1 would presumably count it as such; at any rate, they do not require that a definition assert an equivalence. We shall follow these authorities in taking "definition" in the broad sense.

There is, of course, nothing wrong with also having concepts of definition in a narrower, stricter sense or senses; for such definitions are ordinarily (but not always) preferable. An example of such a case has already been given.

Def. 11. An **equivalential definition** is either an "iffi" definition or a definition that asserts or implies that the definiendum term can replace the defining term—and vice versa—in any proposition without changing the truth-value.[13]

Most advocates of a strict sense for "definition" would include some such limitation as that for an equivalential definition, perhaps combined with other limitations.[14] Example (a) above is not an equivalential definition, but (b) and (c) are.

5B2 Category Differences.

a *Process-Product Ambiguity.* The best authorities on the subject recognize that the word "definition" has, almost inevitably, the kind of double use that is commonly found in words ending in "-tion."[14] This is the duality of process and product; of a human activity on the one hand, and the result of that activity or an object of the act on the other. For example, the word "construction" is used to denote the process of constructing something and is also used to denote an object that has been constructed.

A definition, regarded as a process, is an intellectual activity of defining, of giving a certain kind of explanation. As a product, it is the result of this action, that is, it is a statement that puts the explanation into a formula. There is a tendency for logicians to concentrate on the product-sense as the meaning of "definition", or even to focus on the bare sentence abstracted from its meaning. But this abstracted sentence is, as Robinson says, "a hollow shell" that may express quite different kinds of defining activity. When we discuss purposes of definition, for example, we are considering varieties of defining activity.

We may distinguish these two senses of "definition" by the expressions *definition process* (or defining process) and *definition statement* (or definition formula or defining statement).

Def. 12a. A **definition process** (or **defining process**) is a process intended to explain a meaning of an expression, to explicate a concept, or to indicate the essence of a thing. It normally culminates in a definition statement.

Def. 12b. A **definition statement** (or **defining statement**) is a statement in which the definiendum term is joined with the defining term.

Of the three alternatives in the defining term of Def. 12a, the first is the only intention generally recognized by contemporary English-speaking logicians. Aristotelians give essences. Kant and most German philosophers define concepts, as do some Aristotelians, often (like Joseph) under German influence.

Def. 13. A **definition** is a definition statement or a definition process.

In a given context it may not be necessary to make the distinction between these two senses of "definition" explicit, either because what is said applies to both, or because it is obvious which sense is intended. The alternatives of Definition 13 are not so much different kinds of definitions as they are different senses of the word "definition", referring to different categories of reality.

b *Word-Thing Distinction.* Different categories are also involved in the three alternatives of Def. 12a. For what is defined may be either an expression, a concept, or a 'thing'. This, it would seem, gives rise to a threefold division of definitions by category of object defined. However, logicians have almost always been content with a twofold division: What is defined is either a 'word' or a 'thing'. (See 5A2.)

5C FUNCTIONAL TYPES OF DEFINITION

We divide nominal definitions into two main types according to their purpose or intended function. Either a definition is intended to tell what other people mean by a word, or it is intended to tell what the writer means by the word.[15] The first kind is called a *lexical* definition or dictionary definition; the second a *stipulative* definition.

It is also useful to divide definitions by another principle, in terms of the basic functions of language, according to whether they are cognitive or not. The general purposes or functions of definition are the same as those of language in general. We may abstract five basic linguistic functions: knowledge, imagination, feeling, willing (or wishing), and action. These may be called, respectively, cognitive, imaginative, emotive, directive-optative, and performative functions.[16] Language commonly serves two or more of these functions at once. Lexical definitions are primarily cognitive in purpose. Stipulative definitions, as we shall explain, regularly combine cognitive and non-cognitive functions. The most important definitions that are primarily non-cognitive are the persuasive, in which emotive function is conspicuous.

5C1 Lexical Definition

Def. 14. A **lexical definition** (or **reportive definition**) is a nominal definition intended to report a conventional meaning of the definiendum, that is, to report a meaning established for some group of users of the language.

The "conventional meaning" that the lexical definition intends to report may be a conventional intension (that is, a set of properties), an (conventional) extension (that is, a class of possible objects), a conventional verbal meaning (an expression), or any combination of these, as established by the linguistic conventions of a certain group. (See 4F.)

Almost any dictionary definition is an example of a lexical definition. A dictionary definition may introduce the reader to a word new to him, or give him a more precise conception of a meaning he understands vaguely. The lexicographer usually supplies a distinct defining term for each meaning he can distinguish for a given word. This alerts the reader to a possible ambiguity consisting in an equivocal use of the word, that is, use in a context in which two or more distinct interpretations of the word are possible.

The expression or the specific meaning involved in a lexical definition may be peculiar to a certain group of speakers of the language. It may belong to schoolboy slang, thieves' cant, or sociologists' jargon. It is appropriate that such limitations be indicated.

The lexical definition, logicians commonly say, is true or false according to whether it succeeds or fails in its intention to report a conventional meaning. We would say rather that some lexical definitions give definitely accurate and true reports, and others definitely inaccurate or false reports;

still others are more or less accurate according as they have greater or less success in their intention to report an established meaning.

A definition may be *lexically accurate* (or lexically true) without being a lexical definition at all. This occurs, for example, if the intention of the definer is simply to stipulate a meaning of the term, without claiming or intending to report a conventional meaning, yet, for whatever reason, the definer has chosen a meaning that is in fact a conventional meaning.

It seems natural to use the term "conventional definition" in the following sense:

Def. 15. A **conventional definition** is a definition that defines by means of conventional intension or conventional verbal meaning.

What we said in the paragraph above can be expressed by saying that a conventional definition need not be lexical, since its purpose may be entirely stipulative. The definition statement "A triangle is a three-sided polygon" is a conventional definition, regardless of whether by intention it is lexical, stipulative, or real, and in a given occurrence might perform more than one of these functions.

5C2 Stipulative Definition.[17]

Def. 16. A **stipulative definition** is a definition that tells what one intends a 'word' to mean.

One of the most famous exponents of stipulative definition was Humpty Dumpty, as reported by Lewis Carroll:

> "I don't know what you mean by 'glory,' " Alice said.
>
> Humpty Dumpty smiled contemptuously. "Of course you don't—till I tell you. I meant 'there's a nice knock-down argument for you!' "
>
> "But 'glory' doesn't mean 'a nice knock-down argument,' " Alice objected.
>
> "When *I* use a word," Humpty Dumpty said, in rather a scornful tone, "it means just what I choose it to mean—neither more nor less."
>
> "The question is," said Alice, "whether you *can* make words mean so many different things."
>
> "The question is," said Humpty Dumpty, "which is to be master—that's all."

Alice was too much puzzled to say anything; so after a minute Humpty Dumpty began again. "They've a temper, some of them—particularly verbs: they're the proudest—adjectives you can do anything with, but not verbs—however, *I* can manage the whole lot of them! Impenetrability! That's what *I* say!"

"Would you tell me please," said Alice, "what that means?"

"Now you talk like a reasonable child," said Humpty Dumpty, looking very much pleased. "I meant by 'impenetrability' that we've had enough of that subject, and it would be just as well if you'd mention what you mean to do next, as I suppose you don't mean to stop here all the rest of your life."

"That's a great deal to make one word mean," Alice said in a thoughtful tone.

"When I make a word do a lot of work like that," said Humpty Dumpty, "I always pay it extra."[18]

Humpty Dumpty has clearly abused the privilege of stipulating a meaning. But stipulation is a very useful procedure in a variety of cases.[19]

5C3 Cognitive Functions of Stipulative Definitions. We shall argue that most stipulative definitions combine cognitive with noncognitive functions. This section (a) lists five important functions that stipulative definitions serve in discourse that is primarily cognitive, and (b) distinguishes the cognitive and noncognitive aspects of typical stipulative definitions. Section 5C4 discusses stipulative definitions whose functions are primarily noncognitive.

a *Five Kinds of Stipulation*

(i) *Innovation.* "Something new". When a new thing or concept is discovered, or attention is called to an old thing or concept that has no simple name, the advantage of stipulating that some word or phrase shall be such a (general or discrete) name is evident. One may do this by introducing a new word or symbol into the language—usually adapted from or suggested by a word in the same or another language. Thus van Helmont introduced the word *gas*, suggested by the Greek *khaos*. Or one may add a new meaning to an existing word or phrase. Thus some geometer first used *pencil* for a collection of lines passing through a given point. In either of these cases, the definition is *innovating*.

(ii) *Abbreviation.* The advantages of abbreviation include not only the obvious one of economy, but, even more important, the possibility of grasping more complicated combinations when they are shorter. Besides contractions and ideograms (e.g., Arabic numerals), abbreviations include also the use of a standard expression as short for a longer one within the context of a particular document or occasion. For example: "In this contract, 'the Company' means the Consolidated Widget Company, Incorporated".

(iii) *Eliminating Equivocation.* When a word would be *equivocal* (have distinct possible interpretations) in a given context, it is appropriate to stipulate the meaning intended. Ordinarily this should be one of the established meanings; the definition is then conventional as well as stipulative. It may also be lexical as well as stipulative; for one normally *intends* to state an established meaning, which one chooses or *stipulates* as one's own meaning. The emphasis is probably on the stipulative aspect; for one may be more sure of what one means than of what the word customarily means, and the former is what is needed for understanding the use of the word in the context in question.

(iv) *Precision.* An important type of stipulative definition is what Copi calls a precising definition.[20]

> **Def. 17.** A **precising definition** is a definition that stipulates a more precise meaning within the limits of a lexical (or a conventional) definition.

"Precise" is the opposite of "vague". Greater precision is attained by drawing more sharply the boundary line between what does and what does not fall under a concept. Vagueness is distinct from equivocality—the kind of ambiguity dealt with in case (iii) above.

For example, a dictionary may distinguish ten or more meanings of "man". But when we have stipulated that we take "man" in the sense of "human being", we find the term is vague in more than one direction. When does a human being begin to exist? At conception, at birth, or at a certain point in between? For legal and religious purposes, it is important to decide whether a fetus is to be counted as a human being or not. By a precising definition, one might specify that it becomes human at the end of twelve weeks. Although a principle of distinction may be involved—such as the time it takes on the average for a "sufficiently" human appearance to develop—it is clear that to get a sharp line for practical purposes, one must often draw the line in a way that is to some extent arbitrary.

For the anthropologist, on the other hand, the vagueness of "man" lies in a different dimension. The reader is invited to consider this and other possible ways in which "human being" is a vague term.

A precising definition is usually made by specifying a further property (or properties) in addition to those already included in the conventional intension.

Since the limits set up by a lexical (or conventional) definition are vague in the area where a corresponding precising definition draws a sharper line, one cannot always tell whether an intended precising definition really stays "within the limits" of the related lexical (or conventional) definition. Sometimes it is clear enough whether it is definitely within or not within the limits, but not always. Hence there is not an absolutely precise boundary between a precising definition and an innovating definition of variety (i).

(v) *Purgation.* The last kind of stipulation we list is *purgation*, which purges a useful word of error. For example, the word "atom" was originally a negative term, meaning an indivisible particle of matter. Early modern chemistry applied this term to the unitary particle of the chemical elements. When it was discovered that these 'atoms' were not indivisible, the word "atom" might have been abandoned. Instead, the word was redefined to remove the error involved in applying the original defining term to the particles in question.

If stipulative definition can be advantageous in various ways, it can also be disadvantageous or deceptive in different ways. We return to this question in our discussion of persuasive definitions below.

b *Cognitive and Non-Cognitive Functions of Stipulative Definition.* The function of language is *cognitive* insofar as it is used to obtain, record, or communicate knowledge or belief. Lexical definitions are intended to be primarily, if not purely, cognitive, and usually succeed. The defining term of an emotive term like "murder" is not expected to arouse feeling in the way the term itself does in ordinary use. Such a lexical definition is equivalential (def. 6), that is, it asserts or implies that defining term and definiendum term have the same conventional intension (hence the same analytic intension: 4F, def. 25) and the same extension; but not necessarily the same connotation (in the literary sense, 4F, def. 27).

A definition may be primarily cognitive with appreciable elements of other functions. Such is the case, we hold, with most *stipulative* definitions, though they also have directive and perhaps other functions. Consider, for example, MacKaye's definition: "By a stipulated definition is to be understood a definition adopted independent of custom".[21] That this definition is itself "stipulated"—stipulative in our terminology—is clear from its wording and context, and it is clear that it is of the first or innovating variety of stipulative definitions. The formulation here, that the definiendum "is to be understood" in a certain way, conveys the basically cognitive character of the definition, together with a hint (in "is to be") that the definition is not purely descriptive in character. The author of such a stipulative definition may be interpreted as doing some or all of the following:

(1) He is *establishing* or *making* a definition as a tool for his work ("I hereby define X to mean . . ." or "I hereby stipulate that X mean . . .").

(2) He is *reporting* the meaning he there attaches to the definiendum and intends to attach throughout the work ("By X, I mean . . .").

(3) He is expressing his *will* or intention to use the word with the stipulated meaning ("By X, I intend to mean . . .").

(4) He is *predicting* that he will use the word in the stipulated sense ("By X, I shall mean . . .").

(5) He is making a *request* to the reader to understand the word in the stipulated sense; or expressing a *wish* that the reader so understand it ("By X, let us understand . . .").

(6) He is *recommending* to the reader, or expressing a *wish*, that the reader shall himself use the word in the stipulated sense ("Let us use X to mean . . .").

Of these possible purposes, 2 and 4 are clearly cognitive; 3, 5, and 6 are directive-cognitive, for the action they will or wish to bring about is a cognitive one—understanding an expression to have a certain meaning. Purposes 5 and 6 are *hortatory*: They urge the definition upon the reader. Such a purpose necessarily requires the presentation of the cognitive content of the definition. Purpose 1—the most distinctive and typical for stipulative definitions—may be classed as cognitive-performative; for the action it performs is the cognitive one of assigning a certain meaning to a word.

It should be noted that stipulative definitions fit neatly into formal systems with assumptions of informative character, the whole being a system primarily cognitive in character, constituting theoretical and perhaps practical knowledge (though it may have incidental esthetic value).

We hold, then, that stipulative definitions are usually both cognitive and directive in character, having in most cases an over-all cognitive purpose and also a performative aspect.[22]

5C4 Stipulative Definitions with Non-Cognitive Functions. We have just seen that a stipulative definition may have a secondary hortatory function, in which the cognitive content of the definition is recommended to the reader. Similarly, a lexical definition may be taken as having at least a covert hortatory function; for if use of a given word or meaning is not given an explicitly negative hortatory aspect by being designated as *incorrect, loose, illiterate, vulgar,* or the like, then the definition probably has an implicit positive hortatory aspect, the use being presumably correct.

In some stipulative definitions, however, there is not merely a recommendation of the definition, but an attempt, under cover of definition, to change the attitude toward something. In this case the non-cognitive aspect becomes dominant over the cognitive aspect. The most important case is that of the persuasive definition, as analyzed by Charles S. Stevenson, in which there is a covert transfer of emotive force to a new cognitive content.[23]

> **Def. 18.** A **persuasive definition** is a stipulative definition of a familiar term that (or the defining term of which) has both descriptive and strongly emotive meaning, used to redirect attitudes by transferring the original emotive force of the definiendum to the new content (or the emotive force of the new defining term to the definiendum).

These are examples in which the parenthetic alternatives apply: "Socialism is economic democracy"; "Capitalism is free enterprise". Here the favorable connotations of "democracy", "free", and "enterprise" are to be transferred to the definienda.[24]

Excellent examples of persuasive definitions are given in Huxley's *Eyeless in Gaza.*[25]

> "But if you want to be free, you've got to be a prisoner. It's the condition of freedom—true freedom."
>
> "True freedom!" Anthony repeated in the parody of a clerical voice. "I always love that kind of argument. The contrary of a thing isn't the contrary; oh, dear me, no! It's the thing itself, but as it *truly* is. Ask a die-hard what conservatism is; he'll tell you it's *true* socialism. And the brewer's trade papers; they're full of articles about the beauty of true temperance. Ordinary temperance is just gross refusal to drink; but *true* temperance, *true* temperance is something much more refined. True temperance is a bottle of claret with each meal and three double whiskies after dinner. . . .
>
> "What's in a name?" Anthony went on. "The answer is, Practically everything, if the name's a good one. Freedom's a marvellous name. That's why you're so anxious to make use of it. You think that, if you call imprisonment true freedom, people will be attracted to the prison. And the worst of it is you're quite right.

The name counts more with most people than the thing. . . . And of course 'True Freedom' is actually a better name than freedom *tout court*. Truth—it's one of the magical words. Combine it with the magic of 'freedom' and the effect's terrific".

The persuasive definitions in this quotation are crude, but more subtle ones can be found, as Stevenson illustrates from philosophic definitions of "good" and "justice". Persuasion, of course, may be a perfectly legitimate enterprise, depending on the circumstances. But the persuasive definition, if successful, is somewhat deceptive. For clear thinking, one must be able to detect and analyze the use of such definitions.

There is another fairly common type of definition whose purpose is non-cognitive: the facetious or humorous definition. Samuel Johnson's definition that includes the characterization of "lexicographer" as "a harmless drudge" is an example. Another example: "A statistician is a mathematician who thinks that two plus two is approximately four."

Def. 19. A **facetious** (or **humorous**) **definition** is a definition or pseudodefinition that is not intended to be taken seriously and literally, but is intended to amuse.

The facetious definition may have an ulterior motive, however; if so, it is likely to be persuasive, hence non-cognitive in its ultimate as well as it immediate intent.

5C5 Real Definition as Conceptual Definition. The traditional Aristotelian doctrine of real definition is in disrepute among typical Anglo-American logicians.[26] Not only is the Aristotelian doctrine of essence rejected, but the general tendency is to say that only *words* are defined, not *things*. Then either the term "real definition" is rejected altogether, or it is applied to some kind of definition of words (e.g., to lexical definition). However, we believe that real definition, defined as in our modification of the Aristotelian version, makes good sense. Some careful thinkers who seem at first sight to reject real definition allow a certain kind of definition (called "conceptual" or "explicative") that in fact falls under our notion of real definition.

We defined a real definition (def. 8) as a definition of a 'thing' other than a 'word'—usually an abstract entity or concept. The abstract entity may be a species or natural kind such as the species man or the substance chalk. An ordinary person would probably think of definitions of man or chalk as defining something quite concrete. Reflection shows that one is not defining an individual man nor the actual world society of living men, but a species or kind of animal, abstracting from individuals. One does not define a particular piece of chalk, nor the total discontinuous mass of chalk in the world, but a kind of material substance with a certain chemical composition and physical properties. The ordinary person is right in thinking that what is defined is not merely a word, as opposed to those logicians who think only words are defined. But he has perhaps not realized that what is defined here is not a concrete thing but a form or type of thing, abstracted from the concrete.

We give examples of other abstractions that can be defined: the *class* of unemployed, the *property* or *characteristic* of being cruel, the *relation* of denoting, the *number* 10, the higher abstraction of the *set* of prime numbers.

One may think of oneself as defining a concept or general idea, for example, the concept of a human being. The concept may be mental, an idea or notion in the mind; or it may be that which is conceived, the immediate object of conception. In the latter case, the concept is an actual object existing in time. In the former case, the concept is presumably a species or other abstract entity as discussed above. In either case, it is not a 'word'.[27]

Of the possible kinds of definition of things, definition of concepts has the most support among contemporary logicians, and is most likely to become widely accepted. Consequently, we confine our further discussion of real definition to conceptual definition.

Def. 20. A **conceptual definition** (or **explicative definition**) is a definition that attempts to analyze or explicate a concept or the meaning (especially the intension) of the definiendum term.[28]

To call an analysis or explication of an intensional meaning a conceptual definition or conceptual statement would probably be generally acceptable. Since an intension for us is a property or set of properties, it is not a mental concept, but the object of a concept.

a *Five Kinds of Conceptual Definition.* R. Robinson formulates several important kinds of real definition—specifically, of conceptual definition. These kinds, as he notes, overlap.

(i) *Conceptual definition as the search for a key to a large area.* Many mathematical and scientific definitions are such keys. For example, the definition of a triangle as a plane figure bounded by three straight lines, when added to the assumptions of Euclidean geometry, is the key to a large body of theorems about triangles.[29]

Quite different in exactness is Walter Pater's definition of architecture as "frozen music". This is frankly a metaphor, not intended literally, hence not a proper definition at all according to the traditional doctrine. However, it might serve as a key to the understanding of architecture from a certain point of view.[30]

(ii) *Conceptual definition as analysis of concepts.* In this analysis, one distinguishes 'parts' of the concept, and exhibits the concept as a synthesis of parts into a whole. For example, one comes to realize that a circle is a locus of all the points in a plane equidistant from a given point. Robinson holds that this kind of analysis, a valuable form of insight, is the common meaning of "real definition".[31] Also, "indefinable" has often meant (e.g., in G. E. Moore) unanalyzable in this sense.

(iii) *Conceptual definition as synthesis of a concept into a larger whole.* Sometimes a concept or form is defined by realizing that it is an element in a larger whole, or by discovering its place in a system of concepts or forms. This is often called "analysis" of the concept defined. Thus, when it is said that "terrestrial longitude is defined in terms of Greenwich", Greenwich is being used as the point of reference for a system of longitudes that synthesize all places on the earth's surface.

(iv) *Conceptual definition as the improvement of concepts.* "Real definition" sometimes means improvement of a concept, which is usually the same as to say, replacement of a concept by a similar concept that is better in some way. For some purposes, improvement may come be developing a more general concept; for other purposes, improvement may come by developing a *more specific* concept. Useful as developments in either direction may be, most cases of improvement of concepts probably do not fall under either of these.

Sometimes the improvement consists of purging the concept of error, either a self-contradiction or an empirical error. Thus the concept of an atom was purged of the property of indivisibility erroneously attributed to certain particles. We used the same example under "Stipulative definition", 5C3a (v). This illustrates the point made by Robinson, that improvement of a concept requires "a stipulative redefinition of the word expressing the concept". In this process, "real and nominal definition must both occur together" (p. 187).

In the case of concepts of empirical science, improvement of concepts very often takes the form of increasing the ease or reliability of application to reality. This may be illustrated by the successive definitions of the international unit of length, the meter.

The meter was first defined in 1790 as one ten-millionth of a quadrant of a meridian of the earth passing through Paris, France. The meter was redefined in 1889 as the distance between two lines on a prototype bar kept in Sèvres, France. This improved the accuracy of the definition. Still greater improvement was achieved when the meter was defined in 1960 in terms of the wavelength from a lamp containing the isotope krypton 86.[32]

Improvement of concepts may take the form of altering them so as to fit them into a system, or into a more inclusive system. This is often the case in mathematics and logic.

Robinson finds eight other meanings of "real definition" besides the four forms of conceptual definition we have just described. Some of the others are confused or mistaken notions, and some are useful ideas; but he makes the best case for the four listed. We cannot omit, however, the Aristotelian conception of real definition.

(v) *Conceptual definition as the search for essence.* This is the conception of Aristotle and the scholastics. It is to be made by the method of genus and differentia (5A4); this seems to imply that it is an analysis of concepts. Robinson, with less than his usual patience and perspicacity, claims that there is no such thing as essence in Aristotle's sense, because Aristotle made the most serious attempt ever made to make sense of the notion of essence, but failed completely.[33] Without defining "essence" in Aristotle's sense, we define "definition by essence" in the Aristotelian tradition, mainly by combining the first two senses of conceptual definition above.

> **Def. 21.** A **definition by essence** is a conceptual definition, expressing in a formula an analysis, determined by the nature of the concept rather than by arbitrary decision, which is intended to serve as key for understanding important aspects of the concept or its object.

It is not sufficient to say the definition is a search for a key; for we wish to exclude a metaphorical definition ("frozen music"); and exclude also, for example, "The essence of quick success in war is surprise". (Surprise might often be the key to quick success in war, but the statement quoted is not an analysis of quick success in war.) On the other hand, an analysis by some superficial features would not give the essence. A chemical formula for a compound, for example, "H_2O" (water) or "NaCl" (salt), is an ideal defining term for a definition by essence.

We have omitted from definition 21 one important feature of the Aristotelian tradition: the uniqueness of essence and hence of successful definition by essence. This we take to be the most vulnerable point of the tradition. The essence of a species may differ as it is extracted from the standpoint of different bodies of knowledge. The essence of man may be one thing to an anthropologist (say, "a tool-making primate"), something else to a moral philosopher ("a rational animal" perhaps), and so on.

If a definition by essence is a redefinition (as in a chemical formula) it is almost surely intended to be an improvement of a concept. But a redefinition of a unit of length (e.g., the meter), though an improvement of a concept, is not a definition by essence; for it is rather synthetic than analytic; and its specific quantitative value is determined in one respect by arbitrary decision rather than by the nature of the concept.

b *'Nominalistic' Version of Conceptual Definition.* An important concept related to the five kinds of conceptual definition above has been formulated by Copi: that of a theoretical definition.[34]

Def. 22 (*Copi's Definition*). A **theoretical definition** of a term is one that attempts to formulate a theoretically adequate characterization of the objects to which it is applied.

This is presented as a definition of a term, hence a nominal definition in our terminology. But a term has (extensional and intensional) meaning, and this type of definition involves analysis or synthesis of the meaning. The definition involves characterization of the objects to which it is applied. Since it is characterizing the denotation of the term, it must be a thing-thing as well as a word-thing definition. It takes a word that has an established meaning, and redefines the word and its intension in terms of a theory or system of concepts (scientific, quasi-scientific, philosophic, legal, or other system). There should be little or no shift in the denotation of the term as a result of the redefinition. An improvement of the concept in some respect will be intended. The definition may be analytic or synthetic. The definitions of the virtues aimed at in the Platonic dialogues are cited as examples.

A definition of an acid as "a substance containing hydrogen that can be replaced by a metal or an electropositive group to form a salt" would be classed as a theoretical definition, clearly presupposing chemical theory. The definition of an acid as "a substance with a sour taste" is practical and operational but not theoretical; and the same must be said of the definition of an acid as "a substance that turns blue litmus paper red," though the latter is based on more scientific experience than the former, and the litmus test is the favorite criterion of the chemist. But neither of these practical definitions presupposes any theory of the nature of an acid.

c *Reporting Conceptual Definitions.* When a conceptual definition becomes accepted in a certain discipline such as chemistry, medicine, or grammar, or becomes popular, it usually finds its way into the dictionary. The lexicographers who report the conceptual definition are responsible only for the accuracy of their reporting. They are not responsible for the accuracy of the conceptual definition itself. For example, if chemists define rust as iron oxide, they are asserting a conceptual definition and are responsible for the accuracy of their definition. But the lexicographer who reports that the chemical meaning of the word "rust" is iron oxide need not worry about the truth or falsity of the analysis. His job is accurate reporting of the conventional usage of words, not chemical analysis. To the lexicographer, the chemist's conceptual definition becomes a word-thing or word-word definition (a theoretical definition), since his interest is in how certain people use the word "rust", not primarily in the chemistry of rust. Hence conceptual definitions enter into the dictionary as lexical definitions.

5D WAYS OF DEFINING

In section 5A2 definitions were divided into real definitions and nominal definitions, depending upon whether the definiendum was, respectively, a thing or word. In this section we present another way of classifying definitions (real and nominal), namely, by the kind of definiens. The definiens is the most important meaning, for the purpose at hand, of the definiendum. As explained in 4F, there are three modes of meaning: intensional, extensional, and verbal. Although these modes of meaning were defined for terms, they are applicable to certain kinds of (non-verbal) things. Hence species and concepts, as well as terms, may be defined by one of these modes of meaning.

When a definiens is a set of properties, the definition is called an "intensional definition" (5D1). When the definiens is one specified individual or a class of specified individuals, then the definition is called an "extensional definition" (5D2). When the definiens is a term or expression, then the definition is called a "verbal definition" (5D3).

Intensional and extensional definitions are either thing-thing or word-thing definitions, while verbal definitions are word-word or thing-word definitions.

Since there are three kinds of definiens, there are three major ways of defining the definiendum, but each of these ways can be accomplished by a variety of techniques. In the following subsections the techniques best suited to these kinds of definition will be listed. It will be noted in the text when a technique may be used for more than one way of defining.

5D1 Techniques of Intensional Definition.

Def. 23. An **intensional definition** is a definition (real or nominal) whose definiens is a set of properties.

The definiens of an intensional definition is a set of properties that is intended to be the intension of a concept or word. This way of defining must be used to give the conventional intension of a term or concept. Also almost all conceptual definitions (5C5) are intensional definitions. Lexical as well as stipulative definitions may be intensional. Consequently, intensional definition is one of the most important and most prevalent ways of defining.

We now list and explain seven intensional techniques. We make no claim that the listing is exhaustive or mutually exclusive.

a *Definition by Genus and Difference.* The traditional method of definition by genus and differentia of Aristotle was intended to give a real definition (thing-thing or thing-word) or a species (see 5A2). In this section we explain the modern technique of definition by genus and difference, usually regarded as word-thing rather than thing-thing definition.

The terms *genus* and *species* are used relatively rather than absolutely by modern logicians.[35]

> **Def. 24.** Given two classes C_1 and C_2, each the extension of a general term, C_1 is a **species** of C_2 and C_2 is a **genus** of C_1 iffi C_1 is a proper subclass of C_2.

The plural of "species" is "species", the plural of "genus" is "genera".

For example, the American robin is a species of thrush, also of birds and of vertebrates; the thrush, birds, and vertebrates are all genera of American robins. Red objects are a species of colored objects. A class is, in general, a genus in relation to one class and a species in relation to another. The class of automobiles is a genus of the class of taxicabs and a species of the class of motor vehicles.

> **Def. 25.** A **definition by genus and difference** is an intensional definition in which the definiendum is a species S or a term naming S, and the definiens combines a genus of S with a property (or set of properties) to distinguish S from other species of this genus.

Basically, the technique of definition by genus and differences is a technique whereby a class of things is described by indicating what kind of things they are (the genus) and indicating the difference between them and other things of the same kind (i.e., other species). For example, a square is a rectangle (genus) that differs from other rectangles by having four equal sides (difference). In other words, a square is a species of the genus rectangle that differs from other species of this genus by having four equal sides. Normally this definition would read "A square is a rectangle having four equal sides". Another example of definition by genus and difference is "Man is a species of the genus Animal and differs from other species of this genus by being rational". In short, "Man is a rational animal".

Ideally, only the proximate genus (or *proximum genus*) of the species being defined should be given by the definition. The proximate genus of a species is "that next above it in the series".[36] For example, given the series of classes, *polygon, quadrilateral, parallelogram, rectangle, square;* the proximate genus of square is rectangle, the proximate genus of rectangle is parallelogram, and so on. However, the proximate genus of a species in one classification (expressed as a series of terms) may not be the proximate genus of this species in another classification. For example, the class of vehicles might be the proximate genus of the class of army tanks in one classification and the class of weapons might be the proximate genus to army tanks in another classification.

There is no precise rule for determining the proximate genus of a species, but a good rule of thumb is to look for the nearest genus that can be expressed simply. For example, the class of blood relatives may be an appropriate genus for the class of descendants. An appropriate genus for private (in the army) is enlisted man.

The reason why one is cautioned to use the proximate genus when defining by genus and difference is that a genus that is too broad may not limit the difference sufficiently. For example, to define a square as "a polygon that is a rectangle with four equal sides" is to pick a genus (polygon) that is so broad that all the work of defining has to be done by the difference. In this case, "polygon" is superfluous and should be dropped, as what remains is a complete definition. Often the selection of a genus that is too broad leads to a non-equivalential definition, in this case, a definition where the defining term has a broader extension than the definiendum term. For example, "a square is a polygon with four equal sides" is too broad, since there are polygons with four equal sides that are not squares. The genus "polygon" is too far removed from the species "square".

Whether conceived as a real definition or as a nominal definition, the technique of definition by genus and difference has one limitation. It cannot be used to define a class (or the name of a class) that has no genus (such a class is called a *summum genus*). For example, the class of conceivable entities might well be a class that has no genus, that is, it is a proper subclass to no class.

Unlike Aristotle's method of genus and differentia, the modern technique of definition by genus and difference does not presuppose that there is a unique analysis of the definiendum or its concept. It does not even presuppose that it can be analyzed at all. The modern technique can define a "simple" concept by a synthesis of concepts (5C5,a,iii). For example, "yellow" may be defined as a hue lying between green and orange on the spectrum. It could also be defined by paradigm species (see below): "Yellow is the color of ripe lemons".

b *Definition by Species.*

Def. 26. A **definition by species** is an intensional definition (real or nominal) that defines a given kind or genus by means of a list of species of that genus.

If the definition is equivalential (in intent: def. 11), the list must be intended to be exhaustive. If the list is incomplete, the definition is incomplete.

A definition by species could also be called a *definition by subclasses;* the latter term, however, would also apply to extensional definitions. Here are some statements that might be given as examples of definition by species: "A spouse is a husband or wife". "Categorical propositions are defined to include simple propositions and secondary propositions". "The noun 'feline' refers to lions, tigers, leopards, lynxes, domestic cats, and so on". "A feline is a lion or tiger or leopard or lynx or domestic cat or other feline".

The first is recognized as exhausting the kinds of spouse by anyone knowing the meaning of the term. The second involves technical usage; it is correct and complete according to the usage of this book (though not the definition given in chapter 2). In the third, "and so on" indicates that the list is not claimed to be complete. The fourth also has an incomplete list of species, and is made formally exhaustive only by the phrase "or other feline", which makes the definition circular.

In defining a kind of animal or plant, even a complete list of the known subdivisions will not cover possible unknown species that may be discovered in the future and would be put in the defined kind on the basis of similarity to the species known previously.

A defect in definition by species is lack of sufficient range in the defining species. For example, the definition, " 'Felines' includes lions, tigers, leopards, and so on" would not be as good as the definition, " 'Felines' includes lions, lynxes, domestic cats, and so on". For the former suggests that only the large cats are included in the term defined.

There is a parallel between definition by species and definition by example (Extensional definition, 5D2 below), but they are quite distinct. A definition by species cannot be a definition by example, since a species is not a concrete example of its genus. The horse Bucephalus is an example of a horse but not a species of horse.

c *Definition by Paradism Species.*

Def. 27. A **definition** of a genus *by paradigm species* (or **definition** of a class **by paradigm subclass**) is a definition in which the genus is defined by reference to a species intended to illustrate clearly and non-controversially the conventional intension of the definiendum term.

A paradigm species would more often be called "a paradigm case"; but the latter term is also used for a paradigm example (see 5D2,c below). For example, one might name American robins as a paradigm species of thrushes, or common nouns as a paradigm subclass of general terms.

A definition by paradigm species might run as follows: "The thrushes (*Turdidae*) are a family of birds including the American robins". Here we are told the level of biological classification of the 'genus' defined (technically a Family); it is put in a higher kind (the Class of birds—skipping the Order), and distinguished by reference to one of its species.

The definition just given is not an Aristotelian definition indicating the essence of thrushes (def. 1); but it is a definition by genus and difference (def. 25), and is even equivalential in intent (def. 11). If one offered as a definition of thrushes simply the statement "The thrushes include the American robins", this would be a definition by paradigm species (in the broad sense of "definition"); but the class defined has not been put into a genus.

d *Operational Definition.* In our discussion of theoretical definition (5C5,b), we mentioned, as example of a definition that is not theoretical but operational, the following:

(a) "An **acid** is a substance that turns blue litmus red".

Let us restate this in a form that brings out more explicitly the operational character of the definition:

(b) "Substance x is an **acid** iffi, whenever substance x in liquid state is tested by blue litmus paper, the litmus turns red".

The genus of acids is material substance. For the test to be performed, the substance must be a liquid or be dissolved in water. The test is a public and repeatable operation, namely, inserting blue litmus paper in the liquid. The test has an observable result, which is taken as decisive for the application of the concept defined: As the blue litmus does or does not turn red, the substance is or is not an acid.

Generalizing, we define an operational definition thus:

Def. 28. An **operational definition** of property P is a definition stating that any object x of class K has property P iffi, whenever x is tested by a prescribed procedure (i.e., a sequence of operations), test result R is observed.

Terms such as "soluble", "malleable", "fragile", "lovable", indicating capabilities, are called "disposition terms", and lend themselves readily to operational definitions. For example:

(c) Solid x is **soluble** iffi, whenever a portion of x is put in water, it dissolves.[37]

Not an operational definition in the sense defined would be the definition of a circle in terms of the operation of drawing it by a pair of compasses; for the operation here is one of construction rather than testing. (Such definitions have been called "genetic definitions", like definitions of natural phenomena in terms of their origin.)[38] But the "static" mathematical definition of a circle—as "a closed plane curve consisting of all points equidistant from a given point"—could be reinterpreted as an operational definition, if we test the equidistance by the compasses. In any case, definitions of a circle by compasses, whether constructing or testing, belong to mechanical drawing or applied geometry rather than to pure geometry.

The meaning of definition 28 can be further clarified by two special rules for operational definition.

Rule OpD 1. A test operation must be specified with sufficient detail and precision so that a suitable observer knows exactly how to perform the operation.[39]

An example of a definition that violates this rule: "Atom x is a helium atom iffi, when x is looked at with sufficiently high magnification, it is observed that there are exactly two electrons in orbit around its nucleus". This definition gives no directions as to how to obtain "sufficiently high magnification" to see the electrons. In this case, no such directions can be given, since it is at present technically impossible (if not empirically impossible) to observe electrons directly at any attainable degree of visual magnification.

Rule OpD 2. The test result must be capable of being intersubjectively observed, and must be described with sufficient detail and precision so that it can be identified if observed.

Thus the test result cannot be a private state, such as a feeling, emotion, or mental image. The result must be an event or state of affairs capable of being observed by any suitable observer. A verbal report of a private state is an intersubjective event, hence such reports are acceptable.

Rule OpD 2 also warns against the result of the operation being merely mentioned instead of described. Such vague expressions as ". . . the appropriate result occurs" or ". . . there is some sort of change" are not acceptable.

An operational definition is best regarded as a conceptual (or other kind of thing-thing) definition. It is usually a redefinition, the improvement of a concept. Definition (a) above of an acid would be an arbitrary stipulation were it not a redefinition of a term already having a conventional meaning. But we note that in this case the presupposed conventional definition of an acid, "An acid is a substance with a sour taste", may be taken as a primitive operational definition. Any normal observer, applying the test of taste, can report whether or not the substance tastes sour.[40]

The concept of operational definition was developed by twentieth-century physicists who objected to the unobservable entities, absolute space and absolute time, which were an essential part of the Newtonian world system. Led by Einstein, they set forth theories of relativity in physics, which posited no unobservable entities, and defined space and time in terms of the operations by which they were measured. Physicist P. W. Bridgman introduced the term "operational definition". Behavioristic psychologists extended the concept to psychology. As Aristotle's theory of definition was intimately connected with his worldview, so the theories of operational definition have been related to empiricist theories of science. However, the concept of operational definition seems to be useful regardless of one's philosophical viewpoint.[41]

e *Quantitative Definition.* Quantitative techniques of definition are not ordinarily discussed separately in logic books, but it may be useful to do so.[42] We note, first, that some definitions define quantitatively, though they do not define quantities. For example,

(a) "A **minor** (in British and U.S. law) is a person less than twenty-one years of age".

This definition (which may soon become obsolete) is naturally called quantitative, since it defines a kind of person (hence, in Aristotelian terms, a kind of substance rather than of quantity) by a quantity of time.

Many common terms, once defined qualitatively, are now fitted into a scientific framework by a definition in which a quantitative description is an essential part. Thus, an older dictionary gives as its basic definition of "silver":

> (b) "**Silver,** sil′vėr, *n.* a soft white metal, capable of high polish".[43]

Recent American dictionaries, however, usually include in the definition of silver some quantities such as atomic weight, atomic number, and specific gravity, making the definition precisely quantitative in accord with contemporary science. This gives a partially quantitative definition of a kind of physical substance.[44] Such a definition might run:

> (c) "**sil-ver,** *n.* A lustrous white, ductile metallic element, used for making coins, table utensils, etc. *Symbol* Ag; atomic number 47, atomic weight 107.870, specific gravity 10.5".

A specific type of quantitative definition is especially important in natural science. As Aristotle says: "The most distinctive mark of quantity is that equality and inequality are predicated of it."[45] We call attention to quantitative equational definitions.

> **Def. 29.** A (quantitative) **equational definition** is a definition that defines one measurable quantity as equal to a certain function of another measurable quantity or quantities.[46]

In the simplest form of equational definition, one quantity—say, a unit of length—is defined in terms of another unit of length in the same system.

> (d) "1 kilometer = 1000 meters"

This uses a standard prefix of the metric system.

The U.S. Office of Standard Weights and Measures in 1893 officially defined the yard:

> (e) "1 yard = $\frac{3600}{3937}$ meter"

This definition was based on an earlier evaluation of the meter as 39.37 inches. The yard had previously been defined by a copy of the standard of the British imperial yard.

> (f) "1 meter = 1 ten-millionth of a quadrant of a meridian of the earth passing through Paris, France".

This is the original definition in terms of a natural constant referred to in 5C5,a.

More complex is the definition of a unit of measurement in terms of other variables in the same system. Such is the definition of the unit of force, called the "dyne", in the CGS (centimeter-gram-second) system of units, as equal to the force that produces in each second an acceleration of one centimeter per second on a mass of one gram; that is,

(g) 1 dyne = 1 gram × (1 centimeter/second)/second

The CGS system takes units of length, mass, and time as the basic units by which all other units of measurement are ultimately defined. Modern physics takes the concepts of length, mass, and time as fundamental; all other physical concepts—force, power, momentum, electric current, and so on—are derived concepts, defined directly or indirectly in terms of the fundamental concepts.

Definition (g) is obviously based on Newton's law of motion, that a force action on a body causes an acceleration of motion directly proportional to the force and inversely proportional to the mass of the body. This transforms into the equation

(h) Force = mass × acceleration (see Appendix 5D1,e).

f *Contextual Definition.* A definition often defines a single word—the key word—or its meaning. Often, on the other hand, its definiendum term is not a single word, but combines the key word with other words (not merely the articles "a" and "the"), so that it defines the key word within a certain context or subject to certain conditions. Definitions that supplement the key word in either of these ways are called contextual definitions.

Def. 30. A contextual definition in which *either* (a) the definiendum term combines the key word with expressions other than articles, *or* (b) the definition statement proper is asserted only in a certain context or subject to certain conditions. (For "key word", see note 8 to 5A. A "definition statement proper" is a statement simply uniting definiendum term with defining term unconditionally.)[47]

None of these definitions except (b) may be plausibly taken as extensional. In any case, contextual definitions may be intensional, extensional, or verbal.

g *Synonymous Definition.* One of the simplest ways of giving the meaning of a word is by means of a one-word synonym. For example, we might find the following definitions:

(a) *Fenster* (neuter), window.

(a') "Fenster" is the German word for a window.

(b) **foe,** *n.,* enemy.

(b') A foe is an enemy.

(c) *forte, musical direction,* loud.

Example (a) is a definition of the German word *Fenster* as it may occur in a German-English dictionary. Examples (b) and (c) are definitions that might occur in a dictionary of the English language. Examples (a') and (b') respectively show how one might define the German and English words for an English-speaking friend. These all use one-word synonyms to define a word, and are called synonymous definitions.

Def. 31. A **synonymous definition** (or definition by one-word synonym) is a definition of a single word, using another single word as defining term (not counting definite or indefinite articles).

The synonymous definition defines a word and is therefore nominal. At first sight, it seems that it defines one word by another, and must therefore be a word-word definition. It is indeed often—probably most often—intended to be word-word. However, it may instead—or also—be taken as word-thing definition. Using definition (a'), you may not be thinking of telling your friend what English word corresponds to the German word *Fenster.* You may rather be intending to tell him what kind of object is denoted by the word, or what idea he should have in mind when he hears it. (Put technically, you may be *using* the word "window" to make him think of windows, not *mentioning* the word to call attention to the word.) Then the definition is correlating a word with a thing, and is a word-thing definition. Definition (a) also, to someone who knows English well but not much German, may function in the same way. When a synonymous definition is intended to correlate the word defined with a kind of thing, a species, or a set of properties, it is using an intensional technique and is an intensional form of synonymous definition.

Example (c) has the qualification "*musical direction*", indicating that only where "*forte*" is a musical direction is "loud" a synonym for it. Not even in a discussion of music are "*forte*" and "loud" always interchangeable.

This is a case where the range within which two words are synonymous can be designated rather precisely. For most pairs of synonyms, it is not easy to delimit by a simple formula the cases where the words are interchangeable. Though "big" and "large" are synonyms, in many contexts they are not interchangeable. When we would say "Johnny is a big boy now", we would most likely not say "Johnny is a large boy now". If the maker of a synonymous definition asserts his synonyms to be interchangeable, his definition is "equivalential" by our definition 11, but is likely to be lexically false or inaccurate for some cases. The proportion of English words that have an exact synonym is small.

The technique of synonymous definition is more limited than that of genus and difference. We list some limitations and disadvantages.

(i) Most words have no one-word synonym in their own language, even in English, which is relatively rich in synonyms.

(ii) Only one of a pair of synonyms in a language can be defined by the other. The better-known word of a pair may be used as defining expression, but not as definiendum.

(iii) In most cases, synonyms cannot be used interchangeably in all contexts, and may not convey exactly the same meaning in some cases where both are applicable. For example, synonyms freely interchangeable in English are most often trivial variants, such as "philosophic" and "philosophical". But in Kantian terminology, "transcendent" and "transcendental" are carefully distinguished! Also, in interlingual synonyms, one must beware of false or misleading cognates (i.e., words descended or borrowed from the same form). In French, *conscience* still has the current English meanings of both "conscience" and "consciousness", but the latter sense is now obsolete for the English word "conscience."

(iv) One cannot give a conceptual or theoretical definition by one-word synonym, since no analysis, synthesis, or explication is possible by a single word (except perhaps a compound word: This limitation would not exist in German).

We now describe some cases where the advantages of synonymous definition outweight the disadvantages.

(i) In ordinary discourse and in short dictionaries, the ease and economy of synonymous definition are paramount considerations, and precision is sacrificed if necessary. One does not worry about defining in a circle.

(ii) In bilingual dictionaries, one-word synonyms are the rule, though a string of them may be necessary to convey different meanings of the definiendum, and the defining words may have little or no claim to be synonyms of each other. In translating, one generally wants to replace a word by a single word. It is of course proper to define a German word by an English, and the latter by the former, since the reader is supposed to know one language or the other. An exact synonym—often a cognate—is most likely to be found for a learned or technical term.

(iii) The most scholarly dictionary will define one of a pair of trivial variants (as in iii above) by the other, but will avoid a circle. A scholarly dictionary will define a slang or obsolete word (if found worthy of inclusion) by a more conventional current equivalent, but not conversely. Thus, at the end of a list of meanings of "nutty" may come: "5. *Slang.* insane".

5D2 Techniques of Extensional Definition. A very common technique for communicating the meaning of a term is to list some (or all) of the objects named by the term. For example, one would probably explain what is meant by the expression "West Germanic languages" by giving positive examples of such languages, namely, English, German, Dutch, and so on. Such a definition does not explicitly state what properties a language must have in order to be West Germanic, but instead gives the names of languages that exemplify these properties.

Def. 32. An **extensional definition** (or **definition by example**) is a definition (generally nominal, possibly real) made primarily or entirely by indicating individual objects in the extension of the definiendum term, either by language, by gesture (such as pointing or presenting the object), or by pictorial representation.

Often an extensional definition may be clarified by the addition of negative examples. A negative example is an object that does not possess all the properties signified by the definiendum term, but (if it is a good negative example) shares many of the properties of the positive examples. For instance, Danish, Icelandic, and Gothic are negative examples of West Germanic languages, since they are not West Germanic languages. They are very useful negative examples, since they are Germanic languages. Polish and Welsh are good negative examples, although they are not Germanic, because the areas in which they are spoken overlap those of the West Germanic languages, and because—like Germanic languages—they are Indo-European languages. Hungarian might be a useful negative example, even though it is not an Indo-European language, because of the geographic and historic relations between speakers of Hungarian and German. Chinese, Aztec, and Swahili are of little use as negative examples of West Germanic languages, since they have little in common with Germanic languages beyond being languages. And such negative examples as the Rocky Mountains, George Washington, and the Empire State Building are ridiculous and useless, since they are not even languages.

We distinguish two kinds of extensional definition according to the situation in which it occurs.

a *Ostensive Definition.*

> **Def. 33.** An **ostensive definition** is an extensional definition in which some or all of the objects denoted by the definiendum term are actually produced, presented, or shown to the audience.

Attention may be directed toward these objects by some gesture such as pointing, or by some demonstrative expression, as in "This is a 'such-and-such' ".

For example, the term expression "turquoise blue" is ostensively defined to a person who asks what turquoise blue is by pointing to objects he can observe that exhibit that peculiar shade of blue, or by verbally indicating the presence of this shade of blue by assertions such as "This is turquoise blue", or "That lamp shade is turquoise blue".

b *Citational Definition.* Ostensive definition is a type of extensional definition, but there are extensional definitions that are not ostensive.

> **Def. 34.** A **citational definition** is an extensional definition in which some or all of the objects named by the definiendum are indicated verbally or represented by pictures, drawings, etc., but these objects are not perceptually present to the person for whom the definition is intended.

An example of a citational definition is the extensional definition of "West Germanic language" given above.

Extensional definitions are divided thus:

Extensional Definition

Ostensive Definition	*Citational Definition*
(Examples indicated are perceptually present to audience)	Examples cited are not perceptually present to audience)

c *Definition by Paradigm Example.* This type of definition may be either ostensive or citational.

> **Def. 35.** A **definition by paradigm example** is a non-equivalential extensional definition using as example an object or objects intended to illustrate clearly and non-controversially the conventional intension of the definiendum term. (Cf. Definition by Paradigm Species, 5D1c.)

For example, a person might name Leonardo da Vinci and Rembrandt as paradigm examples of the term "artist". A definition by paradigm example may become the starting point for analyzing the meaning of the definiendum. Such investigations often end in some form of conceptual definition.

d *Limitations of Extensional Definition.* Undoubtedly an extensional definition, in many cases, is a simple and satisfactory way to answer the question "What does this word mean?" For example, if a young boy asks his father "What is a wombat?" or "What does 'wombat' mean?", the father can point to a picture of a wombat in a dictionary and reply "This is a wombat". Such an answer, of course, would be unsatisfactory if the question were asked by a zoologist who wanted to know the classification of wombats in terms of genus, family, and so on.

The meaning of some expressions is difficult if not impossible to communicate by the method of extensional definition. And the definer may find himself in a situation that limits or prevents the use of extensional definitions for certain words.

The following is a list of some common cases in which the use of extensional definitions (ostensive and/or citational) is limited or prevented:

(i) *Examples not perceptually present.* An ostensive definition of a word is impossible if no denotatum of the word is perceptually present. The absence of mutually known denotata may limit the usefulness of a citational definition. For instance, although the expression "turquoise blue" can be citationally defined, if no turquoise blue objects are present and the definer can think of no objects of this color that the audience has seen, then the examples cited will be to no avail.

(ii) *Expressions that have no observable denotata, no known denotata, or no denotata at all.* Terms such as "irrational number", "mind", and "idea" cannot be extensionally defined, since they do not name any observable object. Also there are terms such as "martian" whose denotata (if any) are unknown, hence no examples can be presented or described. Expressions such as "ideal gas" denote nothing and cannot be represented pictorially. Also form words (syncategorematic words) such as "if", "to", "therefore", "but", "and", and so on, have no denotata—form words are not intended to name objects; therefore they cannot be extensionally defined.

(iii) *Ambiguity of the examples.* In most cases of extensional definitions, the examples cited or presented have many properties in common. In such cases, the listener is not sure which property or set of properties is being referred to. For example, an English-speaking person who has no language in common with the listener might attempt to define the word *wood* ostensively by pointing to a wooden table, a wooden desk, a wooden chair, and a wooden stool. Although these objects are all wooden objects, they are also furniture, artifacts, and material objects. Thus the listener might, from these examples, think the word *wood* means wood, furniture, artifact, or material object.

5D3 Techniques of Verbal Definition. A verbal definition is a word-word or a thing-word definition. The word-word interpretation is much more common. But (as we indicated in 5B2,b and in note 18), it seems that Aristotle's real definitions are thing-word definitions.

Def. 36. A **verbal definition** is a definition in which the definiens is a term expression or other linguistic expression.

The purpose of a verbal definition is to give a verbal meaning of the definiendum. For example: *"ME" is an abbreviation for "Middle English". By "bachelor" is meant "unmarried adult male"*.

Any definition that is expressed entirely in words or other linguistic expressions (such as mathematical signs) can be interpreted as—or translated into—a verbal definition. This includes all intensional definitions, and those extensional definitions requiring only linguistic expressions. For example, the real and intensional definition

(a) The essence of **Man** is to be a rational animal

can be translated or replaced by the thing-word (real and verbal) definition

(b) The species **Man** is defined by the phrase "rational animal",

or by the word-word definition

(c) "**Man**" means the same as "rational animal".

Even if we recognize that the definiens of a certain definition is a 'thing'—a concept or non-verbal object—we may acknowledge that the defining expression gives a verbal meaning of the definiendum.

Synonymous definitions (by one-word synonym) are especially likely to be intended as verbal definitions, and to be interpreted as such—in fact as biverbal—whatever the intent.

We find then no peculiar techniques of verbal definition as such, but only peculiar formulas—such as: '*X*' means the same as '*Y*', or '*X*' means what is meant by '*Y*'—to indicate that a technique is being used to express a verbal definition.

Verbal definitions (like intensional definitions) usually use either the technique of genus and difference (def. 25), or the technique of synonymous definition (def. 31); they may at the same time be also examples of specific techniques such as operational definition (def. 28) or contextual definition (def. 30).

In verbal as in other definitions, if a definition is not equivalential (in intent), it is not asserted that defining term and definiendum term are always interchangeable. For example, if one gives the verbal definition (or definitory statement)

(d) "Wombat" means "a kind of Australian marsupial",

it is not intended to authorize replacing the definiendum by the definiens when the former occurs in the sentence "No kangaroo is a wombat". But the definition claims that whatever can be affirmed of any Australian marsupial (e.g., that it is a mammal) can be affirmed of any wombat.

5E RULES OF DEFINITION

5E1 The Traditional Rules of Definition.[48] The first rules for testing definitions were given by Aristotle in the *Topica*, where real definition is the only functional type discussed and definition by genus and differentia the only method considered. For centuries some three to six such rules have been offered in logic textbooks as rules for real and/or nominal definitions. We give a set of five rules equivalent to those found in most modern accounts of the traditional doctrine, giving preference to formulations that express the Aristotelian tradition with greatest clarity.[49]

(1) A definition should give the essence of the species defined.[50] That meant traditionally that the defining term should give the proximate genus and the differentia (difference).

(2) The definiendum term and defining term should be coextensive; i.e., whatever one term applies to, the other must apply to.[51]

(3) A definition should not be circular; the defining term should not contain the definiendum term nor a synonym thereof.[52]

(4) The defining term should be clearer than the definiendum term; the definition should not contain obscure, figurative, or ambiguous language.

(5) The definition as far as possible should be in positive rather than negative language.[53]

Even a cursory examination of these rules shows that they are not all applicable to every functional type or technique of definition. Rule 1 applies only to definition by essence (5C5), a type of conceptual definition. Rule 2 applies only to equivalential definitions (which, to be sure, are the only legitimate definitions, according to many authors). Rule 3 excludes synonymous definition as an acceptable technique.

Appendix 5D1,e: Is $f = ma$ a Law or a Definition?

The question arises whether the equation $F = ma$ is really a law of motion, as it is called, or simply a definition of force. Some writers claim that it is merely a definition. The physicist-philosopher P. W. Bridgman argues that it is not merely a matter of definition.[48]

The first camp—Bridgman calls them the "critics"—argues that, in some cases, one could determine the mass and acceleration of a falling body but has no way of determining independently the force of gravity, and must use the equation as a definition of force. The concept of force, apart from this definition, is, they hold, "nothing more than a glorification of the sensation of muscular tension"—an anthropomorphic feeling that has no place in physics.

Bridgman agrees with the critics that, for the equation to be a law and not a definition, it must be possible to measure force independently of the measure of acceleration and mass. If the equation is a law of physics, it must be possible to determine the value of the left-hand side by an appropriate operation, and to determine the value of the right-hand side by distinct operations, the two values coming out equal. In other words, such an equation "is ostensibly a statement of the possibility of getting to the same terminus by two different paths". Now, the operations for measuring mass and acceleration can be suitably specified, but can an independent operation for measuring force always be specified? In some cases at least, Bridgman points out, we can measure force by a spring balance or an elastic cord, and get a determination independent of that of mass and acceleration. In other cases, there are at least mental experiments that Newton may have done and we may do to give meaning to the application of the law to those cases, even if we cannot actually fasten a spring balance or an elastic cord to the heavenly bodies. So force is here "far from a matter of definition". In general, he concludes, "there *are* elements of conventional [i.e., stipulative] definition here" and in most physical situations. But he does not believe "that any physical situation can ever be completely reduced to a pure convention".

We will not report further Bridgman's interesting discussion with the critics, but make some comments as logicians.

First, if Newton and Bridgman are right (as we think) in holding that equation (h), $F = ma$, really states a law (relating distinct properties of things) and not a mere stipulation of the meaning of the word "force", then the equation also states a real definition, specifically a conceptual definition, which explicates force as a physical concept by its relation to mass and acceleration. The law has held up well experimentally and theoretically, and has served successfully as a definition of force.

Second, the equation was not intended by Newton and has not been generally taken as a mere stipulative definition of the word "force". However, someone who takes it that way should be able to learn physics and do experiments (though perhaps he does not understand the history and logic of the subject as well as Professor

Bridgman). As Bridgman says, "we may have equations of conventional definition, although I believe there are not as many of these as often supposed. . . ."

Third, it is important to know if operational definitions are possible for the terms involved in an equation. It is not a law or real definition unless each side has independent meaning. But it is not necessary to limit the scope of a law to the cases where the operations are now technologically possible. It can be meaningfully extended as a prediction to the cases where only mental operations or expectations of a practical operation are now at hand.

We believe we are in substantial agreement with Bridgman on these points, but differ verbally because he follows those contemporary logicians who recognize only nominal definitions.

Exercises for Chapter 5

EX 5A. Choose the most appropriate answer.

_____ 1. The first extensive treatment of definition was given by: (a) Aristotle. (b) Plato. (c) John Stewart Mill. (d) Prof. R. Robinson. (e) Prof. Leonard.

_____ 2. A nominal definition is a definition that defines a: (a) concept. (b) word or phrase in a foreign language. (c) word or phrase in any language. (d) physical thing. (e) *nom de guerre*.

_____ 3. A real definition is a definition that: (a) is self-evidently true. (b) defines real things like concepts, species, etc. (c) occurs in science and can be demonstrated to be true. (d) gives the meaning of a real number and is used exclusively in mathematics. (e) defines physical things by their chemical or atomic constituents.

_____ 4. Most contemporary British and American logicians take the position that all definitions are: (a) by genus and differentia. (b) intended to give an analysis of certain kinds of physical objects. (c) non-equivalential definitions. (d) nominal definitions. (e) real definitions.

_____ 5. According to Aristotle, a definition is a phrase indicating the: (a) essence of something. (b) constituents of something. (c) meaning of a word or phrase. (d) physical cause of an event. (e) important physical consequences of an event.

_____ 6. Aristotle thought the most important kind of definition to be: (a) real definition. (b) nominal definition. (c) word-thing definition. (d) word-word definition. (e) concise definition.

_____ 7. In real definitions, Aristotle defined only: (a) classes of physical things, like trees, dogs, zebras. (b) individual physical entities. (c) species. (d) philosophical abstractions. (e) mathematical entities.

_____ 8. In the definition " 'house cat' means 'small domesticated feline' ", the definiendum is: (a) the expression *house cat*. (b) the expression *small domesticated felines*. (c) everything

122   Exercises/Chapter 5

named by the term "house cats". (d) everything named by the term "small domesticated feline". (e) the class of all felines.

_____ 9. The term "definiendum" means: (a) a dumb definition. (b) the word or phrase that gives the meaning of what is being defined. (c) what is to be defined or what is defined. (d) that which defines the definiens. (e) a definition that is self-evidently false.

_____ 10. In a nominal definition, the definiendum term is the: (a) same as the definiendum. (b) same as the definiens. (c) expression that signifies the definiendum. (d) expression that signifies the definiens. (e) same as the defining term.

_____ 11. In the real definition "Water is H_2O", the definiendum is: (a) water. (b) the word "water". (c) H_2O. (d) the symbols "H_2O". (e) the sentence "Water is H_2O".

_____ 12. In the definition "A surgeon is a medical doctor who practices surgery", the genus is: (a) medical. (b) medical doctor. (c) surgery. (d) surgeon. (e) medical doctor who practices surgery.

_____ 13. In the definition "A mother is a female parent", the *differentia* is: (a) parent. (b) female. (c) female parent. (d) mother. (e) none of the above.

_____ 14. In the word-word definition " 'Triangle' means the same as 'three-sided figure' ", the defining term is the: (a) same as the definiendum. (b) same as the definiendum term. (c) same as the definiens. (d) expression that signifies the definiens. (e) expression "means the same as".

EX 5B, I. Choose the most appropriate answer.

_____ 1. A nominal definition that says that a certain expression means the same as another expression is a: (a) real definition. (b) word-word definition. (c) word-thing definition. (d) thing-thing definition. (e) thing-word definition.

_____ 2. A statement in which the definiendum term is joined with the defining term is a: (a) definition process. (b) definition statement. (c) nominal definition. (d) word-word definition. (e) word-thing definition.

_____ 3. A nominal definition that says that a certain expression (the definiendum) means a certain thing (property, object, etc.)

is a (an): (a) word-word definition. (b) word-thing definition. (c) thing-thing definition. (d) thing-word definition. (e) equivalential definition.

_____ 4. For a definition to be generally acceptable as a definition in the strict sense, it should be a (an): (a) word-word definition. (b) word-thing definition. (c) thing-thing definition. (d) thing-word definition. (e) equivalential definition.

_____ 5. In the context of the theory of definition, a 'thing' is defined as: (a) any entity whatsoever. (b) anything but a word (or linguistic expression). (c) a concept. (d) a class. (e) a word (or linguistic expression).

EX 5B, II. Judge whether the following definition statements are equivalential. (Reread definition 11.) Answer "yes" or "no".

_____ 1. A gerbil is a small rodent.

_____ 2. Volts equals watts divided by amps.

_____ 3. X is a cousin to Y iffi X is a child of Y's aunt or uncle.

_____ 4. Red is a primary color.

_____ 5. A pencil is a writing instrument.

_____ 6. A square is a kind of rectangle.

_____ 7. A square is a parallelogram whose sides are equal and whose angles are right angles.

_____ 8. Ozone is O_3.

_____ 9. A physical science is physics, chemistry, geology, or astronomy.

_____ 10. A triangle is a three-sided polygon.

EX 5C, I. Choose the most appropriate answer.

_____ 1. We distinguish three main functional types of definition: (a) lexical, cognitive, and non-cognitive. (b) innovative, precising, and persuasive. (c) lexical, stipulative, and conceptual. (d) conventional, facetious, and theoretical. (e) nominal, real, and non-cognitive.

_____ 2. A nominal definition whose intent is to report a meaning established for some group of users of the language is called a:

(a) lexical definition. (b) stipulative definition. (c) conceptual definition. (d) facetious definition. (e) conventional definition.

_____ 3. A nominal definition that establishes the meaning of the definiendum as the person stating the definition intends to use it is called a: (a) lexical definition. (b) stipulative definition. (c) conceptual definition. (d) facetious definition. (e) conventional definition.

_____ 4. A definition or pseudodefinition that is not intended to be taken seriously, but is intended to amuse is called a: (a) lexical definition. (b) stipulative definition. (c) conceptual definition. (d) facetious definition. (e) conventional definition.

_____ 5. A definition that attempts to analyze or explicate the meaning (especially the intension) of the definiendum term would most probably be a: (a) lexical definition. (b) stipulative definition. (c) conceptual definition. (d) facetious definition. (e) conventional definition.

EX 5G, II. Classify the following definitions by selecting the most appropriate label from the key below.

KEY

L lexical definition.
S stipulative definition, primarily cognitive.
F facetious definition.
P persuasive (stipulative) definition.
C conceptual definition.

_____ 1. A statesman is a politician who hasn't been caught.

_____ 2. A square is a quadrilateral with equal sides and all right angles.

_____ 3. The English word "oriel" means a kind of bay window.

_____ 4. The dictionary lists: "IRO, the International Refugee Organization".

_____ 5. Genuine individualism means conformity in dress, action, speech, and thought to the mores of one's culture.

_____ 6. A peony is a flower of the genus *Paeonia*.

_____ 7. Henceforth the letters "IMF" shall be used in this article as an abbreviation for "International Monetary Fund".

Exercises/Chapter 5   125

_____ 8. "Wild carrot" is a name many people use for Queen Anne's Lace.

_____ 9. A logician is a mathematician who can only count up to three.

_____ 10. The accepted meaning of the word "callipygian" is "having beautifully proportioned buttocks".

_____ 11. Real justice means eliminating all those who criticize the current administration.

_____ 12. Let the letters "GAO" stand for General Accounting Officer.

_____ 13. True kindness to another person consists of unrelenting criticism of every facet of his behavior.

_____ 14. Sulphuric acid is H_2SO_4.

_____ 15. Clavicorns are beetles of the group *Clavicornia*.

EX 5C, III. Discussion.

1. Explain the innovative use of stipulative definition.
2. Give three examples of precising definition.
3. Discuss the role that lexical (or conventional) definition plays in constructing a precising definition.
4. In a persuasive definition its non-cognitive aspect is dominant over its cognitive aspect. Why?
5. Give two examples of a synthetic conceptual definition.
6. Give two examples of an analytic conceptual definition.
7. Select three concepts. For each of these concepts give an analytic definition, and for each give a synthetic definition.
8. Give five examples (not in the text) of theoretical definition.
9. Give three examples (not in the text) of facetious (or humorous) definition.
10. Give five examples (not in the text) of persuasive definition, explaining what attitudes they are intended to redirect.

EX 5D, I. Choose the most specific appropriate answer.

_____ 1. A definition whose definiens is a set of properties is a (an): (a) definition by genus and difference. (b) definition by species. (c) definition by paradigm species. (d) intensional definition. (e) extensional definition. (f) verbal definition.

126 Exercises/Chapter 5

_____ 2. A definition that defines a genus by means of a list of species of that genus is a (an): (a) definition by genus and difference. (b) definition by species. (c) definition by paradigm species. (d) intensional definition. (e) extensional definition. (f) verbal definition.

_____ 3. To explain the meaning of *canine* by saying that a canine is a dog, wolf, or fox is to give a (an): (a) definition by genus and difference. (b) definition by species. (c) definition by paradigm species. (d) intensional definition. (e) extensional definition. (f) verbal definition.

_____ 4. The proximate genus of a species is: (a) the genus that contains all the species in a given series. (b) the next above it in a given series of classes, each class except the first being a proper subclass of those above it. (c) any class that is next to another class in a given series. (d) a genus that is approximately equivalent to the species. (e) a genus that doesn't contain that species.

_____ 5. A definition in which some of the objects denoted by the term being defined are indicated verbally though not present is a (an): (a) ostensive definition. (b) verbal definition. (c) citational definition. (d) definition by paradigm species. (e) definition by species.

_____ 6. A definition in which the definiens is a term expression or other linguistic expressions is a (an): (a) ostensive definition. (b) verbal definition. (c) citational definition. (d) definition by paradigm species. (e) definition by species.

_____ 7. Definition by subclasses is another name for: (a) ostensive definition. (b) verbal definition. (c) citational definition. (d) definition by paradigm species. (e) definition by species.

_____ 8. A definition in which some of the objects are actually pointed out is a (an): (a) ostensive definition. (b) verbal definition. (c) citational definition. (d) definition by paradigm species. (e) definition by species.

_____ 9. A species that clearly and non-controversially illustrates the conventional intension of the definiendum term is called a (an): (a) conventional species. (b) operational species. (c) paradigm species. (d) proximate species. (e) genus.

_____ 10. Which one of the following statements is true? (a) The defining term of a synonymous definition may contain two or more words. (b) The definiendum term of a synonymous definition may contain two or more words. (c) Definition by paradigm species is the same as definition by paradigm example. (d) An operational definition is always a kind of theoretical definition. (e) A definition by species may be equivalential.

_____ 11. The definition of acid in terms of the litmus test is called a (an): (a) definition by species. (b) definition by paradigm species. (c) operational definition. (d) quantitative definition.

_____ 12. The kind of definition developed by twentieth-century physicists and used by Einstein was: (a) definition by species. (b) definition by paradigm species. (c) operational definition. (d) quantitative definition.

_____ 13. A definition that defines one measurable quantity as equal to a certain function of another measurable quantity or quantities is called a (an): (a) definition by species. (b) definition by paradigm species. (c) operational definition. (d) quantitative definition.

_____ 14. The kind of definition whose definiens states a procedure or test is a (an): (a) definition by species. (b) definition by paradigm species. (c) operational definition. (d) quantitative definition.

_____ 15. Which one of the following statements is true? (a) An ostensive definition is a type of intensional definition. (b) Synonymous definitions are especially likely to be intended as verbal definitions. (c) A verbal definition is a thing-thing or word-thing definition. (d) A definition by paradigm example is an equivalential definition. (e) A citational definition never uses language.

EX 5D, II. Identify the techniques of the following definitions by choosing a letter (or letters) from the key below:

KEY

a. Definition by genus and difference.
b. Definition by species.
c. Definition by paradigm species.
d. Operational definition.

e. Quantitative definition.
f. Contextual definition.
g. Synonymous definition.
h. Ostensive definition.
i. Citational definition.
j. Verbal definition.

_____ 1. The general definition of power is: $P = \frac{W}{t}$ where P is the power supplied and t is the time taken for the performance of the work W (Semat, *Fundamentals of Physics,* Rinehart & Co., 1958, 485.)

_____ 2. A pachyderm is an elephant, rhinoceros, or hippopotamus.

_____ 3. A professional comedian is an actor like Bob Hope or Charlie Chaplin.

_____ 4. Tin is a metallic element with an atomic number of 50.

_____ 5. The word "between" may be defined by saying that X is *between* Y and Z iff X is in the space or extends through the space that separates Y and Z.

_____ 6. Onomatopoeia is use of a word such as *buzz, ring, boom, crack,* etc.

_____ 7. "Köbenhavn" is the Danish name for Copenhagen.

_____ 8. Electrical power (as measured in watts) equals joules divided by seconds.

_____ 9. "Oneiromancy" means "divination by dreams".

_____ 10. A clairschach is an ancient Celtic harp.

_____ 11. Green is the color that a normal human observer will see if he is visually exposed to light having a wavelength of approximately 530 nanometers.

_____ 12. Board games are chess, checkers, Monopoly, etc.

_____ 13. Alliteration is the use of an expression such as "two tame tigers" or "the wet and weary wind".

_____ 14. A test that a man is physically fit is his ability to do sixty push-ups and two hundred deep knee bends.

_____ 15. "Allegretto" means "somewhat brisk".

EX 5E, I. Answer the following concisely.

Discuss this question: Is the text's definition of "valid argument form" circular?

6

Division and Classification

Many modern logic text books do not treat the subject of division and classification. There was controversy in the nineteenth century regarding the inclusion of division in formal logic.[1] In the opinion of the authors, the subject belongs in formal logic, since it is possible to define division as a formal process, and since the exposition of logic itself requires the use of division and classification. Also, division and definition were inextricably related for Plato and Aristotle; and there is reason to believe that the method of division led Aristotle to his doctrine of syllogisms.[2]

6A KINDS OF DIVISION

Division, according to the dictionary, is "the act, process, or an instance of dividing into parts or portions".[3] Three kinds of division are: logical division, physical division, and metaphysical division.

6A1 Logical Division. To Aristotle, logical division is the process of distinguishing the different species of a genus. In more modern language, it is the process of distinguishing the proper subclasses of a class. Logical division can also be understood as a process of analyzing terms. The result of this process is an arrangement or grouping called a logical division.

Definition 1a defines a logical division as a process. Definition 1b defines logical division as a product of that process.

> **Def. 1a. Logical division** is the process of analyzing a genus or class (or term) into its species or proper subclasses (or subterms).[4]
>
> **Def. 1b.** A **logical division** is an arrangement of species, classes, or terms resulting from a process of logical division.

It is important to note the following characteristics of the process of logical division:

> (i) It is a process that moves from the general to the less general.

> (ii) It analyzes classes into classes, or general terms into general terms.

The result of a logical division is never an enumeration of individuals.

The distinction between logical division and enumeration is illustrated by the following example. The class of mammals may be logically divided into the subclasses (technically, orders) of monotremes, marsupials, primates, and so on. The class of mammals now living in Yonkers, New York is enumerated when the members of the class are referred to individually, either by proper names such as "Fido" and "Tobias Q. Terwilliger", or by definite descriptions such as "This dog", "The mayor", and "The black dog that stole the roast".

We shall henceforth use the term "division" (without qualification) to mean logical division. The rules for division are given in 6B.

6A2 Physical Division.

Def. 2. Physical division (or **partition**) is the process of distinguishing the physical parts of an entity.

For example, the United States can be physically divided into states, and an automobile can be physically divided into engine, exhaust system, shocks, electrical system, and so on. Physical division, like logical division, is a conceptual process. An automobile does not have to be physically disassembled in order to be physically divided. The parts merely have to be distinguished in speech, writing, or thought.

6A3 Metaphysical Division.

Def. 3. Metaphysical division is the process of distinguishing the qualities of an entity.

For example, an apple can be conceptually divided into its qualities of color, shape, size, and taste. A metaphysical division is always conceptual as one cannot physically divide an entity into its qualities.[5]

6B LOGICAL DIVISION

6B1 Definitions. The following terms prove useful in explaining division.

Def. 4. The **summum genus** (or **totum divisum**) is the genus or class (or term) with which the process of division starts.

Def. 5. The **infimae species** (lowest species) are the species or subclasses (or subaltern terms) with which a division ends. (The singular form is *"infima species"*.)

Def. 6. The **subaltern genera** are the genera or classes (or terms) intermediate between the *summum genus* and the *infima species*.

(Of course if there is only one stage of division there will be no subaltern genera.)

An example of a logical division:

(a)

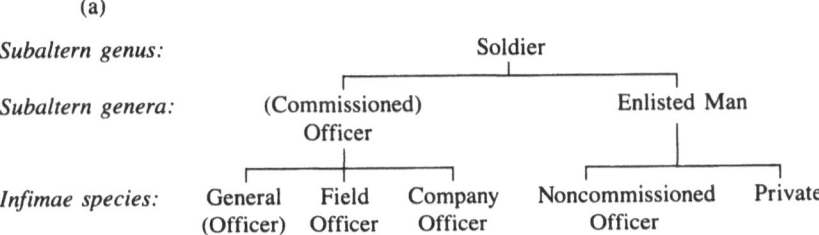

The infimae species are not the classes at which division *must* end, but the classes at which it does end. The infimae species here are "General", "Field Officer", "Noncommissioned Officer", and "Private".

The terms *superordinate, subordinate,* and *coordinate* are used to designate, respectively, a class as related to a class that is a subdivision of it, a class of which it is a subdivision, and a class obtained in the same set of subdivision of a superordinate class. In the above example, "Enlisted Man" is a superordinate class to "Noncommissioned Officer", a subordinate class to "Soldier", and a coordinate class to "Officer".

6B2 The Rules of Logical Division.

Rule D1 Coordinate classes must be *mutually exclusive*.

Rule D2 The coordinate classes must be *jointly coextensive* with the class they divide.

Rule D3 Each stage of a division should be based upon one *principle of division (fundamentum divisionis)*.

Rules D1 and D2 can be combined in compact form: Coordinate classes must be mutually exclusive and jointly coextensive. These two together, as Keynes says, constitute "a precise statement of what is implied when we speak of a logical division". They may, however, be used as rules for testing a supposed logical division.[6]

These rules will now be explained, and an optional Rule D4 added.

Rule D1 *Coordinate classes must be mutually exclusive.*

The division should be made, if possible, by terms whose meaning prevents any overlapping. Otherwise the superordinate class has not been divided into classes that are necessarily exclusive, and there might be no proper division at all. Thus it is not good practice to divide college classes into those with ten members or less, and those with ten members or more, even if it happens that in a given case one has no class with exactly ten members.

Non-exclusiveness results if one divides into classes of which one is subordinate to another. For example, the following violates Rule D1:

(b)

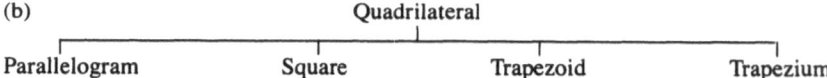

| Parallelogram | Square | Trapezoid | Trapezium |

Squares are parallelograms, so "square" should be subordinate to "parallelogram", not coordinate with it.

Non-exclusiveness may also come from cross-division, a violation of rule D3 (explained below).

Rule D2 *The coordinate classes must be jointly coextensive with the class they divide.*

When a class is divided into parts these parts taken together must contain exactly the same members as the class. This requirement is equivalent to the combination of two subordinate requirements:

(i) Coordinate classes must be *jointly exhaustive* of the class they divide; (i.e., everything in the divided class must be in one of the coordinate classes dividing it).

(ii) Coordinate classes must be *contained* in the class they divide.[7]

That this requirement is necessary is shown by the example of dividing the class of college students into two jointly exhaustive (and mutually exclusive) classes: people less than nineteen years old and people nineteen years old or over. The member of these two classes taken together are all the people in the world and thus do not contain the same members as the class of college students. Dividing the class of college students into college students less than nineteen years old and college students nineteen years old or over obeys requirement (ii) above.

In mathematics, it is usually not difficult to make a priori divisions into suitable subclasses that are mutually exclusive and jointly coextensive. For example, one may divide plane rectilinear figures into triangles, quadrilaterals, pentagons, and polygons of more than five sides. Outside mathematics, one can usually make quantitative divisions of some sort. For example, one may divide rocks—or even animals—into those weighing less than ten grams, those weighing at least ten but less than twenty grams, and so on; but this is likely to be of little use, except perhaps for knowing what it would cost to mail them.

Even in logic, difficulty can arise. We saw in 4B that the division of terms started simply enough in Aristotle, with a dichotomy between a term "which is of such a nature as to be predicated of many subjects" and one "which is not thus predicated". But the traditional division into general and singular terms derived from Aristotle, we found, was not exhaustive; a term such as "the Alps" or "the Smith brothers" does not really fit either category. The traditional division had presupposed that a term must denote either a unique unit, or each of a class of units, not allowing that it might denote a unique plurality as such.

In the social and natural sciences, a priori divisions are generally of relatively limited value. For example, there are various ways in which the class of mammals may be subdivided. The principle way for zoologists is to subdivide into the orders of monotremes, marsupials, rodents, and so on. The concepts of these orders are obtained by empirical and inductive procedures of classification (6D) rather than division, though the result may be presented in the form of a division. There is no guarantee that the classes in such a subdivision of mammals are jointly exhaustive—unless one adds a miscellaneous category, possibly empty, of "other mammals".

Rule D3 *Each stage of a division should be based upon one principle of division (fundamentum divisionis).*

If the principle of division of polygons, for example, is the number of sides, then they are divided into three-sided, four-sided polygons, and so on. If the principle of division is regularity (equality of sides and angles), they are divided into regular and irregular.

Cross-division is the use of more than one principle of division at a given stage of a division, some subclasses being determined by one principle and others by another. Cross-division usually, but not always, results in overlapping or nonexhaustive classes. For example:

(c)

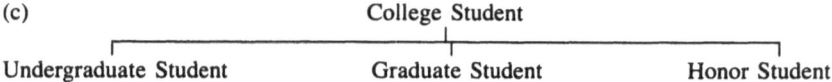

| Undergraduate Student | Graduate Student | Honor Student |

This cross-division, based on the two principles of academic year and scholastic standing, has overlapping classes if there are honor students.

The following cross-division might well have no overlapping classes:

(d)

```
              Teacher
    ┌────────────┴────────────┐
Male Teacher         Teacher Using Lipstick
```

But besides the possibility of overlapping, this division is nonexhaustive if there are women teachers not using lipstick. The adequacy of a cross-division is doubtful, and it is in any case inelegant.

A further specification of rule D3 may be added as an optional rule:

Rule D4 Other things being equal, it is preferable that the same principle of division be used at every stage of a division.

Use of the same principle of division at every stage, where possible, has the advantage of logical simplicity and elegance, but it is not always desirable to do this. For example, the following division uses different principles of division for different stages:

(e)

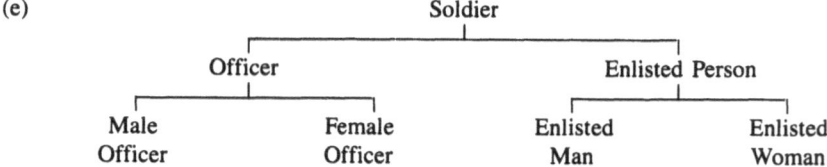

This is not cross-division. This division satisfies the rules, and might well serve a useful purpose.

Essentially the same division as that of (e) may be presented as a two-dimensional array:

(e′)	SOLDIER	Officer	Enlisted Person
	Male	Male Officer	Enlisted Man
	Female	Female Officer	Enlisted Woman

This is also not a violation of rule D3. Soldiers are here divided according to two principles of division, but each is carried through completely. In effect, the division has two stages, though it is arbitrary which is taken as the first stage.

6C DICHOTOMOUS DIVISION

Def. 7. A **dichotomous division** (or **division by dichotomy**) is a logical division of a class—or of each class except the *infimae species*—into two classes by the presence or absence of a given attribute.

A famous example of a dichotomous division is the *Tree of Porphyry*.[8]

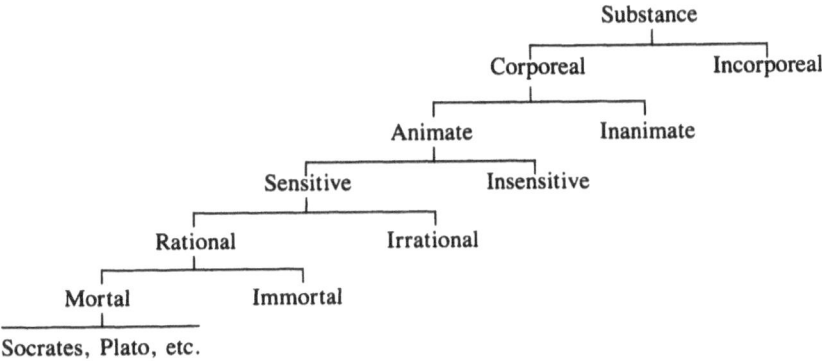

Socrates, Plato, etc.

Here each term is carried down to those dividing it. Thus substance is divided into corporeal substance (i.e., body) and incorporeal substance; animated body is divided into sensitive animated body (i.e., animal) and insensitive animated body; and so on down to mortal rational animal (i.e., man) and immortal rational animal. The last line is not a division of man but an enumeration (6A1).

A dichotomous division automatically satisfies the three basic rules. For this reason, and because of its formal character, some logicians have argued the superiority of dichotomous division.[9] The disadvantages of dichotomous division may be seen by comparison. For example, let us extract from the non-dichotomous division (a) above of the class "Soldier" its division of "(Commissioned) Officer":

(g)
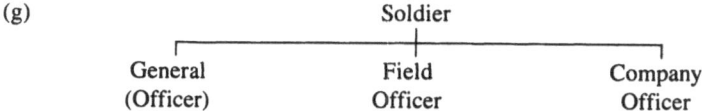

Let us try to do the same thing by dichotomous division. One way would be the following:

(h)
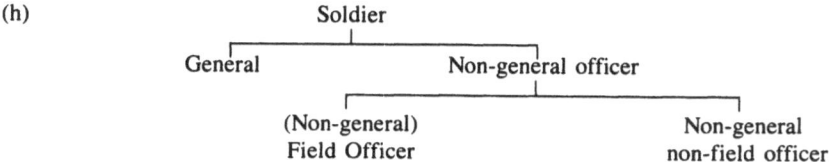

Though we have one more rubric than division (g), we still have not introduced the term "company officer". This could be done, say by setting up the equivalence of "company officer" to "non-general non-field officer" in a supplementary definition. Dichotomous division is here clearly much clumsier than the simple division of example (g), and is increasingly clumsy as division gets more complicated. Nevertheless, division by dichotomy may be favored for purely formal division (as in Bollean albebra or calculus of classes), or for use with a binary system (as in some types of computer/programming calculations).

6D CLASSIFICATION

6D1 Division and Classification. Logical division and classification are closely related. In logical division, one starts with a class (genus) and divides it into subclasses (but not into individuals). In classification, one starts with individuals or classes, and groups them into classes on the basis of properties they share. Like many abstract words ending in "-tion", "division" and "classification" are used both for a process and for the product resulting from the process—in this case, a mental or verbal activity, namely a hierarchical arrangement of concepts or terms. In the sense of such an arrangement, every table that results from logical division may also be regarded as if it were the result of classification.

As a process of knowledge, division is characteristically an a priori process based on meaning. Classification, however, is primarily inductive, and may require empirical knowledge. In less technical language, this means that a table of pure division can be constructed solely from the meanings of the terms in the table; no recourse to experience is necessary. I know, for example, that squares are a subclass of parallelograms, not from experience but from the meanings of the terms "square" and "parallelogram". On the other hand, if I were engaged in the process of classifying plants, I would have to observe the similarities and dissimilarities of actual plants. I could not construct a useful classification of plants unless I had observed the plants I wished to classify.

In the natural sciences, classification is far more important than division, since the principal analyses and relationships are based on empirical data. Division plays an important role in the formal sciences of mathematics and logic, and in the empirical areas to which these disciplines can be applied. But the formal scientist often uses methods partly inductive to develop the knowledge that he will later expound deductively. In such inductive or hypothetico-deductive reasoning, classification plays a role. Logicians' "classifications" of terms, for example, and of fallacies, combine (inductive) classification and (a priori) division.

This is a formal definition of classification.

Def. 8. Classification is a process of grouping individuals or classes into classes on the basis of certain properties that they have in common, these classes in turn being grouped together until the *summum genus* is reached. An arrangement resulting from classification and/or division is also called a "classification".

6D2 Natural and Artificial Classification. Every physical object, whether it is a chemical compound or a living organism, has an indefinite number of properties by which it can be classified, but not all of these properties are of equal theoretical importance. The properties of an object that are of the greatest theoretical importance are the properties that are found to be invariably related to certain other properties. For example, animals that have the property of suckling their young are invariably found to have the characteristics of being warm-blooded and a vertebrate. The basic classifications that science aims at are those founded on the properties that prove to be most important theoretically. Such a classification was traditionally called a **natural classification.**[10] In contrast, a classification is a (more or less) **artificial classification** insofar as the properties on which it is based are relatively thin in invariable relationships with other properties.

A classic example of an artificial or technical classification is the arrangement of plants commonly called the Linnaean classification, based chiefly on the number of stamens and pistils. As Mill said:

> The Linnaean arrangement answers the purpose of making us think together of all those kinds of plants which possess the same number of stamens and pistils; but to think of them in that manner is of little use, since we seldom have anything to affirm in common of the plants which have a given number of stamens and pistils.[11]

Hence, in spite of its simplicity, this principle of classification could not prevail over more pregnant ones that proved to have greater scientific value.

With changes in the accepted theories of science come changes in what is accepted as a natural classification. After the theory of evolution came to be generally accepted in biology, the basic principle of classification of animals and plants was theoretically simple and objective: species and genera were to be grouped together according to family relationships following the supposed line of descent from common ancestors. However, since these relationships are not directly observable, in practice biological classification continue to be based on diverse criteria found empirically to be important.[12]

A classification of division intended to serve a particular purpose is good in so far as it serves that purpose, whether artificial or not. To primitive man, a classification of animals on the basis of their danger to him, or their utility to him, is of great practical value, though likely to contribute little toward the development of a scientific zoology. With the development of scientific interest comes a shift away from such an anthropocentric view toward greater objectivity, and the artificiality of the primitive view is recognized.

6D3 Rules of Classification. There are six rules: four formal rules and two informal. It should be noted that the first three formal rules correspond exactly to the first three rules of division (6B2). The fourth is more general than the optional fourth rule of division.

a *Formal rules*

Rule C1 Coordinate classes in the classification must be *mutually exclusive*.

Rule C2 The coordinate classes must be jointly *coextensive* with the class immediately superordinate (their proximate genus).

Rule C3 Each stage of a classification should be based on one *principle of classification.*

Rule C4 Other things being equal, the classification using the *fewest principles* of classification is preferred. This is the criterion of logical *simplicity.*

b *Informal rules*

Rule C5 The classification should serve the purpose for which it was constructed.

Rule C6 Unless the classification is constructed to serve one specific function, it is desirable that it be as *fruitful* as possible.

A classification is fruitful to the extent that it suggests new hypotheses, explanations, and theories concerning its subject matter. For example, the Periodic Table—the classification of the elements—proved extremely fruitful, since it suggested the existence of hitherto unknown elements and even suggested what physical properties they would have. It should be noted that natural classifications, by definition, are more fruitful than artificial ones.

Exercises for Chapter 6

EX 6A–6D. Choose the most appropriate letter for each blank.

_____ 1. The process of analyzing a genus or class into its species or proper subclasses is called: (a) classification. (b) division. (c) dichotomy. (d) *infimae species.*

_____ 2. In the natural sciences: (a) classification and division are of equal importance. (b) division is of more importance than classification. (c) classification is of more importance than division. (d) neither classification nor division are of any importance.

_____ 3. The process of distinguishing the qualities of an entity is called: (a) classification. (b) metaphysical division. (c) physical division. (d) qualitative division.

_____ 4. The class with which the process of division starts is called the (a) *summum genus.* *(b) subaltern genera. (c) infimae species.* (d) coordinate class.

_____ 5. The subclasses with which a division ends are called the: (a) *summum genus.* (b) subaltern genera. (c) *infimae species.* (d) subordinate classes.

_____ 6. The logical division of a class, except for the last classes in the division, into two classes by the presence or absence of a given attribute, is called: (a) metaphysical division. (b) physical division. (c) short division. (d) dichotomous division.

_____ 7. The only kind of division that automatically satisfies the rules of division is: (a) metaphysical division. (b) physical division. (c) dichotomous division. (d) long division.

_____ 8. Which one of the following processes depends most upon induction? (a) metaphysical division. (b) classification. (c) physical division. (d) deductive reasoning.

_____ 9. A natural classification is one which is: (a) found in nature. (b) based on properties that prove to be important theoretically. (c) based solely upon the meaning of words. (d) not a scientific classification.

_____ 10. By definition: (a) natural classifications are more fruitful than artificial ones. (b) artificial classifications are more fruitful than natural ones. (c) division is more fruitful than classification. (d) physical division is more fruitful than metaphysical division.

Ex 6A–6B. For each of the three examples listed below comply with the following instructions.

1. Name the *summum genus*, the subaltern genera, and the *infimae species*. State the principle of division for each stage.
2. Test each example to see if the formal rules of classification are complied with.
3. Give your reasoned opinion as to what useful purpose or purposes each classification might serve. State your opinion as to the fruitfulness of each classification.

Example 1.

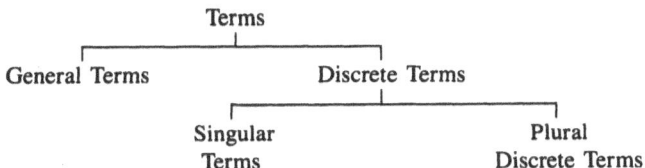

For the definitions of *term, general term, discrete term* etc., see chapter 4.

Example 2.

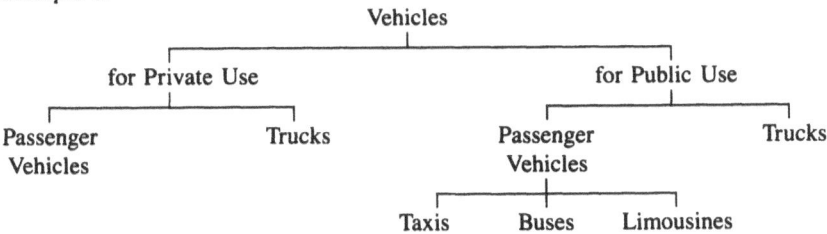

For definitions of terms consult a dictionary.

Example 3.

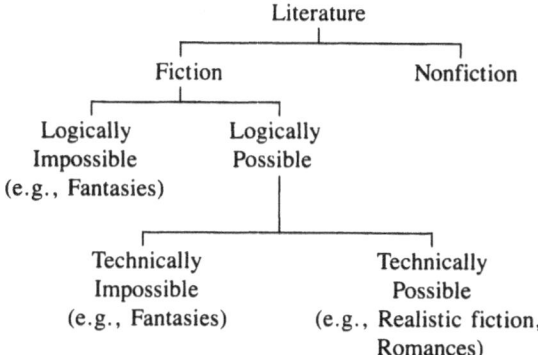

The definitions of terms in Example 3 are as follows: *Fiction* is a story about non-actual people and/or non-actual events and/or non-actual places. (Generally at least its characters are non-actual.) A state-of-affairs or event is logically possible if a proposition that asserts it is consistent with all known confirmed statements that state laws of nature (scientific laws). An event is *technically possible* if the propositions that assert it is consistent with all known confirmed statements that assert that such an event can be achieved by *known* scientific techniques.

II

Basic Concepts of Aristotelian Logic

7

Standard Categorical Propositions

A categorical proposition has been defined as a subject-predicate proposition. In Aristotelian logic four types of categorical proposition are taken as standard. The propositional forms of these four types are called the standard categorical forms. Propositions of these types are called **standard categorical propositions** or **standard categoricals**.

The four **standard categorical forms** are, with examples:

Code Letter	The Standard Categorical Forms	Standard Categorical Propositions
A	All S are P	*All shrubs are plants.*
E	No S are P	*No sows' ears are purses.*
I	Some S are P	*Some Scots are Presbyterians.*
O	Some S are not P	*Some sailors are not prosperous.*

7A THE PARTS OF A STANDARD CATEGORICAL

7A1 Quantifiers. Every standard categorical proposition must have one of the following quantifiers: "all", "no", "some", or "some . . . not. . . ." We take the "not" in the O proposition as part of the quantifier, as one would if "Not all S are P" were the standard form (though it is usually taken as part of the copula: see 7A2).

The logician takes "all" and "no" strictly. "All Scots are patriots" means "Each and every Scot, without exception, is a patriot". However, logic—unlike ordinary usage—does not take the plural form of subject and verb to imply that there is more than one instance of the subject term.

If "Some S are P" is given the minimal meaning "At least one S is P", then it is possible to make a true statement about S and P, using the standard categorical forms, no matter what relation holds between S and P.

For example, in the case where exactly one S is P and exactly one S is not P, we can say (incompletely but truly) that "Some S are P and some S are not P". But if "some" were defined as meaning "at least two", (or "at least three", etc.) then none of the four quantifiers could be used to make a true statement about this case with the given terms. This means that there could be real objects about which no true statement could be made by use of the standard categorical forms. To make the system of quantifiers always applicable, "some" is given the meaning of *at least one*.

An equivalent formulation of the **I** (for example) "Some Scots are Presbyterians" is "Something real is both a Scot and a Presbyterian". Corresponding formulations of the **O** proposition "Some Scots are not Presbyterian" are: "At least one Scot is not a Presbyterian" and "Something real is a Scot and not a Presbyterian".

7A2 The Copula.

Def. 1. The **copula** in a standard categorical proposition is a form of the verb "to be", usually "are" or "is", serving as the main verb.

A simple proposition whose main verb is not a form of the verb "to be" must be replaced by one with this verb to obtain a standard categorical form. (See chapter 25, Standardizing Propositions.)

It is possible—and often advisable—to reduce propositions not in present tense to present tense. The rules for categorical arguments presuppose that the propositions are in the same tense. For example, "Some painters were not subsidized by Royalty" equals "Some painters of the past are not people subsidized by Royalty".

The copula may be immediately followed by "not" only in the **O** proposition. "All S are not P" is an ambiguous form and is non-standard.

7A3 The Subject Term.

Def. 2. The **subject term** (or **logical subject**) of a standard categorical proposition is the entire expression between the quantifier and the copula.

The quantifier and the copula are not part of the subject term. When we use the word *subject* without qualification we shall mean the subject term, that is, the logical subject, not the grammatical subject. The grammatical subject consists of the quantifier (if any) together with the subject term.

7A4 The Predicate Term.

Def. 3. The **predicate term** (or **logical predicate**) of a standard categorical is the entire expression after the (principal) "are" in the **A, E,** and **I** propositions and after the "are not" in the **O** proposition.

When we use the word *predicate* without qualification we shall mean the predicate term. The grammatical predicate of a categorical proposition consists of the main verb and its objects and modifiers; in a standard categorical, it consists of the copula and everything following it.

7A5 Code-Letter Notation for Standard Categorical Forms.

Code-Letter Notation	Categorical Forms
A*sp*	All S are P
E*sp*	No S are P
I*sp*	Some S are P
O*sp*	Some S are not P

7A6 Four-Part Analysis of Categoricals.

Code Letter	Quantifier	(*Subject*)	Copula	**Q'r**	(*Predicate*)
A	All	(*popular kings*)	are		(*happy men*).
E	No	(*married men*)	are		(*bachelors*).
I	Some	(*fine painters*)	are		(*neurotics*).
O	Some	(*Europeans*)	are	**not**	(*Frenchmen*).

7B QUANTITY AND QUALITY OF STANDARD CATEGORICAL PROPOSITIONS

7B1 Quantity.

Def. 4. The **quantity** of a categorical proposition is either universal or particular.

Def. 5. A **universal proposition** is one that affirms or denies the predicate of everything named by the subject.

The standard universal quantifiers of traditional logic are "all" and "no". The standard forms of universal propositions are "All S are P" and "No S are P".

Def. 6. A **particular proposition** is one that affirms or denies the predicate of *at least one* thing named by the subject.

The standard particular quantifiers are "some" and "some . . . not . . .". The standard forms of particular propositions are "Some S are P" and "Some S are not P".

For any specific S and P, the truth of "Some S are P" does not exclude the possibility that all S are P nor that some S are not P, nor that exactly one S is P. (It does exclude the possibility that no S are P.)

Numerous other particular quantifiers ("at least two", "most", "several", etc.) are not treated systematically in traditional logic (except by some who erroneously treat them as equivalent to "some").

7B2 Quality.

Def. 7. The **quality** of a categorical proposition is either affirmative or negative.

The standard forms of affirmative propositions are "All S are P" and "Some S are P".

The standard forms of negative propositions are "No S are P" and "Some S are not P".

7B3 Quantity-Quality Table.

Table 7.1: Quantity-Quality Table

Quantity	Quality	Code Letter	Categorical Form	Code-Letter Notation
Universal	Affirmative	A	All S are P	Asp
Universal	Negative	E	No S are P	Esp
Particular	Affirmative	I	Some S are P	Isp
Particular	Negative	O	Some S are not P	Osp

In generalized statements, we use "Xsp" to refer to any of the four categorical forms. The "**X**" is a variable (or dummy letter) standing for "A", "E", "I", or "O".

7C EXISTENTIAL PRESUPPOSITIONS OF STANDARD CATEGORICAL PROPOSITIONS

In this section we discuss a problem concerning one aspect of the meaning of standard categorical propositions. This problem, which is related to the meaning of standard quantifiers, discussed in 7A1, is concerned with the implications and especially with the presuppositions of the existence or nonexistence of the things named by the terms of standard categorical propositions.

One of the presuppositions of existence made in traditional logic is that the subject term of a standard categorical is never empty, that is, it is presupposed that there are real things that the subject term names. (See 4F1.) If this presupposition of existence is not made for the subjects of the categoricals, then these categoricals are "meaningless" in traditional logic, in the sense of being neither true nor false.

For example, the universal affirmative "All centaurs are quadrupeds" has an empty term as subject, that is, a term that applies to nothing. This sentence is neither true nor false in traditional logic because the assumption of either its truth or its falsity, it will be shown, leads to a contradiction.

Let us assume (1) that "All centaurs are quadrupeds" is *true*. Now, traditional logic holds that the argument from "All S are P" to "Some S are P" is valid. (See 8B4.) Then it follows that "Some centaurs are quadrupeds" should be true. But this is not true, since it means "At least one centaur is a quadruped" or "Something real is both a centaur and a quadruped", and we know that nothing real is a centaur. Therefore, if the conclusion of this valid argument is not true, our initial assumption must be wrong and the sentence "All centaurs are quadrupeds" *cannot be true* in traditional logic.

Now let us assume (2) that "All centaurs are quadrupeds" is *false*. Traditional logic holds that if it is false that all S are P, then it is true that some S are not P (See 8B1). Then it should follow from this assumption that "Some centaurs are not quadrupeds" is true. But this conclusion, which means "At least one centaur is not a quadruped" (or "Something real is a centaur and not a quadruped"), is not true, because there are no centaurs. Therefore, our assumption—that "All centaurs are quadrupeds" is false—*cannot be true*.

We conclude that "All centaurs are quadrupeds" can be neither true nor false in traditional logic, and in this sense is meaningless in traditional logic. Similarly it can be demonstrated that no other categorical proposition with an empty term for subject can be meaningful within this system of traditional logic.

7D DIAGRAMS OF STANDARD CATEGORICALS

We present here two related and complementary systems of diagrams, which we believe to be those best suited for representing standard categorical propositions taken with an Aristotelian interpretation, and arguments composed of them.

The first system we call the "five-Case diagrams", diagramming the five distinct relations that *S*'s may have to *P*'s, given that there are *S*'s and *P*'s. (This system appears in many twentieth-century logic books under the misnomer "Euler's diagrams" or "Eulerian diagrams". If anyone's name is to be attached to this system, it should be that of J. D. Gergonne; these five relations are now called the Gergonne relations, since his paper of 1817[1] is the first known systematic study of them and their relation to the standard categorical propositions and syllogisms.)

The second system we use is a system of Eulerian diagrams, in which each of the four forms of standard categorical propositions is represented by a single distinctive diagram.

The five-Case Diagrams

If we have two terms—say *f* and *g*—each denoting something, there are just five specific and incompatible relations in which *f* can stand to *g*, called the "Gergonne relations".

In only one of the five cases does the Gergonne symbol stand for one of the four standard categorical forms: his "f*H*g" for Exclusion means the same as "E*fg*". Gergonne believes the logician should use a symmetrical sign for a symmetrical relation. Also, he writes: "The letter (H), initial of the word *Hors*, designates the system of two ideas one absolutely outside the other, like the two vertical legs of this letter."[2] His symbols for Identity and Intersection are also symmetrical, and intended to express the identity (or unity) of extensions in the first case, and the intersection crossing or overlapping of extensions in the other. In contrast, the "C" for Being Contained and the inverted "C" for Containing are asymmetrical, one the converse of the other, like the relations they symbolize. The "C" also, like a less-than sign, indicates that the extension of the first term is less than that of the second; the inverted "C" indicates that the extension of the first is greater than that of the second.

(The numbering of the five cases above is not from Gergonne, but follows the numbers assigned by J. A. Faris in an article in the *Journal of Symbolic Logic*.)[3]

Name: Diagram	Relational form and Example	Standard categorical equivalent; (Gergonne symbol)
Identity 1) (circle with f g together)	The f are **identical** with the g; e.g., French idioms are identical with Gallicisms.	Afg & Agf (f*I*g)
Being *Contained* 2) (f inside g)	The f are **contained** in the g; e.g., furniture workers are contained in the gainfully employed.	Afg & Ogf (f*C*g)
Intersection 3) (f and g overlapping)	The f **intersect** the g; e.g., the freshmen intersect the girls.	Ofg & Ifg & Ogf (f*X*g)
Containing 4) (g inside f)	The f **contain** the g; e.g., the French contain the Gascons.	Agf & Ofg (f*O*g)
Exclusion 5) (f and g separate)	The f **exclude** the g; e.g., the featherless bipeds exclude the gorillas.	Efg (f*H*g) (f *est hors de* g)

Exercises for Chapter 7

EX 7, I. Put the appropriate letter in the margin: "Y" for yes, "N" for no.

_____ 1. Is "most" a standard quantifier?

_____ 2. Is the grammatical predicate of a categorical proposition its main verb without its objects and modifiers?

_____ 3. The quantifier "some" in logic means at least two?

_____ 4. Does the grammatical subject consist of the quantifier (if any) together with the subject term?

_____ 5. Is the quantity of the **O** proposition negative?

_____ 6. Is a universal proposition one that affirms or denies the predicate of everything named by the subject?

_____ 7. Are the universal quantifiers "no" and "some"?

_____ 8. Are the universal standard forms "No S are P" and "Some S are not P"?

_____ 9. Are the affirmative standard forms "All S are P" and "Some S are P"?

_____ 10. Is the quantifier a part of the subject term?

EX 7, II. Put the appropriate letter in the margin.

_____ 1. The quantity of a categorical proposition is: (a) affirmative or negative. (b) simple or compound. (c) universal or particular. (d) categorical or compound.

_____ 2. The predicate term of a categorical is the entire expression: (a) after the "are". (b) after the "are" in the **A**, **E** and **I** propositions and after the "are not" in the **O** proposition. (c) after the subject term. (d) after the quantifier.

_____ 3. The subject term of a categorical proposition is the entire expression: (a) after the copula. (b) before the copula. (c) between the quantifier and the predicate term. (d) between the quantifier and the copula.

Exercises/Chapter 7   153

_____ 4. The copula in a standard categorical proposition is a: (a) verb in the past tense. (b) form of the verb "to be". (c) quantifier. (d) term.

_____ 5. "Only S are P" is a: (a) standard categorical proposition. (b) standard categorical form. (c) non-standard categorical proposition. (d) non-standard categorical form.

_____ 6. The number of distinct categorical forms taken as standard in the Aristotelian logic is: 1, 2, 3, 4, . . . ; or (X) indefinite.

_____ 7. Every categorical proposition in standard form must begin with one of the following: (a) "some", "no", "almost all". (b) "some", "most", "all". (c) "some", "over half", "few". (d) "some", "no", "all".

_____ 8. We take the "not" in the O proposition as part of the: (a) predicate term. (b) verb. (c) subject. (d) quantifier.

_____ 9. In logic "some" means: (a) at least one. (b) at least one but not all. (c) at least two. (d) at least two but not all.

_____ 10. The standard universal quantifiers of traditional logic are: (a) "no" and "all". (b) "some" and "some . . . not . . .". (c) "no" and "some". (d) "all" and "some".

EX 7, III. For each proposition:

1. Identify (subject term) and [predicate-term] by brackets.

2. Indicate the quantity and quality: *univ. af.,* . . . , *part. neg.*

3. Write the code letter.

Example:
I a. Some (friends of mine) are [noncommissioned officers.] *part. af.*

1. Some cats are fat animals.

2. All hairless wombats are funny-looking creatures.

3. No dictators are Zen Buddhists.

4. Some logicians are females.

5. Some sociologists are not scientists.

6. All people who smoke more than a pack of cigarettes a day are people who are either neurotic or foolish.

7. Some hornbills are brightly colored birds.
8. Some cats and dogs are not animals that are overweight.
9. All devoted military men are neurotics.
10. All people who profit from war are people who are likely to favor war.
11. No nationalists are supporters of the United Nations.
12. All people who are opposed to a strong United Nations are ones who are opposed to world peace.
13. No sane men are men who want the armament race.
14. No supporters of the United Nations are advocates of imperialism.
15. Some military officers who served in the First World War are not movie stars.
16. Some soldiers are not people who favor war.
17. Some students who are not in class today are students who are going to fail logic.
18. No men who believe some of the people all of the time are men who are to be trusted.
19. All men and women and children are beings that are entitled to protection of the United Nations Bill of Rights.
20. Some insects are beetles that are not green.
21. Some students who are not cat lovers are students who are not dog lovers.
22. All senators and congressmen are men who are either doves, hawks, or owls.
23. All people who are concerned about the population explosion are people who are concerned about human welfare.
24. Some people who have no money are people who are not dishonest.
25. Some men who have all the luck are people who are not there when you need them.

8

The Traditional Square of Opposition

In chapter 7 we introduce the four standard categorical forms: **A, E, I,** and **O**. In this chapter we name the relation between standard categoricals having the same subject term and the same predicate terms and determine what inferences may be based on these relations. Only standard categoricals are considered here, though analogous relations hold for nonstandard categoricals.

8A THE OPPOSITION OF STANDARD CATEGORICALS

Def. 1. Two standard categoricals are **opposed** to one another (or are **opposites**) iffi they have the same subject term and the same predicate term and differ in form.[1] (The four forms are **A, E, I,** and **O**.)

Given opposed proposition of the four standard forms, there are six pairs as shown in figure 8.1.

These pairs of opposed propositions have the following names: "contradictories", "contraries", "subcontraries", and "alterns", as shown in figure 8.2.

These relationships form the basis of certain valid argument forms that, having just one premiss, are called "immediate inferences".[2]

Def. 2. An **immediate inference** is an argument containing exactly one premiss and one conclusion.

Figure 8.1: Opposed Pairs

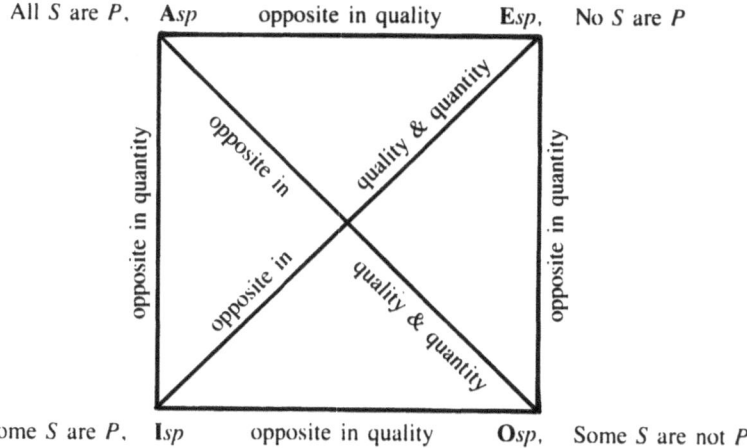

Figure 8.2: The Traditional Square of Opposition

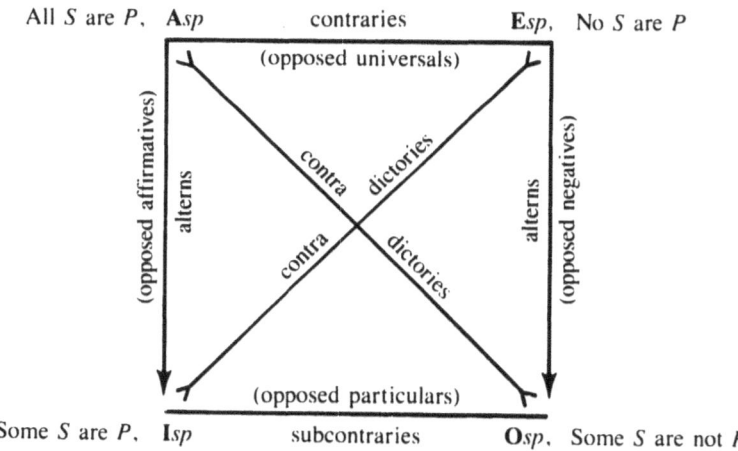

In the immediate inferences in chapters 8 to 27, both premiss and conclusion will be categorical (but not necessarily standard).[3]

An example of a valid immediate inference is: *All prudes are moral persons; therefore some prudes are moral persons.*

The arrows (→) in figure 8.2 represent entailment (or logical implication) referred to in 1B, after definition 7. In 8B1,b, "entailment" is defined (def. 9) and discussed. The sign for contradictories is explained below in 8B1,c.

We now define the relations that exist between pairs of opposed standard categoricals. Our definitions apply to all standard categoricals (and so do some Inference Rules of 8B; but many Inference Rules in 8B—beginning with R2—require knowledge of the distinction in modality made in 2B).

All the relations between categoricals on the square of opposition are defined in terms of quality and quantity. Assuming that we are talking only about opposed standard categoricals, we may informally define the pairs of propositions on the square of opposition as follows:

i **Contradictories** are categoricals that differ in quality and quantity.

ii **Contraries** are universals that differ in quality.

iii **Subcontraries** are particulars that differ in quality.

iv **Alterns** are categoricals that differ *only* in quantity.

We now define these terms formally, also the corresponding relations.

Def. 3a. A standard categorical is the **contradictory** (or the **contradictory opposite**) of an opposed proposition iffi they differ in quantity and quality.

Def. 3b. Contradiction (of opposites) (or **contradictory opposition**) is the relation between a proposition and its contradictory.[4]

Opposed **A** and **O** propositions are contradictories, and opposed **E** and **I** propositions are contradictories. An **A** proposition is the contradictory of the opposed **O**, and an **O** is the contradictory of the opposed **A**. Similarly for **E** and **I** propositions. For example, *All ascetics are philosophers* is the contradictory of *Some ascetics are not philosophers;* and *Some girls are good archers* is the contradictory of *No girls are good archers.*

Def. 4a. A standard categorical is the **contrary** (or the **contrary opposite**) of an opposed proposition iffi they are both universal and differ in quality.

Def. 4b. Contrariety (of opposites) (or **contrary opposition**) is the relation between a universal proposition and its contrary.[5]

Opposed **A** and **E** propositions are contraries. An **A** proposition is *the* contrary of the opposed **E** proposition, and the **E** is *the* contrary of the opposed **A**. For example, *All politicians are liars* is *the* contrary of *No politicians are liars*. *No bank robbers are professors* is *the* contrary of *All bank robbers are professors*.

> **Def. 5a.** A standard categorical is the **subcontrary** (or the **subcontrary opposite**) of an opposed proposition iffi they are both particular and differ in quality.
>
> **Def. 5b. Subcontrariety** (of opposites) (or **subcontrary opposition**) is the relation between a particular proposition and its subcontrary.

Opposed **I** and **O** propositions are subcontraries. The **I** proposition is *the* subcontrary of the **O** proposition, and the **O** is *the* subcontrary of the **I**. For example, *Some logicians are not philosophers* is *the* subcontrary of the opposed proposition *Some logicians are philosophers;* and *Some xats are sacred objects* is *the* subcontrary of *Some xats are not sacred objects*.

> **Def. 6.** A standard categorical is the **altern** of an opposed proposition iffi they have the same quality and differ in quantity.[6]

Opposed **A** and **I** propositions are alterns, likewise opposed **E** and **O** propositions. For example, *All tigers are cats* and *Some tigers are cats* are alterns.

> **Def. 7a.** A universal proposition is the **superaltern**[7] of its altern.
>
> **Def. 7b. Superalternation** of opposites (or **superaltern opposition**) is the relation of a universal to its altern.

An **A** proposition is the superaltern of the opposed **I**, and an **E** proposition is the superaltern of the opposed **O**.

> **Def. 8a.** A particular proposition is the **subaltern** (or the **subalternate**)[8] of its superaltern.
>
> **Def. 8b. Superalternation** of opposites (or **subaltern opposition**) is the relation of a subaltern to its superaltern.

An **I** proposition is the subaltern of the opposed **A**, and an **O** proposition is the subaltern of the opposed **E**.

8B INFERENCE RULES FOR THE SQUARE OF OPPOSITION

In this section we give rules for judging immediate inferences. A proposition justified by these rules, which state logical principles, is a logically necessary proposition. A logically necessary proposition is necessarily true by virtue of the meaning of its words (see 2B, def. 13).

Two new signs are introduced: "X" and "Y". These signs, with the arrow for entailment and canceled arrow for nonentailment, will be used to symbolize rules. In this chapter the letters "X" and "Y" are variables whose substitution instances are propositions in quotes, that is, names of propositions. Read "X^T" as "X is true". Read "X^F" as "X is false".

8B1 Inference Rules for Contradictories.

a *Rules Stated and Justified.*

> **R1** *(Law of Contradiction)* **Contradictories cannot both be true nor both be false.**

(In other words, contradictories must have opposite truth-values.)[9] R1 is equivalent to the following pair of conditionals:

> **R1a** If a proposition is true, its contradictory is false.

> **R1b** If a proposition is false, its contradictory is true.

R1 can be justified intuitively by appealing to concrete pairs of contradictories. For example, it is obvious that the (contingent) contradictories "All students are studious" and "Some students are not studious" cannot both be true and cannot both be false. The rule also holds for any pair of noncontingent contradictories, for example, "All men are animals" and "Some men are not animals". It is not difficult to see that R1 holds for any pair of contradictory **A** and **O** propositions; they cannot both be true and cannot both be false.

This result is not an accident, of course. As explained in 7A1, the meaning of the standard particulars is fixed as "at least one S is—or is not—P" so that either "All S are P" or "Some S are not P" will be true, but not both; and either "No S are P" or "Some S are P" will be true but not both.

R1a and R1b follow directly from R1. Since contradictories cannot both be true, if one is true the other must be false (R1a). And since contradictories cannot both be false, if one is false the other must be true (R1b).

b *Abbreviations and New Signs.*

Opposed standard categorical forms will be abbreviated in this chapter by using just their code letters: **A**, **E**, **I** and **O**. Thus instead of writing "If '**A**sp' is true, then '**O**sp' is false", we may write "If **A** is true, then **O** is false".

We also use "T" for "true" and "F" for "false", written as a superscript or "exponent". For example, "$\mathbf{A}^T$" stands for the form "It is true that all S are P". More concisely, we may read "$\mathbf{A}^T$" as "**A** is true". Thus the statement "If **A** is true, then **O** is false" now becomes "If $\mathbf{A}^T$ then $\mathbf{O}^F$".

It is convenient to express necessary conditionals as entailments. For this purpose we define entailment in terms of conditionals and necessity.

Def. 9. "X **entails** Y" means "If X then Y" is necessarily true.[10]

For example, the statement "If $\mathbf{A}^T$ then $\mathbf{O}^F$" may be expressed as "$\mathbf{A}^T$ entails $\mathbf{O}^F$". The first statement is justified by R·1a, since **O** is the contradictory of **A**.

We now introduce the arrow ($\rightarrow$) as the entailment sign to stand for the word *entails*.

Def. 10. $(X \rightarrow Y)$ iffi (X entails Y).

Thus for "$\mathbf{A}^T$ entails $\mathbf{O}^F$" we write "$\mathbf{A}^T \rightarrow \mathbf{O}^F$".

A **two-headed arrow** ($\leftrightarrow$) is the symbol for reversible entailment or logical equivalence. Read "$X \leftrightarrow Y$" as "X entails Y and Y entails X".

Def. 11. "$X \leftrightarrow Y$" means "$X \rightarrow Y$ and $Y \rightarrow X$"

For example, "$\mathbf{A}^T \leftrightarrow \mathbf{O}^F$" means "That **A** is true entails that **O** is false and that **O** is false entails that **A** is true".

To assert a proposition is logically equivalent to asserting that the proposition is true. For example, asserting "All hornbills are birds" is the same as asserting "It is true that all hornbills are birds".

Generalizing the relation of contradictory opposites, we define the relation that holds between propositions when one is contradictory to—or a contradictory of—the other.

Def. 12a. X is **contradictory to** (or **a contradictory of**) Y iffi $X \leftrightarrow Y^F$, i.e. X reversibly entails the falsity of Y.

The following are contradictories related by entailment:

$$A \leftrightarrow O^F, \quad O \leftrightarrow A^F, \quad E \leftrightarrow I^F, \quad I \leftrightarrow E^F, \quad X \leftrightarrow (X^F)^F$$

c *Symbol for Contradictories*

We introduce a symmetrical symbol, reversed arrowheads, for the relation of contradictories defined in definition 12a.

Def. 12b. "$X \succ\!\!\prec Y$" means "$X \leftrightarrow Y^F$".[11]

This symbol can be used for the pairs of contradictory opposites of the square of opposition, as it already was in figure 8.2 in 8A: $A \succ\!\!\prec O$, $E \succ\!\!\prec I$. But it is not limited to such pairs. For example, one may write: "$Esp \succ\!\!\prec Ips$", though they are not contradictory opposites, since they are not opposed forms (neither their subjects nor predicates are identical).

The following are pairs of contradictories as such:

$$A \succ\!\!\prec O \quad O \succ\!\!\prec A \quad X \succ\!\!\prec X^F \quad X^F \succ\!\!\prec X$$
$$E \succ\!\!\prec I \quad I \succ\!\!\prec E \quad X^T \succ\!\!\prec X^F \quad X^F \succ\!\!\prec X^T$$

8B2 Inference Rules for Contraries.

a *Rules Stated and Justified.*

R2 (*Law of Contraries*) **Contraries cannot both be true; both are false or just one.**

From this we derive a definition and a rule of inference.

R2a If a universal proposition is true, its contrary must be false.

R2b From the falsity of a universal proposition, the truth-value of its contingent contrary cannot be determined.

It is evident that contrary propositions cannot both be true. To have "All sailors are Presbyterians" and "No sailors are Presbyterians" both true, for example, each sailor would have to be a Presbyterian and also not be a Presbyterian. This is impossible if there *are* any sailors, as we assume. Since contraries cannot both be true, it follows that if one is true, the other is false (R2a).

162   *Aristotelian Logic*

It is easy to find examples in which contraries are both false, and others in which one is true and the other false. In general, when a universal is false, its contrary may be true or may be false. One is tempted to formulate a rule: "If a universal is false its contrary is undetermined". But this overlooks the case where the contrary to be determined is a necessarily true proposition (e.g., "All men are animals") or a necessarily false proposition (e.g., "All propositions are true"). The truth-value of such a priori propositions is already determined regardless of what antecedent is proposed for them. We exclude such cases by limiting to contingent contraries the propositions whose truth-value is undetermined by the falsity of a universal (R2b).

b *Rules for Contraries: Entailments and Non-entailments.* As was the case with contradictories, a definite or positive rule—for example, with "cannot be true" or "must be false" (R2a)—is equivalent to an entailment. With contraries we also have an indefinite or negative rule, for example, with "cannot be determined" (R2b). Such a rule is equivalent to a pair or pairs of non-entailments.

R2a ($\rightarrow$) $A \rightarrow E^F$, $E \rightarrow A^F$

R2b ($\not\rightarrow$) (i) If E is contingent, then:
$A^F \not\rightarrow E$ and $A^F \not\rightarrow E^F$; i.e.,
Given that A is false, the truth-value of E is undetermined.

(ii) If A is contingent, then:
$E^F \not\rightarrow A$ and $E^F \not\rightarrow A^F$; i.e.,
Given that E is false, the truth-value of A is undetermined.

8B3 Inference Rules for Subcontraries.

a *Rules Stated and Justified (in Part).*

R3 (*Law of Subcontraries*) **Subcontraries cannot both be false; both are true or just one.**

From R3 may be derived a definite rule (R3a) and an indefinite or negative rule (R3b).

R3a If a particular proposition is false, its subcontrary must be true.

R3b From the truth of a particular proposition, the truth of a contingent subcontrary cannot be determined.

The rules for subcontraries may be derived from the rules for contraries taken together with those for contradictories. We illustrate this by an indirect proof of R3's first clause, which is equivalent to R3a.

Given: Inference rules for contradictories (8B1,a) and for contraries (8B2,a).
To Prove: Subcontraries cannot both be false.
Proof. Suppose (1) the subcontraries **I** and **O** are both false.
Then the contradictory of **I**, namely **E**, would be true (by R1b), and the contradictory of **O**, namely **A**, would be true (by R1b).
But **E** and **A** cannot both be true (by R2).
Therefore, the supposition (1) must be false; i.e., subcontraries cannot both be false. Q.E.D.

In R3b, the restriction to "a *contingent* subcontrary" is required by the same cases that made us restrict R2b to "a contingent contrary". For example, since "All men are animals" is necessarily true, "Some men are not animals" is necessarily false. Consequently, we cannot say that, given that "Some men are animals" is true, the truth-value of its subcontrary "Some men are not animals" is undetermined.

b *Rules for Subcontraries: Entailments and Non-entailments.*

R3a ($\rightarrow$) $I^F \rightarrow O$, $O^F \rightarrow I$

This rule may be stated as the (inclusive) disjunction: **I***sp* or **O***sp*.

R3b ($\nrightarrow$) (i) If **O** is contingent, then:
$I \nrightarrow O$ and $I \nrightarrow O^F$; i.e.,
Given **I***sp*, the truth-value of **O***sp* is undetermined.

(ii) If **I** is contingent, then:
$O \nrightarrow I$ and $O \nrightarrow I^F$; i.e.,
Given **O***sp*, the truth-value of **I***sp* is undetermined.

8B4 Inference Rules for Alterns.

a *Rules Stated and Justified in Part.*

R4 (*Law of Alterns*) **A universal entails but (if contingent) is not entailed by its subaltern.**

From this follow two definite and two indefinite (or negative) rules.

R4a If a universal is true, its subaltern must be true.

R4b If a particular is false, its superaltern must be false.

R4c From the truth of a particular, the truth-value of its contingent superaltern cannot be determined.

R4d From the falsity of a universal, the truth-value of its contingent subaltern cannot be determined.

The rules for alterns may be derived from those for contraries and contradictories. We show this for two of the rules that follow from R4.

Proof of R4b. If a particular proposition X is false, its contradictory X' is a true universal. But the contrary of X' is then (by R2a) a false universal, which is the superaltern of X'.

Proof of R4c. If and only if X is a true particular, its contradictory X' is a false universal. But from this fact, (by R2b) the truth-value of a *contingent* contrary of X' cannot be determined; and this contrary would be the contingent superaltern of X.

b *Rules for Alterns: Entailments and Non-entailments.*

R4a ($\rightarrow$) $\quad$ $A \rightarrow I, \quad E \rightarrow O$

R4b ($\rightarrow$) $\quad$ $I^F \rightarrow A^F, \quad O^F \rightarrow E^F$

R4c ($\nrightarrow$) $\quad$ (i) If **A** is contingent, then:
$\quad\quad\quad\quad I \nrightarrow A$ and $I \nrightarrow A^F$; i.e.,
Given I*sp*, the truth-value of A*sp* is undetermined.

(ii) If **E** is contingent, then:
$\quad\quad\quad\quad O \nrightarrow E$ and $O \nrightarrow E^F$; i.e.,
Given O*sp*, the truth-value of E*sp* is undetermined.

R4d ($\nrightarrow$) $\quad$ (i) If **I** is contingent, then:
$\quad\quad\quad\quad A^F \nrightarrow I$ and $A^F \nrightarrow I^F$; i.e.,
Given (A*sp*)^F, the truth-value of I*sp* is undetermined.

(ii) If **O** is contingent, then:
$\quad\quad\quad\quad E^F \nrightarrow O$ and $E^F \nrightarrow O^F$; i.e.,
Given (E*sp*)^F, the truth-value of O*sp* is undetermined.

8B5 Incorporating Rules in the Square of Opposition. In this subsection we incorporate more information of the previous subsections of 8B into the square of opposition. We first introduce the entailments, which hold for all standard categoricals, contingent or not, on the Aristotelian interpretation. At each corner of a square of opposition, we join to the standard form—by the two-headed arrow of reversible entailment—the equivalent expression stating the falsity of its contradiction, as in 8B1,b.

Figure 8.3: The Aristotelian Square of Opposition with Entailments and Non-Entailments

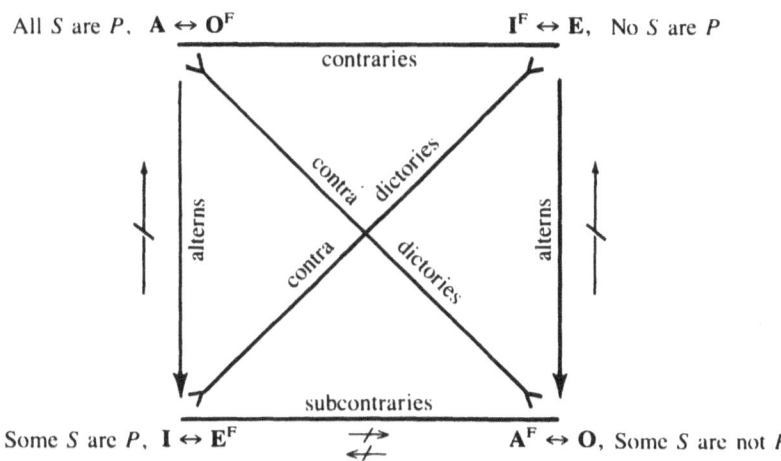

From the arrows and two-headed arrows of figure 8.3, we can read off all the definite relationships—that is, the entailments—that hold for opposed propositions on the Aristotelian interpretation, whether the propositions are contingent or not. The downward arrow on the left tells us that:[12]

    i (for alterns) **A** entails **I** (by R4a),
    ii (for contraries) **A** entails $\mathbf{E}^F$ (by R2a),
    iii (for subcontraries) $\mathbf{O}^F$ entails **I**, (by R3a),
    iv (for alterns) $\mathbf{O}^F$ entails $\mathbf{E}^F$ (by R4b).

The downward arrow on the right side tells us that:

    v (for alterns) **E** entails **O** (by R4a),
    vi (for contraries) **E** entails $\mathbf{A}^F$ (by R2a),
    vii (for subcontraries) $\mathbf{I}^F$ entails **O** (by R3a),
    viii (for alterns) $\mathbf{I}^F$ entails $\mathbf{A}^F$ (by R4b).

Unlike the entailments of the square, the nonentailments hold for contingent opposites, but not in general for necessary or impossible propositions. With this qualification, the pair of canceled arrows pointing from the **I** corner to the **A** and **O** corner tells us that:

ix (for alterns) **I** entails neither **A** nor its falsity (by R4c),
x (for subcontraries) **I** entails neither **O** nor its falsity (by R3b),
xi (for contraries) E^F entails neither **A** nor its falsity (by R2b),
xii (for alterns) E^F entails neither **O** nor its falsity (by R4d).

Similarly, the pair of canceled arrows pointing from the **O** corner to the **E** and **I** corners tells us that:

xiii (for alterns) **O** entails neither **E** nor its falsity (by R4c),
xiv (for subcontraries) **O** entails neither **I** nor its falsity (by R3b),
xv (for contraries) A^F entails neither **E** nor its falsity (by R2b),
xvi (for alterns) A^F entails neither **I** nor its falsity (by R4d).

8C SQUARE-OF-OPPOSITION PROBLEMS

These problems are all of this type: Given the truth-value of a standard contingent categorical, determine, if possible, the truth-value of the propositions in the remaining three forms. Below are some typical examples of this type of problem with their solutions.

8C1 Problems of Inference from Truth.

PROBLEM 1. Given that *All men are cowards* is true, determine the truth-values of propositions 1 to 3.

SOLUTIONS

1. No men are cowards.   Given A^T: $A^T \rightarrow E^F$, by R2a (contrariety)
Answer: Prop. 1 is false.

2. Some men are cowards.   Given A^T: $A^T \rightarrow I^T$, by R4a (superalternation).
Answer: 2 is true.

3. Some men are not cowards.   Given A^T: $A^T \rightarrow O^F$, by R1a (contradiction).
Answer: 3 is false.

PROBLEM 2. Given that *Some cats are rat catchers* is true, determine, if possible, the truth-values of propositions 4 to 6.

SOLUTIONS

4. All cats are rat catchers.   Given I^T: **I** $\nrightarrow$ **A** and **I** $\nrightarrow A^F$, by R4c (subalternation).
Answer: From information given, 4 is undetermined.

5. No cats are rat catchers. Given I^T: $I^T \to E^F$, by R1a (contradiction).
Answer: 5 is false.

6. Some cats are not rat catchers. Given I^T: $I \not\to O$ and $I \not\to O^F$, by R3b, (subcontrariety).
Answer: From information given, 6 is undetermined.

8C2 Conditions That Determine Truth-Values.

a When a universal proposition is given as true, or when a particular proposition is given as false, then the truth-values of all the opposed propositions can be determined.

b When a universal proposition is given as false, or a particular proposition is given as true, then only the truth-value of its contradictory can be determined, and the other two opposed propositions have undetermined truth-values.

8C3 Problems of Inference from Falsity. A knowledge of contradiction and the inferences from truth (R1a, R2a, R3b, R4a, R4c) is sufficient to work a square-of-opposition problem. Given a proposition as false and asked to determine the truth-value of the other opposed propositions the procedure is as follows:

Step 1. From the falsity of the proposition, infer the truth of its contradictory.

Step 2. From the truth of this contradictory, infer, if possible, the truth-values of the other propositions.

An example using this procedure is:

PROBLEM 3. Given that the proposition *Some owls are not bald birds* is false, determine, if possible, the truth-values of the propositions 7 to 9.

Step 1. From the falsity of the given proposition we may infer the truth of its contradictory, *All owls are bald birds*.

SOLUTIONS

7. All owls are bald birds. Given O^F: $O^F \to A^T$, by R1b (contradiction).
Answer: 7 is true.

Step 2. From the truth of **A**, the truth-values of the following propositions can be determined:

SOLUTIONS

8. No owls are bald birds. Given A^T: $A^T \to E^F$, by R2a (contrariety).
Answer: 8 is false.

168   *Aristotelian Logic*

9. Some owls are bald birds.   Given A^T: $A^T \rightarrow I^T$, by R4a (superalternation).
Answer: 9 is true.

8D THE OPPOSITION OF A PRIORI CATEGORICALS.

If the standard categoricals are a priori (necessary or impossible), then, though the names of the pairs of opposed propositions remain the same (and the names of the relations), changes occur in the inference rules.

8D1 A Square of Opposed A priori Categoricals.

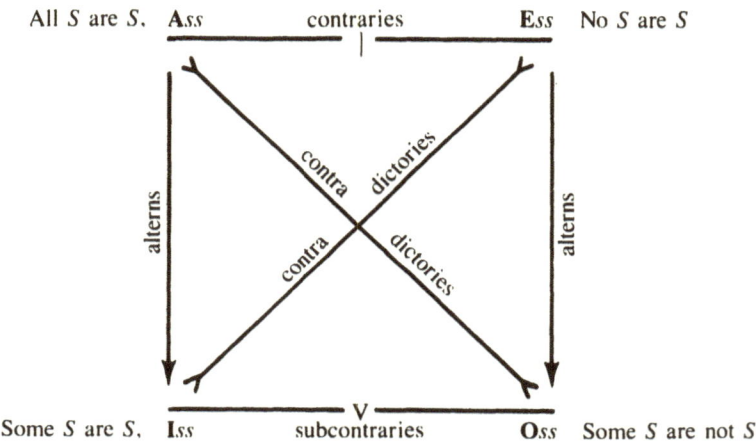

Propositions of the forms "All S are S" and "Some S are S" are necessary, and those of the forms "No S are S" and "Some S are not S" are impossible.[13]

8D2 Inference Rules Based on the Opposition of A priori Categoricals, Where One of the Universals is Necessary.[14]

    APR1 Contradictories have opposite truth-values.
    APR2 Contraries have opposite truth-values.

    APR3 Subcontraries have opposite truth-values.
    APR4 Alterns have identical truth-values. (Alterns mutually entail one another.)

The diagram of 8D1 (which is the same as that for the traditional square except that the variables are identical) may be modified by using symbols of more specific relations for the sides of the square. For the top and bottom, as well as for the diagonals, the double reversed arrowheads (sign for contradiction ">——<") may be used. And for the sides, the two-headed arrow of reversible entailment may be used. (By our definitions, for example, a pair of opposed categoricals of different quantity remain alterns even if they entail each other by virtue of their specific meaning.)

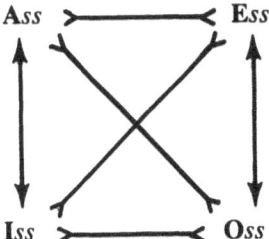

8D3 Diagrams: Inferences of Secondary Propositions, Where One Universal is Necessary.

A, E, I, and O are opposed a priori categoricals. The diagrams merge into two diagrams of equivalences for secondary a priori propositions with one universal necessary, distinguished by whether the affirmatives are said to be both true or both false.

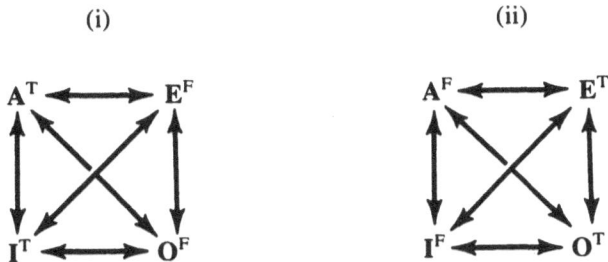

For example, the truth of "All S are S" is equivalent to that of "Some S are S", and to the falsity of "No S are S" and "Some S are not S".

Appendix 8E

8E SCHOLASTIC VS. MODERN DOCTRINES OF THE SQUARE OF OPPOSITION

The scholastics defined the relations of the square of opposition in terms of formal properties such as quantity and quality. For example, they defined "contraries" as opposed universal propositions differing in quality. Many modern logicians define the relations in terms of truth-values. For example, contraries are commonly defined as propositions that cannot both be true but may both be false: We shall write "contraries$_2$" for this concept. Likewise, contradictories$_2$ are defined as propositions that cannot both be true nor both false: similarly for subcontraries and so on. In other words, these modern logicians are defining the relations in terms of those possible combinations of truth-value that are the basis of rules of inference. These two ways of defining the relations of the square of opposition do not yield equivalent results.

The definitions given by the scholastics apply to *a priori* as well as contingent propositions, but many of the *rules* of inference were recognized to apply *only to contingent propositions*. That many of these rules were restricted to contingent propositions is a fact that most modern logicians seem to have overlooked. The consequences of this will now be explored.

8E1 Examples of the Modern Relations. By the scholastics' definition of contraries, *A priori* propositions of the forms "All S are S" and "No S are S" are contraries. But by the modern definitions, propositions of these forms are not contraries but contradictories. They are not contraries$_2$ because one of the propositions ("All S are S") is necessary; hence they cannot both be false. Likewise, "Some S are S" and "Some S are not S" are not subcontraries$_2$, because they cannot both be true; They are contradictories$_2$. Further, "Some S are S" is not subaltern$_2$ but equivalent to "All S are S"; for if some S are S, it must be true that all S are S. And "Some S are not S" similarly is not subaltern$_2$ but equivalent to "No S are S".

A more embarrassing difficulty is presented by such a problem as the following: Are *All mugwumps are bolters* and *No mugwumps are bolters* contraries$_2$? They are plainly inconsistent on an Aristotelian interpretation. Before deciding whether they are contraries$_2$ or not, the logician—not well versed in American political history—must consult the dictionary. Here he finds that, in the original historical sense of "mugwumps" in English ("Republicans who bolted the Blaine ticket"), it is necessarily true that all mugwumps are bolters; hence *All mugwumps$_1$ are bolters* and *No mugwumps$_1$ are bolters* cannot both be false; so the propositions are not contraries$_2$ but contradictories$_2$. In the derived senses of "mugwump", however, it is not necessarily true that all mugwumps are bolters; so *All mugwumps$_2$ are bolters* and *No mugwumps$_2$ are bolters* are contraries$_2$. The scholastic, on the other hand, need only know that "mugwumps" and "bolters" are meaningful terms used consistently to say that "All mugwumps are bolters" and "No mugwumps are bolters" are contraries.

We give some examples of pairs of propositions, at least one being *a priori*, for which the modern relations hold, perhaps unexpectedly.

(i) **Contradictories$_2$** cannot both be false nor both true.

All dogs are mammals;	$2 = 3$.
All dogs are mammals;	*Some dogs are rats.*
All men are animals;	*No men are animals.*
Some dogs are not cats;	*Some dogs are cats.*
Some integers are prime;	*All integers are prime.*

In the above pairs, the first proposition cannot be false, so both cannot be false; the second cannot be true, so both cannot.

(ii) **Contraries$_2$** cannot both be true, both may be false.

Some dogs are cats;	$2 = 3$
Some dogs are cats;	*Some cats are dogs.*
Some men are not animals;	*No men are animals.*
Some dogs are cats;	*Some elephants live in canary cages.*
All integers are prime;	*All integers greater than 3 are prime.*

In the above pairs, the first *cannot* be true; both are false.

(iii) **Subcontraries$_2$** cannot both be false, both may be true.

All dogs are mammals;	$2 + 2 = 4$
All men are animals;	*Some men are animals.*
No dogs are cows;	*Some cows are sick.*

(iv) **Superaltern$_2$-Subaltern$_2$**: It is impossible to have the first and not the second; possible to have the second and not the first.

Some men are not animals;	*Some men are animals.*
Some men are not animals;	*All men are animals.*
No men are animals;	*Some men are animals.*
No men are animals;	*All men are animals.*

8E2 Modern and Scholastic Squares for A priori Categoricals. Let us consider the square of opposition for propositions relating "men" and "animals" (a paradigm case for Peter of Spain and many scholastics, following Aristotle). We find that *All men are animals* is not contrary$_2$ to *No men are animals* (since they cannot both be false), but contradictory$_2$ and also subaltern$_2$ to *No men are animals*. Further, *All men are animals* is not superaltern$_2$ to *Some men are animals* (since it is not possible to have the second true and the first false), but it is equivalent and also subcontrary$_2$ to *Some men are animals*. Hence we cannot get a traditional square from these terms if **A, E, I,** and **O** are put in their usual positions. But we get the relations of the traditional square by writing the propositions in an unusual order:

Figure 8.4: "Modern" Square of Opposition for A priori Categoricals

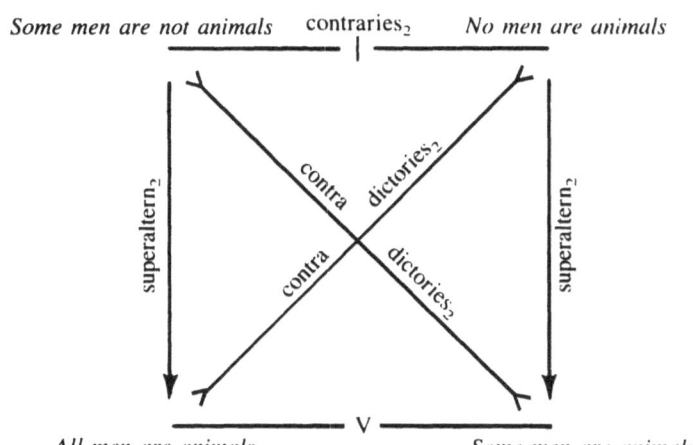

Following the scholastic definitions, however, Peter of Spain is able to put the propositions in their usual positions for the traditional square. But he noted that the universals with this necessary (or 'natural') matter—that is, *All men are animals* being necessarily true—must have opposite truth-value (1.16). And William of Sherwood noted that the subcontraries in this case (particulars as usual) "cannot be true at the same time, and the truth of the particular subaltern entails the truth of the subalternant universal" (Kretzman ed., 34). Hence the diagram for these a priori categoricals with the scholastic definitions may be either the same as our usual one (in 8A or 8D1), or it may use the more specific symbols indicated in 8D2: the two-headed arrows of mutual entailment at the sides, the double reversed arrow heads elsewhere.

8E3 Summary. The two ways of defining the relations of the square of opposition are listed below.

(1) Scholastic way: This goes back to Aristotle, was developed by the commentators and scholastics, and is continued by some modern scholastics and neo-scholastics. The relations are defined by formal properties of categorical propositions, especially quantity and quality. The rules of inference depend upon whether the propositions are a priori or contingent.

(2) Modern way: This begins by ignoring the distinction of a priori and contingent matter (as in the *Port-Royal Logic*); then it can turn the truth-value rules of inference for contingent categoricals into definitions, finally dropping the limitation to categoricals. If a priori categoricals are brought back, unexpected results appear.

We prefer to follow the scholastic way, for the following reasons: It has a longer tradition; it is more formalistic; and the modern way gives anomolous results when a priori categoricals are reintroduced. The one advantage of the modern way—a greater generality of the relations—is attained at too great sacrifice. This kind of generality can be supplied by concepts such as compatibility and incompatibility.

Exercises for Chapter 8

EX 8A–B. Put the appropriate letter in the margin.

_____ 1. A pair of opposed **A** and **E** propositions are:
(a) contraries. (b) subcontraries. (c) contradictories. (d) alterns.

_____ 2. A pair of opposed **E** and **O** propositions are:
(a) contraries. (b) subcontraries. (c) contradictories. (d) alterns.

_____ 3. A pair of opposed **I** and **O** propositions are:
(a) contraries. (b) subcontraries. (c) contradictories. (d) alterns.

_____ 4. If two opposed standard categorical propositions are both particular, then they are:
(a) contraries. (b) subcontraries. (c) contradictories. (d) alterns.

_____ 5. If two opposed standard categorical propositions are both universal, then they are:
(a) contraries. (b) subcontraries. (c) identical. (d) alterns.

_____ 6. Two opposed standard categorical propositions that differ both in quantity and quality are:
(a) contraries. (b) subcontraries. (c) contradictories. (d) alterns.

_____ 7. Two opposed standard categorical propositions that have the same quantity and differ in quality are:
(a) contraries. (b) subcontraries. (c) contradictories. (d) contraries or subcontraries.

_____ 8. Two opposed standard categorical propositions that differ in quantity but have the same quality are:
(a) contraries. (b) subcontraries. (c) contradictories. (d) alterns.

_____ 9. The name of the relation between alterns in the direction superaltern to subaltern is:

(a) subalternation. (b) superalternation. (c) alternation. (d) alienation.

_____ 10. An argument having just one premiss and a conclusion is called a(n) (a) syllogism. (b) deductive argument. (c) immediate inference. (d) mediated inference.

EX 8C. Assume that the propositions referred to in the following fifteen exercises are contingent.

Instructions: Complete each of the following to make a true statement by writing "True", "False", or "Und." (Undetermined) in the blank.

1. If an **I** proposition is true, then the opposed **A** proposition is _____.
2. If an **I** proposition is true, then the opposed **O** proposition is _____.
3. If an **O** proposition is false, then the opposed **I** proposition is _____.
4. If an **O** proposition is false, then the opposed **A** proposition is _____.
5. If an **A** proposition is true, then the opposed **E** proposition is _____.
6. If an **A** proposition is true, then the opposed **I** proposition is _____.
7. If an **E** proposition is false, then the opposed **A** proposition is _____.
8. If an **O** proposition is false, then the opposed **E** proposition is _____.
9. If an **A** proposition is true, then the opposed **O** proposition is _____.
10. If an **A** proposition is false, then the opposed **I** proposition is _____.
11. If an **I** proposition is true, then the opposed **E** proposition is _____.
12. If an **E** proposition is false, then the opposed **O** proposition is _____.
13. If an **E** proposition is true, then the opposed **O** proposition is _____.
14. If an **O** proposition is true, then the opposed **E** proposition is _____.
15. If an **O** proposition is true, then the opposed **A** proposition is _____.

EX 8D. Assume that the first proposition (a) in each set of four is true; then determine, if possible, the truth-values of the other three propositions.

Place the appropriate letter in the left margin. Repeat the exercise, assuming that the first proposition in each set is *false*.

T = True, F = False, or U = Undetermined

Given:
(a) T
(b) ____
(c) ____
(d) ____

1. (a) No philosophers are military officers.
   (b) All philosophers are military officers.
   (c) Some philosophers are not military officers.
   (d) Some philosophers are military officers.

Given:
(a) F
(b) ____
(c) ____
(d) ____

(a) T
(b) ____
(c) ____
(d) ____

2. (a) Some men are wicked people.
   (b) All men are wicked people.
   (c) No men are wicked people.
   (d) Some men are not wicked people.

(a) F
(b) ____
(c) ____
(d) ____

(a) T
(b) ____
(c) ____
(d) ____

3. (a) All Harvard students are native Bostonians.
   (b) Some Harvard students are native Bostonians.
   (c) Some Harvard students are not native Bostonians.
   (d) No Harvard students are native Bostonians.

(a) F
(b) ____
(c) ____
(d) ____

(a) T
(b) ____
(c) ____
(d) ____

4. (a) Some shrimp fishermen are not union members.
   (b) No shrimp fishermen are union members.
   (c) All shrimp fishermen are union members.
   (d) Some shrimp fishermen are union members.

(a) F
(b) ____
(c) ____
(d) ____

(a) T
(b) ____
(c) ____
(d) ____

5. (a) No lame kangaroos are good rat catchers.
   (b) All lame kangaroos are good rat catchers.
   (c) Some lame kangaroos are good rat catchers.
   (d) Some lame kangaroos are not good rat catchers.

(a) F
(b) ____
(c) ____
(d) ____

Exercises/Chapter 8   177

(a) T   6. (a) Some barons are accordionists.   (a) F
(b) _____   (b) All barons are accordionists.   (b) _____
(c) _____   (c) Some barons are not accordionists.   (c) _____
(d) _____   (d) No barons are accordionists.   (d) _____

(a) T   7. (a) Some deaf gophers are nervous   (a) F
                animals.
(b) _____   (b) No deaf gophers are nervous   (b) _____
                animals.
(c) _____   (c) Some deaf gophers are not nervous   (c) _____
                animals.
(d) _____   (d) All deaf gophers are nervous   (d) _____
                animals.

(a) T   8. (a) All bullfrogs are poor jumpers.   (a) F
(b) _____   (b) No bullfrogs are poor jumpers.   (b) _____
(c) _____   (c) Some bullfrogs are poor jumpers.   (c) _____
(d) _____   (d) Some bullfrogs are not poor jumpers.   (d) _____

(a) T   9. (a) Some philosophers are not brilliant   (a) F
                men.
(b) _____   (b) Some philosophers are brilliant men.   (b) _____
(c) _____   (c) No philosophers are brilliant men.   (c) _____
(d) _____   (d) All philosophers are brilliant men.   (d) _____

(a) T   10. (a) No people who smoke are prudent   (a) F
                men.
(b) _____   (b) Some people who smoke are not   (b) _____
                prudent men.
(c) _____   (c) All people who smoke are prudent   (c) _____
                men.
(d) _____   (d) Some people who smoke are prudent   (d) _____
                men.

9

Existential Presuppositions of Aristotelian Logic

9A UNIVERSE OF DISCOURSE AND PRESUPPOSITION OF EXISTENCE

9A1 Universe of Discourse. Every proposition refers to some realm of existence or to some limited part of such a realm. For example, the proposition "All men are mortal" refers to all men, past, present, and future, in the realm of physical existence. It does not refer to any fictitious or imaginary man. On the other hand the realm of existence referred to by the proposition "All fairies have magical powers" is conventional folklore, specifically, the descriptions of fairies.[1]

> **Def. 1.** The **universe of discourse** of a proposition, argument, or deductive system is the realm of existence or some limited part of such realm to which it refers.[2]

It is quite common to limit the universe of discourse to some specific aspect of the realm of existence to which the proposition refers. For example, in the realm of physical existence the universe of discourse could be *animals, plants, trees, early American furniture,* and so on. A proposition that asserts or denies membership in any of these limited universes is, respectively, asserting or denying the physical existence of an object in these universes.

Henceforth, when we use the word "existence", we will mean existence within a universe of discourse. This existence may or may not be a physical existence.

9A2 Presupposition and Implying Existence. In order to understand the problem of existential import (discussed in 9B1) it is important to distinguish between the presupposition of existence and the implication of existence. The former implies the latter, but not vice versa.

Propositions such as *Twilliger's wife's name is Mary, Lovejoy's stock dropped four points today,* and *Harrison's computer was made in Japan,* presuppose, respectively, the existence of Twilliger's wife, Lovejoy's stock, and Harrison's computer. For it would sound very odd indeed to assert that Twilliger's wife's name is Mary if Twilliger has no wife. The important thing to note is that the nonexistence of Twilliger's wife would *not* make the proposition about his wife's name false. The existence of Twilliger's wife is a precondition for the truth and falsity of the proposition about his wife's name.[3]

The proposition *Twilliger's wife's name is Mary,* if it has truth-value (if it is true or false), implies that Twilliger has a wife. Hence if a proposition presupposes the existence of the entities it refers to, it also implies that such entities exist. The converse, however, does not hold. For example, the proposition *There is a goblin in my basement* implies the existence of a goblin in my basement and if there is no such creature there then the proposition is false. Such a proposition *There is a goblin in my basement* asserts the existence of a goblin, therefore it implies that there *is* a goblin. However, no presuppositions concerning the existence of goblins has to be made in this case.

In short, if a proposition presupposes the existence of x, then the proposition implies that existence of x, but a proposition may imply the existence of x without presupposing the existence of x.

When propositions imply existence, they do so implicitly or explicitly. When they do so explicitly they are called "existential propositions".

> **Def. 2.** An **existential proposition** is a proposition that explicitly affirms or denies the existence of an entity or entities within its realm.

Examples of existential propositions are: *There are black swans, Hamlet is one of Shakespeare's characters, Unicorns do not exist,* and *Pink elephants are hallucinations.*

9B PRESUPPOSITIONS OF EXISTENCE IN TRADITIONAL LOGIC

By "traditional logic" we mean the system consisting of the square of opposition, the valid immediate inferences (as listed in 16A), and the twenty-four forms of the syllogism.

9B1 The Problem of Existential Import. The problem of existential import is the problem of finding a consistent set of existential presuppositions for standard categorical propositions so that traditional logic will remain unchanged. By "remain unchanged" we mean that all the arguments and only the arguments judged valid in traditional logic will in fact be valid when the standard propositions are given a consistent existential interpretation.

A fair question to ask at this point is this: Why is there a problem of existential import? Why not assume that standard propositions make no presuppositions of existence and let it got at that? The reasons for assuming that the traditional logic, if it is to remain unchanged, must make presuppositions of existence for its standard propositions are outlined below:

First, the particular propositions in the traditional logic imply the existence of their subjects (i.e., they imply the existence of entities to which the subject term applies), for it is reasonable to assume that "some", which means "at least one", implies existence. Hence the I and O propositions are existential propositions.

Second, since particulars imply existence of their subjects and can be deduced from universals, it follows that universals imply existence of their subjects. (If the conclusion of an argument implies existence, the premiss must imply existence.)

Third—therefore, all the standard propositions imply existence of at least their subjects.

Fourth, the standard propositions must presuppose as well as imply the existence of their subjects. Because if they only imply existence and do not presuppose existence then they would all be false. If all the four opposed propositions (A, E, I, and O) on the square of opposition are false then the relations (contrariety, contradiction, etc.) on the traditional square of opposition do not hold. Consequently, in order to preserve these relations the standard propositions must presuppose as well as imply existence of their subjects.

9B2 The Two-Pair Existential Presupposition (Two-PEP) of the Traditional Logic.

> **Def. 3.** A standard proposition makes a **two-pair existential presupposition** (two-PEP) when the proposition presupposes the existence of entities to which both its subject and predicate and their contradictories apply.

For example, the proposition *All wombats are mammals* makes a two-PEP when it presupposes the existence of wombats, non-wombats, mammals, and non-mammals.

One solution to the problem of existential import is to assume that every standard proposition makes a two-PEP. This assumption we will demonstrate in 9B3 is sufficient to keep the traditional logic unchanged.

9B3 Demonstration of the Existential Implication of the Standard Propositions.

First we will make explicit several rules that have been assumed without formal explanation.

Rule EI (Rule of Existential Implication): If the conclusion of a valid argument implies the existence of entities to which its subject S or predicate P or their contradictories non-S or non-P apply, then the premises of this argument (respectively) imply the existence of entities to which these terms apply.

Rule EI is saying that whatever kinds of things are implied to exist by the conclusion of a valid argument must also be implied to exist by the premises of this argument.

Rule EF (Rule of Existential Falsity): If a categorical proposition implies but does not presuppose the existence of entities to which its subject or predicate or their contradictories apply, then it is false if any of these terms are empty.[4]

We shall now informally demonstrate the implications and presuppositions of existence of the standard proposition making use of rules EI and EF, the immediate inferences, the square of opposition, and Axiom 1:

Axiom 1. The I proposition implies existence of both its subject and predicate.[5]

PROBLEM A: To prove that the A proposition in traditional logic implies the existence of both its subject and predicate.

Proof A

(1) All S are P implies Some S are P. (Superalternation)

(2) All S are P implies the existence of at least one S and at least one P. (Line 1, Axiom 1, and Rule EI)

(3) All S are P implies Some non-S are non-P. (Inverse)

(4) All S are P implies the existence of at least one non-S and at least one non-P. (Line 3, Axiom 1, and Rule EI)

(5) All S are P implies the existence of at least one S, at least one P, at least one non-S, and at least one non-P. (Lines 2 and 4).

We have now proved that the A proposition implies the existence of both its subject and predicate and their contradictories.

Existential Presuppositions 183

PROBLEM B: To prove that the **O** proposition in traditional logic implies existence of its subject and the contradictory of its predicate.

Proof B

(1) Some *S* are not *P* implies Some *S* are non-*P*. (Obversion)

(2) Some *S* are not *P* implies the existence of at least one *S* and at least one non-*P*. (Line 1, Axiom 1, and Rule EI).

Therefore, the **O** proposition implies the existence of its subject and the contradictory of its predicate. Now we prove that the **E** proposition makes the same implications of existence as the **A** proposition.

PROBLEM C: To prove that the E proposition in traditional logic implies existence of both its subject and predicate and their contradictories.

Proof C

(1) No *S* are *P* implies Some *S* are not *P*. (Superalternation)

(2) No *S* are *P* implies the existence of at least one *S* and at least one non-*P*. (Line 1, Proof B, and Rule EI)

(3) No *S* are *P* implies Some non-*S* are not non-*P*. (Inverse)

(4) No *S* are *P* implies the existence of at least one non-*S* and at least one *P*. (Line 3, Proof B, and Rule EI)

(5) No *S* are *P* implies the existence of at least one *S*, at least one *P*, at least one non-*S*, and at least one non-*P*. (Lines 2 and 4).

The existential implications of each standard proposition are shown in parentheses in the following square of opposition:

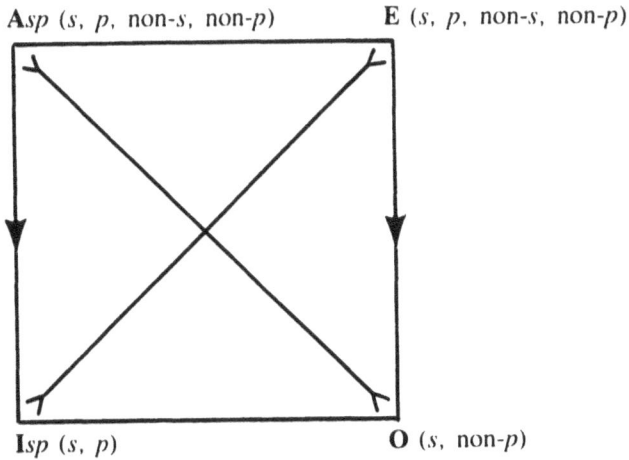

A*sp* (*s*, *p*, non-*s*, non-*p*)   **E** (*s*, *p*, non-*s*, non-*p*)

I*sp* (*s*, *p*)   **O** (*s*, non-*p*)

9B4 The Existential Presuppositions (EP) of the Standard Propositions.

a *The Opposed Particulars.* The **I** and **O** propositions presuppose existence of their subjects, because if they did not they would both be false. But on the contingent square of opposition they cannot both be false. Therefore their subjects are presupposed.

b *The Opposed Universals.* The **A** and **E** propositions presuppose existence of their subjects. Both **A** and **E** propositions imply the existence of their subjects, hence they would both necessarily be false if their subjects did not exist. But on the contingent square of opposition it is possible for all propositions to be either true or false. Therefore as long as it is possible for the universals to be true they must presuppose the existence of their subjects.[6]

It will be left to the students to demonstrate that every existential implication of the standard propositions must also be existentially presupposed.

Standard Proposition	Existential Implications	Existential Presuppositions
All S are P	s, p, non-s, non-p	s, p, non-s, non-p
No S are P	s, p, non-s, non-p	s, p, non-s, non-p
Some S are P	s, p	s, p
Some S are not P	s, non-p	s, non-p

It suffices to describe the existential presuppositions of the standard propositions by stating that they presuppose the existence of their subjects. The other existential presuppositions are redundant since they can be deduced from this information and the existential implications of the propositions.

9B5 The Two-PEP of the Standard Propositions.

We have given in 9B4 the minimal existential presuppositions for each standard proposition. Hence, it is quite obvious that if we assume that every standard proposition presupposes the existence of both its subject and predicate and their contradictories that this would be more than sufficient to preserve the traditional system.

Why do we assume more than what we have to? Because a TWO-PEP is the minimal number of explicit presuppositions (based on Axiom 1) that we can have for *all* four standard propositions.

9B6 Difference between Relative and Absolute Existential Interpretations.

In the foregoing section (9B4) we have given one solution to the problem of existential import. The solution is, if we assume that every standard proposition makes a TWO-PEP, then the traditional logic remains unchanged.

The solution we have given makes the relations of the square of opposition relative to presuppositions of existence. In short, our traditional relations of the square of opposition remain intact and unchanged because we made a number of presuppositions designed for that purpose. These existential presuppositions are not stated on the square of opposition. They are in the background, out of sight, but in force. When the existential presuppositions of the standard proposition are not part of what the proposition explicitly states, then this interpretation is called a "relative interpretation".

An absolute existential interpretation of the standard propositions occurs when the relations of the square of opposition hold between the standard propositions and their existential interpretations. An example of such an interpretation is:[7]

Standard Propositions	*Absolute Existential Interpretation*
All S are P	There is nothing that is an S and not a P, and there is a S, and there is a non-P.
No S are P	There is nothing that is both S and P, and there is a S, and there is a P.
Some S are P	At least one thing is both S and P, or there is no S, or there is no P.
Some S are not P	There is at least one thing that is an S and not a P, or there is no S, or there is no non-P.

The advantage of the absolute existential interpretation of the traditional logic is that no existential presuppositions are necessary. Existential statements have to be made, but these statements are explicitly part of the standard propositions. The inferences of the traditional square of opposition will hold for the absolute interpretation given above as well as the valid immediate inferences of the traditional system.

Exercises for Chapter 9

EX 9A, I. Identify which of the following proposition are true and which are false.

1. The term "existence" will be used in chapter 9 to mean any object that has mass and occupies space.
2. The presupposition of existence implies the implication of existence.
3. The implication of existence implies the presupposition of existence.
4. The universe of discourse of a proposition is the realm of existence (or a part of this realm) to which the proposition refers.
5. An existential proposition is one that presupposes the existence of entities to which its subject applies.

EX 9A, II. Which of the following propositions presupposes and implies existence of entities to which their subjects apply, and which of the following are existential propositions.

1. Nothing is real but the mind of God.
2. The present king of France is bald-headed.
3. The integer between 2 and 4 is an odd number.
4. The integer between 4 and 6 is an odd number.
5. The dog owned by Socrates was named "Fido".
6. All UFOs are illusions or hoaxes.
7. There is a pot of gold at the end of the rainbow.
8. Few centaurs are fast enough to catch a unicorn.
9. Twilliger's youngest daughter is named "Maralyn".
10. God is omnipotent.

EX 9. Explain the following:

1. Explain why existential presuppositions must be made for the standard propositions in traditional logic.

2. Explain why it is reasonable to assume that the standard particular propositions in Aristotelian logic are existential propositions.

3. Explain, using examples, why propositions that imply existence but do not presuppose it are false.

4. Explain why the **A**, **E**, **I**, and **O** propositions in Aristotelian logic would be false if no presupposition of existence were made for these propositions.

5. Explain what is meant and give an example of a two-pair existential presupposition (two-PEP).

6. Explain why conditions that allow the opposed **I** and **O** propositions to both be false are not allowed in Aristotelian logic.

7. Explain with examples what is meant by saying that if a proposition presupposes existence, then it implies existence, but not conversely.

8. Explain why an empty subject term may make one proposition false and another proposition meaningless.

9. Explain with examples what kind of sentences neither imply existence nor presuppose existence.

10. Explain the difference between relative and absolute existential interpretations. What are the advantages of the latter over the former?

10

Distribution of Terms in Categorical Propositions

The doctrine of distribution developed out of medieval discussion of the properties of terms.[1] It proved useful for testing validity of syllogisms and conversions, and survived in modern logic only in this form. When it was applied injudiciously to arguments involving negative terms, a contradiction arose (examined in the chapter of inversion). Some logicians[2] have concluded that distribution is theoretically and practically indefensible. But there is more than one satisfactory clarification of the concept. It can be extended to non-standard categorical forms; and its application is simpler on a non-Aristotelian than on an Aristotelian interpretation. In this chapter, however, we deal with its application to standard categorical forms on an Aristotelian interpretation.

Section 10A is a minimal account of distribution of terms in categorical propositions. A precise explanation of distribution is given in 10B, and a different explanation based on the medieval doctrine is in Appendix 10A5.

For the purpose of using rules of distribution to determine the validity of arguments, as we shall do for conversions (chapter 11), categorical syllogisms (chapter 21), and other chain arguments (chapter 22), 10A gives a sufficient account of distribution. However, a more precise concept of distribution provides a sound theoretical basis for its use, allaying the suspicions that have been aroused. It also provides a basis for extending the application of distribution to other cases, and helps avoid the two errors that may arise from taking the syllogistic distribution rules as defining distribution: either generalizing the application of the rules without warrant; or, since this leads to untenable results, rejecting distribution altogether.

10A DISTRIBUTED AND UNDISTRIBUTED TERMS

10A1 Preliminary Exposition.

Def. 1. *(Preliminary)*. A term *'B'* in a categorical proposition is **distributed** in that proposition iffi what the proposition asserts it asserts of every *B* or of any *B* (taken universally).

Def. 2. A term in a categorical proposition is **undistributed** in that proposition iffi it is not distributed in that proposition.

Distribution of terms in a proposition is determined by what the proposition asserts, not by what happens to be true. In judging distribution of terms in the proposition "Some students of elementary logic are undergraduates", we ignore the fact (if it is a fact) that all students of elementary logic are undergraduates, because the quoted proposition does not assert this fact.

Instead of saying that a term is distributed in a proposition, we may say that the proposition **distributes** the term. The concept of distribution is applied in this chapter only to subject-terms and predicate-terms, and mostly to standard categorical propositions, though it could be applied to the terms (in the broader sense) that are part of complex terms; and applications to non-standard categoricals is briefly indicated.

10A2 Determination of Distribution in the Standard Categoricals.[3]

a *The Standard Universals.* The **A** proposition *All cougars are mammals* is obviously making its assertion about every cougar (namely that each one is a mammal), so the term "cougar" is distributed in this proposition. The same manner of reasoning would hold for the subject term of any **A** proposition, so the subject term of every **A** proposition is distributed.

However, the proposition *All cougars are mammals* is not asserting that every cougar is John Doe or any other human, though humans are mammals, so it is not making its assertion about every mammal. Therefore, "mammals" in this proposition is undistributed. An **A** proposition has an undistributed predicate term.

The **E** proposition *No women are monks* asserts of every woman that she is not a monk, and asserts that no woman is any monk. We may also say it denies that any woman is any monk. It is making its assertion of every woman and any monk; therefore, both terms are distributed. An **E** proposition distributes both subject term and predicate term.

b *The Standard Particulars.* The **I** proposition *Some Frenchmen are logicians* makes its assertion about some Frenchmen, but not about every

Frenchman, hence the term "Frenchmen" in this proposition is undistributed. The term "logicians" is also undistributed in this proposition, since it does not assert that some Frenchmen is every logician. Both subject term and predicate term of an **I** proposition are undistributed.

The **O** proposition *Some books are not novels* does not say of every book that it is a novel, so the term "books" in the proposition is undistributed. The proposition does, however, assert something with reference to any novel, namely that "some book" is not any novel. There is some book that is not *Moby Dick* and not *Catcher in the Rye* and not *Fanny Hill* . . . and not any other novel. Therefore, an **O** proposition has an undistributed subject term and a distributed predicate term.

10A3 Table of Distribution in Standard Categoricals. Distributed terms are indicated by a square or rectangle; undistributed terms are underlined by a dotted line.

Table 10.1: Distribution in Standard Categoricals

STANDARD CATEGORICALS	Affirmatives: predicate undistributed	Negatives: predicate distributed
Universals: subject distributed	All ⬚S⬚ are P	No ⬚S⬚ are ⬚P⬚
Particulars: subject undistributed	Some S are P	Some S are not ⬚P⬚

In standard categorical propositions, the universals alone distribute the subject, and the negatives alone distribute the predicate.

10A4 THE DISTINCTION BETWEEN "UNDISTRIBUTED" AND "NOT DISTRIBUTED"

The term "mammals" is neither distributed nor undistributed in the proposition *Some men are philosophers* because it does not occur in this proposition. It would be incorrect to say that "mammals" is undistributed in this proposition. In general, if a term does not occur in a categorical proposition, it is neither distributed nor undistributed in that proposition.

If a term is undistributed in a proposition, then it is also not distributed in that proposition. For example, the term "men" is undistributed in the proposition *Some men are philosophers* and is therefore not distributed in this proposition.

10B EXPLANATION OF DISTRIBUTION BASED ON SUBTERM SUBSTITUTION

Recent criticism of the traditional doctrine of distribution has demonstrated the need for a more precise definition of the concept of a distributed term in the context of categorical propositions. In this section we present a more precise explanation of this concept and define it in the recent tradition of De Morgan, Curry, and Barker.[4]

The definitions and tests for distribution given in this section apply to all categoricals, standard and non-standard. Since the distribution of terms in standard categoricals is readily memorized, the tests described in this section are of practical value only for determining the distribution of terms in non-standard categoricals. This section provides a theoretical justification for the traditional account of the distribution of terms in standard categoricals (other than the medieval explanation reported in Appendix 10; however, our explanation in 10A1–A2 followed the medieval explanation rather than that of this section).

An essential concept for the forthcoming discussion is *subterm* (introduced in 4D). For the present purpose, a *term* is the subject term or predicate term of a categorical proposition.

Def. 3. A general term 'X' is a **subterm** of a general term 'Y' iffi every X is a Y or everything X is Y.

For example, subterms of the term "polygon" include "polygon", "quadrilateral", "rectangle", and "square". Subterms of the term "colored" include "colored", "red", and "bright red".

Now, as explained in 7C and chapter 9, traditional logic presupposes that the subject term of a standard categorical proposition is not empty. This fact is also expressed by saying that the Aristotelian interpretation of a standard categorical proposition presupposes the existence of something denoted by the subject term of the proposition. For example, if the proposition *All ghosts are spirits* is asserted, it implies that some ghosts are spirits, which says that something is both a ghost and a spirit, hence that something is a ghost. On the other hand, if it is denied that all ghosts are spirits, the contradictory must be true, namely, some ghosts are not spirits, which says that something is a ghost but not a spirit, hence again that something is a ghost. In either case, then, whether the original **A** proposition is true or false, it follows that there are ghosts, and the term "ghosts" is not an empty term.

We note, next, that if a term is non-empty, it does not follow that all its subterms are non-empty. The term "cat" is non-empty, but it does not follow that its subterm "cat with three tails" is non-empty. It may be empty or non-empty. We find we must explicitly restrict the subterms we make use of in the following definition of non-empty subterms in order to make the results agree with the Aristotelian doctrine. (This restriction would not be necessary for the Boolean or hypothetical interpretation.)

Def. 4. A term in the subject (or predicate) position in a categorical proposition is **distributed in** that proposition iffi, for each true proposition of the same distinctive form, every substitution of a non-empty subterm for the term in that position makes a true proposition.[5]

Def. 5. A term in the subject (or predicate) position in a categorical proposition is **undistributed in** that proposition iffi it is not distributed in that proposition.[6]

Definition 5 is (by def. 4) equivalent to:

Def. 5a. A term in the subject (or predicate) position in a categorical proposition is **undistributed in** that proposition iffi, for some true proposition of the same distinctive form, substituting some non-empty subterm for the term in that position makes a false proposition.[7]

These definitions are a bit tricky, but their application is not too difficult. Note that whether a term is distributed or not in a proposition does not depend on the specific term but on the form of the proposition and the position of the term. However, the choice of terms or subterms to try out in the form does make a difference.

In applying our definitions, it is easier to show that a term is undistributed in a proposition than that it is distributed, since a single instance can show lack of distribution. We begin therefore with an example in which the term is shown to be undistributed.

Let us examine the distribution of the predicate term in the proposition *All dogs are pets*. Having heard of wild dogs, we judge that the given proposition is not true. To use definition 5a (or 5b), we must take a true proposition of the same distinctive form, that is, of the form "All *S* are *P*". Let us take the true proposition *All dogs are mammals* (true by definition), as our test proposition. Next we must think of subterms of the predicate "mammals". When the non-empty subterms "dogs" or "carnivorous mammals" are substituted for the predicate in the test proposition, we get true propositions. But when we substitute the non-empty subterm "cats", we get the false proposition *All dogs are cats*. This shows, in the words of definition 5a, that there is some true proposition (e.g., *All dogs are mammals*) of the same distinctive form as the original proposition *(All dogs are pets)*, such that substituting some non-empty subterm (e.g., "cats") for the predicate makes a false proposition. So the predicate term in this—and any—**A** proposition is undistributed. In a similar way, we can show that subject and predicate are undistributed in the true **I** proposition *Some dogs are pets*, substituting to get the false propositions, respectively, *Some wild dogs are pets* and *Some dogs are pet cats*.

We turn now to the question of the distribution of the subject term of an **A** proposition. Again, we must take true propositions as the starting point for substitution of non-empty subterms. We take *All dogs are mammals* again. If this is true, it follows that *All wild dogs are mammals*, and also that *All tame dogs are mammals*, given that both wild dogs and tame dogs exist. Likewise, it follows that *All male dogs are mammals* and *All female dogs are mammals*. In general, from *All dogs are mammals*, it follows that *All dogs of any kind are mammals*, as long as we limit ourselves to non-empty kinds. (On an Aristotelian interpretation, we cannot accept such a sentence as "All dogs that are not mammals are mammals" as standing for either a true or false proposition.) Generalizing further, the reader can see that if a proposition of the form "All S are P" is true, then a corresponding proposition of the form "All S of kind K are P" is true, where the values of "S of kind K" are non-empty subterms of the corresponding values of the variable S.

Similarly, given the true proposition *No dogs are cats*, it follows that *No male dogs are cats*, *No female dogs are cats*, and in general, *No dogs of any kind are cats*. So the subject term of this and all **E** propositions is distributed. Likewise, from *No dogs are cats*, it follows that *No dogs are cats of any kind;* so the predicate term of this and all **E** propositions is distributed.

Textbook explanations of the distribution of the predicate of the **O** proposition often are unable to explain it in the same way they explain distribution in the universal propositions. However, the subterm method works here in the same way as for universals. Since it is true that *Some people are not logicians*, it follows that *Some people are not Aristotelian logicians*, and also that *Some people are not non-Aristotelian logicians*, and in general *Some people are not logicians of any kind*. Hence the predicate term is distributed in this and all **O** propositions.

Finally, we apply this method to certain non-standard categorical propositions. Let us examine the form "Most S are P", which we interpret as "More than half the S are P". We start from the true proposition *Most Americans are females*. It is certainly false that *Most male Americans are females*, and also false that *Most Americans are females over eighty.* So neither term is distributed in the "most" proposition.

Now consider the form contradictory to the preceding: "No more than half the S are P", equivalent to "At most half the S are P". We start from the true proposition *At most half the Americans are males.* It is false that *At most half the male Americans are males,* so the subject term is undistributed. However, it is true that *At most half the Americans are males of a specific kind,* whatever kind we take, since less than half are males the males altogether; so the predicate is distributed in the from "At most half the S are P". Note that these two contradictory forms agree in having the subject term undistributed. Thus the rule that holds for standard categoricals, that a term is distributed in a standard categorical proposition iffi it is undistributed in the contradictory proposition, does not hold for non-standard categoricals. However, rules of distribution prove useful for determining validity of arguments with non-standard categoricals as well as for those with only standard categoricals.

Appendix to 10A

HISTORICAL INTRODUCTION TO DISTRIBUTION

10A5 Distribution and the Doctrine of *Suppositio*. The modern doctrine of distribution had its origin in the medieval doctrine of supposition *(suppositio)*, a theory of the ways in which a term in a proposition may stand for things.[1] This doctrine was part of their theory of the properties of terms, which "took shape in the second half of the twelfth century, and it seems to have grown out of the discussions of Abelard and his contemporaries about the structure of categorical propositions".[2] Full accounts of supposition appear in William of Sherwood (or Shyreswood) and the influential Peter of Spain. We shall base our account on the relatively clear and simple teachings of William of Ockham. Furthermore, we limit ourselves to his analysis of common personal supposition, which is the normal supposition of general terms as used, for example, in standard categorical propositions.

a *Ockham's Division of Common Personal Supposition.* Common personal supposition is divided into determinate and confused supposition; the latter is further divided.

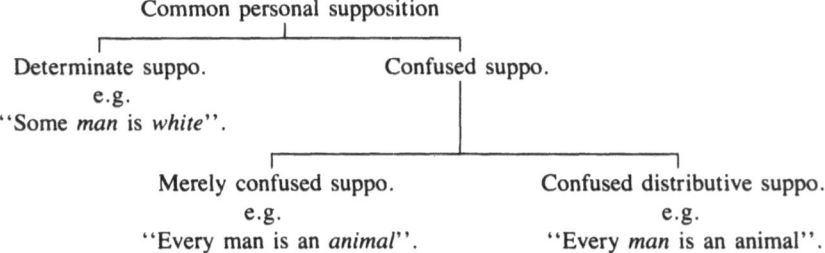

The italicized terms exemplify the supposition in question.

The distributed terms of modern logic have confused distributive supposition. The undistributed terms have either determinate or merely confused supposition. We now explain these kinds of supposition.

b *Determinate Supposition.* Ockham defines determinate supposition thus:

> ... When (1) the logical descent from a common term to its singular inferior terms can legitimately be made by a disjunctive proposition, and

(2) from any singular proposition such a proposition is inferable, then this term has determinate personal *suppositio*.[3]

For example, in the proposition *Some man is a philosopher*, the subject "man" has determinate supposition. The inference is valid: "Some man is a philosopher; therefore this man is a philosopher, or that man is a philosopher (and so on for each man)". And secondly, from the singular proposition *This man is a philosopher*, *Some man is a philosopher* follows.

c *Merely Confused Supposition.* Confused personal supposition is defined by Ockham as any personal supposition of a common (general) term that is not determinate.[4] This is divided into merely confused supposition and confused distributive supposition.

Of the standard categorical forms, only the predicate of the **A** has merely confused supposition. Ockham defines it:

> Merely confused *suppositio* occurs when (1) a common term has personal *suppositio*; (2) we are unable to make the logical descent to the singulars by means of a disjunctive proposition without any change of the other extreme; (3) we can, however, make the logical descent by way of a proposition with a disjunctive predicate; and (4) the original proposition can be inferred from any singular.[5]

For example, the term "marsupial" in the proposition *Every wombat is a marsupial* has merely confused supposition, because (1) it is a common (or general) term having personal supposition; (2) *Every wombat is a marsupial* does not entail *Every wombat is this marsupial or every wombat is that marsupial* (and so on for each individual marsupial); (3) *Every wombat is a marsupial* does entail *Every wombat is either this marsupial or that marsupial or* that *marsupial* (and so on for each marsupial); and (4) the singular proposition *Every wombat is this marsupial* entails *Every wombat is a marsupial*.

d *Confused Distributive Supposition.* Ockham defines it thus:

> Confused distributive *suppositio* occurs when it is licit to make a logical descent in some way to a copulative [i.e., conjunctive] proposition if the term has many inferiors, but a formal inference cannot be made to the original proposition from one of the instances.[6]

For example, the subject of *Every dog is a animal* has confused distributive supposition, because this proposition entails *This dog is an animal, and that dog is an animal* (and so on for each dog). But the inference *This dog is an animal; therefore every dog is an animal* is not formally valid.

The same criteria apply to the predicate of the **O** proposition, and to both terms of an **E**. For example, *Some female is not mother* entails *Some female is not* *this mother and some female is not that mother* (and so on for each mother). *No whale is a fish* entails *This whale is not a fish, nor is that whale a fish* (and so on for each whale). But inference from one instance to the original proposition is not formally valid.

Terms with this kind of supposition were called "distributed" by Pseudo-Scotus, who noted the necessity that the middle term of a syllogism be distributed in at least one premiss. And elsewhere he remarked, "From the non-distributed the distributed never follows formally", that is, a term not distributed in the premiss cannot be distributed in the conclusion.[7] He thus anticipated the method of testing validity of syllogisms by rules, including rules of distribution, which is found in a textbook printed in 1489. This rule method became standard in modern logic; the origin of the doctrine of distribution in the doctrine of supposition became lost in what Bochenski has called the "Dark Ages" of early modern logic.

Appendix to Chapter 10

10C THE ANALYSIS OF DISTRIBUTION BY INTERPRETING STANDARD CATEGORICAL PROPOSITIONS AS IDENTITY STATEMENTS

10C1 Introduction. One way in which categorical propositions can be analyzed is by stating that things named by one term in the proposition are identical with certain things named by the other term in the proposition. This is, perhaps, easiest to see in the case of singular propositions. For example, the singular proposition "Robert Graves is the author of *Count Belisarius*" states that Robert Graves is identical with the author of *Count Belisarius*.

If we change the example to "The author of *Count Belisarius* is a poet", we may interpret this as stating that the author of *Count Belisarius* is identical with a certain poet (namely, Robert Graves, though he is not named). The propositions last quoted have the same meaning but a different form than the I proposition "some poet is the author of *Count Belisarius*", which states that some poet is identical with the author of *Count Belisarius*.

The O proposition "Some poet is not the author of *Count Belisarius*" states that some poet is not identical with the author of *Count Belisarius*, that is, some poet is distinct from the author of *Count Belisarius*. These introductory examples illustrate how the verb *to be* ("is" or "are") in the categorical proposition can be interpreted as identity.

10C2 Identity Statements and Quantification of the Predicate. As we have seen in section 10A, the subject is distributed in a standard categorical proposition when preceded by a universal quantifier. On the other hand, the subject is undistributed when preceded by a particular quantifier. Hence, the universal categorical propositions have distributed subject terms.

However, the predicate terms in the standard categorical propositions are not immediately preceded by a quantifier. Consequently, there is some difficulty in determining whether or not the predicate terms are distributed.

The advantage of interpreting the standard categorical proposition as identity statements is that identity statements may be formulated so that both the subject and predicate terms are quantified in a standard way. For example, we may interpret the I proposition *Some poets are novelists* as stating that some poet is identical with some novelist. Since both terms are preceded by a particular quantifier, it is easy to see that both are undistributed.

10C3 Interpreting the Standard Categorical Propositions as Identity Statements.

a *The A proposition.* For example, "All men are animals" is interpreted as stating that *every* man is identical with some animal or other. Since the term *man* is preceded by the universal quantifier *every,* this term is distributed. The term *animal* is undistributed, because it is preceded by the particular quantifier *some.*

Suppose one tried to interpret the above example as "*Every* man is identical with *every* animal". This interpretation of the A proposition is not correct, because one seldom, if ever, when he asserts a proposition of the form "All *S* are *P*" means to assert a proposition of the form "Every *S* is every *P*".[1] In other words, "All *S* are *P*" is not equivalent to "*Every S* is identical with *every P*".

b *The E proposition.* For example, "No fish are whales" is interpreted as "No fish is identical with any whale", or (better) "*Every* fish is distinct from *every* whale". Since both terms are preceded by a universal quantifier, both are distributed.

c *The I proposition.* For example, "*Some* plastics are electrical conductors" is interpreted as "*Some* plastic is identical with *some* electrical conductors". Since both terms are preceded by a particular quantifier, both are undistributed.

It is apparent that the categorical form "Some *S* are *P*" cannot be translated as "Some *S* is identical with every *P*"; this would imply that every *P* is (some) *S*. In fact, some *S* can be identical with every *P* only if there is only one *P.* Some Scotsman is (identical with) every author of *Waverley.*

d *The O proposition.* For example, "Some poets are not novelists", is interpreted as "*Some* poet is distinct from *every* novelist". In this proposition, only the predicate term is distributed, since only the predicate term is preceded by a universal quantifier.

To interpret the above example as "Some poet is distinct from some novelist" is incorrect, because this interpretation merely states that there is at least one poet and at least one novelist that are not the same person. Consequently, this interpretation would allow the possibility that all poets are novelists. This, however, should not be allowed, since the proposition "Some poets are not novelists" means that it is false that all poets are novelists.

10C4 Summary.

a *A Definition of Distribution by Identity Statements.* A term *T* is distributed in a categorical proposition, if the proposition (restated in quantified-identity form) states something of *every T.*

b *Summary by Table.* In Column 1, distributed terms are indicated by being boldfaced. Undistributed terms are in regular type. In Column 2, the distributed terms are indicated by "every" immediately preceding the term; undistributed terms are indicated by "some" immediately preceding the term.

Column 1	Column 2
Standard Categorical Forms	*Quantified Identity Forms*
All S are P	Every S is identical with some P (or other).
No S are P	Every S is distinct from every P.
Some S are P	Some S is identical with some P (or other).
Some S are not P	Some S is distinct from every P.

Exercises for Chapter 10

EX. 10A, I. Put the appropriate letter in the margin.

_____ 1. All negative standard categorical propositions have: (a) distributed subjects. (b) undistributed subjects. (c) distributed predicates. (d) undistributed predicates.

_____ 2. All affirmative standard categorical propositions have: (a) distributed subjects. (b) distributed predicates. (c) undistributed subjects. (d) none of the above.

_____ 3. Universal standard categorical propositions have: (a) distributed subjects. (b) distributed predicates. (c) undistributed subjects. (d) undistributed predicates.

_____ 4. Particular negative standard categorical propositions have: (a) distributed subjects. (b) undistributed predicates. (c) distributed predicates. (d) undistributed subjects and undistributed predicates.

_____ 5. The **A** and **I** propositions have: (a) distributed subjects. (b) undistributed subjects. (c) distributed predicates. (d) undistributed predicates.

_____ 6. The **E** and **O** propositions have: (a) distributed subjects. (b) undistributed subjects. (c) distributed predicates. (d) undistributed predicates.

_____ 7. The **A** and **E** propositions have: (a) distributed subjects. (b) undistributed subjects. (c) distributed predicates. (d) undistributed predicates.

_____ 8. If a standard categorical proposition has both subject and predicate distributed, then it must be an: **A, E, I, O**.

_____ 9. The **I** and **O** propositions have: (a) distributed subjects. (b) undistributed subjects. (c) distributed predicates. (d) undistributed predicates.

_____ 10. If a standard categorical proposition has neither its subject nor predicate distributed, then it must be an: **A, E, I, O**.

Exercises/Chapter 10   203

_____ 11. If a standard categorical proposition has a distributed predicate, then it must be: (a) affirmative. (b) negative. (c) universal. (d) particular.

_____ 12. If a standard categorical proposition has a distributed subject and an undistributed predicate then it is an: **A, E, I, O.**

_____ 13. If a standard categorical proposition has an undistributed predicate then it is: (a) affirmative. (b) negative. (c) universal. (d) particular.

_____ 14. If the subject is undistributed in a standard categorical proposition then it is: (a) affirmative. (b) negative. (c) universal. (d) particular.

_____ 15. If the subject of a standard categorical proposition is distributed then it is: (a) affirmative. (b) negative. (c) universal. (d) particular.

_____ 16. In the proposition *All oboes are wind instruments* the term "cow" is: (a) distributed. (b) undistributed. (c) not distributed and not undistributed. (d) none of the above.

_____ 17. If a standard categorical proposition has an undistributed subject and a distributed predicate, then it is an: **A, E, I, O.**

_____ 18. In non-standard particular propositions such as "At least two S are P" or "A few S are P" the subject is: (a) distributed. (b) undistributed. (c) not distributed and not undistributed. (d) distributed and undistributed.

_____ 19. The subject of a false **A** proposition is: (a) distributed. (b) undistributed. (c) not distributed. (d) not distributed and not undistributed.

_____ 20. The predicate of a false **I** proposition is: (a) distributed. (b) undistributed. (c) collective. (d) not distributed and not undistributed.

EX. 10A, II. Underline the distributed terms in the following propositions. Draw dotted line under the undistributed terms.

1. Some snowflakes are things imperfectly formed.
2. Some panpipes are wooden instruments.
3. No porcupines are cuddly animals.

4. All crustaceans are hard-shelled animals.

5. Some cucumbers are not edible vegetables.

6. No demagogues are demigods.

7. All decorous delinquents are deluded deceivers.

8. Some carved stone idols are not idols as large as those found on Easter Island.

9. Some optometrists are skilled physicians.

10. No orangutans owned by movie stars are animals now living in Africa.

EX. 10B. Test the distributed and undistributed terms in EX 10A, II, 1–5, by the subterm substitution method explained in 10B.

11

Conversion

Conversion seems to be a trivial operation; but next to inferences based on the square of opposition, it is the most important of the traditional forms of immediate inferences.

11A DEFINITIONS

Def. 1. Conversion of a standard categorical proposition is an immediate inference in which the conclusion contains exactly the same terms as the premiss, but in reverse order, and has the same quality.[1]

These are examples of conversion (some valid and some invalid): (a) *All snakes are reptiles; therefore, all reptiles are snakes.* (b) *Some mammals are flying creatures, hence all flying creatures are mammals.* (c) *No wombats are camelopards; therefore, some camelopards are not wombats.*

Def. 2. The **convertend** is the premiss of a conversion.

Def. 3. A **converse** is the conclusion of a conversion.

Example (d): Premiss (convertend):   *No chubs are cherubs.*
↓
Conclusion (converse): ∴ *No cherubs are chubs.*

Def. 4. A **simple conversion** is a conversion in which the converse has the same quantity (and quality) as the convertend. A **simple converse** is the conclusion of a simple conversion.

205

(See examples (a) and (d) above.)

Def. 6. A **conversion** *per accidens*—also called **conversion by limitation**—is a conversion in which the permiss is universal but the conclusion is particular. (The premiss and conclusion have the same quality by definition 1.)

(See example (c) above.)

11B TRANSFORMATION TO SUBSTANTIVAL FORM

If the predicate in a proposition is in adjectival form, it must be replaced by an equivalent substantival form before conversion. For example, if the proposition "Some dogs are black" is to be converted, the adjectival predicate "black" must first be replaced. Substituting an equivalent substantival term for it, we have "Some dogs are black things". The resulting conversion would be: "Some dogs are black things; therefore, some black things are dogs".[2]

11C TABLE OF CONVERSIONS

Table 11.1: Conversions (Valid and Invalid)

Convertend	Simple Converse	Conversion per accidens
All S are P	All P are S	Some P are S
No S are P	No P are S	Some P are not S
Some S are P	Some P are S	None
Some S are not P	Some P are not S	None

Our definition of "conversion" allows for two other forms, both invalid, going from a particular to the universal of which it would be the converse *per accidens*. (See example (b) after definition 1.)

11D VALID CONVERSION

Not all simple conversions are valid inferences, though all conversions *per accidens* are valid (assuming, as we do, an Aristotelian interpretation, namely, that there is something the terms denote).

11D1 Rule for Valid Conversion. A conversion is valid iffi it obeys the following rule:

Rule of Distribution. No term is distributed in the conclusion that is not distributed in the premiss.

Violation of this rule is called (fallacy of) **illicit process.**

11D2 Table of Valid Conversions.

Table 11.2: Valid Conversions

Convertend	*Simple Converse*	*Conversion per accidens*
All S are P	(Not valid)	Some P are S
No S are P	No P are S	Some P are not S
Some S are P	Some P are S	None
Some S are not P	(Not valid)	None

As the table shows, simple conversion is valid only for **E** and **I** propositions. The simple conversions of **A** and **O** propositions are invalid, since they violate the rule of distribution. Their invalidity can be demonstrated by counterexample. For instance, the following counterexample shows that simple conversion of the **A** proposition is not a valid form of inference.

True premiss: *All dogs are mammals.*
 ↓
False conclusion: ∴ *All mammals are dogs.*

A valid argument cannot have a true premiss and a false conclusion. The propositions *Some females are not mothers* and *Some mothers are not females* provide a counterexample for simple conversion of the **O** proposition when used as premiss and conclusion, respectively. The **A** proposition does, however, have a valid conversion *per accidens,* while the **O** proposition has no valid conversion of any kind.

11D3 The Strongest Valid Converse.

Def. 7. To **find** (or **take**) **the converse** of a categorical proposition is to find the strongest valid converse, i.e., the simple converse if it is valid, otherwise the converse *per accidens* if that is valid.

For each standard categorical, there are two possible forms of conversion, of which both may be valid, just one, or neither (see 11D2). It would be confusing, then, to speak in general of "*the* converse" (as if there were only one); but we may use the expression in certain contexts.

Table 11.2: Strongest Valid Converse

Convertend	The Strongest Valid Converse
All S are P	Some P and S
No S are P	No P are S
Some S are P	Some P are S
Some S are not P	None

11D4 How to Find the Converse of a Categorical Proposition. Remember that "to find the converse" means "to find the strongest valid converse". Remember also that if the predicate is not substantival in form, there is no converse strictly speaking, and we must first change the predicate. (See 11B.)

If the convertend is E*sp* or I*sp*, then the simple converse is the converse we find. For the forms **E** and **I**, both terms are distributed or both undistributed, so inferring the simple converse does not violate the rule of distribution—that is, does not commit the fallacy of illicit process.

If the convertend is A*sp* (e.g., "All hornbills are birds"), then the converse *per accidens* I*ps* (e.g., "Some birds are hornbills") is the converse we find. Inference from A*sp* to its simple converse A*ps* would commit an illicit process, but inference of the converse *per accidens* does not. Note that the rule of distribution does not forbid decreasing the distribution.

If the convertend is O*sp* (e.g., "Some animals are not cats"), then no conversion is valid. For inference of the simple converse (e.g., "Some cats are not animals") commits an illicit process, as would inference to a universal negative (e.g., "No cats are animals").

Exercises for Chapter 11

Ex. 11A. Place the appropriate letter in the margin.

_____ 1. Conversion is: (a) an immediate inference. (b) an argument with two or more premisses. (c) a non-standard proposition. (d) a collection of general terms.

_____ 2. A convertend is: (a) a false conversion. (b) a false converse. (c) the premiss of a conversion. (d) the conclusion of a conversion.

_____ 3. A converse is: (a) a true convertend. (b) a true conversion. (c) the premiss of a conversion. (d) a conclusion of a conversion.

_____ 4. Which statement is false? (a) Every conversion contains a convertend and a converse. (b) No conversion has more than one convertend. (c) The converse of a conversion may differ in quantity from its convertend. (d) A simple conversion has no convertend.

_____ 5. Which statement is true? (a) Every conversion contains exactly three distinct terms. (b) Only the convertend of a conversion can be a standard categorical proposition. (c) Each term in a conversion occurs exactly once. (d) The quality of the convertend and the converse must be the same.

_____ 6. A conversion *per accidens* is a conversion in which: (a) both the quality and quantity change. (b) the quality changes but not the quantity. (c) the quality and quantity remain the same. (d) the quality remains the same but the quantity changes.

_____ 7. In a simple conversion: (a) both the quality and quantity change. (b) the quality changes but not the quantity. (c) the quality and quantity remain the same. (d) the quality remains the same but the quantity changes.

_____ 8. Another name for conversion *per accidens* is: (a) invalid conversion. (b) conversion by limitation. (c) accidental conversion. (d) conversion on account.

_____ 9. Which statement is true for valid conversion? (a) The convertend must be universal. (b) The converse must be particular.

(c) A conversion may have a particular convertend and a universal converse. (d) If a convertend is particular, the converse must be particular.

_____ 10. Which statement is false? (a) A simple conversion may have a universal converse. (b) A conversion *per accidens* may have a particular convertend. (c) A conversion may contain exactly two distinct terms. (d) In both simple conversion and conversion *per accidens* the convertend and the converse must have the same quality.

EX. 11B. After each proposition whose predicate is in adjectival form, write an equivalent substantival form of the predicate.

1. All violets are blue. _____

2. Some glittering things are not golden. _____

3. All women are essentially beautiful persons or beautiful objects. ____
_____

4. Some people are fanatical. _____

5. No molecules are capable of being seen by the human eye. _____
_____

6. Some experiences are as detrimental as they are unforgettable. ____
_____

7. Some wolves are crippled by traps. _____

8. All hermits are used to being lonely. _____

9. Some enterprises are not profitable. _____

EX. 11C–D, I. Place "V" for valid or "I" for invalid in each blank. Also place "L" in the blank if the conversion is by limitation *(per accidens);* write "Not C" if the inference is not a conversion.

_____ 1. All men are mortals; therefore, all mortals are men.

_____ 2. No camelopards are wombats, so some wombats are not camelopards.

_____ 3. Since some rodents are mice, some mice are rodents.

_____ 4. No mice are moose; therefore, some moose are not mice.

_____ 5. Some mongooses are not geese, hence no geese are mongooses.

_____ 6. All potted plants are flora; so some flora are potted plants.

_____ 7. No flora are fauna; consequently no fauna are flora.

_____ 8. No kangaroos are kings; ergo*, some kings are not kangaroos.

_____ 9. Some Martians are logicians, so some logicians are not Martians.

_____ 10. All asteroids are planetoids; therefore some planetoids are not asteroids.

EX. 11B–D, II. Find the strongest valid converse of the following propositions. If no valid conversion is possible, write "None". If a transformation to substantival form is needed, do in it your head, then proceed as if it had been made. (You may abbreviate an individual word that remains unchanged by its initial letter.)

1. No barons are accordionists.

2. Some bullfrogs are celebrated jumpers.

3. All fire hydrants are red.

4. Some intoxicated tightrope walkers are not good insurance risks.

5. No seasick naval captains are hearty eaters.

6. Some bald-headed barbers are rabbit breeders.

7. All deaf gophers are nervous animals.

8. Some shrimp fishermen are nonunion members.

9. No Ku Klux Klan members are Civil Liberties Union lawyers.

10. Some poetic sheepherders are dedicated beekeepers.

---

*"Ergo" is Latin for "therefore".

11. All hatcheck girls are women who admire the Greek gods.

12. No lame kangaroos are good rat catchers.

13. Some myopic, henpecked astronomers are not ballad-singing bigamists.

14. Some bearded philosophers are highly respected in their community.

15. All deep-sea divers who smoke over three packs of cigarettes a day are short-winded.

III

Immediate Inferences
Not Needed for Standard Syllogism

12

Negative Terms

Negative terms were of course known to Aristotle, but they were not much studied by logicians (except Boethius in the fifth century) until De Morgan in 1847 extended the traditional doctrine to include complementary terms. At the same time, they played an important role in Boole's algebra of classes. Ordinary language has other kinds of negative terms that have still not received much systematic attention from logicians.

12A DEFINITIONS

12A1 Negative, Positive, and Privative Terms.

Def. 1. An **explicit negative term** is a term that has a negative prefix or suffix.

Examples of explicit negative terms with the negative prefix or suffix italicized are: "*il*legal action", "*im*moral person", "color*less* liquid", "*un*lawful act", and "*non*-animals". Unless otherwise indicated we shall use "negative term" to mean "explicit negative term".

Def. 2. An **explicit positive term** is a term that is not explicitly negative, that is, it is a term that does not have a negative prefix or suffix.

Examples of explicit positive terms are: "toy dog", "visible celestial body", "tree", "yellow flower", "yellow", and "blind". Unless otherwise indicated we shall use "positive term" to mean "explicit positive term".

Def. 3. A **privative term** is a term whose definition signifies the absence or lack of a quality that is normally present.

Examples of privative terms are: "stupid" (lacking intelligence), "blind" (lacking sight), "lame", and "deaf". These privative terms are explicitly positive, since they have no negative prefix nor suffix. They are semantically negative. Privative terms are of little importance in traditional logic.

12A2 Contradictory and Contrary Terms.

Def. 4. A pair of terms is **contradictory** if and only if by virtue of their meaning alone each and every entity in the universe must be named by one or the other but not both.[1]

A term T and its negation non-T are contradictory terms. To say that something is a non-T is the same as saying that it is not a T. For example, "John is a non-mathematician" means "John is not a mathematician".

The term "non-mathematician" is called the contradictory of the term "mathematician", and vice versa. This means simply that a thing (or person) is a non-mathematician if and only if it (or he) is not a mathematician. The contradictory of "mathematician" could also be written: "thing or person that is not a mathematician".

Examples of contradictory terms are: "temporal", "non-temporal"; "red beach ball", "thing that is not a red beach ball"; and "horse", "non-horse". Contradictory terms are readily recognized because there is no third alternative. One of the two terms must always apply to every entity and both terms are never applicable to the same entity.

Def. 5. Two general terms are **contraries** if and only if, by virtue of their meaning alone, they apply to possible cases on opposite ends of a scale. Both terms cannot apply to the same possible case, but neither may apply.

Examples of contrary terms on the scale of intelligence are "genius" and "idiot". The letter grades "A" and "F" used in most colleges are contraries. Relative terms such as "tall" and "short", "big" and "small", may be regarded as contraries.

"Pencil" and "pig" are **inconsistent** terms, that is, terms that by virtue of their meaning alone cannot both apply to the same possible case. However, they are not contrary terms because there is no reasonable scale of which they are on opposite ends.

Contradictory terms must be distinguished from contrary terms. For example, "kind" and "unkind" are contrary, not contradictory terms. For an act cannot be both kind and unkind (in the same way to the same person), but may be neither kind nor unkind, just indifferent.

ACTS		
	Non-Kind Acts	
Kind acts	Indifferent acts	Unkind acts

The term "indifferent" in this case means "neither kind nor unkind"; for example, sneezing or blowing my nose. The non-kind acts are those that are not kind, hence either unkind or indifferent.

The term "non-kind" is subaltern to (weaker than) the term "unkind", because being unkind implies being non-kind, but not conversely.

12B HOW TO FORM THE CONTRADICTORY OF A TERM

12B1 Forming the Contradictory of Simple Terms.

Def. 6. Negating a term is the operation of forming its contradictory by prefixing "non-" or, if "non-" is already prefixed, canceling it.[2]

Consequently, the following rule:

R1 The contradictory of a simple term may be formed by negating it.

Examples:

Given Term	*Contradictory of the Given Term*
horses	non-horses
pencils	non-pencils
red	non-red
beautiful	non-beautiful

If there is already a "non-" prefixed to the given term, then we negate by canceling the "non-", since non-non-T is equivalent to T.

Examples:

Given Term	Contradictory of the Given Term
non-horses	horses
non-pencils	pencils
non-red	red
non-beautiful	beautiful

If one term is the contradictory of the other, the other is the contradictory of the first. For example, "non-horses" is the contradictory of "horses" and "horses" is the contradictory of "non-horses."

12B2 Forming the Contradictory of Complex Terms. The rule is:

R2 The contradictory of a complex term may be formed by placing parentheses around the entire term and then prefixing "non-".

Examples:

Given Complex Term	Contradictory of Given Term
Austrian bankers	non-(Austrian bankers)
men with guns	non-(men with guns)
beautiful paintings	non-(beautiful paintings)
redheaded people	non-(redheaded people)

It may not be apparent to the student why the complex terms are negated in this way. This will be explained in detail.

PROBLEM: What is the contradictory of the term "Austrian bankers"? The question asks us to formulate a term that applies to all things that are not Austrian bankers, such as Russian bankers, Austrian policemen, cats, trees, and so on.

There are four likely candidates for the answer. They are:
(1) non-Austrian bankers
(2) Austrian non-bankers
(3) non-Austrian non-bankers
(4) non-(Austrian bankers)

The first term, "non-Austrian bankers", is not the answer. This term applies only to bankers who are not Austrians. It incorrectly leaves out the cats, trees, and Austrian policemen who are not Austrian bankers. The second term, "Austrian non-bankers" applies only to Austrians who are not bankers, hence Russian bankers and Russian policemen, as well as cats and trees, are wrongly omitted. Unfortunately, the third term, "non-Austrian non-bankers", is also inadequate, as it incorrectly omits both Russian bankers and Austrian policemen, none of whom are Austrian bankers.

The correct answer is the fourth term, "non-(Austrian bankers)", which is a term applicable to everything that is not both an Austrian and a banker. To express this without parentheses, we may write: "Entities that are not Austrian bankers". The following diagram clarifies the divisions involved:

AUSTRIAN BANKERS	NON-(AUSTRIAN BANKERS)		
All those who are both Austrian and bankers	Austrian non-bankers	Non-Austrian bankers	Non-Austrian non-bankers
	Austrian firemen Austrian policemen etc.	Russian bankers British bankers etc.	Russian policemen cats trees etc.

12B3 The Universe of Discourse. Terms such as "honest men" and "non-honest men" are not, strictly speaking contradictory terms, because they do not exhaust between them everything in the universe. There are many things in the universe—cows, pencils, trees, hatracks—that are neither honest men nor non-honest men. Such terms, however, can be regarded as contradictory terms, if we limit the *universe of discourse*—the class that contains everything to which we will refer—to men. Since all men are either honest or non-honest, but not both at once (in the same respect), the terms "honest men" and "non-honest men" are contradictory terms within the universe of discourse *men*, though not contradictory in an unlimited universe.

A serviceable definition of "universe of discourse" is as follows:

Def. 7. A **universe of discourse** (UD) is a class that includes all the things we wish to talk about. It may also be referred to as a **limited universe** (or simply "universe").

UD = men

honest men	non-honest men

In general, if the UD is the class B, AB and non-AB are contradictories within that universe (although not contradictories in the unlimited universe). The rule is:

R3 Within a limited UD, say B, the terms AB and non-AB are contradictories.

$$UD = B$$

| AB | non-AB |

Regardless of the universe of discourse the contradictory of a term may be found by either rule **R1** or **R2**.

12B4 The Difference Between "Not" and "Non-".

The prefix "non-" is part of a term. The prefix "non-" in front of a term in a proposition does not make the proposition negative. We call the proposition "Some animals are non-horses" an affirmative proposition, because it is of the affirmative form "Some S are P", though it has a negative term "non-horses". On the other hand, the equivalent proposition "Some animals are not horses" is a negative proposition, because it is of the negative form, "Some S are not P".

The word "not" may also be used as part of a term (rather than a form word). For example, "Some persons who were not invited are present" is an affirmative proposition with a negative subject term.

12C COMPLEMENTARY AND CONTRADICTORY TERMS

Complementary terms and contradictory terms are distinguished even though both are jointly exhaustive and mutually exclusive.

> **Def. 8.** A pair of terms is **complementary** within a given universe iffi each entity in that universe is named by one or the other of the terms, but not by both.

Comparing definition 3 with the one above, one sees that contradictory terms are terms that are necessarily complementary by virtue of their meaning alone. Hence all contradictory terms are complementary terms, but not conversely. The exhaustive and exclusiveness of contradictory terms can be determined from their meanings alone; this may or may not be the case with complementary terms. A pair of terms are complementary if each names a set of entities within a given universe such that each entity is a member of one set or the other but not both. The exhaustiveness and exclusiveness of these sets may be determined by the meaning of these terms or it may be determined as a matter of fact. For example, if the given universe consists of the pieces of fruit in a basket, the terms "apples" and "pears" are complementary *as a matter of fact* if only apples and pears are in the basket.

Complementary terms must also be distinguished from complimentary terms (eulogistic terms) such as "honorable", "beautiful", "good", "splendid", etc.

12C1 Complementary Classes.

Def. 9. The **complementary class** (or **complement** of a class) is the class of all things not in the given class. (Or: The complementary class is the class of things named by a complementary term.)

For example, the complement of the class of animals is the class of non-animals. The compliment of the class of books is the class of non-books.

If *A* is the complementary class of *B*, *B* is the complementary class of *A*. Since the complement of the class of animals is the class of non-animals, the complement of the class of non-animals is the class of animals.[3]

12D ORDINARY-LANGUAGE FORMS OF NEGATIVE TERMS

12D1 Negative Prefixes other than "Non-". Ordinary language has many ways of forming negative terms, other than by prefixing "non-". For example, it uses the Germanic prefix *un-*, the Latin prefix *in-* (with variant forms depending on the next letter: *il-*, *im-*, *ir-*, *ig-*), and others. Sometimes, by using these prefixes, the contradictory term is formed; for example, "unobserved" seems to be the contradictory to "observed". More often, the negative term is not contradictory, but contrary. Thus, "illogical" does not mean "non-logical": The statement "The artist's creative though is non-logical" does not imply that it is *il*logical.

It may be a matter of fine judgment to decide whether terms are contradictory. For example, if perfection is though of as an absolute matter, "perfect" and "imperfect" are contradictory. But, say De Morgan, "we have *not perfect* which is not so strong a term as *imperfect;* and *not imperfect,* . . . which is not so strong as *perfect*". Thus, we might say that a car just off the production line is "not imperfect", since it need not be rejected; but we might not wish to say that it is perfect (since it might be improved). In this example, "not imperfect" is *not* equivalent to "perfect".

Terms that are exclusive but not exhaustive within a broader universe may become contradictories within a narrower universe. Take the terms "vertebrate" and "invertebrate". These terms are not exhaustive in a universe of physical things, since it would be as unnatural to call a river or even a plant an "invertebrate" as to call it a "vertebrate"; but animals were commonly divided into vertebrates and invertebrates (though contemporary biologists find some primitive *chordata* they would not call by either name). Hence, within the universe of discourse of animals, the terms "vertebrate" and "invertebrate" have been considered contradictory.

Animals (narrower universe)	
Vertebrates	Invertebrates

In the universe of living things, "vertebrate" and "invertebrate" are exclusive but not contradictory.

LIVING THINGS (broader universe)		
Animals		Plants
Vertebrates	Invertebrates	

12D2 Formal Treatment of Negative Prefixes other than "Non-". Given an argument containing a term *T* and a negative term other than "non-*T*", say "un-*T*"; for example, "wise" and "unwise".

Step 1. Take, as a universe of discourse, a term broad enough to include all other terms of the given argument. Possibilities in reference to the terms "wise" and "unwise" might be "animals", "people", "students", depending upon the context.

Step 2. Decide whether *T* and "un-*T*" are contradictory in this universe. If they are, replace "un-*T*" by "non-*T*", thus making the terms explicitly contradictories. If our universe is students, we might decide that they are either wise or unwise; then we could use "non-wise" for "unwise".

Step 3. If *T* and "un-*T*" are not contradictory, we must use "non-*T*" for contradictory of *T*, and "non-un-*T*" for contradictory of "un-*T*" (if we need such a contradictory).

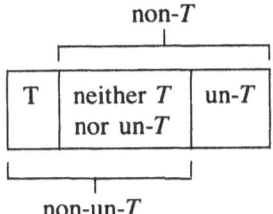

An example of the above is:

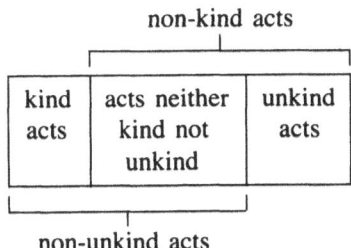

Exercises for Chapter 12

EX. 12, I. Place the appropriate letter in each blank.

_____ 1. Which of the following is an explicitly negative term? (a) Black cat. (b) Tailless cat. (c) Sleeping cat. (d) Catnap.

_____ 2. The terms "scissors" and "paste" are: (a) contraries. (b) contradictories. (c) explicitly negative terms. (d) inconsistent terms.

_____ 3. Contradictory terms are: (a) jointly exhaustive and mutually exclusive. (b) jointly exhaustive, but not mutually exclusive. (c) mutually exclusive, but not jointly exhaustive. (d) neither jointly exclusive nor mutually exhaustive.

_____ 4. If both terms cannot apply to the same thing, but neither may apply, such as the terms "strong men" and "weak men", then these terms are: (a) contraries. (b) contradictories. (c) inconsistent terms. (d) explicitly negative terms.

_____ 5. If both terms cannot apply to the same thing, but neither may apply, like the terms "airplane" and "duck", then these terms are (a) contraries. (b) contradictories. (c) inconsistent terms. (d) explicitly negative terms.

EX. 12A, II. Determine whether each of the following pairs of terms are contradictories, contraries, or inconsistent terms by placing the appropriate letters in each blank.

Cd = contradictories, Ct = contraries, Ic = inconsistent

_____ 1. "typewriter", "ballpoint pen"
_____ 2. "everything of which I am thinking", "everything of which I am not thinking"
_____ 3. "fat", "skinny"
_____ 4. "wombats", "non-wombats"
_____ 5. "gophers", "chipmunks"

EX. 12B. Determine, within the universe of discourse given for each pair of terms, whether the terms are contradictories or not. If they are contradictories, place a "Y" for "yes" in the blank; if not, place an "N" for "no" in the blank.

TERMS		UNIVERSE OF DISCOURSE
_____	1. "non-white horses", "white horses"	Horses
_____	2. "non-white horses", "white horses"	Mammals
_____	3. "non-(white horses)", "white horses"	Mammals
_____	4. "white horses", "non-horses"	Animals
_____	5. "white non-horses", "non-white non-horses"	Non-horses
_____	6. "white non-horses", "non-white horses"	All real things
_____	7. "female white horses", "male white horses"	Horses
_____	8. "female white horses", "male white horses"	White horses
_____	9. "female non-(white horse)", "male white horse"	Mammals
_____	10. "non-(female white horse)", "female white horse"	Horses

13

Obversion

13A DEFINITIONS

Def. 1. Obversion of a standard categorical proposition is an immediate inference in which the conclusion differs from the premiss only in quality and in having as predicate the contradictory of the predicate of the premiss.

Examples of obversion (all valid) are: (a)"All hornbills are birds; therefore, no hornbills are non-birds". (b) "Some Greeks are non-philosophers, hence some Greeks are not philosophers". (c)"Some birds are dodoes; therefore, some birds are not non-dodoes".

Def. 2. The **obvertend** is the premiss of an obversion.

Def. 3. The **obverse** is the conclusion of an obversion.

Example (d): Premiss (obvertend): *All sharks are carnivores.*
Conclusion (obverse): *No sharks are non-carnivores.*

13B Table 13.1: Valid Obversions

OBVERTEND	OBVERSE
All S are P	No S are non-P
No S are P	All S are non-P
Some S are P	Some S are not non-P
Some S are not P	Some S are non-P

13C RULE FOR VALID OBVERSION

All inferences by obversion are valid and reversible.

13D HOW TO FIND THE OBVERSE OF A CATEGORICAL PROPOSITION

Step 1. Change the quality of the proposition. Affirmative changes to negative and negative changes to affirmative. The quantity of the proposition remains the same. When the **A** proposition is obverted, it changes to an **E** proposition, and vice versa; and when an **I** proposition is obverted, it changes to an **O** proposition, and vice versa.

Step 2. Keep the subject the same and in the same position, and negate the predicate (i.e., form the contradictory term). For instance, in example (d) the subject "sharks" remains the same and in the subject position, but the predicate of the obvertend "carnivores" is negated and becomes "non-carnivores" in the obverse.

13E FOUR COMMON ERRORS IN ATTEMPTING OBVERSION

The first common error is pseudo-obversion of **E** to the amphibolous form "All *S* are not *P*", or of **A** to "No *S* are not *P*". It should be noted that "All *S* are not *P*" and "No *S* are not *P*" are not standard forms. The correct obverse of **E** is "All *S* are non-*P*" and the correct obverse of **A** is "No *S* are non-*P*".

The second mistake is the use of prefixes that do not necessarily indicate a contradictory term. If negative prefixes other than "non-" are used, there is risk that a contradictory term will not be formed. For example, "unkind" is not contradictory to "kind". Therefore, only "non-" should be used to form a negative term. (See 12D1.)

The third error is negating part(s) of a compound term. As stated in 12C2, the contradictory of a complex term may be formed by placing parentheses around the entire term and then prefixing "non-". A complex term is not negated by negating its parts. Hence neither "non-white horses", "white non-horses", nor "non-white non-horses" is the contradictory term of "white horses." The contradictory of "white horses" is "non-(white horses)".

Negating the subject is the fourth common mistake. This error may be avoided by remembering that only the predicate of the obvertend is negated. The subject—see 13D(2) above—remains the same.

13F EXAMPLES ILLUSTRATING FINDING THE OBVERSE (13D)

PROBLEM 1. To find the obverse of the   *All* rodents *are* mammals.
A proposition:

Step 1. Change quality, quantity remains the same:	*No. . . are. . . .*
Step 2. Fill in the subject and negate the predicate:	*No* rodents *are* non-mammals.

Hence, the obverse of *All rodents are mammals* is *No rodents are non-mammals.*

PROBLEM 2. To find the obverse of the **I** proposition:	*Some* Turks *are* redheaded men.
Step 1. Change quality, quantity remains the same:	*Some. . . are not. . . .*
Step 2. Fill in the subject and negate the predicate.	*Some* Turks *are not* non-(redheaded men).

Hence, the obverse of *Some Turks are redheaded men* is *Some Turks are not non-(redheaded men).*

13G SUMMARY OF OBVERSION

1. Quantity remains the same.
2. Change quality.
3. Keep subject the same and in the same position.
4. In negating, form *true* contradictory of the predicate.

Compound predicates are placed in brackets, prefixed by "non-". (see 13E, problem 2).

We diagram obversions as follows:

$$A sp \overset{ob}{\leftrightarrow} E s\bar{p} \quad E sp \overset{ob}{\leftrightarrow} A s\bar{p}$$

$$I sp \overset{ob}{\leftrightarrow} O s\bar{p} \quad O sp \overset{ob}{\leftrightarrow} I\, s\bar{p}$$

This diagram shows that when **A** proposition is obverted, it changes to an **E** proposition, and vice versa; and when an **I** proposition is obverted, it changes to an **O** proposition, and vice versa. It also shows that we keep the subject the same and negate the predicate. The bar over a letter is read as "non-". Hence "$\bar{p}$" is read as "non-p."

Exercises for Chapter 13

EX 13A–D. Select the most appropriate letter for each question.

_____ 1. Obversion is a (an): (a) argument having two or more premisses. (b) kind of immediate inference. (c) invalid conversion. (d) false convertend.

_____ 2. An obvertend is: (a) a false obverse. (b) an omitted obverse. (c) the conclusion of an obversion. (d) the premiss of an obversion.

_____ 3. All inferences by obversion: (a) contain a negative conclusion. (b) contain a negative premiss. (c) are valid. (d) are by limitation.

_____ 4. If the obvertend is negative, the obverse must be: (a) universal. (b) particular. (c) affirmative. (d) negative.

_____ 5. If the obvertend is universal, the obverse must be: (a) universal. (b) particular. (c) affirmative. (d) negative.

_____ 6. The subject of the obverse is the: (a) predicate of the obvertend. (b) negation of the predicate of the obvertend. (c) negation of the subject of the obvertend. (d) subject of the obvertend.

_____ 7. If the premiss and the conclusion of an immediate inference are of opposite quantity, then the inference: (a) must be invalid. (b) cannot be an obversion. (c) must be valid. (d) must be an obversion.

_____ 8. The predicate of an obverse is the: (a) negation of the predicate of the obvertend. (b) negation of the subject of the obvertend. (c) subject of the obvertend. (d) predicate of the obvertend.

_____ 9. The number of standard categorical propositions in an obversion is: (a) one. (b) two. (c) three. (d) four.

_____ 10. The obverse of a universal negative is a: (a) universal affirmative. (b) particular affirmative. (c) particular negative. (d) nonstandard categorical proposition.

EX 13B–E. Are the following inferences valid obversions? Answer "Y" for "yes" or "N" for "no".

_____ 1. All men are mortals; therefore, no non-men are mortals.

_____ 2. No camelopards are wombats, hence all camelopards are not wombats.

_____ 3. Some rodents are mice, so some rodents are not non-mice.

_____ 4. All potted plants are flora, hence no potted plants are not flora.

_____ 5. Some Martians are brilliant logicians; therefore, some Martians are not non-brilliant logicians.

_____ 6. No acts of God are immoral acts, hence all acts of God are moral acts.

_____ 7. All priests are theists, hence no priests are atheists.

_____ 8. Some mongooses are not geese, hence some mongooses are non-geese.

_____ 9. Some stallions are black horses, hence some stallions are non-(black horses).

_____ 10. All non-people are non-fanatics, therefore no non-people are fanatics.

EX 13D–F. Find the obverse of the following propositions.

_____ 1. All lobsters are crustaceans.

_____ 2. All swan maidens are beautiful women.

_____ 3. Some cudgels are museum pieces.

_____ 4. No flintlocks are modern weapons.

_____ 5. Some limericks are poems that children enjoy.

_____ 6. Some landlords are not kindhearted men.

_____ 7. Some expensive curios are objects that weigh less than an ounce.

_____ 8. No czars are people who had to work for a living.

_____ 9. All husky lumberjacks who are hearty eaters are men.

_____ 10. Some blind mice and white whales are neurotic animals.

_____ 11. Some lunatics are not Pentagon personnel.

_____ 12. All persons who live by the sword are persons who will die by the sword.

_____ 13. Some sword swallowers are men with sore throats.

_____ 14. No fireflies are dangerous insects.

_____ 15. All camel drivers are men who have infinite patience.

14

Contraposition

Next to conversion and obversion, contraposition is the best known of the immediate inferences from standard categorical propositions.[1]

14A DEFINITIONS

Def. 1. Contraposition of a standard categorical proposition is an immediate inference in which the conclusion contains the terms of the premiss, negated and in reverse order, and has the same quality. (See 12B, How to Form the Contradictory of a Term.)

Examples of contraposition (not all of them valid) are: *All snakes are reptiles; therefore, all non-reptiles are non-snakes. Some birds are hornbills, hence all non-hornbills are non-birds. No bats are non-mammals; therefore, some mammals are not non-bats.*

Def. 2. A **contrapositive** is the conclusion of a contraposition.

Def. 3. A **simple contraposition** is a contraposition in which the conclusion has the same quantity (and quality) as the premiss. The conclusion of a simple contraposition is called the **simple contrapositive.**

Def. 4. A **contraposition by limitation** is a contraposition in which the quantity changes from universal to particular (the quality remaining the same).

Def. 5. To **find** (or **take**) **the contrapositive** of a standard categorical proposition is to find the strongest valid contrapositive if any, i.e., the simple contrapositive if it is valid, otherwise the contrapositive by limitation if that is valid.

Though there is some kind of contrapositive for any standard categorical, we are usually interested only in the valid forms, and where (as for the A) there is more than one valid form, we are usually interested only in the strongest valid contrapositive.

14B CONTRAPOSITIVES (VALID AND INVALID)

Table 14.1: Contrapositives (Valid and Invalid)

Premiss	Simple Contrapositive	Contrapositive by Limitation
All S are P	All non-P are non-S	Some non-P are non-S
No S are P	No non-P are non-S	Some non-P are not non-S
Some S are P	Some non-P are non-S	None
Some S are not P	Some non-P are not non-S	None

Taking a form in the second column as premiss, the corresponding form in the first column is its simple contrapositive. We may start with just one of the terms negated. The simple contrapositive of "All non-S are P" is "All non-P are S"; and so on.

(Our definition counts as contraposition an inference from "Some S are P" to "All non-P are non-S", and from "Some S are not P" to "No non-P are non-S". Such strengthened inferences would be invalid if the propositions are contingent and they are very rare.)

14C VALID CONTRAPOSITION

Not all contrapositions are valid inferences, though all contrapositions by limitation are valid (assuming, as we do when obversion and contraposition are add to Aristotelian logic, that each term and also its negation denote something).

14C1 How to Find the Contrapositive of a Standard Categorical Proposition. Contraposition, by definition, negates both terms and changes their order. This can be done by obverting, then converting, then obverting again.

a *Steps for Finding the Contrapositive.*

Step 1. Obvert the proposition.

Step 2. Find the strongest valid converse of the obverse (if any: see 11D).

Step 3. Obvert the result of step 2.

If no valid conversion is possible in step 2, there is no valid contrapositive. Note that any contrapositive obtained by the above three steps must be the conclusion of a valid inference, since each step is a valid inference.

b *Short Method of Finding the Contrapositive.*

The **A** and **O** propositions: Negate subject and predicate, interchange them.

The **E** proposition: Negate subject and predicate, interchange them, reduce quantity. The result is an **O** proposition.

The **I** proposition has no valid contrapositive.

14C2 Examples of Finding the Contrapositive by Steps

PROBLEM 1. To find the contrapositive of the **E** proposition *No prairie dogs are auks.*

Premiss (to be contraposed): *No prairie dogs are auks.* (a)

Step 1. Obvert (a): *All prairie dogs are non-auks.* (b)

Step 2. Convert (b): *Some non-auks are prairie dogs.* (c)

Step 3. Obvert (c): *Some non-auks are not non-(prairie dogs).*

In step 2, the strongest valid converse is a converse by limitation, hence the quantity of the proposition is reduced. The result is a contrapositive by limitation.

PROBLEM 2. To find the contrapositive of the **I** proposition *Some camels are dromedaries.*

Premiss (to be contraposed): *Some camels are dromedaries.* (a)

Step 1. Obvert (a): *Some camels are not non-dromedaries.* (b)

Step 2. Cannot be performed, since the **O** proposition has no valid converse. Hence, the premiss cannot be validly contraposed.

Table 14.2: Strongest Valid Contrapositive

Premiss	The Strongest Valid Contrapositive
All S are P	All non-P are non-S
No S are P	Some non-P are not non-S
Some S are P	None
Some S are not P	Some non-P are not non-S

Table 14.3: Valid Contrapositives

Premiss	Simple Contrapositive	Contrapositive by Limitation
All *S* are *P*	All non-*P* are non-*S*	Some non-*P* are non-*S*
No *S* are *P*	(Not valid)	Some non-*P* are not non-*S*
Some *S* are *P*	(Not valid)	None
Some *S* are not *P*	Some non-*P* are not non-*S*	None

As the table shows, there is a valid simple contrapositive only of **A** and **O** propositions. (Compare this with the table of valid conversion, 11D2.) That there is no valid simple contrapositive of the **E** and **I** propositions, and no valid contrapositive of any kind for the **I** proposition may be demonstrated by counterexample.[2]

Exercises for Chapter 14

EX 14A, I. Choose the appropriate letter for each question.

_____ 1. The simple contrapositive of an **A** proposition is an **A, E, I, O.**

_____ 2. Contraposition is an inference that is: (a) always valid. (b) never valid. (c) sometimes valid. (d) valid only if the premiss is a universal.

_____ 3. A contraposition by limitation is a contraposition where: (a) both propositions have the same quantity. (b) both propositions have the same subject. (c) the premiss is particular and the conclusion is universal. (d) the premiss is universal and the conclusion is particular.

_____ 4. The propositional form that has no valid simple contrapositive and no valid contrapositive by limitation is: **A, E, I, O.**

_____ 5. The two propositional forms that have a valid simple contrapositive are: (a) **A** and **O**, (b) **E** and **I**, (c) **A** and **E**, (d) **I** and **O**.

EX 14, II. Place "V" for valid contrapositive, "I" for invalid contrapositive, or "Not C" for "not a contrapositive" in each blank. Also place "L" in the blank if it is a contrapositive by limitation.

_____ 1. All men are mortals; therefore all non-men are non-mortals.

_____ 2. Some reptiles are not birds, hence some non-birds are not non-reptiles.

_____ 3. No guys are dolls, so some non-dolls are not non-guys.

_____ 4. All spices are condiments, hence all non-condiments are non-spices.

_____ 5. Some rodents are mice, therefore some non-rodents are not non-mice.

_____ 6. Some batteries are not dry cells, so some non-(dry cells) are non-batteries.

_____ 7. No bees are birds, therefore, no non-birds are non-bees.

_____ 8. All one-eyed cats are half-blind felines, hence some non-(half-blind felines) are non-(one-eyed cats).

_____ 9. Some jewels are diamonds, so some non-diamonds are non-jewels.

_____ 10. No bats are birds, so all non-birds are non-bats.

EX 14, III. Find the contrapositive of the following propositions:

1. Some mammals are baffled bats.
2. No logicians are fishmongers.
3. Some cataleptics are intelligent people.
4. All turtles are patient animals.
5. Some Arabs are not followers of Islam.
6. No chaplains are acknowledged atheists.
7. Some frustrated sociologists are aggressive people.
8. Some four-wheeled carriages are not broughams.
9. All Ceylonese are islanders.
10. No men are demigods.
11. Some non-Germans are not atomic scientists.
12. Some non-parrots are non-birds.
13. All three-legged elephants are creatures that should be pitied.
14. No songless birds are bullfinches.
15. Some binaries are not objects visible to the naked eye.

15

Inversion and Partial Inversion

"Inversion" is an odd sort of inference; no one but a traditional logician would think of making it. But it has had a startling result; some logicians, examining the "partial inverse" of an **A** proposition, discovered that they had been maintaining an inconsistent doctrine.

15A INVERSION

15A1 Definitions.

Def. 1 Inversion of a standard categorical proposition is an immediate inference in which the conclusion has the same quality as the premise and has as subject the contradictory of the premiss's subject and has as predicate the contradictory of the premiss's predicate.

Examples of inversion (not all of which are valid) are: *All octagons are polygons; therefore, some non-octagons are non-polygons*, *No rabbis are priests, hence, no non-rabbis are non-priests*, and *Some parrots are birds, therefore, all non-parrots are non-birds.*

Def. 2. An **inverse** is the conclusion of an inversion.

Def. 3. A **simple inversion** is an inversion in which the inverse has the same quantity as the premiss. The conclusion of a simple inversion is called the **simple inverse.**

Def. 4. Inversion by limitation is an inversion in which the quantity changes from universal (premiss) to particular (conclusion).

Table 15:1: Inversions

Premiss	Simple Inverse	Inverse by Limitation
All S are P	All non-S are non-P	Some non-S are non-P
No S are P	No non-S are non-P	Some non-S are not non-P
Some S are P	Some non-S are non-P	None
Some S are not P	Some non-S are not non-P	None

15A2 Valid Inversions.

Table 15.2: Valid Inversions

Premiss	Inverse by Limitation
All S are P	Some non-S are non-P
No S are P	Some non-S are not non-P
Some S are P	None
Some S are not P	None

As the table shows, no simple inversion is a valid inference, and all inversions by limitation are valid inferences. Proof that simple inversion in not a valid inference can be shown by counterexample.

15A3 The Inverse.

Def. 5. The **inverse** of a standard categorical proposition is the inverse that the proposition validly implies.

When we say "take the inverse" or "find the inverse" we refer to the valid inverse. (See Table of Valid Inversions, 15A2.)

15A4 How to Find the (Valid) Inverse.

The inverse of the **A** proposition is obtained by taking its contrapositive and then converting.

$$\text{All } S \text{ are } P \xleftrightarrow{oco} \text{All non-}P \text{ are non-}S \xrightarrow[pa]{c} \text{Some non-}S \text{ are non-}P.$$

The inverse of *All S are P* is *Some non-S are non-P.*

The inverse of the **E** proposition is obtained by taking its converse and then contraposing.

$$\text{No } S \text{ are } P \xleftrightarrow{c} \text{No } P \text{ are } S \xrightarrow{oco} \text{Some non-}S \text{ are not non-}P.$$

The inverse of *No S are P* is *Some non-S are not non-P.*

A simple method of finding the (valid) inverse of a universal proposition (**A** or **E**) is to reduce its quantity, keep quality the same, and replace its subject and predicate with their contradictory terms.

15B PARTIAL INVERSION

15B1 Definitions.

Def. 6 Partial inversion of a standard categorical proposition is an immediate inference in which the conclusion is the opposite quality of the premiss and had as subject the contradictory of the premiss's subject and has as predicate the premiss's predicate.

Examples of partial inversion (not all of which are valid) are: *All martins are mammals; therefore no non-martins are mammals*, *No porbeagles are beagles, hence, some non-porbeagles are beagles*, and *Some pessimists are alcoholics; therefore, some non-pessimists are not alcoholics.*

Def. 7. A **partial inverse** is the conclusion of a partial inversion.

Def. 8. A **simple partial inversion** is a partial inversion in which the inverse has the same quantity as the premiss. The conclusion of a simple partial inversion is called the **simple partial inverse.**

Def. 9. A **partial inversion of limitation** is an inversion in which the quantity changes from universal (premiss) to particular (conclusion). The conclusion of a partial inversion by limitation is called a **partial inverse by limitation.**

15B2 Valid Partial Inversions.

Table 15.3: Valid and Invalid Partial Inversions

Premiss	Simple Partial Inverse (all invalid)	Partial Inverse by Limitation (all valid)
All S are P	No non-S are P	Some non-S are not P
No S are P	All non-S are P	Some non-S are P
Some S are P	Some non-S are not P	None
Some S are not P	Some non-S are P	None

As the table shows, no simple partial inversion is a valid inference, and all partial inversions by limitation are valid inferences.

15B3 The Partial Inverse.

Def. 10. The **partial inverse** of a standard categorical proposition is the partial inverse that the proposition validity implies.

When we say "take the partial inverse" or "find the partial inverse" we refer to the valid partial inverse.

15B4 How to Find the (Valid) Partial Inverse. The partial inverse of a proposition may be found by observing it inverse. Particular propositions, since they have no inverse, have no partial inverse.

The partial inverse of the **A** proposition is formed by obverting its inverse.

$$\text{All } S \text{ are } P \xrightarrow{\text{inverse}} \text{Some non-}S \text{ are non-}P \xleftrightarrow{o} \text{Some non-}S \text{ are not } P.$$

The partial inverse of *All S are P* is *Some non-S are not P*.

Or the partial inverse of the **A** may be formed by the three steps of contraposition, conversion by limitation, and obversion:

$$\text{All } S \text{ are } P \xrightarrow{oco} \text{All non-}P \text{ are non-}S \xrightarrow[pa]{c} \text{Some non-}S \text{ are non-}P$$
$$\updownarrow o$$
$$\text{Some non-}S \text{ are not } P.$$

The partial inverse of the **E** proposition is formed by obverting its inverse.

$$\text{No } S \text{ are } P \xrightarrow{\text{inverse}} \text{Some non-}S \text{ are non-}P \xleftrightarrow{o} \text{Some non-}S \text{ are } P$$

The partial inverse of *No S are P* is *Some non-S are P*.

Or it may be formed by the three steps of conversion, obversion and conversion by limitation.

$$\text{No } S \text{ are } P \xleftrightarrow{c} \text{No } P \text{ are } S \xleftrightarrow{o} \text{All } P \text{ are non-}S \xrightarrow[pa]{c} \text{Some non-}S \text{ are } P.$$

A simple method of finding the partial inverse of a universal proposition (**A** or **E**) is to reduce its quantity, replace subject with its contradictory term, and leave predicate unchanged.

Exercises for Chapter 15

EX 15A, I. Place the appropriate letter in each blank.

_____ 1. The valid inverse (simple or by limitation) has: (a) the same quantity as its premiss. (b) the same quality as its premiss. (c) the opposite quantity as its premiss. (d) the opposite quality as its premiss.

_____ 2. The number of distinct terms in a valid inversion is: (a) one. (b) two. (c) three. (d) four.

_____ 3. The number of negative terms a valid inversion must contain is: (a) one. (b) two. (c) three. (d) four.

_____ 4. All simple inversions are: (a) valid inferences. (b) invalid inferences. (c) inferences with two premisses. (d) inferences with more than two premisses.

_____ 5. All inversions by limitations are: (a) valid inferences. (b) invalid inferences. (c) inferences that have a particular premiss. (d) inferences that have a particular conclusion.

EX 15A, II. Find the (valid) inverse of the following propositions.

1. No rabbits are raccoons.
2. All dinghies are boats.
3. No cowbirds are hornbills.
4. Some silly sycophants are simpering supervisors.
5. All palliums are cloaks.
6. No ocelots are non-cats.
7. All non-introverts are non-psychotics.
8. Some fungi are not non-mushrooms.
9. All non-lions are canines.
10. No pugilists are non-boxers.

EX 15B, I. Place the appropriate letter in each blank.

_____ 1. The valid partial inverse of a proposition may be found by: (a) obverting its inverse. (b) converting its inverse. (c) inverting its obverse. (d) obverting its converse.

_____ 2. All partial inversions are: (a) valid. (b) invalid. (c) immediate inferences. (d) mediated inferences.

_____ 3. A proposition has no valid partial inverse by limitation if the proposition has no: (a) simple converse. (b) valid inverse by limitation. (c) obverse. (d) simple contrapositive.

_____ 4. The two propositional forms that have no valid partial inverse are: (a) **A** and **E**. (b) **I** and **O**. (c) **A** and **O**. (d) **E** and **I**.

_____ 5. In a partial inverse by limitation the premiss and conclusion: (a) have the same quantity and quality. (b) have the same quantity, but differ in quality. (c) have the same quality, but differ in quantity. (d) differ in both quantity and quality.

EX 15B, II. Find the (valid) partial inverse of the following propositions.

1. All dabchicks are grebes.
2. All cabals are secret organizations.
3. Some caricaturists are insecure people.
4. Some dinosaurs are not vegetarians.
5. No cacophonies are pleasant sounds.
6. No housewives are non-females.
7. Some monks are not cenobites.
8. Some non-lawyers are not non-photographers.
9. All great works of art are valuable objects.
10. All dendriform objects are things shaped like trees.

16

Tables of Immediate Inferences

16A TRADITIONAL IMMEDIATE INFERENCES BY COMBINED CONVERSIONS AND OBVERSIONS

16A1 Traditional Immediate Inferences from the A Proposition.

I	II	III
1) **All S are P (A)** $\xrightarrow[pa]{c}$	Some P are S (A^c) $\xrightarrow{c}$	Some S are P (A^{cc})
(*Premiss*)	(*converse per acc.*)	(*subaltern*)
↓ ob	↓ ob	↓ ob
2) No S are $\bar{P}$ (A^o)	Some P are not $\bar{S}$ (A^{co})	Some S are not $\bar{P}$ (A^{cco})
(*obverse*)	(*converse obverted*)	(*subaltern overted*)
↓ c		
3) No $\bar{P}$ are S (A^{oc})	Some $\bar{S}$ are not P (A^{ococo})	Some $\bar{P}$ are not S (A^{ococco})
(*obverse converted*)	(*partial inverse*)	(*subaltern of* A^{oc})
↓ ob	↑ ob	↑ ob
4) All $\bar{P}$ are $\bar{S}$ (A^{oco}) $\xrightarrow[pa]{c}$	Some $\bar{S}$ are $\bar{P}$ (A^{ococ}) $\xrightarrow{c}$	Some $\bar{P}$ are $\bar{S}$ (A^{ococc})
(*contrapositive*)	(*inverse*)	(*contrapositive p.a.*)

16 A2 Traditional Immediate Inferences from the E Proposition.

(obtained by substituting non-P for P, or P for non-P, in table above)

I	II	III
1) All S are $\bar{P}$ (E^o) $\xrightarrow[pa]{c}$	Some $\bar{P}$ are S (E^{oc}) $\xrightarrow{c}$	Some S are $\bar{P}$ (E^{occ})
(*obverse*)	(*obverse converted*)	(*subaltern obverted*)
↑ ob	↓ ob	↓ ob
2) **No S are P (E)**	Some $\bar{P}$ are not $\bar{S}$ (E^{oco})	Some S are not P (E^{occo})
(*Premiss*)	(*contrapositive p.a.*)	(*subaltern*)
↓ c		
3) No P are S (E^c)	Some $\bar{S}$ are not $\bar{P}$ (E^{coco})	Some P are not S (E^{cocco})
(*converse*)	(*inverse*)	(*converse per acc.*)
↓ ob	↑ ob	↑ ob
4) All P are $\bar{S}$ (E^{co}) $\xrightarrow[pa]{c}$	Some $\bar{S}$ are P (E^{coc}) $\xrightarrow{c}$	Some P are $\bar{S}$ (E^{cocc})
(*converse obverted*)	(*partial inverse*)	(*subaltern of* E^{co})

Analysis of Table for **A**.

   i Column I: universals. Columns II and III: particulars.
  ii Columns I and II: obtained by alternate obversion and conversion from premiss.
Column III: Each is subaltern of universal in same row; here obtained through two successive conversions.
 iii Row 1: **A** and **I** forms in *S* and *P*; **I**-forms obtained by conversions from **A**-form.
  iv Row 4: **A** and **I** forms with both terms negated; **I**-forms obtained by conversions from **A**-form.
   v Rows 2 and 3: **E** and **O** forms with one term negated; could go by contraposition from column I to column II, and from column II to column III.
  vi Each form in rows 1 and 3 has its obverse directly below it.
 vii Each form in row 2 has its simple converse directly below it (whether inferrable or not).
viii Each form in row 1 has its simple contrapositive below it in row 4 (whether inferrable or not).

Analysis of Table for **E**.

Same as analysis of Table for **A**, *except:*
iii' Row 1: **A** and **I** forms in *S* and non-*P*.
iv' Row 4: **A** and **I** forms in non-*S* and *P*.
 v' Rows 2 and 3: **E** and **O** forms with zero or terms negated.

16A3 Traditional Immediate Inferences from the I Proposition.

1) **Some *S* are *P*** (**I**) $\xrightarrow{c}$ Some *P* are *S* (I^c)
   (*Premiss*)   (*converse*)
       ↓ ob   ↓ ob
2) Some *S* are not $\bar{P}$ (I°) Some *P* are not $\bar{S}$ (I^{co})
   (*obverse*)   (*converse obverted*)

16A4 Traditional Immediate Inferences from the O Proposition.

(obtained by substituting non-*P* for *P*, or *P* for non-*P*, in table for **I**)

1) Some *S* are $\bar{P}$ (O°) $\xrightarrow{c}$ Some $\bar{P}$ are *S* (O^{oc})
   (*obverse*)   (*obverse converted*)
       ↑ ob   ↓ ob
2) **Some *S* are not *P*** (**O**) Some $\bar{P}$ are not $\bar{S}$ (O^{oco})
   (*Premiss*)   (*contrapositive*)

Analysis of Tables for **I** *and* **O**.

i Row 1: affirmatives.   Row 2: negatives.
ii Each form in row 1 has its obverse directly below it.

The four tables 16A1–4 were suggested by those in F. Chapman & P. Henle, *Fundamentals of Logic* (Scribner's 1933), page 53.

16B THE TRADITIONAL IMMEDIATE INFERENCES, LISTED BY OPERATIONS

	I	II	III	IV
Premise (*X*)	A*sp*	E*sp*	I*sp*	O*sp*
1. Converse (*X*ᶜ)	I*ps*	E*ps*	I*ps*	—
2. Obverse (*X*°)	E*sp̄*	A*sp̄*	O*sp̄*	I*sp̄*
3. Converse obverted (*X*ᶜᵒ)	O*p̄s*	A*p̄s*	O*p̄s*	—
4. Obverse converted (*X*ᵒᶜ)	E*p̄s*	I*p̄s*	—	I*p̄s*
5. Contrapositive (*X*ᵒᶜᵒ)	A*p̄s̄*	O*p̄s̄*	—	O*p̄s̄*
6. Inverse (Aᵒᶜᵒᶜ, Eᶜᵒᶜᵒ)	I*sp*	O*sp*	—	—
7. Partial inverse (Aᵒᶜᵒᶜᵒ, Eᶜᵒᶜ)	O*s̄p*	I*s̄p*	—	—
8. Converse *per accidens*	I*ps*	O*ps*	—	—
9. Subaltern	I*sp*	O*sp*	—	—
10. Subaltern obverted	O*sp̄*	I*sp̄*	—	—
11. Subaltern of converse obverted	—	I*p̄s*	—	—
12. Subaltern of obverse converted	O*p̄s*	—	—	—
13. Subaltern of contrapositive	I*p̄s̄*	—	—	—

A dash occurs where the operation cannot be validly applied to the given categorical form. Table suggested by that in Keynes, *Formal Logic*, 4th ed. p. 140.

Figure 16.1: The Octagon of Opposition[1]

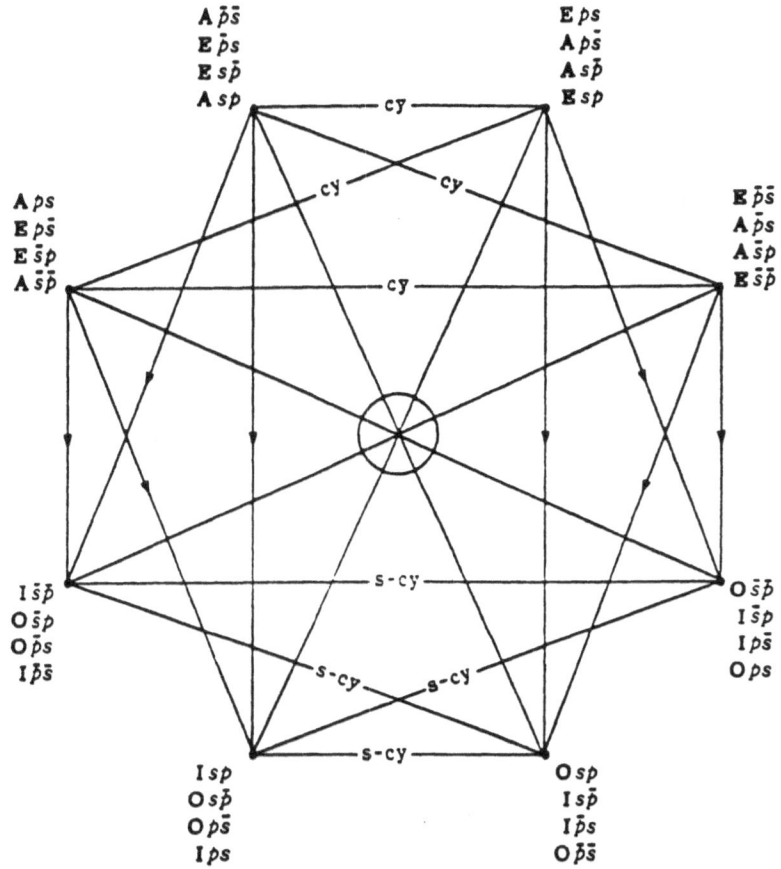

The key to reading the octagon is:

a. Contrariety: —— cy ——
b. Subcontrariety: —— s-cy ——
c. Implication: ——▶
d. Contradiction: ——⊝——
e. Independence: Categorical forms on corners not connected by a straight line are independent of each other.

The purpose of the octagon of opposition is to show in one diagram the logical relations between the thirty-two categoricals in standard form.

---

1. Edward A. Hacker, "The Octagon of Opposition," *Notre Dame Journal of Formal Logic*, XVI, No. 3 (July 1975), 352. Reprinted by permission of *Notre Dame Journal of Formal Logic*.

17

Relations

Relations play an indispensable role in the inference of Aristotelian logic, as in all deductive systems. Relations such as *deducible-from, equivalent-to, contradictory-of,* and others, must be used in all reasoning.

Though the authority of Aristotle is blamed for the dominance of the subject-predicate analysis of propositions in logic and philosophy—not without reason—it was Aristotle who began the study of the logic of relations, as he began so many studies. Discussing relative terms such as "double" and "master" in his *Categories*, he points out that every relative term has its correlative: "By the term 'slave' we mean the slave *of a master;* by the term 'master', the master *of a slave*". Elsewhere he deals with some arguments containing relational propositions. It is remarkable that for over two thousand years very little was added to Aristotle's beginning. De Morgan in the 1850s made the decisive breakthrough—the first successful systematic study of relations in general.

This chapter will not go very far into the subject. It introduces some terms that are useful for analyzing relations in logic and all other fields.

17A SOME BASIC CONCEPTS

We take the term *relation* as basic; we give an explanation rather than a definition in the strict sense.

> **Def. 1.** A **relation** is a connection of any sort between two or more objects.

The objects need not exist at the same time; for example, Queen Victoria descended from George I, though he was dead long before she was born. The objects may be abstractions such as numbers.

The fact or possibility that a relation holds between certain objects is expressed by a relational proposition.

Def. 2. A **relational phrase** (or **relator**) is a word or phrase that expresses a relation.

In the following examples of relational propositions, the relational phrase is italicized:

Cassius *was an object of suspicion to* Caesar.

Caesar *suspected* Cassius.

Cassius *was suspected by* Caesar.

Caesar *was in* the senate house.

The key word in the relational phrase may be a noun or noun phrase, an adjective, a verb (active or passive), or a preposition.

It is not incorrect to analyze such relational propositions as subject-predicate propositions, as is usually done in traditional logic. "Brutus stabs Caesar" may be taken as "Brutus [is one who] stabs Caesar", analyzed as "Brutus |is| one who stabs Caesar". This analysis is adequate for some purposes; but for considering its relation to "Caesar is stabbed by Brutus", for example, it is inadequate.

Def. 3. The **degree** of a relation is the maximum number of objects it relates in a given occurrence.

A relation may be dyadic, triadic, tetradic, and so on. (It gets much harder to find examples as the number increases; our knowledge of Greek roots for the names may give out, too.)

(a) Dyadic (binary, two-place) relations were expressed above.

(b) Triadic (ternary, three-place) relations are expressed by the italicized phrases:

Judas *was paid* thirty pieces of silver *to identify* Jesus.
New Haven *is between* Boston *and* New York.
Aristotle *distinguished* "Pleasure is good" *from* "Pleasure is the good".

(c) Tetradic (quaternary, four-place) relations:

I *bought* the book *at* the bookstore *for* ninety-five cents.
I *substituted* "man" *for* the letter "S" *in* the formula.

A few logicians generalize "relations" to include properties as "monadic relations"; we follow the more usual usage. Henceforth, we deal almost exclusively with dyadic relations.

Def. 4. The **field** of a relation R is the class of all objects that have the relation R to something or to which something has the relation R.

Thus the field of the relation *father-of* consists of whatever is or has a father.

17B CONVERSE RELATION AND RELATIONAL CONVERSION

17B1 Definitions.

Def. 5. The **converse relation** or **converse** of a given relation R is the relation that holds between any x and any y if and only if relation R holds between y and x.

The converse of the realtion *less-than* is *greater-than;* the converse of *parent-of* is *child-of*. We may also speak of the relational phrase for the converse of a relation as the converse of the relational phrase for the original relation. Thus the phrase "is greater than" is the converse of "is less than".

Def. 6. Correlative expressions (words, phrases) are pairs of expressions (words, phrases) such that one expression of a pair stands for a relation and the other for its converse relation.

Def. 7. Relational conversion or **immediate inference by converse relation** is inference, from a premise stating that a is in relation R to b, to the conclusion that b is in the converse relation of R to a. Here "a" and "b" may be replaced by singular terms; one of them may be replaced by a quantified general term such as "Every man" or "Some married men".

For example, such inferences are:

(a) Giap captured Dien Bien Phu;
therefore, Dien Bien Phu was captured by Giap.

(b) Giap took Dien Bien Phu;
∴ Dien Bien Phu fell to Giap.

Both forms are valid. But the first is formally valid, by the relation of active and passive forms of a transitive verb (see below). The second is valid semantically, not formally, that is, it is valid by virtue of the meaning of the verbs. An example with a quantified noun:

(c) Lieutenant Fuzz outranks every noncommissioned officer; therefore, every noncommissioned officer is outranked by Lieutenant Fuzz.

However, if both a and b in definition 7 are replaced by quantified terms, the inference may not be valid. For example, from the premiss "Every teacher teaches some student", there does not follow a conclusion "Some student is taught by every teacher" (in the most natural sense of the latter, that there is some one student who is taught by every teacher).

17B2 Relational Conversion with Verbs. Relational conversion can be effected in a regular manner with a transitive verb, by passage from active to passive, or vice versa.

Where V stands for a transitive verb, the following pattern of inference is formally valid and reversible:

$a \; V \; b$;
∴ b is V'd by a.

For example:

(d) The Yezidis worship the Devil;
∴ the Devil is worshipped by the Yezidis.[1]

Examples (a) and (c) under definition 7 are also examples of this pattern, except that (a) is in the past tense.

17B3 Relational Conversion with Adjectives. Where Ad stands for an adjective, the following pattern of inference is formally valid and reversible:

a is more Ad than b (or a is Ad-er than b);
∴ b is less Ad than a.

For example:

(e) The sofa is more comfortable than the chair;
∴ the chair is less comfortable than the sofa.

17B4 Relational Conversion with Nouns. Finding the correlative of a relational noun may be a little tricky, as Aristotle pointed out.[2] The converse of the relation *father-of* is not *son-of*, because, if John is father of Pat, Pat may be a daughter of John. Neither is the converse *child-of*; although if a is the father of b, b is child of a. The relational conversion must be reversible; however, if b is child of a, it doesn't follow that a is father of b.

If we analyze "a is father of b" as "a is male parent of b", we see the relational converse may be expressed: "b is child of the male a", or "b is child of (its) father a", or "b has a as father". The last of these forms does not require any semantic analysis of "father", hence is best for logical generalization.

In general, if *RN* stands for a relational noun or noun phrase, then the following pattern of inference is valid and reversible:

a is *RN* of b;
therefore, b has a as *RN*.

For example: "Tom is (an) uncle of Jean; therefore, Jean has Tom as uncle". "Lindsay is mayor of New York; therefore, New York has Lindsay as mayor".

In practice, when a simpler or more idiomatic expression is known for the converse relation, this will ordinarily be used. Thus one would use "y is child of x" rather than "y has x as parent" for relational conversion of "x is parent of y". But for *formal* logic we need to be able to express relationships according to formal patterns, without reference to the meaning of concrete words.

However, if both a and b are replaced by quantified terms, the inference may not be valid. For example, from the premiss "Every teacher is god of some student", there does not follow a conclusion "Some student has as god every teacher" (in the most natural sense of the latter, that there is some one student to whom every teacher is a god).

17B5 Relational Conversion with Prepositions. Where *prep* stands for a preposition, and b for a concrete singular term or quantified general term, the following schema is commonly valid and reversible:

a is *prep* b;
∴ b has a *prep* it (him, her).

For example: "The pencil is on the table; therefore, the table has the pencil on it". "The King is in the counting room; therefore, the counting room has the King in it".

With all formulas of 17B, but especially with prepositions, one must watch out for idiomatic forms that do not conform to rule. It is important that the value of b after *prep* be a concrete singular term or a quantified general term. "The motion is in order" cannot be transformed by this formula; nor can "The train is on time". These are excluded by our restriction on substitution for b.

17C SOME PROPERTIES OF RELATIONS

17C1 Transitivity. Every dyadic relation is transitive, intransitive, or mediotransitive.

> **Def. 8.** A relation is **transitive** iffi, whenever it relates x to y and y to z, it also relates x to z. In other words, relation R is transitive iffi, for every x, y, and z, if $x R y$ and $y R z$ then $x R z$.

Here x, y, and z need not be distinct. If Andrew is brother of Bob, and Bob is brother of Charlie, it doesn't follow that Andrew is brother of Charlie; for "Charlie" may be Andrew's nickname. So *brother-of* is not a transitive relation. Examples of transitive relations are deducibility and equality:

For every p, q, and r, if p is deducible from q, and q is deducible from r, then p is deducible from r.

For every x, y, z, if x equals y and y equals z, then x equals z.

> **Def. 9.** A relation is **intransitive** iffi, whenever it relates x to y and y to z, it does not relate x to z. That is: relation R is intransitive iffi, for all x, y, and z, if $x R y$ and $y R z$ then it is false that $x R z$.

Examples of intransitive relations are *father-of* and *contradictory-of*:

For all x, y, z, if x is the father of y and y is the father of z, then x is not the father of z.

For all p, q, r, if p is the contradictory of q, and q is the contradictory of r, then p is not the contradictory of r.

> **Def. 10.** A relation is **medio-transitive** iffi it is neither transitive nor intransitive.[3]

Hence relation R is medio-transitive iffi for some x, y, and s, $x R y$ and $y R z$, but it is false that $x R z$; and for some x, y, and z, $x R y$ and $y R z$ and $x R z$.

Examples of medio-transitive relations are *loves and incompatible-with* (for terms).

To some cases, a loves b and b loves c, but a does not love c; so the relation is not transitive. In some cases, d loves e and e loves f and d loves f; so the relation is not intransitive.

Red is incompatible with blue, and blue is incompatible with crimson, but red is not incompatible with crimson; therefore *incompatible-with* is not transitive. Red is incompatible with blue, blue with green, and red with green; therefore the relation is not intransitive.

17C2 Symmetry. Every dyadic relation is symmetrical, asymmetrical, or mediosymmetrical.

> **Def. 11.** A relation is **symmetrical** iffi whenever it relates x to y it also relates y to x. That is, relation R is symmetrical iffi, for all x and y, if $x R y$ then $y R x$.

Examples of symmetrical relations are *equals* (for numbers) and *contradictory-of* (for propositions or terms).

For all a and b, if a equals b, then b equals a.

For all p and q, if p is the contradictory of q, then q is the contradictory of p.

> **Def. 12.** A relation is **asymmetrical** iffi, when it relates x to y, it does not relate y to x. That is, relation R is asymmetrical iffi, for all x and y, if $x R y$ then it is false that $y R x$.[4]

Examples of asymmetrical relations are *subaltern-of* and *father-of*.

For all p and q, if p is the subaltern of q, then q is not the subaltern of p.

For all a and b, if a is father of b, then b is not father of a.

> **Def. 13.** A relation is **medio-symmetrical** if it is neither symmetrical nor asymmetrical.

Hence relation R is medio-symmetrical iffi, for some x and y, $x R y$ but it is false that $y R x$, and for some (other) x and y, $x R y$ and $y R x$.

Examples of medio-symmetrical relations are *deducible-from* and *loves*.

In some cases, p is deducible from q but q is not deducible from p; in other cases, p is deducible from q and q is deducible from p.

17C3 Reflexiveness. Every dyadic relation is reflexive, irreflexive, or medioreflexive.

Def. 14. A relation is *reflexive* iffi every object in the field of the relation has the relation to itself. That is, relation R is reflexive iff, for all x and y, if $x R y$ or $y R x$, then $x R x$.

Examples of reflexive relations are *equals* and *deducible-from*.
For every a and b, if a equals b or b equals a, then a equals a.
For every p and q, if p is deducible from q or q is deducible from p, then p is deducible from p.

Def. 15. A relation is **irreflexive** (or aliorelative) iffi it never relates an object to itself. That is, a relation R is irreflexive iffi, for all x, it is false that $x R x$.

Examples of irreflexive relations are *complementary-to*, *father-of*, and *belongs-to*.[4]
No term (or class) is complementary to itself.
For any a, a is not the father of a.
Ockham remarked that every *belongs-to* proposition with identical terms, such as "Socrates belongs to Socrates" (or "Socrates is Socrates's"), is false.[5]

Def. 16. A relation is **medio-reflexive** when it is neither reflexive nor irreflexive.

Hence, relation R is medio-reflexive iffi, for some x, it is false that $x R x$, and for some x, $x R x$.

Examples of medio-reflexive relations are *equals-the-square-of*, *hates*, and *sees*.
$1 = 1^2$; but $3 \neq 3^2$.

The example of *sees* is suggested by Ockham, who says that "Socrates sees Socrates" is true. We add that, on the other hand, someone, for example, a blind man, does not see himself.

Exercises for Chapter 17

EX 17A. Place the appropriate letter in each blank.

_____ 1. A connection of any sort between two or more objects is called, (an): (a) relation. (b) formal link. (c) association. (d) formal binder.

_____ 2. A word or phrase that expresses a relation is called a: (a) connector. (b) relation phrase. (c) degree. (d) binder.

_____ 3. The class of all objects that have the relation R to something or to which something has the relation R is called the: (a) degree of relation R. (b) force of relation R. (c) field of relation R, (d) significance of relation R.

_____ 4. The number of objects a relation relates in a given instance is called the relation's: (a) field. (b) degree. (c) force. (d) significance.

_____ 5. The relation *distinct-from* is: (a) dyadic. (b) triadic. (c) tetradic. (d) monadic.

EX 17B, I. Write the relational converse of each of the following.

1. The king loves the queen.
2. The king ate the apple.
3. The king licked the frosting off.
4. The queen ill-used her servants.
5. He imitated the king.
6. The king activated the guard.
7. The rebels overthrew the king.
8. The king regained the throne.
9. The king requested the rebel leader's oath of allegiance.
10. The people cheered the king.

EX 17B, II. Write the relational converse of each of the following.

1. Sir Roger is more adroit than the king.
2. The king is more obese than Sir Roger.

3. Sir Roger is more skillful at swordmanship than the king.
4. Sir Roger is less cunning than the king.
5. The king is less honest than Sir Roger.

EX 17B, III. Write the relational converse of each of the following. If it cannot be done, try to explain why.

1. Plato was teacher of Aristotle.
2. Schmidt was head scientist of Project Venus.
3. Sir James is a social leader in our community.
4. Dr. Butler is the minister of North Church.
5. Taylor is the president of Local 192.
6. Hawkins is assistant dean of the college.
7. Everyone is a relative of someone.
8. George Washington was the father of our country.
9. Every person is captain of his fate.
10. Every actress is the idol of some girl.

EX 17B, IV. Write the relational converse of each of the following. If it cannot be done, try to explain why.

1. Sir Roger Leyton is for the king.
2. The queen is with the king.
3. The queen is by the king.
4. The king's pen is in the desk.
5. The flag is above the king's tower.
6. Sir Roger Leyton is behind the king.
7. The king's sword is through the stone.
8. The king's scepter is on the table.
9. The king is without the royal bodyguard.
10. The king's dog is under the king's bed.

EX 17C. After each dyadic relation indicate its relational properties by placing the appropriate letters in each of the first three blanks.

1st blank	2nd blank	3rd blank
T = transitive	S = symmetrical	R = reflexive
IT = intransitive	AS = asymmetrical	IR = irreflexive
MT = medio-transitive	MS = medio-symmetrical	MR = medio-reflexive

In blank 4 write the field of the relation, for example, physical objects, numbers, thinking being, and so on.

Relation	Blank 1	Blank 2	Blank 3	Blank 4
1. contrary of				
2. logically independent of				
3. logically equivalent to				
4. spatially outside of				
5. spatially inside of				
6. offspring of				
7. kills				
8. is thinking of				
9. not logically independent of				
10. physically touches				
11. greater in weight than				
12. older than				
13. owes money to				
14. larger number than				
15. is the obverse of				

18

Reversible and Non-reversible Inferences

Valid immediate inferences are either reversible or non-reversible. Reversible inferences are like two-way streets—one can travel in either direction. Therefore, a reversible inference, based on a reversible entailment (symbolized by a double-headed arrow "↔"), is a two-way valid inference. The premiss entails (or implies) the conclusion and the conclusion entails the premiss.

A non-reversible inference is a one-way street; travel is permitted in only one direction and that is from premiss to conclusion. Therefore, in a non-reversible inference, based on a non-reversible entailment, the premiss entails the conclusion but the conclusion does not entail the premiss.[1]

The distinction between reversible and non-reversible immediate inferences is important for an understanding of the procedures given in chapter 20, *A Deductive System of the Standard Syllogism*, and chapter 23, *Reducing the Number of Terms in Arguments*.

18A REVERSIBLE INFERENCES

Def. 1. A **reversible inference** is a valid immediate inference in which the conclusion also entails the premiss.

Examples of reversible inferences are: *No racoons are possums; therefore no possums are racoons. All non-goblins are non-orcs, hence all orcs are goblins. No wizards are morals; therefore all wizards are non-mortals.* The definition itself supplies the test for reversible inferences. If the premiss entails the conclusion and the conclusion entails the premiss, the inference is reversible.

18B NON-REVERSIBLE INFERENCES

Def. 2 A **non-reversible inference** is a valid immediate inference in which the conclusion does not entail the premiss.

Examples are: *All halflings are hearty eaters; therefore some hearty eaters are halflings. It is true that all dwarfs are short people, hence it is false that no dwarfs are short people. No politicians are honest men; therefore some honest men are politicians.* A non-reversible inference can be detected simply by testing the immediate inference for validity in both directions. If the premiss entails the conclusion, but the conclusion does not entail the premiss, the inference is non-reversible.

18C TABLE 18.1: REVERSIBLE AND NON-REVERSIBLE INFERENCES

Reversible Inferences

Inferences based on contradictories: $A^T \leftrightarrow O^F$, $E^T \leftrightarrow I^I$ etc.
The (simple) conversion of the **E** and **I** propositions.
All obversions.
The contraposition of the **A** and **O** proposition.
Immediate inference by converse relation.

Non-Reversible Inferences

All inferences based on contrariety, subcontrariety, superalternation-subalternation.
The conversion *per accidens* of the **A** and **E** propositions.
The contrapositive of the **E** proposition.
The inverse and partial inverse.

IV

Aristotelian Logic:
Mediated Inferences

19

The Standard Syllogism: Definitions

19A DEFINITIONS

Def. 1. A **standard categorical syllogism** is a deductive agrument consisting of three standard categorical propositions: two premisses, and a conclusion which comes last (or first). It contains three terms, each shared by two propositions.[1]

Unless otherwise specified, by the term "standard syllogism" or (prior to chapter 24) "syllogism" we shall mean "standard categorical syllogism". An example of a standard categorical syllogism follows:

(Premiss:) *All cats are felines.*
(Premiss:) *No dogs are felines.*
(Conclusion:) ∴ *No cats are dogs.*

The terms and premisses in the syllogism have special names.

Def. 2. The **major term** of a syllogism is the predicate of its conclusion.

Def. 3. The **minor term** of a syllogism is the subject of its conclusion.

Def. 4. The **extreme terms** of a syllogism are the terms in its conclusion (i.e., the major and minor terms).

Def. 5. The **middle term** of a syllogism is the term that occurs once in each of its premisses (but not in its conclusion).

266   *Aristotelian Logic*

Def. 6. The **major premiss** of a syllogism is the premiss that contains its major term.

Def. 7. The **minor premiss** of a syllogism is the premiss that contains its minor term.

19B STANDARD-ORDER SYLLOGISMS

19B1 Standard Order of the Propositions. The order of the propositions in a syllogism is, of course, irrelevant to the validity of the argument. Consequently, the propositions of a syllogism may occur in any order. For instance, the conclusion may be stated first, or either premiss may come first. Furthermore, the most common methods of determining validity of a syllogism, such as formal rules (to be given in chapter 21) or diagrams, do not depend on the order of the propositions.

However, the order of the propositions in a syllogism is important for describing its specific form, which is done by means of the mood and figure, as we shall explain. Without a standard order, there would be a multiplication of forms with trivial differences, complicating the task of description. It is also possible to prove useful derived rules in terms of mood or figure. We now define what is meant by a standard syllogism in *standard order*, or for short, a standard-order syllogism.

Def. 8. A **standard-order syllogism** is a standard syllogism in which the major premiss is first, the minor premiss is second, and the conclusion is last. (If written horizontally, the count is from left to right; if written vertically, the count is from top to bottom.)

Here is an example of a standard-order syllogism:

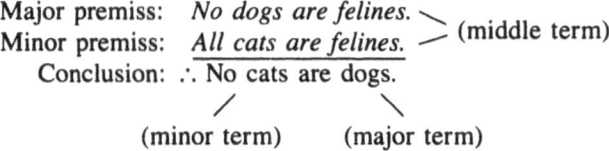

Major premiss: *No dogs are felines.*
Minor premiss: *All cats are felines.* (middle term)
Conclusion: ∴ No cats are dogs.
              (minor term)   (major term)

Compare this syllogism with the example in 19A. Note that the premisses had to be transposed, because "dogs", the predicate of the conclusion, occurred in the second premiss. The predicate of the conclusion, the major term, has to occur in the first premiss of a standard-order syllogism.

19B2 Moods of the Standard Syllogism.

Def. 9. The **mood** of a standard syllogism is the sequence of code letters of its three propositions in standard order (major premiss, minor premiss, conclusion).

The mood of the syllogism in the example after definition 8, which is in standard order, is EAE. Note that we define "mood" for standard syllogisms in general, whether written in standard order or not; but if the argument is not written in standard order, we must think of it as if it were.

Let us turn back to the syllogism in 19A just after definition 1. One might hastily judge that this is in mood AEE. But the major term—the predicate of the conclusion (by definition 2)—is "dogs", which occurs also in the second premiss, the E premiss. So the E premiss is the major premiss (by definition 6). The mood of this example is then EAE—the same as for the example definition 8, in which the same propositions are written in after standard order.

There are sixty-four moods of standard syllogism. Proof: There are three propositions in a syllogism and four possible standard categorical forms for each proposition (i.e., the major premiss could be an **A, E, I,** or **O**; the minor premiss and the conclusion could also be any one of these four forms). So the number of moods equals $4 \times 4 \times 4 = 64$.

19B3 Figures of the Standard Syllogism.

Def. 10. The **figure** of a standard syllogism is determined by the position of its middle term when it is in standard order. There are only four possible arrangements of the middle term, so there are just four figures. They are:

	Fig. 1	Fig. 2	Fig. 3	Fig. 4
Major premiss:	M — P	P — M	M — P	P — M
Minor premiss:	S — M	S — M	M — S	M — S
Conclusion:	S — P	S — P	S — P	S — P

(S = minor term, P = major term, M = middle term)

Observe that the pattern of figure 3 is a "C", which is the third letter of the alphabet. The pattern of the fourth and last figure is a "Z", which is the last letter of the alphabet. The pattern of figure 1 is the mirror image of figure 4, and the pattern of figure 2 is the mirror image of figure 3.[2]

It is essential that the figure and mood of a syllogism be determined from its standard order. That is, the propositions must be in the order of major premiss, minor premiss, conclusion—or be thought of in this order—before its mood and figure can be determined.

19B4 Syllogistic Form.

Def. 11. A (standard) **syllogistic form** is a distinctive form (2 definition 6) of a standard-order syllogism.

The mood and figure of a standard-order syllogism determine its syllogistic form, which is designated by code letters for the mood and the number for the figure. The example following definition 8 above has the mood **EAE** in figure 2, which we write "**EAE** fig. 2" or "**EAE-2**".

Since a syllogistic form in any of the sixty-four moods may be of any of the four figures, there are (64 × 4 =) 256 standard syllogistic forms (of which, we shall see, just twenty-four are valid on the Aristotelian interpretation).

By definition 1 above, we accept as "standard categorical syllogisms" not only certain arguments written in the order (1) major premiss, minor premiss, conclusion, but also certain arguments in the orders (2) minor, major, conclusion; (3) conclusion, major, minor; and (4) conclusion, minor, major. There are then four times as many forms of standard syllogism as of standard-order syllogism (1024 instead of 256). It is unnecessary, however, to have special labels for those not in standard order; we designate these by the mood and figure of the corresponding standard-order syllogism. Thus the example following definition 1 is said to be EAE fig. 2, just as if it were rewritten in the order major, minor, conclusion.

Exercises for Chapter 19

EX 19, I. Place the appropriate letter in the margin.

_____ 1. The form of a standard-order syllogism is determined by: (a) the position of the middle term in the syllogism. (b) the position of the conclusion in the syllogism, that is, whether it is first, second, or last. (c) the position of the major and minor terms in the syllogism. (d) the mood and figure of the syllogism.

_____ 2. The figure of a standard-order syllogism is determined by the positon of the: (a) major term. (b) minor term (c) middle term. (d) conclusion.

_____ 3. A standard syllogism can occur in any of: (a) 4 figures. (b) 32 figures. (c) 64 figures. (d) 256 figures.

_____ 4. A standard syllogism can occur in any of: (a) 32 moods. (b) 64 moods. (c) 128 moods. (d) 256 moods.

_____ 5. A standard-order syllogism can occur in any one of: (a) 4 forms. (b) 64 forms. (c) 128 forms. (d) 256 forms.

_____ 6. The major and minor terms of a standard syllogism are called the: (a) final terms. (b) conclusion terms. (c) extreme terms. (d) statement terms.

_____ 7. A syllogism has: (a) one premiss. (b) two premisses. (c) three premisses. (d) any number of premisses.

_____ 8. The term in the syllogism that occurs once in each premiss but not in the conclusion is called the: (a) middle term. (b) minor term. (c) major term. (d) extreme term.

_____ 9. The subject of the conclusion in a syllogism is called the: (a) middle term. (b) minor term. (c) major term. (d) final term.

_____ 10. The predicate of the conclusion in a syllogism is called the: (a) middle term. (b) minor term. (c) major term. (d) final term.

EX19, II. State the mood and figure of each of the following forms, which are not all in standard order.

1. All *M* are *P*
    All *S* are *M*
    ∴ All *S* are *P*

2. Some *M* are *P*
    All *M* are *S*
    ∴ No *S* are *P*

3. All *P* are *M*
    Some *S* are not *M*
    ∴ No *S* are *P*

4. All *P* are *M*
    All *M* are *S*
    ∴ All *S* are *P*

5. Some *Y* are *Z*
    Some *X* are not *Y*
    ∴ Some *X* are *Z*

6. No *X* are *Z*
    All *Y* are *Z*
    ∴ All *Y* are *X*

7. All *X* are *Z*
    Some *X* are not *Y*
    ∴ Some *Z* are not *Y*

8. Some *X* are *Y*, since all *Z* are *X* and some *Z* are *Y*.

9. No *X* are *Z* and all *Y* are *X*, therefore some *Z* are not *Y*.

10. Some *X* are *Y*; so, since no *X* are *Z*, some *Z* are not *Y*.

EX 19, III. Using "S" for the minor term, "P" for the major term, and "M" for the middle term, construct the following syllogistic forms:

1. **AAA** fig. 1
2. **EIO** fig. 2
3. **OAO** fig. 3
4. **IAI** fig. 4
5. **AIO** fig. 1
6. **IOE** fig. 3
7. **AEE** fig. 2
8. **IOI** fig. 4
9. **EAE** fig. 1
10. **IOA** fig. 3

20

A Deductive System of the Standard Syllogism

This chapter presents the doctrine of the standard syllogism as a deductive system. We give the traditional doctrine in its modern form, with twenty-four valid forms in four figures, rather than Aristotle's doctrine of fourteen forms in three figures. However, we follow Aristotle's method of showing validity by reduction to first-figure forms, and invalidity by counterexample.

20A AXIOMATIC METHOD

20A1 Axiomatic Method in General. The *axiomatic method* (or *postulational method*) is a method of presenting a subject-matter as a system of proofs. Such a system contains the following elements: undefined terms, definitions that introduce defined terms, assumptions (axioms and/or postulates), rules of deduction, and theorems.

Definitions might, in principle, be lacking; but almost all important systems contain them. Since not every term can be defined without circularity (which is rejected), there must be undefined terms. These have no official definition within the system, but may of course be explained informally. The assumptions are propositions that are not proven in the given system, but are assumed without proof.[1] Theorems are proved by deducing them by the rules of deduction from the assumptions and/or theorems already proved. The classic example of an axiomatic system has for centuries been Euclid's *Elements*. Modern systems of geometry have followed essentially his method, but have attained greater rigor; for example, making explicit the tacit assumptions.

20A2 Aristotle's Deductive System. In his *Prior Analytics,* Aristotle developed a deductive system as a way of demonstrating the valid forms of syllogism. He did this for both assertoric and model syllogisms; but we shall omit all consideration of the modal syllogisms, which are much more complicated and confusing. Aristotle's work preceded Euclid; in fact, his systems for the syllogism are the first known deductive systems. It is not surprising, therefore, that Aristotle's standards of rigor are not as high as those later attained in mathematics; for the general trend of mathematics and logic has been to attain even greater strictness in this regard. However, the usual modern treatment of syllogism by rules of quality and distribution is a lapse from Aristotelian rigor.[2] We generally aim in this chapter at no greater rigor than Aristotle himself, except that we make explicit the main principles of propositional logic involved.

a *Aristotle's Terminology.* In Aristotle's system, he defines certain terms ("premiss", "term", etc.) much as we did in chapters 1, 2, and 19. But Aristotle's concepts differ from those that are now traditional in at least two ways that lead to different results.[3] First, by his conception of the figure of a syllogism, there are not four figures, but only three, corresponding to the first three of the traditional four.[4] The arguments that we count as valid fourth-figure syllogisms he would accept as valid, but not as "syllogisms" in his strict sense.[5] Second, Aristotle saw no use in drawing a particular conclusion from premisses that justify a universal conclusion. Hence, of the traditional eighteen valid forms in figures 1, 2, and 3, Aristotle did not count the four known as subaltern forms, which infer a particular where they could have inferred a universal. This leaves fourteen forms—the same fourteen in these figures that are listed in the medieval mnemonic verses (see 20D2). In this chapter, we shall accept the four figures and subaltern forms, while using Aristotle's methods of reduction and counterexamples.

b *Aristotle's Axiomatic Syllogisms.* Aristotle's method was to assume certain syllogistic forms as primitive or axiomatic,[6] and prove the others by reduction to the axiomatic forms. He was aware that there were different sets of assumptions he could make. His best-known proposal is to assume the four first-figure forms that he regarded as 'perfect'.[7] He also proposed assuming just the two first-figure forms with universal conclusions, AAA and EAE (later known as Barbara and Celarent).[8] We shall follow the latter more elegant procedure. These are written:[9]

AXIOMATIC SYLLOGISTIC FORMS

AAA-1   **EAE**-1
All M are P No M are P
<u>All S are M</u>   <u>All S are M</u>
∴ All S are P ∴ No S are P

c *Aristotle's Rules of Deduction: Reduction and Immediate Inferences.* The deductive method requires rules of deduction for deriving theorems from axioms. Aristotle's method is based on his procedure of reduction, including direct and indirect reduction. These are procedures by which an argument is shown to be valid by its relation to another argument already known to be valid. Reduction is also used to derive one argument form from another argument form. (For convenience, we shall sometimes speak of reduction of "arguments" or "syllogisms" when what we say applies to both argument and argument forms.)

The basic principles of direct and indirect reduction are complex, and will be explained in sections 20B and 20C. The procedures also require immediate inferences relating propositions of the arguments involved. Aristotle used only the following: simple conversion of **E** and **I**, conversion *per accidens* of **A**, and repetition (identity); also, for indirect reduction, contradictory opposition. We use these, and also subalternation.

Reduction of arguments may be subdivided into the following kinds:

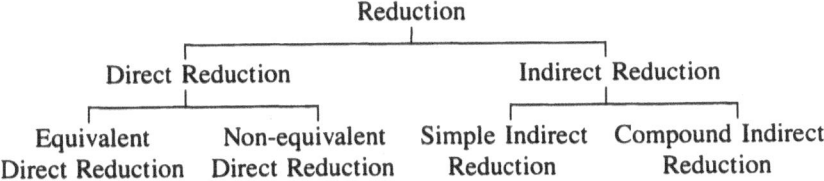

The overall pattern of Aristotle's deductive system, and the system of this chapter, is as follows:

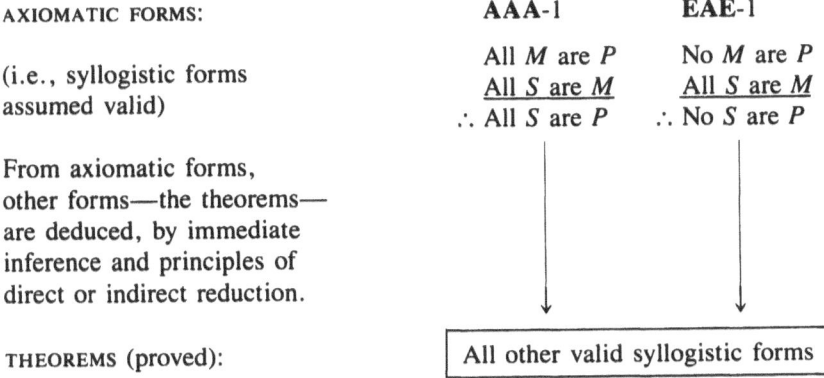

20B DIRECT REDUCTION

20B1 Direct Reduction in General.

Def. 1. Direct reduction (or **ostensive reduction**) of argument II to argument I is the demonstration that, from the premises of II or immediate inferences therefrom, there follows by argument I the conclusions of II or one from which it may be immediately inferred.

It is first shown that the premises of argument II entail all the premises of argument I; the premises of argument I (by hypothesis) jointly entail its conclusion *(r);* the conclusion *(r)* of argument I is shown to entail the conclusion *(r')* of argument II; therefore, the premises of argument II jointly entail its conclusion *(r')*. Hence, argument II is valid. Argument II is then said to be **directly reduced** to argument I. (We may also say that the validity of argument I directly implies the validity of argument II, or that argument I implies argument II.)

The following is the general scheme of direct reduction of syllogisms, reducing II to I (where p, q, r, p', q', r', are propositions):

$$
\begin{array}{ccc}
\text{Argument I} & & \text{Argument II (to be proved)} \\
p & \leftarrow & p' \\
\underline{q} & \leftarrow & \underline{q'} \\
\downarrow & & \\
r & \rightarrow & r'
\end{array}
$$

(1) Argument I should be an axiomatic syllogism or have been reduced to one. Consequently, its validity has been assumed or already proved.

(2) Argument II is the syllogism that is being reduced, that is, proved valid.

(3) The horizontal arrows stand for reversible or nonreversible inferences (including identity).[10] The vertical arrow (which we usually omit) indicates the inference from premises to conclusion in the syllogism assumed valid.

(4) The chain of reasoning runs thus: p' and q' together entail p and g; p and q together entail r; r implies r'; therefore, p' and q' together entail r'. The general form of this argument is: P entails Q, Q entails R, R entails S; therefore, P entails S. ("P entails Q"is equivalent to "Q is deducible from P". Entailment is a transitive relation.)

20B2 Equivalent Direct Reduction.

Def. 2. Equivalent direct reduction is direct reduction in which each premiss in one argument is equivalent to a premiss in the other argument, and the conclusions are equivalent. In this case the arguments are said to be equivalent, and either could be reduced to the other.

The general scheme of equivalent direct reduction by syllogisms follows:

$$\begin{array}{ccc} \text{Argument I} & & \text{Argument II} \\ p & \leftrightarrow & p' \\ \underline{q} & \leftrightarrow & \underline{q'} \\ r & \leftrightarrow & r' \end{array}$$

Argument I is equivalent to argument II and either could be reduced to the other. For example:

$$\begin{array}{ccc} \text{EIO-1} & & \text{EIO-4} \\ \text{No } M \text{ are } P & \xleftarrow{c} & \text{No } P \text{ are M} \\ \underline{\text{Some } S \text{ are } M} & \xleftarrow{c} & \underline{\text{Some } M \text{ are } S} \\ \text{Some } S \text{ are not } P & = & \text{Some } S \text{ are not } P \end{array}$$

Here the major premises and minor premises are respectively equivalent by simple conversion, and the conclusions are identical. Hence the arguments are equivalent, and either could be reduced to the other. In the Aristotelian tradition, however, valid syllogisms in the first figure are regarded as "perfect". Hence the fourth-figure argument is ordinarily reduced to the first figure. To indicate this direction of the reduction, we have written it with one-way arrows for conversions. Whichever way we write it, it fits the definition of equivalent direct reduction.

It is important to note that in the Aristotelian tradition (and in this chapter), simple conversion of **E** and **I** and repetition (identity) are the only reversible inferences used for direct reduction. However, other reversible inferences, such as obversion, and contraposition of **A** and **O**, could be used.

Four distinct syllogistic forms can be shown to be equivalent to one another by direct reduction, using only simple conversion and identity.

$$\begin{array}{cccc} \textbf{EIO-1} & \textbf{EIO-2} & \textbf{EIO-3} & \textbf{EIO-4} \\ \text{No } M \text{ are } P & \xleftrightarrow{c} \text{No } P \text{ are } M & \xleftrightarrow{c} \text{No } M \text{ are } P & \xleftrightarrow{c} \text{No } P \text{ are } M \\ \underline{\text{Some } S \text{ are } M} & = \underline{\text{Some } S \text{ are } M} & \xleftrightarrow{c} \underline{\text{Some } M \text{ are } S} & = \underline{\text{Some } M \text{ are } S} \\ \text{Some } S \text{ are not } P & = \text{Some } S \text{ are not } P & = \text{Some } S \text{ are not } P & = \text{Some } S \text{ are not } P \end{array}$$

Direct reduction sometimes requires converting the conclusion. In this case it is customary to change the order of the premises, in order to keep the standard order with major premiss first (though of course the validity of the argument is not affected by the order). For example, we reduce AEE figure 2 to EAE figure 1 thus:

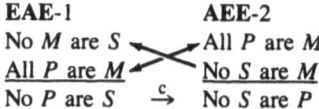

EAE-1   AEE-2
No M are S All P are M
All P are M No S are M
No P are S $\xrightarrow{c}$ No S are P

There is a set of four forms including EAE figure 1 that are equivalent to one another by direct reduction:

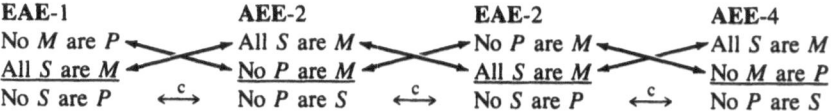

Another such set including AII figure 1 is:

AII-1		AII-3		IAI-3		IAI-4
All M are P	=	All M are P		Some M are S	$\xleftrightarrow{c}$	Some S are M
Some S are M	$\xleftrightarrow{c}$	Some M are S		All M are P	=	All M are P
Some S are P	=	Some S are P	$\xleftrightarrow{c}$	Some P are S	=	Some P are S

Note that proving two syllogisms to be equivalent to one another is not proof of their validity unless one of them is an axiom or has been reduced to an axiom.

20B3 Non-equivalent Direct Reduction.

Def. 3. Non-equivalent direct reduction is direct reduction based upon at least one non-reversible immediate inference together with reversible inferences.

The non-reversible inferences traditionally used in direct reduction are conversion *per accidens* (conversion by limitation), and less frequently subalternation (inferring **I** from **A** or **O** from **E**).

When non-reversible inferences are used, it is necessary to take care that the entailments go in the right direction: from the premisses of argument II (to be reduced) to the premisses of argument I (assumed valid), and from the conclusion of argument I to the conclusion of argument II. It is found that only one non-equivalent inference may be used in a given reduction to a valid standard syllogism (see note 10 to B1). Equivalent inferences must be used for the other two pairs of propositions. A rule to remember: We may strengthen a premiss or weaken the conclusion of a valid argument.

CONVERSION PER ACCIDENS OF A PREMISS

AII-1   AAI-3
All M are P =   All M are P
Some S are M $\xleftarrow{cpa}$ All M are S
Some S are P =   Some S are P

AAI figure 3 is thus reduced to AII figure 1, but not conversely. (The validity of AII figure 1 will be demonstrated in C2 by compound indirect reduction to EAE figure 1, an axiomatic syllogism.)

SUBALTERNATION OF CONCLUSION

EAE-1   EAO-2
No M are P $\xleftarrow{c}$ No P are M
All S are M =   All S are M
No S are P $\xrightarrow{sub}$ Some S are not P

EAO figure 2 is valid because it can be directly reduced to an axiomatic syllogism. This last reduction would rarely be made, since we could infer "No S are P" from the given second-figure premisses. However, for completeness of the system, we have given a way of proving this so-called "subaltern" form.

20C INDIRECT REDUCTION

Indirect reduction (also called *reductio per impossibile*) is either simple indirect reduction or compound indirect reduction.

20C1 Simple Indirect Reduction.

Def. 4. Simple indirect reduction of argument II to argument I is the demonstration, assuming the validity of argument I, of an argument II constructed as follows: the contradictory of the conclusion of argument I is taken as premiss, together with all the original premisses but one, while the contradictory of this one becomes the conclusion.

a *General Scheme of Indirect Reduction.* The general scheme of simple indirect reduction for syllogisms, and two-premiss arguments generally, may take either of these two forms;

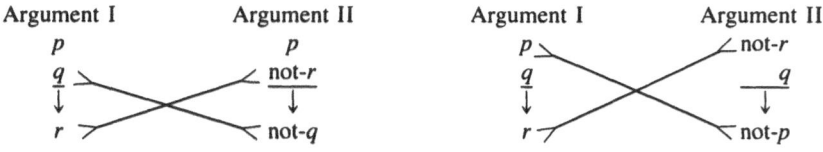

(1) Argument I is assumed to be valid.

(2) The contradictory of r is not-r; of q, not-q. "$p{>}\!\!-\!\!{<}q$" expresses the mutual entailment of p and not-q.

(3) Argument II (or III) is being reduced to argument I. However, since the two arguments are equivalent, the validity of either argument implies the other.

b *The Principle of Indirect Reduction.* Simple indirect reduction may be thought of as based on a scheme for inferring one condition from another, in either of two forms:

    i.   If p and q, then r;
          ∴ If p and not-r, then not-q.

    ii.   If p and q, then r;
          ∴ If not-r and q, then not p.

These forms are especially appropriate if syllogisms (and syllogistic forms) take the form of conditionals rather than arguments (or argument forms).

In i, p may be replaced by a conjunction of any number of propositional letters, giving, for example,

    iii. If (p_1 and p_2) are q, then r;
          ∴ If (p_1 and p_2) are not-r, then not-q.

Similarly, q in (ii) may be replaced by a conjunction. Likewise, in the reduction schemas in C1a above, the variable p in argument II (or q in argument III) could be replaced by a conjunction. Hence indirect reduction applies to arguments with any number of premisses greater than one.

c *Indirect Reduction by Indirect Proof.* Indirect reduction may also be justified by an indirect proof or *reductio ad absurdum*. We demonstrate the simple indirect reduction of **AOO** figure 2 to **AAA** figure 1 by an indirect proof, in the style currently known as "natural deduction". The principle of indirect proof or *reductio ad absurdum* may be stated thus: Given the truth of certain premisses, if adding an arbitrary supposition leads logically to contradictory results, the supposition must be false.

An indirect proof of the indirect reduction of an argument of form II—*p*, not-*r* ∴ not *q*—to an argument of form I—*p*, *q* ∴ r—is as follows:

	JUSTIFICATION
(1) *p* and not-*r* are both true,	by hypothesis.
(2) *Suppose* *q* is true:	arbitrary supposition.
(3) Then *p* and *q* are true,	by (1) and (2);
(4) so *r* would be true	by argument I and (3).
(5) But this is impossible; not-*r* is true	by (1).
(6) ∴ supposition (2) is false,	by Indirect Proof, (2)–(5)

i.e., *q* is false, not-*q* is true.

∴ not-*q* follows from (1), i.e., argument II is valid. Q.E.D.

d *Purposes of Indirect Reduction.* Indirect reduction was introduced by Aristotle for a specific purpose; but it is useful in a quite general way.

The valid syllogisms **AII** fig. 1, **EIO** fig. 1, **AOO** fig. 2, and **OAO** fig. 3 cannot be directly reduced to the axiomatic syllogisms by any of the immediate inferences regularly used by Aristotle, namely, conversion (simple or by limitation) and repetition (identity). Hence another procedure was needed which Aristotle found in indirect reduction. (If obversion is used as well as conversion, and their combinations, all valid syllogisms can be directly reduced either to **AAA** or to **AII** in figure 1.)

In general, simple indirect reduction may be used to derive, from any valid argument with *n* premisses, *n* other arguments, each having as conclusion the contradictory of a premiss of the original argument. Simple indirect reduction may be combined with direct reduction to yield yet other valid arguments.

20C2 Examples of Simple Indirect Reduction.

a *Abstract Example:* Reduction of **AOO** figure 2 to **AAA** figure 1.

Axiomatic Syllogism	To Prove Valid
AAA fig. 1	**AOO** fig. 2
All *M* are *P*	All *P* are *M*
<u>All *S* are *M*</u>	<u>Some *S* are not *M*</u>
All *S* are *P*	Some *S* are not *P*

By the reduction schema of C1a above (arg. I–arg. II), the validity of **AAA** figure 1 implies the validity of a transposed argument as follows:

      AAA-1   Transposed Argument
      All M are P =   All M are P
      <u>All S are M</u>   <u>Not all S are P</u>
      All S are P Not all S are M

By the square of opposition, the minor premiss and conclusion of the transposed argument are restated in standard **O** form, and the transposed argument is equivalent to:

      All M are P
      <u>Some S are not P</u>
      Some S are not M

Substituting P for M, M for P in the last argument, to obtain the conventional use of "M" for the middle term, "P" for major term, gives:

      AOO-2
      All P are M
      <u>Some S are not M</u>
      Some S are not P

This completes a proof that validity of **AAA** figure (Barbara) implies validity of **AOO** figure 2 (Baroko). In short, Baroko has been reduced to Barbara. The names "Barbara" and "Baroko" are those given to these arguments in the medieval mnemonic lines (20D2 below).

In indirect reduction, we shall usually take for granted the use of the square of opposition, and write the contradictories of the original propositions directly in standard form, omitting the first form of transposed argument above.

b *Compact Reduction of Baroko to Barbara.* A simple indirect reduction such as that above will ordinarily be written thus:

      AXIOMATIC FORM   REDUCED FORM

      AAA-1   **AOO**-2
      All D are C =   All D are C
      <u>All F are D</u>   <u>Some F are not C</u>
      All F are C Some F are not D

(Letters *S*, *M*, *P* could have their conventional use in only one argument at a time in the transposition.)

c *Indirect Reduction of a Concrete Argument.* Indirect reduction of a concrete argument of the form **OAO** figure 3 (Bokardo) to one of the form **AAA** figure 1 (Barbara) is written similarly:

AXIOMATIC SYLLOGISM   REDUCED SYLLOGISM
AAA-1   **OAO**-3

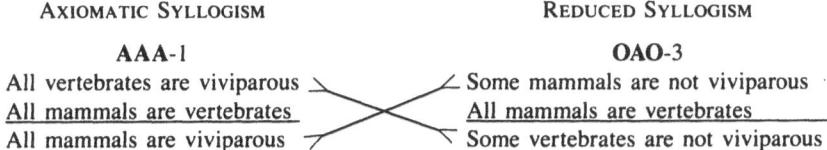

All vertebrates are viviparous   Some mammals are not viviparous
All mammals are vertebrates   All mammals are vertebrates
All mammals are viviparous   Some vertebrates are not viviparous

Of course, both arguments do not have true premisses. It happens that the one in Bokardo has true premisses; only this one proves its conclusion.

20C3 Compound Indirect Reduction. To reduce an argument to one known to be valid, it may be necessary to go through two stages, using both direct and indirect reduction.

Def. 5. Compound indirect reduction (or Indirect with direct reduction) is reduction of an argument to another through a third argument, using direct reduction once and simple indirect reduction once.

For example, Aristotle (*Prior Analytics* 29b) remarks that **AII** figure 1 (Darii)—though it is "perfect" by itself—may be reduced indirectly to **AEE** figure 2 (Camestres), which in turn is reduced directly to **EAE** figure 1 (Celarent).

AXIOMATIC FORM   REDUCED FORM

EAE-1   **AEE**-2   **AII**-1

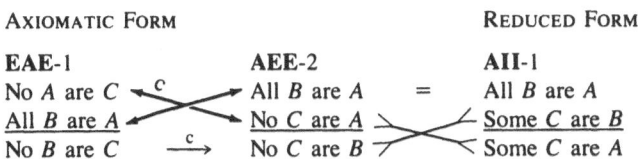

No *A* are *C*   All *B* are *A*   =   All *B* are *A*
All *B* are *A*   No *C* are *A*   Some *C* are *B*
No *B* are *C*   No *C* are *B*   Some *C* are *A*

The validity of **AII** figure 1 (Darii) may also be established by reducing it directly to **IAI** figure 3 (Disamis), and the latter indirectly to **EAE** figure 1 (Celarent).

Either of these reductions of Darii is a two-stage reduction. Reductions of three or more stages are possible but not necessary in the present system.

20D THE TWENTY-FOUR VALID SYLLOGISTIC FORMS

There are twenty-four valid syllogistic forms in all, six in each figure, in the modern traditional doctrine, counting the axiomatic forms Barbara and Celarent, and the forms that can be reduced to them by direct or indirect reduction.

20D1 Table 20.1: Valid Syllogistic Forms.

Figure 1	Figure 2	Figure 3	Figure 4
AAA	AEE	AAI	AEE
EAE	EAE	AII	AAI
AII	AOO	IAI	IAI
EIO	EIO	EAO	EAO
AAI	AEO	EIO	EIO
EAO	EAO	OAO	AEO

The five forms below the horizontal lines are the subaltern forms (explained in D2d).

The same twenty-four are obtained if the four "perfect" syllogisms of the first figure, **AAA, EAE, AII,** and **EIO** are accepted as axiomatic.

20D2 Mnemonic Names.

a *The Mnemonic Verses.* Medieval logicians constructed names for the valid syllogistic forms—with the exception of five subaltern forms (see d below)—designed to indicate the manner of reduction to the first figure. These were put together into mnemonic (memory-aiding) verses, of which we give the version usual in English-language textbooks.

> Bárbara, Célarént, Darií, Ferió-*que prióris.*
> Césare, Cámestrés, Festíno, Baróko *secúndae.*
> *Tértia* Dáraptí, Disamís, Datísi, Felápton,
> Bokárdo, Feríson *hábet. Quárta ińsuper áddit*
> Brámantíp, Camenés, Dimarís, Fesápo, Freśison.

We add accents to suggest stress for the verses. But in prose, stress first syllable if only third is marked above, and stress second syllable if two are marked.[11] The student is not expected to memorize the verses, but it is useful to know how to use them.

The first line has names of the four forms of the first figure *(prioris)* to which reduction is to be made. The second line names four forms of the second figure *(secundae).* All six forms of the third figure *(tertia)* are named, and five of the fourth *(quarta).*[12]

b *Significance of Mnemonic Names.*

(1) The vowels in order give the mood (in standard order).

(2) The initial B, C, D, or F in lines 2 through 5 matches the initial in the first line, indicating the form to which reduction is made.

(3) "K" (or "c") following "o" indicates simple *indirect reduction*, the conclusion and the **O** premiss being contradicted.

(4) "S" immediately after the first or second vowel indicates *simple conversion* of the corresponding premiss in the syllogism being reduced.

(5) "S" after the third vowel indicates *simple* conversion of the conclusion of the first-figure form to which reduction is made.

(6) "P" immediately after the first or second vowel indicates conversion *per accidens* of the corresponding premiss in the syllogism being reduced.

(7) "P" after the third vowel indicates conversion *per accidens* of the conclusion of the first-figure form to which reduction is made.

(8) "M" indicates direct reduction in which interchange of the premisses (*mutatio* or *metathesis*) is made to keep standard order.

(9) No letter indicates the figure.[13] The remaining letters are without significance. A numerical "exponent" or subscript may be added to indicate figure.

c *Examples of Reduction by the Mnemonic Names.*

EXAMPLE 1. To reduce **EAO** figure 4 to the first figure.

EAO figure 4 is named "Fesapo"; therefore it is to be reduced to Ferio, as indicated by the initial "F". The "e" is followed by "s", and the "a" by "p", so the **E** and **A** premisses of Fesapo are to be converted, simply and *per accidens* respectively, without transposing the premisses, since there is no "m". The conclusions will be identical, since there is (and could be) no "s" or "p" after the "o".

This is written:

	Ferio		Fesapo
	No M is P	←c—	No P is M
	Some S is M	←cpa—	All M is S
	Some S is not P	=	Some S is not P

An abbreviated way of rendering it is:

	Ferio		Fesapo
	Emp	←c—	Epm
	Ism	←pa—	Ams
	Osp	=	Osp

Hence the validity of Ferio implies the validity of Fesapo. This is a non-equivalent reduction.

EXAMPLE 2. To reduce **AEO** fig. 4 to the first figure.

AEO figure 4 is named "Camenop"; therefore, since the initial letter is "C", it is reduced to Celarent. The "m" indicates that the premisses of Camenop are transposed. The final "p" signifies that the conclusion of Celarent is converted *per accidens*.

Using our abbreviated method of writing we have:

$$\text{Celarent} \quad \begin{array}{c} E mp \\ \underline{A sm} \\ E sp \end{array} \underset{pa}{\overset{c}{\longrightarrow}} \begin{array}{c} A sm \\ \underline{E mp} \\ O ps \end{array} \quad \text{Camenop}$$

d *Subaltern Forms of Syllogisms.* The mnemonic verses list nineteen names, lacking names for five forms called "subaltern" forms, sometimes said to have "no name nor use", often simply ignored.

Def. 6. A **subaltern syllogistic form** is one derived from a valid syllogistic form having a universal conclusion, by substituting for that conclusion its subaltern.

We mention these subaltern forms because, though they have little practical use, their omission leaves a gap in the theory. The subaltern forms are: **AAI, EAO** in figure 1; **AEO, EAO** in figure 2; and **AEO** figure 4. We name them respectively: Barbarix, Feraxo; Camestrop, Cesarox; Camenop.[14] Camestrop[2] and Camenop[4] are reduced to Celarent in the usual way, though they could also be reduced to Camestres[2] and Camenes[4] respectively by subalternation.

Here it is appropriate to complete the list of the significance of mnemonic names:

(10) An "x" is a mnemonic name immediately after the second vowel indicates subalternation of the minor premiss.

(11) An "x" after the last vowel indicates subalternation of the conclusion of the first-figure syllogism to which reduction is made.

Hence Barbarix is reduced to Barbara by subalternation of Barbara's conclusion. Feraxo[1] is reduced by subalternation of its minor premiss to Ferio. But it could also be reduced to Celarent by subalternation of the latter's conclusion.[15]

Cesarox is reduced thus:

$$\begin{array}{lcl} \text{Celarent} & & \text{Cesarox} \\ \text{No } M \text{ is } P & \xleftarrow{c} & \text{No } P \text{ is } M \\ \underline{\text{All } S \text{ is } M} & = & \underline{\text{All } S \text{ is } M} \\ \text{No } S \text{ is } P & \xrightarrow{sub} & \text{Some } S \text{ is not } P \end{array}$$

20D3 Table 20.2: Reduction of the Twenty-four Valid Forms of Aristotelian Syllogism.

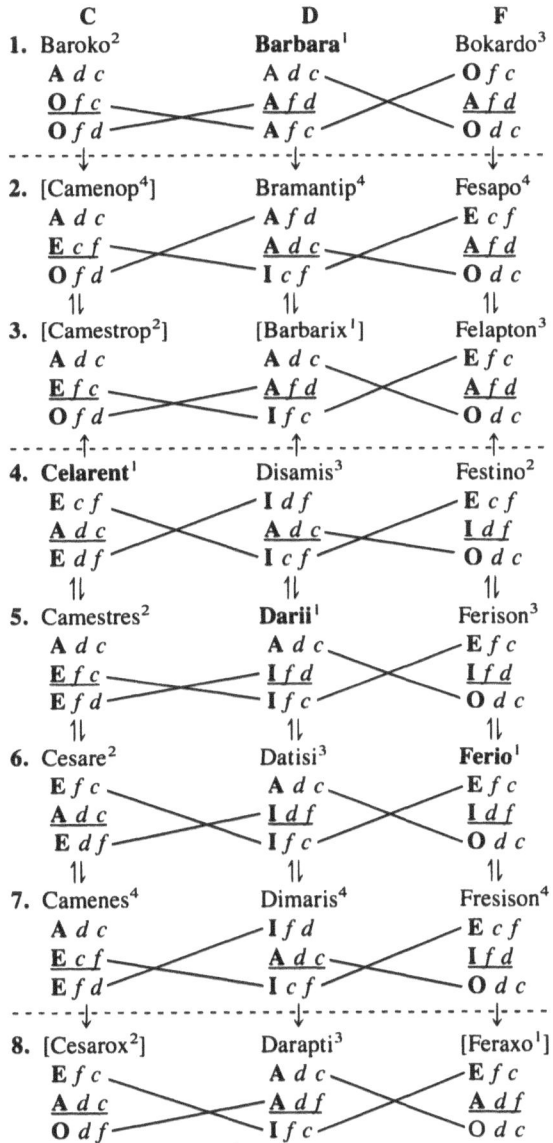

20D4 Key to the Table of Reductions

P>————<O: **P** is contradictory of *O*.

⤳̶ simplified to ×

⇅ Equivalent direct reduction. Any form reduces directly in one stage to any other in same column not separated by dotted line; Celarent to for example, Camenes.

↓ Non-equivalent direct reduction. The form above implies the form below but not conversely. The lower reduces directly to the higher.

↑ Non-equivalent direct reduction. The form below implies the form above but not conversely.

[ ] Names of subaltern forms, lacking names in mnemonic verses, in brackets.

The column letter (C, D, or F) is used for the middle term, which is not changed by direct reduction. (The middle is changed by indirect reduction; and direct reduction often changes the major and minor terms; so use of *S*, *M*, and *P* in this table would be confusing.)

The first and third forms in a row reduce to each other by simple indirect reduction.

Forms in row 1 cannot be reduced by the prescribed means except by simple indirect reduction to each other. The mnemonic names of Baroko and Bokardo indicate their reduction to Barbara.

Any form in rows 2 through 8 reduces directly in one stage to any other in the same column in rows 4 through 7. For example, any form in column C except Baroko reduces directly to Celarent; we may ignore the intervening arguments, though we could reduce by way of them if we wished. The mnemonic names—except those beginning with "B"—indicate the details of direct reduction to the first-figure forms of rows 4 through 6. "Bramantip" and "Barbarix" indicate direct reduction to Barbara.

Any form in rows 2 and 3 reduces directly in one stage to any other in the same column in rows 1 through 7. For example, Fesapo and Felapton reduce directly to Bokardo, as well as to Ferio and to each other.

Any form in rows 2 through 8 reduces by compound indirect reduction to any other form in a different column and row in rows 4 through 7. This reduction can always be made in two distinct ways. For example, Derapti can be reduced directly to Disamis, the latter indirectly to Celarent. Darapti can also be reduced indirectly to Cesarox, the latter directly to Celarent.

Any form in rows 2 through 8 reduces in one or two stages to any other form in rows 4 through 7. For example, twenty forms reduce to Celarent; twenty reduce to Camestres; and so on.

The twenty-two other forms reduce to Barbara or Celarent; the other forms reduce to Barbara or Camestres; and so on, for twelve pairs in all,

A Deductive System   287

each containing Barbara and one of the forms in rows 4 through 7. (Question for the reader: What pairs *not* containing Barbara are possible?)

20E COUNTEREXAMPLES TO SYLLOGISTIC FORMS

By reduction, we can prove that there are at least twenty-four valid syllogistic forms, given that Barbara and Celarent are valid. There are 232 syllogistic forms that cannot be reduced either directly or indirectly to an axiomatic form. This, however, is no proof that these forms are invalid; just as the fact that we cannot reduce Barbara to Celarent does not prove that Barbara is invalid. It is fallacious to argue that since all reducible syllogistic forms are valid, all irreducible syllogistic forms are invalid. The absence of proof of validity is not proof of invalidity.

Aristotle's method of reduction is a way of proving validity of syllogistic forms. The basic method used by Aristotle, and still in use, to prove that an argument form is invalid is that of counterexample.

A counterexample to an argument form, as we have said (3B), is a concrete argument of the same form with true premises and a false conclusion. The existence of a counterexample to an argument form proves that the argument form is invalid.

To illustrate the method of counterexample we shall show, as Aristotle did, that there is no valid syllogism with **AE** premises in the first figure.

(a) To show the following syllogistic form is invalid:

AEE fig. 1

All *B* are *A*
No *C* are *B*
∴ No *C* are *A*

Taking for *A*, *B*, *C*, the terms *animal, man, horse*, respectively as Aristotle suggests,[16] we get the syllogism:

All men are animals.
No horses are men.
∴ No horses are animals.

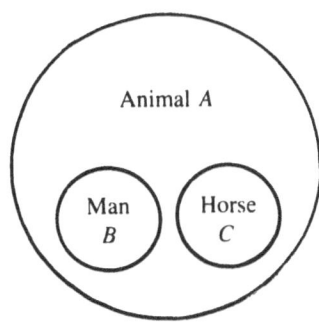

Here we know from the meaning of the terms that the premisses are true and the conclusion false. The diagram represents the actual situation, not merely what the premisses imply. (The size of the circles has no significance.) This syllogism is a counterexample to **AEE** figure 1, which is therefore invalid.

With the same true premisses, the conclusion "Some horses are not animals" is also false; so **AEO** figure 1 is invalid.

We must not hastily infer from our counterexample that, with **AE** premisses in figure 1, the situation is necessarily as it is above, and that we may infer an affirmative conclusion. This is not the case, as another counterexample shows.

(b) To show the following syllogistic form is invalid:

AEA fig. 1

All *B* are *A*
<u>No *C* are *B*</u>
∴ All *C* are *A*

We could interpret *A, B, C* as in example (a) above, and make an argument in which all the propositions are true. This, however, would prove nothing, since valid as well as invalid arguments may have all true propositions. But if we interpret *A, B, C* as animal, man, stone, respectively, as Aristotle suggests in the passage cited, we have the counterexample:

All men are animals.
<u>No stones are men.</u>
∴ All stones are animals.

This syllogism has true premisses and a false conclusion. It is a counterexample to **AEA** figure 1, which is therefore invalid. The same interpretation also shows that **AEI** figure 1 is invalid, since "Some stones are animals" is also false.

Summarizing what has been established, we see that **AE** premisses can give neither **A, E, I,** nor **O** conclusion in the first figure. (The do indeed give a conclusion in the fourth figure: what conclusion? But this does not concern us at the moment.)

Note that neither of the two diagrams above diagrams just what the premisses "All *B* are *A*" and "No *C* are *B*" assert, since either of these two situations is consistent with the premises. (And a third is possible, in which the minor term *C* is partly in, partly out, of the major term *A*.) In showing an argument invalid with this style of diagram, we diagram a situation in which the premises are true and the conclusion false.

Aristotle goes on to consider **EE** premises in figure 1; and similarly considers all possible pairs of premises in the three figures he recognizes, to show that there are no valid syllogisms other than those reducible to the axiomatic of the first figure. We shall not repeat this account (to which we would have to add a similar consideration of fourth-figure forms); but we shall consider invalid forms systematically in the next chapter.

20F SUMMARY OF CHAPTER

(Section A) Aristotle presented the doctrine of the syllogism as a deductive system. He took syllogisms of the first figure as axiomatic; **AAA** and **EAE** in figure 1 are sufficient. Other forms are proved valid by reduction to these.

(Section B) Where possible, syllogisms are usually reduced by direct reduction. This may take the form of equivalent direct reduction, which uses only reversible immediate inferences (for Aristotle, only simple conversion of **E** and **I,** and repetition); or non-equivalent direct reduction, which uses a nonreversible immediate inference (only conversion *per accidens* of **A** and **E** in Aristotle; we add subalternation) combined with reversible inferences. In nonequivalent reduction, one must observe the proper order of the entailments, to make use of the transitivity of the entailment relation.

(Section C) Reduction may also be made by indirect reduction, which is needed to reduce **AOO** figure 2 and **OAO** figure 3 to the first figure. In simple indirect reduction, the conclusion and one premiss of one syllogism are contradicted and transposed to give a syllogism equivalent in validity. Indirect may also be combined with direct reduction. Twenty-four forms in all—six in each of the four figures—are valid by reduction to the axiomatic forms.

(Section D) Mnemonic verses provide names for nineteen forms—excluding five subaltern forms—that show how they may be reduced to the first figure. All twenty-four forms are presented in the Table of Reduction.

(Section E) Aristotle showed the invalidity of invalid forms by counterexample. This is illustrated for syllogisms with **AE** premises in the first figure.[16]

21

Rules of the Standard Syllogism

Medieval and modern logicians have developed sets of rules for testing standard categorical syllogisms. It was found that relatively simple rules of distribution, quality, and quantity permitted direct judgment of the validity of a syllogism, without resort to reduction or comparison with a complete list of valid forms. While the principles of Aristotelian reduction to the first figure can reasonably claim self-evidence, such a claim is doubtful for these rules, plausible though they are. But for quick determination of validity, rules of this sort are unsurpassed.

The rules are commonly applied to the 256 standard forms of syllogism, and pick out the twenty-four valid forms of the previous chapter. But the order in which the premisses are written is immaterial.

21A FORMAL RULES

A standard syllogism is formally valid if and only if it satisfies the four formal rules:

21A1 Rules of Quality.

R1 (*Rule of Affirmative Conclusion:* Rule Af) **If the conclusion is affirmative, both premisses are affirmative.**

R2 (*Rule of Negative Conclusion:* Rule Neg) **If the conclusion is negative, just one premiss is negative.**

21A2 Rules of Distribution.

R3 (*Rule of Distributed Middle:* Rule DMid) **The middle term is distributed at least once.**

R4 (*Rule of Distributed Extreme:* Rule DX) **Any Term distributed in the conclusion is distributed in the premiss.**

21A3 Comments on Formal Rules.

On R1: The converse of Rule Af holds for valid syllogisms (by Rule Neg).

On R2: The converse of Rule Neg holds for valid syllogisms (by Rule Af). Also, since there are just two premisses, the consequent of Rule Neg is equivalent to "just one premiss is affirmative", and to "one premiss is negative, one affirmative". The form chosen for Rule Neg is one that holds also for chain arguments with more than two premisses. (See chapter 22.)

On R3: The middle term may be distributed twice in a valid syllogism (on the Aristotelian interpretation). This occurs in just three forms (of the nine that infer a particular from two universals: see Table of Reduction 20D3).

On R4: The converse of Rule DX does not hold for every valid form (on the Aristotelian interpretation). A term distributed in a premiss is undistributed in the conclusion in six of the forms that infer a particular from two universals.

21.B FORMAL FALLACIES OF THE SYLLOGISM

A (standard) syllogism violating a formal rule commits a formal fallacy. These are the fallacies of quality and fallacies of distribution.

21B1 Fallacies of Quality.

F1 The fallacy of **affirmative from negative** (AFN) occurs when the syllogism has an affirmative conclusion and one or more premisses negative. For example:

> *All snapdragons are plants.*
> *No snapdragons are carnivores.*
> ∴ *All carnivores are plants.*

F2 The fallacy of **inequality of negatives (IN)** occurs when a syllogism has a negative conclusion and does not have exactly one negative premise. For example:

All equiangular triangles are 60–60–60 degree triangles.
All 60–60–60 degree triangles are equilateral triangles.
∴ *Some equilateral triangles are not equiangular triangles.*

(Note: An **EEE** syllogism, for example, may also be characterized as a fallacy of *negative premisses;* and so may an **EEI** syllogism, which violates Rule Af.)

21B2 Fallacies of Distribution.

F3 The fallacy of **undistributed middle (UM)** occurs when the middle term is undistributed in both premisses. For example:

All mothers are females.
All women are females.
∴ *All women are mothers.*

F4 The fallacy of **illicit Process (IP)** occurs when a term is distributed in the conclusion but not distributed in the premisses. Two cases are distinguished:

The fallacy of **illicit major** (i.e., illicit process of the major term) occurs when the major term is distributed in the conclusion but not in its premiss. For example:

All salamanders are amphibians.
No toads are salamanders.
∴ *No toads are amphibians.*

The fallacy of *illicit minor* occurs when the minor term is distributed in the conclusion but not in its premiss. For example:

No tigers are vegetarians.
All tigers are mammals.
∴ *No mammals are vegetarians.*

21C TESTING VALIDITY OF AN ARGUMENT BY RULES

21C1 First Step. Check argument by the definition of a standard syllogism, that is, see that (a) its two premisses and conclusion are all standard categorical propositions, and (b) subject and predicate of conclusion are terms of different premisses, joined to a middle term.

If the argument is not a standard syllogism as defined, these formal rules cannot be used to determine its validity directly. But if we can translate the argument into a standard syllogism, we can then use the rules. (See chapter 23, on reducing number of terms, and chapter 25, on non-standard propositions.)

21C2. Second Step. Check standard syllogism by formal rules. If it violates one or more of the rules, it is formally invalid. If it satisfies all the rules, it is formally valid.

The quality may be checked at a glance, from the mood or the quantifies. It can be seen at once if it has one of the two permissible patterns: all propositions affirmative, or premisses differing in quality with conclusion negative.

To check distribution, one may mark the distributed terms till one sees whether the middle term is distributed, and whether every term distributed in the conclusion is distributed in its premiss. (If either premiss is an **E**, the middle term must be distributed. If the conclusion is an **I**, there can be no illicit process.)

21C3 Third Step. Check semantic rules; that is, decide if context or content of the argument give reason to doubt whether (a) each expression is used in the same sense in every occurrence throughout the argument (identical expressions with different meaning are different terms); and (b) the form words ("All . . . are", etc.) are used in the appropriate way—here meaning "according to the traditional (Aristotelian) interpretation". This third step belongs to the art of applying logic, not to the science of formal logic.

21D DERIVED RULES FOR THE SYLLOGISM

The following rules are deducible theorems from the four basic formal rules (R1–R4) of section 21A. They are useful for direct judgment of validity of syllogisms, and for proving other rules and principles. If a standard syllogism is valid, the seven following rules hold:

21D1 Derived Rules of Quality.

DR1 Not both premisses are negative.

PROOF. The conclusion is either affirmative or negative. If it is affirmative, both premisses are affirmative (by Rule Af). If it is negative, just one premiss is negative (by Rule Neg). Therefore, in either case, not both premisses are negative. DR1, and the fallacy in an argument that violates it, may be called "Negative premisses".

DR2 If a premiss is negative, so is the conclusion. (Corollary of Rule Af.)

Violation of DR2 (as of Rule Af) is the fallacy of affirmative from negative.

DR3 If both premisses are affirmative, so is the conclusion.

Further proofs are left to the reader.

21D2 Derived Rule of Distribution.

DR4 The number of distinct terms distributed in the premisses is at least one more than in the conclusion.

This can be proved by using Rules DMid and DX.

21D3 Derived Rules of Quantity.

DR5 Not both premisses are particular.

To prove, consider each of the possible forms with particular premisses. DR5 and the corresponding fallacy are called "Particular premisses".

DR6 If a premiss is particular, so is the conclusion.

21D4 Derived Rule of Quantity and Quality.

DR7 If the major premiss is particular, the minor premiss is an A.

If the major premiss is an **I**, the major term is undistributed in it, and hence in the conclusion (by Rule DX), which must be affirmative. And so on.

21E ALTERNATIVE SETS OF RULES

Many other sets of formal rules have been or could be given for the standard syllogism (not counting non-Aristotelian interpretations). In contemporary textbooks, we find sets of rules ranging from three (J. Culbertson,

W. Salmon) to eight (Chapman and Henle). Some sets are incomplete; the longer ones commonly contain redundant rules. (A rule of a given set of rules is called "redundant" if any argument invalidated by the rule is also invalidated by another rule of the set. Any of our derived rules would be redundant if added to our set of four formal rules. If DR6 or DR7 appears in a set, it is likely to be redundant.)

21E1 Concise Rules for Syllogism. We give a set of two rules, one of quality and one of distribution. A categorical syllogism is valid if and only if:

CR1 The number of negative premisses equals the number of negative conclusions; and

CR2 Every term is either distributed in a premiss or undistributed in the conclusion.

The reader can show that Rule CR1 is equivalent to the two rules Af and Neg together. (The number of negative conclusions is of course either one or zero.)[1]

Rule CR2 is equivalent to rules DMid and DX together. Rule CR2 requires that the middle term (which is not *un*distributed in the conclusion) be distributed in a premiss; and that an extreme term, if it is distributed in the conclusion (hence not undistributed there), must be distributed in a premiss.[2]

21E2 Other Sets of Rules. Rules of distribution differ from our rules DMid and DX (if at all) only in details of wording. For rules of quality, one commonly finds DR1 (negative premisses), plus a pair or rules that may be put into a single sentence such as: "The conclusion is negative if and only if just one premiss is negative". Starting from the conclusion, there are two cases; starting from the premisses, there are three cases, as presented in our rules DR1–3. The reader may prove that the rules DR1–3 are equivalent to our pair of rules Af and Neg, without using any rules of distribution.

Often included are such "rules" as: "Every standard syllogism must consist of three categorical propositions and contain just three terms". This statement should not be included in the rules, because it is implicitly contained in the definition of the standard syllogism. If the rules are stated as rules for validity of standard syllogisms as defined above, the statement is redundant. If the rules are intended to apply to "syllogisms" in some broader sense—perhaps containing four terms—then this statement (and other rules as well) is not true; for a quasi-syllogistic argument may contain four terms and yet be valid. (See chapter 23 on reducing number of terms.) The statement, if thought of as defining "standard syllogism", is misleading, since it does not contain the complete definition.

21F THE ARISTOTELIAN ANTILOGISM[3]

The antilogistic method of testing a syllogism for validity is worth knowing, since it is relative simple and can be extended to the sorites. An analogous method can be used for other types of argument (e.g., the hypothetical syllogism, etc.).

21F1 Definitions and Principles.

Def. 1. An **antilogistic triad** is the set of three propositions formed from a standard syllogism by taking its premisses together with the contradictory of its conclusion. For example:

SYLLOGISM	ANTILOGISTIC TRIAD
All romantics are daydreamers.	All romantics are daydreamers.
Some clergy are romantics.	Some clergy are romantics.
∴ Some clergy are daydreamers.	No clergy are daydreamers.

Def. 2. An **antilogism** is the assertion that an antilogistic triad is inconsistent.[4]

For example, the antilogism of the above syllogism is the assertion that the triad *All romantics are daydreamers, Some clergy are romantics, No clergy are daydreamers* is inconsistent. The relation between a syllogism and its antilogism is stated in principle 1.

Principle 1. A standard syllogism is valid iffi its antilogism is true.

This principle is equivalent to principle 1a.

Principle 1a. A standard syllogism is valid iffi its antilogistic triad is inconsistent.[5]

Consequently, a standard syllogism is tested for validity by testing its antilogistic triad for inconsistency. If this triad is inconsistent, then the antilogism is true and the syllogism is valid. If the triad is consistent then the antilogism is false and the syllogism is invalid.

21F2 Testing the Syllogism for Validity. Principle 1a can be used to test a syllogism for validity if we know how to test the antilogistic triad for inconsistency.

a *Antilogistic Rules.*

An antilogistic triad is inconsistent iffi the triad obeys rules AR1 and AR2:

AR1 Exactly one proposition in the triad is negative.[6]

AR2 Each term in the triad is distributed at least once.[7]

A rule of quantity can be proved from rules AR1 and AR2. Its use sometimes expedites matters.

AR3 At most one proposition in the triad is particular.[8]

Using these antilogistic rules, we will test the following triads (which we assume have been formed from corresponding syllogisms) for inconsistency:

(a) All X are Y
All Z are X
Some Z are not Y

(b) Some X are Y
All X are Z
Some Z are not Y

(c) Some A are not B
All B are C
No A are C

(d) No B are C
All C are D
All B are D

Triad (a) is inconsistent, since it obeys all the rules. Triads (b), (c), and (d) are consistent. Triad (b) has two particulars (and a term that is not distributed), triad (c) has two negatives, and triad (d) has a term that is not distributed.

b *Procedure for Testing.* The procedure for testing a standard syllogism for validity by the antilogistic rules is quite simple.

Step 1. Form the antilogistic triad by taking the premisses of the syllogism together with the contradictory of its conclusion.

Step 2. Test this triad for inconsistency by rules AR1 and AR2. (AR3 may be used also.) The triad is consistent if it breaks any one of the rules. The triad is inconsistent iffi it satisfies AR1 and AR2.

Solution. The syllogism is valid iffi its triad is inconsistent.

c *Example* Two concrete examples illustrating the antilogistic method follows.

(A)   SYLLOGISM   ANTILOGISTIC TRIAD

No zebus are reptiles.   *No zebus are reptiles.*
All zebus are mammals.   *All zebus are mammals.*
∴ *No mammals are reptiles.*   *Some mammals are reptiles.*

The triad is consistent, since it violates rule 1: "Mammals" is undistributed in both occurrences. Therefore (by principle 1a) the syllogism is invalid.

(b)   SYLLOGISM   ANTILOGISTIC TRIAD

No women are priests.   *No women are priests.*
Some pacifists are women.   *Some pacifists are women.*
∴ *Some pacifists are not priests.*   *All pacifists are priests.*

This triad is inconsistent, since it obeys rules AR1–2. Consequently the syllogism is valid (principle 1a).

21G TABLE 21.1: VALID FORMS OF STANDARD ORDER SYLLOGISMS

1) **AAA**-1
All M are P
All S are M
All S are P

   EAE-1
No M are P
All S are M
No S are P

   AII-1
All M are P
Some S are M
Some S are P

   EIO-1
No M are P
Some S are M
Some S are not P

2) **AAI**-1
All M are P
All S are M
Some S are P

   EAO-1
No M are P
All S are M
Some S are not P

3) **AEE**-2
All P are M
No S are M
No S are P

   EAE-2
No P are M
All S are M
No S are P

   AOO-2
All P are M
Some S are not M
Some S are not P

   EIO-2
No P are M
Some S are M
Some S are not P

4) **AEO**-2
All P are M
No S are M
Some S are not P

   EAO-2
No P are M
All S are M
Some S are not P

5) **AII**-3
All M are P
Some M are S
Some S are P

   IAI-3
Some M are P
All M are S
Some S are P

   EIO-3
No M are P
Some M are S
Some S are not P

   OAO-3
Some M are not P
All M are S
Some S are not P

6)   **AAI**-3
All M are P
All M are S
Some S are P

   EAO-3
No M are P
All M are S
Some S are not P

7) **AEE**-4
All P are M
No M are S
No S are P

   IAI-4
Some P are M
All M are S
Some S are P

   EIO-4
No P are M
Some M are S
Some S are not P

8) **AEO**-4
All P are M
No M are S
Some S are not P

   AAI-4
All P are M
All M are S
Some S are P

   EAO-4
No P are M
All M are S
Some S are not P

The forms in rows 2 and 4, and **AEO**-4 in row 8, are subaltern forms; that is, the conclusion is a subaltern to a universal conclusion from the same premisses in the same figure (in row above). These five forms are omitted from the medieval mnemonic verses.

All the forms in rows 2, 4, 6, and 8 draw a particular conclusion from two universals, hence presuppose an Aristotelian interpretation.

Exercises for Chapter 21

21, I. Test the following forms of syllogism for validity by the four traditional rules. If the form is invalid, name a fallacy it commits by placing the appropriate letters in the margin.

KEY

AFN affirmative from negative
IN   inequality of negatives
UM   undistributed middle
IP   illicit process
V   valid

_____ 1. All *P* are *M*
       All *S* are *M*
       ∴ All *S* are *P*

_____ 2. Some *S* are not *M*
       No *P* are *M*
       ∴ Some *S* are not *P*

_____ 3. All *P* are *M*
       No *S* are *M*
       ∴ No *S* are *P*

_____ 4. All *P* are *M*
       Some *S* are *M*
       ∴ Some *S* are *P*

_____ 5. All *P* are *M*
       All *M* are *S*
       ∴ All *S* are *P*

_____ 6. All *P* are *S*
       Some *M* are *S*
       ∴ Some *M* are not *P*

_____ 7. All *M* are *S*
       Some *P* are *M*
       ∴ All *P* are *S*

_____ 8. No *M* are *S*
       No *P* are *S*
       ∴ No *P* are *M*

_____ 9. Some *S* are *P*
       All *S* are *M*
       ∴ No *M* are *P*

_____ 10. Some *M* are not *S*
       All *P* are *S*
       ∴ No *P* are *M*

_____ 11. Some X are not Y
       All X are Z
       ∴ Some Z are not Y

_____ 12. No X are Z
       All Y are Z
       ∴ All Y are X

_____ 13. No Z are Y
       All X are Y
       ∴ No X are Z

_____ 14. All X are Y
       Some Z are not X
       ∴ Some Z are Y

_____ 15. Some X are Z, since some X are not Y and some Y are Z.

_____ 16. Some *M* are *P*, so some *S* are *P*, since all *S* are *M*.

_____ 17. Some *P* are *M* and no *S* are *M*, therefore some *S* are not *P*.

_____ 18. Some *S* are not *M*, hence no *S* are *P*, since all *P* are *M*.

_____ 19. Some *S* are *P*, for all *M* are *S* and some *M* are not *P*.

_____ 20. Some *M* are not *S* and no *M* are *P*, so some *S* are not *P*.

21, II. Test the following standard syllogisms for validity by the four traditional rules. If the syllogism is invalid state the formal fallacy that it commits.

KEY

AFN Affirmative from negative
 IN Inequality of negatives
 UM Undistributed middle
 IP Illicit process
  V Valid

_____ 1. All allies of the United States are enemies of the Third Reich.
All Allies of Great Britain are enemies of the Third Reich.
∴ All allies of Great Britain are allies of the United States.

_____ 2. No large, fierce, sharks are nice house pets.
All porbeagles are large, fierce sharks.
∴ No porbeagles are nice house pets.

_____ 3. All chorus girls are professional dancers.
No nuns are chorus girls.
∴ Some nuns are not professional dancers.

_____ 4. All objects that are denser than water are objects that will float in water.
Some objects that are denser than water are not things that are soluble in water.
∴ Some things that are soluble in water are not objects that will float in water.

_____ 5. Some troubadours of ancient France are men who were members of the heretical Cathars.
All the troubadours of ancient France are men who were advocates of courtly love.
∴ Some men who were advocates of courtly love are men who were members of the heretical Cathars.

_____ 6. Some large pills are not placebos.
       All boluses are large pills.
       ∴ Some boluses are not placebos.

_____ 7. Some circus acrobats are guitar players.
       No geisha girls are guitar players.
       ∴ No geisha girls are circus acrobats.

_____ 8. All horses are winged sharks.
       All winged sharks are quadrupeds.
       ∴ All horses are quadrupeds.

_____ 9. No cooling drinks are hot drinks.
       Some beverages are cooling drinks.
       ∴ Some beverages are hot drinks.

_____ 10. All good hikers are nature lovers.
       All soldiers are good hikers.
       ∴ All soldiers are nature lovers.

_____ 11. All successful politicians are good speakers.
       All successful lawyers are good speakers.
       ∴ All successful politicians are successful lawyers.

_____ 12. No numbers evenly divisible by two are numbers evenly divisible by four.
       No odd numbers are numbers evenly divisible by two.
       ∴ No odd numbers are numbers evenly divisible by four.

_____ 13. All devils are barb-tailed creatures.
       All imps are devils.
       ∴ All imps are barb-tailed creatures.

_____ 14. No sultans are bus drivers.
       All bus drivers are union members.
       ∴ No union members are sultans.

_____ 15. All cowboys are bowlegged people.
       Some Wall Street bankers are not cowboys.
       ∴ Some Wall Street bankers are not bowlegged people.

_____ 16. Some athletes are prudent people.
       No prudent people are smokers.
       ∴ Some athletes are smokers.

_____ 17. Some parrots are not talkative birds.
       All macaws are parrots.
       ∴ Some macaws are not talkative birds.

304 *Exercises/Chapter 21*

_____ 18. No ballet dancers are stout people.
All stout people are people who dislike hot weather.
∴ No people who dislike hot weather are ballet dancers.

_____ 19. All people who are alcoholics are people who are considered to be maladjusted.
Some society matrons are people who are alcoholics.
∴ Some society matrons are people who are considered to be maladjusted.

_____ 20. No men willing to die for their beliefs are cowards.
All men indistinguishable from Socrates are men willing to die for their beliefs.
∴ No men indistinguishable from Socrates are cowards.

21, III. The following arguments are standard syllogisms, except that the conclusion may be in the middle. Write 1, 2, or 3 in the first blank accordingly as the conclusion is the first, second, or third proposition respectively. Then test for validity by the four traditional rules, and write AFN, IN, UM, IP, or V in the second blank.

_____, _____ 1. All mushrooms are fungi, and all mildews are fungi; therefore all mushrooms are mildews.

_____, _____ 2. Some teachers are married men; for some teachers are bachelors, and no bachelors are married men.

_____, _____ 3. All nudists are suntanned people; so all nudists are nature lovers, for all suntanned people are nature lovers.

_____, _____ 4. All red bugs are chiggers, and no fleas are red bugs; hence no chiggers are fleas.

_____, _____ 5. Some lawyers are not dishonest people, but all judges are lawyers; so some judges are not dishonest people.

_____, _____ 6. Some crimes of passion are not voluntary actions; therefore no moral acts are crimes of passion, since all moral acts are voluntary actions.

_____, _____ 7. Some cenobites are not gold prospectors, for no gold prospectors are gregarious, and some cenobites are not gregarious.

_____, _____ 8. Since no military generals are circus midgets, and all circus midgets are undersized people, no undersized people are military generals.

_____, _____ 9. No theological hierarchies are democracies; so, since all hierarchies are theological hierarchies, all hierarchies are democracies.

_____, _____ 10. Some athiests are obscure people, and no obscure people are famous people; consequently some athiests are famous people.

_____, _____ 11. All gin drinks are alcoholic beverages; for all alcoholic beverages are intoxicating beverages, and all gin drinks are intoxicating beverages.

_____, _____ 12. No members of the Diogenes Club are members of the Aristotelian Society; so no people interested in philosophy are members of the Diogenes Club, since all members of the Aristotelian Society are people interested in philosophy.

_____, _____ 13. No retired gamblers are good insurance risks; so, since some jet pilots are not good insurance risks, some jet pilots are not retired gamblers.

_____, _____ 14. No band conductors are ballet dancers, because some ballet dancers are not musically inclined people and all band conductors are musically inclined people.

_____, _____ 15. No union members are antisocial people; therefore some mountain climbers are antisocial people, since some mountain climbers are union members.

_____, _____ 16. No stingrays are whales, and all whales are mammals; ergo no mammals are stingrays.

_____, _____ 17. No Texan cowboys are professional jockeys, but some professional tennis players are not professional jockeys; hence some professional tennis players are not Texan cowboys.

_____, _____ 18. All dictionaries are books, and some books are not great literary works, so some dictionaries are not great literary works.

_____, _____ 19. Some Australian bushmen are not poor insurance risks, because no Australian bushmen are alcoholic jet pilots, and all alcoholic jet pilots are poor insurance risks.

_____, _____ 20. All sharks are carnivores; therefore no carnivores are camelopards, because no camelopards are sharks.

21, III, B. Draw the strongest valid syllogistic conclusion (if any) from each of the following pairs of premisses.

1. No military generals are Olympic athletes, and some Olympic athletes are women.
2. All concert musicians are people who love music, and some revolutionists are not concert musicians.
3. Some Buddhist monks are not readers of the *New York Times,* but all informed New Yorkers are readers of the *New York Times.*
4. Some spies are code experts and all code experts are crossword puzzle fans.
5. No chess players are jazz musicians and some checker players are not jazz musicians.
6. No airline pilots are exconvicts, but some airline pilots are grandfathers.
7. All extraverts are friendly people, but some Zen Masters are not friendly people.
8. All dogs are mammals and all canines are mammals.
9. Some philosophers are not men, but all philosophers are wise people.
10. All alcoholics are insecure people and some alcoholics are women.

21, IV. Prove derived rules DR2–DR7. In each case the proof may use any basic formal rule (R1–R4) or any derived rule having a lower number than the one being proved.

21, V. For the following proofs, any formal rule or derived rule may be used. A proof of the first exercise is presented in detail.

1. Prove that any valid syllogistic form in figure 1 must have a universal major premiss.
   PROOF. Figure 1
   $$\begin{array}{c} M \text{ - } P \\ \underline{S \text{ - } M} \\ S \text{ - } P \end{array}$$

(a) *Suppose* there is a valid syllogism in figure 1 that has a *particular* major premiss.

(b) Then M is undistributed in the major premiss (since the subject of a particular is undistributed).

(h) Neg	(b) M̤ -[P]	(g)
(d) Neg	S -[M]	(c)
(e) Neg	S -[P]	(f)

Letters refer to steps in the proof.

Distribution indicated by square, lack of it by dots.

(c) So M must be distributed in the minor premiss (by rule DMid).

(d) Then the minor premiss is negative (since *only* negatives distribute the predicate).

(e) Hence the conclusion is negative (by DR2).

(f) And so the major term P is distributed (since all negatives distribute the predicate).

(g) Then the major term must be distributed in the major premiss (by rule DX).

(h) Hence the major premiss also must be negative.

(i) But it is impossible that (d) and (h) both be true (by DR1).

(j) Hence the supposition (1)—that the valid figure-1 syllogism has a *particular* major premiss—is impossible.

(k) Therefore, the major premiss must be universal in figure 1.

We have given an indirect proof, that is, a proof that starts by supposing the contradictory of what we want to prove. Then we proceed until we get results that cannot both be true, which shows that the original supposition was false. The advantage of this kind of proof is that it gives an extra premiss to start from.

2. Prove that a valid syllogistic form in figure 1 must have an affirmative minor premiss.

3. Prove that a valid syllogistic form in figure 2 must have a universal major premiss.

4. Prove that a valid syllogistic form in figure 2 must have a negative conclusion.

5. Prove that a valid syllogistic form in figure 3 must have an affirmative minor premiss.

6. Prove that a valid syllogistic form in figure 3 must have a particular conclusion.

7. Prove that a valid syllogistic form in figure 4 with an affirmative major premiss must have a universal minor premiss.

8. Prove that a valid syllogistic form in figure 4 with one negative premiss must have a universal major premiss.

9. Prove that a valid syllogistic form must have at least one subject term distributed.

10. Prove that a valid syllogistic form must have either zero or two predicate terms distributed.

11. Prove that a valid syllogistic form with an O premiss must have an O conclusion.

12. Prove that no valid syllogistic form in figure 3 can have the subject term of each proposition distributed.

13. Prove that a valid syllogistic form in figure 2 must have the predicate term of exactly one premiss distributed.

14. Give the valid syllogistic forms that have only one occurrence of one term distributed.

15. Prove that no valid syllogistic form in figures 2, 3, and 4 can have an A conclusion.

21, VI. For each of the following construct a valid syllogism having the stated proposition as the conclusion. Try to find premisses for these syllogisms that are as reasonable as possible (i.e., do not select premisses that are obviously false).

1. All dictators are insecure people.

2. No atheists are theists.

3. Some philosophers are not materialists.

4. Some acts of aggression are moral actions.

5. All physical entities are observable entities.

6. No pleasures are intrinsic evils.

7. Some Greeks are not philosophers.

8. Some wars are morally justified acts.

9. No beliefs common to all religions are false beliefs.

10. Some statements in the Bible are not false statements.

22

Chain Arguments Including Sorites

22A DEFINITIONS

Def. 1. A **chain argument** is a deductive argument (i) consisting of n (n = two or more) standard categorical propositions, with (ii) n distinct terms, (iii) each term occurring in just two propositions, (iv) with conclusion last (or first) and (v) two successive propositions always sharing a term.

It follows from definition 1 that the conclusion of a chain argument will share a term with the first premiss and another with the last premiss.

Def. 2. A **middle term** of a chain argument is a term shared by two premisses.

Def. 3. The **major term** of a chain argument is the predicate of the conclusion.

Def. 4. The **minor term** of a chain argument is the subject of the conclusion.

Def. 5. An **extreme term** of a chain argument is the minor or major term.

Def. 6. A **standard sorites** is a chain argument with four or more propositions.

An example of a standard sorites follows:

All dogs are mammals.
No reptiles are mammals.
All snakes are reptiles.
All cobras are snakes.
∴ No dogs are cobras.

If the premisses in the above example were written in reverse order, the sorites would still be standard. By "sorites" we mean a standard sorites unless otherwise specified.

A standard categorical syllogism (19A, def. 1) could be defined as a chain argument with three propositions. A **two-term argument** could be defined as a chain argument with two propositions. A chain argument is either a two-term argument, a standard syllogism, or a standard sorites.

22B DETERMINING THE VALIDITY OF A CHAIN ARGUMENT

22B1 Formal Rules. A chain argument is formally valid if and only if it satisfies the following four formal rules:

Rules of Quality

R1 (Rule of Affirmative Conclusion: Rule Af) **If the conclusion is affirmative, all the premisses are affirmative.**

R2 (Rule of Negative Conclusion: Rule Neg) **If the conclusion is negative, just one premiss is negative.**

Rules of Distribution

R3 (Rule of Distributed Middle: Rule DMid) **Any middle term is distributed at least once.**

R4 (Rule of Distributed Extreme: Rule DX) **Any term distributed in the conclusion is distributed in a premiss.**

These four rules provide a test for formal validity for two-term arguments, for standard syllogisms, and for standard sorites, since they are all chain arguments. (A two-term argument is a chain argument containing just two propositions.)

The Rule of Distributed Middle, R3, is "satisfied vacuously", as the mathematicians say, by two-term arguments, since they have no middle term.

22B2 Formal Fallacies. A chain argument violating a formal rule commits a formal fallacy. The names of these are:

1. The fallacy of **affirmative from negative** occurs when the chain argument has an affirmative conclusion and one or more premisses negative.
2. The fallacy of **inequality of negatives** occurs when the chain argument has a negative conclusion and does not have exactly one negative premiss.
3. The fallacy of **undistributed middle** occurs when a middle term in a chain argument is undistributed in both of its premisses.
4. The fallacy of **illicit process** occurs when a term in a chain argument is distributed in the conclusion but not distributed in the premisses.

22B3 Concise Rules. The set of two concise rules for the syllogism (21E1) also holds for all chain arguments. A chain argument is formally valid iffi:

CR1 The number of negative premisses equals the number of negative conclusions; and
CR2 Every term is either distributed in a premiss or undistributed in the conclusion.

The reader can show that CR1 is equivalent to the two rules R1 and R2 (Af and Neg) of 22B taken together. Likewise CR2 is equivalent to R3 and R4 (DMid and DX) taken together.

22B4 Antilogistic Test. The antilogistic method of testing syllogisms (21F) can be generalized with slight changes to give a test for validity of chain arguments.

Def. 7. An **antilogistic polyad** is a set of (two or more) propositions formed from a chain argument by taking its premiss(es) together with the contradictory of its conclusion.

Antilogistic Principle: A chain argument is valid iffi its antilogistic polyad is inconsistent. **Antilogistic Rules**: The rules for antilogistic polyad are the same as for an antilogistic triad (21F2), replacing "triad" by "polyad".

An antilogistic polyad is inconsistent iffi it satisfies rules A1 and A2:

A1 Exactly one proposition in the polyad is negative.
A2 Each term in the polyad is distributed at least once.

It may be shown easily that these rules are equivalent to the concise rules of 22B3.

An example of testing a sorites by antilogistic method:

Sorites	Antilogistic Polyad
All dogs are mammals.	All *dogs* are mammals.
No reptiles are mammals.	No *reptiles* are *mammals*.
All snakes are reptiles.	All *snakes* are reptiles.
All cobras are snakes.	All *cobras* are snakes.
∴ Some dogs are not cobras. >—<	All *dogs* are cobras.

Exactly one proposition in the polyad is negative; and every term in the polyad is distributed at least once. Hence the polyad is inconsistent and the sorites is valid.

Exercises for Chapter 22

22,I (for 22A). For each of the following arguments, indicate whether it is a chain argument (Yes or No). If it is, indicate what kind: two-term argument (2-T), standard syllogism (Syl), or sorites (Sori).

1. All dogs are vertebrates; therefore, no dogs are non-vertebrates.
   Chain arg.? _____ If so, what kind? _____
2. Some men are liars, therefore some men are not liars.
   Chain arg.? _____ If so, what kind? _____
3. Some men are liars, and some men are not liars; so some liars are not liars.
   Chain arg.? _____ If so, what kind? _____
4. All professors are scholars; so all absent-minded professors are scholars.
   Chain arg.? _____ If so, what kind? _____
5. All professors are scholars, some scholars are absent-minded; hence some scholars are professors.
   Chain arg.? _____ If so, what kind? _____
6. Some professors are absent-minded; for all professors are scholars, and some scholars are absent-minded.
   Chain arg.? _____ If so, what kind? _____
7. All men are bipeds; some mammals are not bipeds; some vertebrates are mammals; and all mammals are vertebrates. Therefore, some vertebrates are not men.
   Chain arg.? _____ If so, what kind? _____
8. All fish are aquatic animals; all sharks are fish; no cats are sharks; therefore, no cats are aquatic animals.
   Chain arg.? _____ If so, what kind? _____
9. All whales are mammals; all trout are fish; all sharks are fish; no trout are sharks; no mammals are reptiles; therefore, no whales are reptiles.
   Chain arg.? _____ If so, what kind? _____
10. All entrepreneurs are after a large profit.
    No cautious investors are after a large profit.
    Some businessmen are cautious investors.
    So, some businessmen are not entrepreneurs.
    Chain arg.? _____ If so, what kind? _____

22, II (For 22B1). For each argument of Exercise I above that is a chain argument, determine its validity by the rules of 22B1. If it is invalid, name the rule it violates (Af, Neg, DMid, DX).

22, III (For 22A, B1). For the arguments of Exercise I above that are *not* chain arguments, try to determine their validity by some means. (Hint: In some cases, from an argument that is not a chain argument, a chain argument may be obtained by deleting one or more premisses.)

22, IV (For 22 B2). Test the following forms of standard sorites for validity by the four formal rules. Place the appropriate letters in the margin, naming the fallacy if any.

KEY

AFN Invalid: affirmative from negative
IN Invalid: inequality of negatives
UM Invalid: undistributed middle
IP Invalid: illicit process
V Valid

_____ 1. All A are B
      All B are C
      All C are D
    ∴ Some A are D

_____ 2. No C are D
      Some D are B
      Some A are not B
    ∴ Some A are not C

_____ 3. No C are B
      All B are D
      Some D are E
    ∴ Some C are not E

_____ 4. All A are C
      All C are B
      Some D are B
      All D are E
    ∴ Some E are A

_____ 5. All E are B
      All B are C
      All C are A
      Some A are D
    ∴ Some E are D

_____ 6. All D are B
      All A are D
      Some A are not C
      All C are E
    ∴ Some B are E

_____ 7. All D are C
      All D are A
      All A are E
      All E are B
    ∴ All C are B

_____ 8. All A are D
      All D are E
      No E are C
      All B are C
    ∴ All B are A

_____ 9. All C are E   _____ 10. All D are A
         All E are A   All A are E
         All A are D   All E are B
         All D are B   No B are C
         Some F are B   Some C are not F
      ∴ Some F are not C   ∴ Some D are not F

22, V. Test the following sorites for validity by the four formal rules. Place the appropriate letters (AFN, IN, UM, IP, or V) in the margin.

_____ 1. All warm-blooded animals are mammals.
         All horses are warm-blooded animals.
         Some quadrupeds are not horses.
      ∴ Some quadrupeds are mammals.

_____ 2. No college presidents are beatniks.
         All beatniks are believers in flowerpower.
         All believers in flowerpower are pot smokers.
      ∴ No college presidents are pot smokers.

_____ 3. All canaries are yellow birds.
         All yellow birds are tropical birds.
         Some tropical birds are song birds.
      ∴ Some canaries are song birds.

_____ 4. Some Germans are circus strongmen.
         No circus strongmen are logicians.
         All logicians are rational men.
      ∴ Some Germans are rational men.

_____ 5. Some fat people are vegetarians.
         All vegetarians are food faddists.
         All food faddists are fanatics.
      ∴ Some fat people are not fanatics.

_____ 6. Some leopards are not friendly animals.
         All leopards are cats.
         All cats are carnivores.
      ∴ Some carnivores are not friendly animals.

_____ 7. All military generals are people with rigid personalities.
         All military generals are aggressive people.
         Some politicians are aggressive people.
      ∴ Some people with rigid personalities are politicians.

_____ 8. All haflings are hobbits.
Some successful farmers are haflings.
No successful farmers are stupid people.
∴ Some hobbits are not stupid people.

_____ 9. No Orcs are Brandybucks.
All Brandybucks are Shirefolk.
All Shirefolk are Haflings.
All Halflings are Hobbits.
∴ No Orcs are Hobbits.

_____ 10. No felines are dogs.
All dogs are canines.
Some mammals are not canines.
All warm-blooded bipeds are mammals.
∴ No felines are warm-blooded bipeds.

_____ 11. All extant beings are mortals.
No magical creatures are extant beings.
All fairies are magical creatures.
All goblins are fairies.
∴ No goblins are mortals.

_____ 12. All exiled kings are lonely people.
Some authoritarians are exiled kings.
No compassionate people are authoritarians.
All happy people are compassionate people.
∴ Some lonely people are not happy people.

_____ 13. All paranoids are psychotics.
No psychotics are trustworthy people.
All federal agents are trustworthy people.
All federal agents are government employees.
All government employees are poorly paid individuals.
∴ Some paranoids are poorly paid individuals.

_____ 14. All sea captains are well-traveled men.
All well-traveled men are men of experience.
All men of experience are sophisticated men.
All sophisticated men are congenial men.
All congenial men are potentially good husbands.
All potentially good husbands are good lovers.
∴ All sea captains are good lovers.

_____ 15. All Zen Monks are practitioners of meditation.
            All practitioners of meditation are introspective people.
            All introspective people are persons inclined to be moody.
            All persons inclined to be moody are emotional people.
            All emotional people are temperamental people.
            All temperamental people are nervous people.
            No nervous people are demolition experts.
        ∴ No Zen Monks are demolition experts.

23

Reducing the Number of Terms in Arguments

Many argument forms in Aristotelian logic are tested for validity by using the rules of quality and distribution; but, as we have seen, the rules are not applicable to an argument, even one composed solely of standard categorical propositions, unless its terms and propositions are equal in number. However, an argument that contains more terms than propositions may, by certain changes, be brought under the traditional rules. Such cases may arise under these three conditions, among others:

A. The argument contains distinct terms equivalent in meaning.

B. The argument contains one or more pairs of contradictory terms.

C. The argument contains one or more pairs of correlative expressions.

An argument that is not a chain argument (ch. 22, def. 1) because of one or more of the conditions listed above can be reduced to a chain argument by one of the procedures described below, and then tested for validity by the traditional rules.

23A ELIMINATING DISTINCT EQUIVALENT TERMS IN ARGUMENTS

23A1 Occurrences of Equivalent Terms in Arguments. Arguments may have a greater number of terms than propositions because they contain distinct equivalent terms.

For example:

(a) *All prime numbers greater than two are odd numbers, and no odd number is even; therefore, no prime number greater than two is divisible by two.*

This argument has three propositions and four terms. However, the distinct terms "even" (as applied to integers) and "divisible by two" are equivalent in meaning and in intention as well as denotation (see 4F). Another example is:

(b) *Since wood alcohol is a light, volatile, inflammable liquid, and methanol is used as a solvent, it follows that some solvents are light, volatile, inflammable liquids.*

The above argument contains three categorical propositions and four distinct terms, but two of these terms, "wood alcohol" and "methanol", are equivalent in meaning, in the sense of intention.

23A2 Recognizing Equivalent Terms in Arguments. There are no clear-cut rules to aid a person in the recognition of distinct equivalent terms (terms that differ linguistically, but are equivalent in meaning). There are relatively few term expressions in the English language that are interchangeable in all contexts. For example, "even" and "divisible by 2" are not equivalent expressions in all uses of "even", but only as applied to integers. As far as it goes, the dictionary is generally the best guide to equivalence in meaning. However, one must consider the usage of a particular writer or speaker.

23A3 Procedure for Eliminating Equivalent Terms in Arguments. Once a pair of synonyms or other equivalent terms are recognized in an argument, either one may be substituted for the other, thus reducing the number of terms by one. For example:

(c) *No camelopards are carnivores and some ruminant mammals are giraffes; so some ruminant mammals are not carnivores.*

Since "camelopards" is a synonym for "giraffes", either term can be substituted for the other. Substituting "giraffes" for "camelopards" we obtain:

(d) *No giraffes are carnivores, and some ruminant mammals are giraffes; so some ruminant mammals are not carnivores.*

This argument contains the same number of terms as propositions and meets the criteria for a chain argument. It can be tested by the traditional rules:

23B ELIMINATING PAIRS OF CONTRADICTORY TERMS IN ARGUMENTS

23B1 The Need for a Reduction Procedure. As we have seen, arguments that contain a greater number of terms than propositions should not on this account alone be judged invalid. For example, consider:

(e) *All visible objects are tangible objects.*
     All immaterial objects are intangible objects.
     ∴ *All immaterial objects are invisible.*

This argument contains five terms, two more than the number of propositions; but it should not be hastily judged invalid. The argument contains two pairs of terms that are contradictory within the universe of objects:

visible objects, invisible objects = (non-visible objects)

tangible objects, intangible objects = (non-tangible objects)

By the use of reversible inferences, the argument may be reduced to one containing three distinct terms, thus making it a chain argument, in this case, a standard syllogism. This reduction can be accomplished by using the standard prefix "non-" for "in-" and applying contraposition to the first premiss. The result would be:

(f) *All non-tangible objects are non-visible objects.*
     All immaterial objects are non-tangible objects.
     ∴ *All immaterial objects are non-visible objects.*

The argument now is a standard syllogism (i.e., a chain argument with three propositions) and can be tested for validity by the traditional rules. Not all arguments can be reduced as simply as the above, hence the following procedures that use only reversible inferences will prove useful. These are an extension of the procedures for reducing two-pair dyads to two-term dyads.

23B2 Procedures for Reducing N-Pair Argument to Chain Arguments

Def. 1. An **n-pair argument** is an argument such that if all occurrences of "non-" as initial prefix of its terms are canceled, the result is a chain argument.

Every two-term argument, standard syllogism, and standard sorites is an n-pair argument, but not conversely. Examples of n-pair argument forms are:

(g) Some *B* are non-*C*
∴ Some *B* are *C*

(h) All *S* are *P*
∴ All non-*P* are non-*S*

(i) No non-*P* are non-*M*
All non-*S* are *M*
∴ Some *S* are *P*

(j) All non-*M* are *P*
Some *S* are *M*
∴ Some *S* are *P*

(k) No *A* are non-*B*
All *B* are *C*
Some *C* are non-*D*
∴ Some *A* are not *D*

(l) All *E* are *D*
No *C* are non-*D*
No non-*C* are *B*
Some non-*A* are *B*
∴ Some *A* are non-*E*

Procedures will be presented for reducing a three-pair argument to a standard syllogism (i.e., a chain argument with three propositions) and reducing a (3 + n)-pair argument (a non-standard sorites) to a standard sorites.

a *Procedure for Reducing Three-Pair Argument to Standard Syllogism.*

Def. 2. A **three-pair argument** is an argument such that if all occurrences of "non-" as initial prefix of its terms are canceled, the result is a standard syllogism.

Examples of three-pair argument forms are (i) and (j) above.

Step 1. Given any three-pair argument: Either it is a standard syllogism or it is not. (a) If it is a standard syllogism, it can be tested for validity by the traditional rules. (b) If it is not a standard syllogism, go on to step 2.

Step 2. Either the number of terms in the three-pair argument can be reduced by two by *contraposing* one of the propositions or it cannot. (a) If the number of terms can be reduced by two by contraposing an **A** or **a** proposition, then do so. The result either is a standard syllogism or it is not. If it isn't, go on to step 3. (b) If contraposing one of the propositions will not reduce the number of terms by two, go on to step 3.

Reducing the Number of Terms

Step 3. Either the number of terms can be reduced by *obverting* one or more of the propositions or it cannot. (a) If it can then do so. The result either is a standard syllogism or it is not. If it is not, go on to step 4. (b) If the number of terms cannot be reduced by obverting one or more propositions, go on to step 4. (If step 4 is needed the argument must contain a pair of contradictory subjects.)

Step 4. Locate the propositions that have contradictory subjects. Either one of the propositions is an **E** or an **I** or neither is. (a) If one is an **E** or **I**, take the *converse obverted* of this proposition. The result is a standard syllogism. (b) If neither is an **E** or an **I**, identify the one of this pair that contains the predicate of the third proposition. Contrapose the identified proposition and obvert the third proposition. The result is a standard syllogism.

Shortcut. A shortcut that can often be used: If at any step in the procedure the three-pair argument has just one pair of contradictory terms and both occur as subject, skip to step 4.

b *Reduction Procedure for Three-Pair Argument Illustrated*

Problem: To reduce the three-pair argument form

All non-M are non-P
No non-S are M
∴ All S are P

to a standard syllogism and test for validity by the traditional rules.

Step 1. It is not a standard syllogism. Proceed to step 2.

Step 2. Contraposing the first proposition will reduce the number of terms by two. After contraposing we have:

All P are M
No non-S are M
∴ All S are P

This three-pair argument has only one pair of contradictory terms and these occur as subjects. Therefore by our shortcut we skip to step 4.

Step 4. The last two propositions in the above argument contain contradictory subjects and the second premiss is an **E**. Therefore we obvert the converse of this premiss. The result is:

All P are M
All M are S
∴ All S are P

The above argument is a standard syllogism and may be tested for validity by the traditional rules. It is invalid, since it commits a fallacy of illicit process.

c *Reducing the Number of Terms in Non-Standard Sorites.* "Sorites" that are non-standard because they contain pairs of contradictory terms may be reduced to standard sorites (i.e., chain arguments with three or more premisses) by the following procedure.

Step 1. Arrange the propositions so that any two successive propositions have a term in common or have a term in one proposition and its contradictory in the other. An example is:

(m) *Some catamounts are not non-pets.*
All non-catamounts are non-cougars.
No cougars are non-felines.
No felines are herbivores.
∴ *Some pets are not herbivores.*

Step 2. By the use of three reversible immediate inferences—namely, obversion, simple contraposition of **A** or **O**, and conversion obverted of **E** or **I**—eliminate the pairs of contradictory terms, thus reducing the number of terms to the number of propositions in the argument. For example, if we take the contrapositive of the second premiss in the above sorites and the obverse of the first and third premiss we have a standard sorites (namely, a chain argument with five propositions).

(n) *Some catamounts are pets.*
All cougars are catamounts.
All cougars are felines.
No felines are herbivores.
∴ *Some pets are not herbivores.*

This sorites is invalid, as "catamounts", one of its middle terms, is undistributed. The construction of a mechanical procedure, like that given in 23B2a, will be left to the reader.

23C ELIMINATING CORRELATIVE EXPRESSIONS IN ARGUMENTS

23C1 Definitions. These definitions were given in chapter 17, but we repeat them for convenience.

Def. 3. The **converse relation** (or **converse**) of a given relation R is the relation that holds between any x and any y iffi relation R holds between y and x.

Def. 4. Correlative expressions are pairs of expressions such that one expression of a pair stands for a relation and the other for its converse relation.

The following are examples of pairs of correlative expressions (in boldface).

(o) A **is greater than** B; B **is less than** A.
(p) Pat **is a parent** of Leslie;   Leslie **is a child** of Pat.
(q) Herman **is taller than** Otto;   Otto **is shorter than** Herman.
(r) P **entails** Q Q **is deducible from** P
(s) X **equals** Y Y **equals** X

These relational propositions can be analyzed into three parts: subject, correlative expression, and object. For example:

SUBJECT	CORRELATIVE EXPRESSION	OBJECT
A	is greater than	B
Pat	is a parent of	Leslie
P	entails	Q

23C2 Procedure for Eliminating Correlative Expressions in Arguments. An argument may contain a greater number of terms (by subject-predicate analysis) than propositions because the argument contains pairs of correlative expressions. The procedure for eliminating correlative expressions from an argument follows.

Step 1. Identify any pair of correlative expressions.

Step 2. In one proposition, replace one member of a pair of correlative expressions by the other member of the pair in the argument and interchange, in the latter, the subject with the object. For example, the following argument has five terms (by subject-predicate analysis):

(t) *Since Jonathan is an ancestor of all the natives on this island, and William is a native of this island, it follows that William is a descendant of Jonathan.*

The five terms are (1) Jonathan, (2) ancestor of all the natives on this island, (3) William, (4) native of this island, (5) descendant of Jonathan.

The correlative expressions are "descendant of" and "ancestor of". Substituting "descendant of" for "ancestor of" in the first proposition and interchanging the subject and object of this proposition we have:

(u) *Since all the natives of this island are descendants of Jonathan, and William is a native of this island, it follows that William is a descendant of Jonathan.*

By subject-predicate analysis, the argument now has three terms.

23D SUMMARY

An argument cannot be tested for validity by the traditional rules unless it is a chain argument, which implies that it has the same number of terms as it has number of propositions. Therefore, arguments having more terms than propositions must have the number of terms reduced, if possible, by one or more of the above procedures before they can be tested for validity by the traditional rules.

Exercises for Chapter 23

EX 23A. Count the number of propositions and the number of distinct terms in each argument. Reduce, as far as possible, the number of terms in each argument by eliminating distinct equivalent terms.

1. Some asteroids are bodies that have their orbits beyond the orbit of Mars. All bodies that have their orbits beyond the orbit of Mars are bodies that are more distant from the sun than the earth. Hence, some planetoids are bodies that are more distant from the sun than the earth.

2. Abraham Lincoln was a person born in Kentucky. The sixteenth President of the United States was a person who was assassinated. Therefore, some person who was assassinated was a person born in Kentucky.

3. The author of *The Jungle Book* was a person who was awarded the Nobel prize for literature in 1907. Rudyard Kipling was the husband of Caroline, sister of Charles Wolcott Balestier. Hence, the husband of Caroline, sister of Charles Wolcott Balestier, was a person who was awarded the Noble prize for literature in 1907.

4. The man who created Donald Duck is the person who made at least four films, since Walt Disney is the person who made the films *Pinocchio* and *Fantasia*, and the creator of Mickey Mouse is the person who made the films *Dumbo* and *Snow White and the Seven Dwarfs*.

5. The star Polaris is a star that can be used to find north. The Big Dipper is a constellation that can be used to find the pole star, hence the Big Dipper is a constellation that can be used to find the North Star.

EX 23B. Count the number of propositions and the number of distinct terms in each argument. Reduce, as far as possible, the number of terms in each argument by eliminating pairs of contradictory terms.

1. No fragile things are movable objects, since no immovable objects are lightweight objects and all lightweight objects are fragile things.

2. Some infertile areas are dairy farms and no fertile areas are lands in the arctic zone; therefore, some dairy farms are not areas in the arctic zone.

3. No illiterate people are logicians and all logicians are college graduates. Hence, all college graduates are literate people.

4. All unknown geniuses are frustrated people and some frustrated people are neurotics; therefore, some known geniuses are not frustrated people.

5. Some Christian actions are peaceful activities for all peaceful activities are non-violent actions and all violent actions are non-Christian actions.

EX 23C. Count the number of propositions and the number of distinct terms in each argument. Reduce, as far as possible, the number of terms in each argument by eliminating correlative expressions in each argument.

1. A quart is smaller than a gallon and a quart is larger than a pint; therefore, a gallon is larger than a pint.

2. An inch is longer than a centimeter and an inch is shorter than a foot, hence a foot is longer than a centimeter.

3. Herb is the son of Tom, and Bill is the father of Tom; hence Bill is the grandfather of Herb.

4. If proposition P entails proposition Q and if proposition P is deducible from proposition R, then proposition R entails proposition P.

5. Seventeen is greater than five, since seventeen is greater than thirteen and five is less than seven.

EX 23A–C. Review: Count the number of propositions and the number of distinct terms in each argument. Reduce, as far as possible, the number of terms in each argument.

1. All animated things are organic beings. No inorganic beings are sentient beings. Some insentient beings are valuable things. Therefore, some valuable things are inanimate beings.

2. The integer between 3 and 5 is an even number. All numbers over 2 that are evenly divided by 2 are non-primes. Hence the integer 4 is not a prime.

3. Mr. Hogsbottom is a person who weighs more than Lady Plushfoot. Lady Plushfoot is a person who weighs more than Mr. Hogsbottom's father. Mr. Hogsbottom's father is a person who weighs less than his wife. Therefore, Mr. Hogsbottom is a person who weighs more than his mother.

24

Singular Propositions

24A SINGULAR TERMS AND SINGULAR PROPOSITIONS

In 4B, we divided terms into general and discrete terms, and subdivided the latter into singular terms and plural discrete terms. A singular term, in its context, purports to denote just one thing. A singular term may be a proper name, a singular description ("this man", "the tallest man here"), or a pronoun referring to a previous singular term. It may also be an abstract term ("generosity", "the class of Austrian non-bankers", "the number 4").

Def. 1. A **singular proposition** (or a **singular**) is a proposition whose grammatical subject is a singular term.

Examples:

(a) *Socrates is an Athenian.*

(b) *The king is dead.*

(c) *This old man came rolling home.*

(d) *She is my best friend and severest critic.*

(e) *Beauty is in the eye of the beholder.*

These examples have different kinds of singular terms as subject. The first four have concrete singular terms; the fifth has an abstract singular term as subject. They also have different kinds of predicates. Example (d) predicates one singular term of another.

The following are not singular propositions:

(f) *Someone who loves Plato loves truth more.*

(g) *No one is as mighty as the Lord.*

(h) *He jests at scars who never felt a wound.*

Singular propositions do not begin with standard quantifiers, nor (in most cases) with *any* quantifier. Hence, though they are categoricals, they are not standard categoricals, nor is there any natural and obvious way of translating them into standard form. They therefore are not part of the doctrine of immediate inferences and syllogisms as we have expounded it up to this point.[1]

How are singulars to be introduced into traditional logic? This has been done in two ways. One way is to assert an equivalence between singulars and some kind of standard-form proposition, so that arguments with singulars may be reduced to standard form. The other way is to enlarge the range of standard forms, incorporating some varieties of singulars without change. Most modern exponents of traditional logic adopt the first way in theory and the second way in practice. We present the first way in 24B, the second in 24C.

24B STANDARDIZING SINGULAR PROPOSITIONS

24B1 The Quantity of Singulars. If singulars are to be assimilated to the standard categorical forms, the first question is, are they universal or particular? They are traditionally taken to be universal.

a *Affirmative Singulars.* One's first thought, because of the ordinary connotations of "particular", is to say that singulars must be particular rather than universal. And some examples seem to bear this out. Let us take an argument that is very old, though it does not appear in Aristotle:

(a) *All men are animals; Socrates is a man;
therefore, Socrates is an animal.*

If one regards the singulars as particulars, as if they began "Some Socrates" or "Something that is Socrates", this is a syllogism in Darii (fig. 1).[2] This agrees with our intuitive recognition of the argument as valid. But then it is also valid if we take the singulars as **A** propositions, and have an argument in Barbara.

Let us try again with what the medievals called an **expository syllogism**—a third-figure syllogism with two singular premises:

(b) *Socrates is running, and Socrates is a white thing, therefore, some white thing is running.*

If the singulars are particulars, we have two particular premisses, and an undistributed middle term; so the argument could not be valid. But it seems clear that the argument *is* valid. (It is traditionally presupposed that a proper noun—at least as subject—actually applies to something, like the subject terms of standard categorical propositions.) So the premisses must be taken as universals.

If affirmative singulars are to be given the form of universal affirmatives, how shall this be done? The form "All Socrates is running" is not only not idiomatic, but its meaning is obscure. When "All" modifies a singular term, it usually means *the whole of;* for example, "All Gaul is divided into three parts" says that *the whole of Gaul,* or Gaul as a whole, is so divided. The subject is still a singular term logically, as it is grammatically singular. If we use plural forms, as in "All Platos are running", we seem to be speaking of every person named "Plato", which is not what we intend.

A correct way of standardizing "Socrates is running" is to express it thus: "All persons identical with Socrates are running" or (to use a noun that is always applicable)

(c) *All objects (or entities) identical with Socrates are running.*

Now the subject term is general in form, though there can be only one thing to which it applies; we call it a *unit term.* And the standard categorical means the same as the original singular—assuming that the name "Socrates" has the same meaning in both.[3]

Def. 2. A **unit term** is a consistent general term whose meaning is such that it cannot apply to more than one object.

With this formulation, the expository syllogism (b) above becomes an AAI form (Darapti):

(d)   All objects idential with Socrates are running;
   All objects identical with Socrates are white things;
 therefore, some white thing is running.

This is valid, the middle term being now a general term distributed twice.

This expansion of the singular term is cumbersome. We may abbreviate it if we wish by enclosing the singular term in braces:

Def. 3. {s} = objects identical with s.

Then we standardize "Socrates is running" by writing "All {Socrates} are running" (or, if both terms must be noun phrases, "All {Socrates} are running objects".)

b. *Negative Singulars.* Negative propositions with singular subjects, such as "Socrates is not running", are also taken as universals—universal negatives of course. "No Socrates is running" or "No Socrates are running" would be confusing (though not as bad as "All Socrates . . . " for the affirmative). We resort to the same device as before: "No objects identical with Socrates are running (objects)", abbreviated "No {Socrates} are running (objects)". As usual with E propositions, both terms are said to be distributed. The validity of syllogisms can be determined by the traditional rules of quality and distribution (ch. 21).[4]

Consider the following examples:

(1) *Socrates is not running.*   ↔   *No {Socrates} are running.*
     Socrates is a Greek.   ↔   *All {Socrates} are Greeks.*
     ∴ *Some Greek is not running.* ↔   ∴ *Some Greeks are not running.*

This satisfies the rules of quality and distribution, and is valid (by Felapton).

(2) *Socrates is running.*   ↔   *All {Socrates} are running.*
     Socrates is not a Roman.   ↔   *No {Socrates} are Romans.*
     ∴ *Some Roman is not running.* ↔   ∴ *Some Romans are not running.*

This has an illicit process of the major term, and is invalid.

If we limit ourselves to the rendering of propositions with singular subjects as universals, there are just six valid forms, two in each figure but the fourth. We have illustrated the forms in Barbara in the first figure, Darapti and Felapton in the third. There are also forms in Celarent in the first, Cesare and Camestres in the second.[5] We invite the reader to illustrate these.

24B3 Singular Terms as Predicates. We have considered singular terms only as subjects; but they may also occur as predicates in ordinary language. Thus "Socrates is a Greek" may be converted to "Some Greek is Socrates". Standardized as above, "All objects identical with Socrates are Greeks" may be converted to "Some Greeks are objects identical with Socrates". Although this is a conversion *per accidens*, the converse is equivalent to the convertend. The unit term is distributed even in the predicate, contrary to the usual rule for affirmatives.

Also, "Socrates is not a paid teacher" is equivalent by conversion to "No paid teacher is Socrates". Hence we may standardize either of these two equivalent propositions as "No objects identical with Socrates are paid teachers" or "No {Socrates} are paid teachers".

With an **I** or **E** form, nothing substantial is lost if we require that a proposition with singular or unit term in the predicate be standardized with unit term in the subject.[6]

The case is different with *doubly singular* propositions, that is, categoricals with a singular term for subject and another for predicate; for example, "Socrates is the master of Plato"; "Tully is Cicero"; "The author of *Ivanhoe* is the author of *Waverley*". Here, of course, conversion cannot free us from having a singular or unit term in the predicate as well as the subject. To standardize doubly singular affirmatives, we might write them as:

(i) All objects identical with s are objects identical with p, *abbreviated:* All $\{s\}$ are $\{p\}$;

or:

(ii) All objects identical with s are all objects identical with p, *abbreviated:* All $\{s\}$ are all $\{p\}$.

Form (i) is shorter and less unnatural; form (ii), on the other hand, makes explicit the distribution of the predicate. We shall use form (i), but use "**U**" for its code letter (instead of "**A**"), indicating an affirmative with both terms distributed.[7] We standardize "Socrates is the master of Plato" as "All objects identical with Socrates are objects identical with the master of Plato" or "All {Socrates} are {the master of Plato}".[8]

There are also doubly singular negatives: "Russell is not the author of *Ivanhoe*"; "This article is not the best on the subject". These may be standardized in the form "No objects identical with s are objects identical with p", and abbreviated "No $\{s\}$ are $\{p\}$". While the distribution is as for **E**, it is more convenient for us to use a special symbol, namely, "$\bar{\mathbf{U}}$". We use "**E**" if the predicate is not a singular or unit term.

Let us consider first a syllogism where all the terms are unit terms, that is, all the propositions are **U** or $\bar{\mathbf{U}}$. There are just two possibilities for a valid syllogism: either all the propositions are **U**, or the conclusion and just one premiss is $\bar{\mathbf{U}}$, the other premiss **U**. (The traditional rules of quality hold; the reader can easily construct a counterexample for any case where they fail.) All terms are distributed. There are three possible valid moods: UUU, U$\bar{\mathrm{U}}\bar{\mathrm{U}}$, $\bar{\mathrm{U}}$U$\bar{\mathrm{U}}$. In the first figure we have:

All {m} are {p}	All {m} are {p}	No {m} are {p}
<u>All {s} are {m}</u>	<u>No {s} are {m}</u>	<u>All {s} are {m}</u>
∴ All {s} are {p}	∴ No {s} are {p}	∴ No {s} are {p}

Since **U** and **Ū** are both simply convertible, either or both premisses can be converted in the above forms; so each of the three moods is found in each of the four figures.

There remain the syllogisms with just two singular (or unit) terms, hence with one double singular and two propositions with singular (or unit) subject. (We omit propositions with a singular term in the predicate only.) The valid forms can be determined by the traditional rules of quality and distribution, taking each unit term as distributed. Six forms are valid. For example:

AUA-1	**AEŪ**-2
All {d} are P	All {d} are P
<u>All l{f} are {d}</u>	<u>No {f} are P</u>
∴ All {f} are P	∴ No {f} are {d}

These could be obtained by substitution in Barbara and Camestres respectively. **EUE**-1 can be obtained by substitution in Celarent. The other three can be obtained by simple conversion of the **U** or **Ū** in the first three.

Summarizing, we find six forms valid with one singular term as subject—two in each of figures 1, 2, and 3—and six forms also valid with two singular terms, two in each of the first three figures. With three singular terms, twelve forms are valid, three in each of the four figures. The fallacies are named as in 21B.

24C SINGULAR PROPOSITIONS AS SUCH

The method of standardizing singulars presented in 24B has the advantage of reducing propositions and arguments with singular terms to standard forms, thus extending the traditional doctrine to cover some singulars. It has the disadvantage of unnaturalness, and would be unbearably lengthy without a suitable abbreviation.

A more natural method is to let the singulars stand as such, writing "Socrates is a Greek", "Socrates is not a Roman", "The author of *Ivanhoe* is the author of *Waverley*", and so on. But we say that a singular term serving as subject or predicate is distributed. This follows clearly enough from our preliminary explanation of distribution, 10A1, definition 1, slightly vague though this may be: for the singular proposition "makes an assertion about everything named" by the singular term, only one thing being named by it. Then we may directly apply the traditional rules of quality and distribution for testing syllogisms (and other chain arguments) that are in standard form (as hitherto defined). The validity of the arguments in 24B1 can be tested just as well with the original singular terms as with the translations into unit terms with quantifiers.

We must allow for one discrepancy: our singulars are grammatically singular, where the standard forms are grammatically plural. Thus we combine "All *men* are animals" with "Socrates is a *man*". Here we must take sameness of terms in a broad rather than a strict sense.[9]

Syllogisms with two or three singular terms may also be tested directly by the rules. The following is an example of $A E \overline{U}$-2, (cf. last form of 24B):

His greatest danger is a physical weakness;
His fear is not a physical weakness;
∴ His fear is not his greatest danger.

The terms are distributed in every occurrence except the predicate of the first premiss, and the quality of the propositions is as follows: affirmative, negative, negative. The argument is valid.

The following is $A \overline{U} E$-1:

The mumps is a physical ailment;
His sickness is not the mumps;
∴ His sickness is not a physical ailment.

This has an illicit process.

As in 24B, there are six valid syllogistic forms with one singular term (as subject), six with two singular terms, and twelve with all three terms singular. There would be more forms if we admitted categoricals with only the predicate a singular term, as in "Some philosopher is not Socrates".

Exercises for Chapter 24

EX 24A, I. Put the appropriate letter in the margin.

S = singular proposition   N = not a singular proposition

_____ 1. Helen's face launched a thousand ships.
_____ 2. Someone loves everyone.
_____ 3. Somebody up there loves me.
_____ 4. The man who gave me directions was mistaken.
_____ 5. The voters have a right to know the issues.
_____ 6. My enemies are dead.
_____ 7. Everyone except Smith did his homework.
_____ 8. Only Smith did his homework.
_____ 9. He who lives by the sword shall die by the sword.
_____ 10. The man who takes what is mine will be punished.

EX 24B. Standardize the following syllogisms by standardizing the singular propositions and putting the conclusion last.

1. Bill is not the barber; the barber is the mayor; therefore Bill is not the mayor.
2. All Italians are good singers, therefore Joe is a good singer, since Joe is Italian.
3. Socrates is not a god, since no men are gods and Socrates is a man.
4. The man in the grey overcoat is a thief and some thieves are not Zen Buddhists, so the man in the grey overcoat is not a Zen Buddhist.
5. Plato is a Greek and Socrates is a Greek. Hence, Plato is not Socrates.
6. Professor Braun is a teacher, and Professor Braun is not a deist, therefore some teachers are not deists.
7. Scott is the author of *Ivanhoe;* George Eliot is not the author of *Ivanhoe*; therefore, George Eliot is not Scott.

8. Aristotle is Greek and Cicero is not. Therefore, Aristotle is not Cicero.

9. Brown is not Smith and Smith is no mechanic. Consequently, Brown is a mechanic.

10. Green is a mechanic and Smith is no mechanic. Hence Smith is not Green.

EX 24B, II. Test by rules of quality and distribution the syllogisms of Exercise I as standardized. If invalid, name fallacy: AFN, NFL, (or IN), UM, IP.

EX 24C. Without rewriting the arguments in Exercise I above: (1) Underline the distributed terms. (2) Indicate conclusion if it is not final. (3) Indicate fallacy if any, or mark "V".

25

Standardizing Categorical Propositions

25A THE PROBLEM OF STANDARDIZING NON-STANDARD PROPOSITIONS

In this chapter we deal with problems of translating some of the common non-standard categorical forms of ordinary language into the standard categorical forms (**A, E, I,** or **O**). This process of translating non-standard forms into standard forms is called **standardizing.**

Most spoken and written propositions in ordinary language are not in standard form. Categoricals such as "None but the brave deserve the fair", "Almost all the people voted", "Dogs are mammals", occur frequently, but are not in standard categorical form. Consequently most arguments encountered, whether in scholarly or ordinary discourse, are not in standard form and cannot be tested for validity as they stand by the rules of traditional logic. Often, however, these non-standard arguments may be changed into standard chain arguments by standardizing the non-standard propositions.

Because of the various ambiguities and complexities of natural languages, as well as the peculiar idioms and nuances of English, there are few definite and infallible translation rules. Also, the meaning of a sentence may vary according to the context in which it occurs; hence it is often difficult, if not impossible, to determine the meaning of a sentence unless its context is known.

Besides non-standard quantifiers such as "None but" and "Most", there are other problems of standardization. There may be no expressed quantifier. An adjectival or verbal predicate may need to be transformed into substantival form (noun or noun phrase). The order of words in the sentence may need to be changed in order to get it into standard form. More radical changes may be needed, including the introduction of words such as "times", "places", "cases"—called "parameters"—in order to transform compound propositions into standard categorical propositions.

25B NO QUANTIFIER AND NON-STANDARD QUANTIFIERS

25B1 No Quantifier. When there is no quantifier, the context or a plausible interpretation will generally determine what quantifier should be used. Let us note that what is intended may not be a standard quantifier— "All", "Some", or "No"—but a non-standard quantifier such as "Most", "Almost all", and so on. Examples:

(a) *Sheep are gentle animals* is standardized as *All sheep are gentle animals.*

(b) *Sophomores are in my logic class* is standardized as *Some sophomores are in my logic class.*

(c) *Bats are not birds* is standardized as *No bats are birds.*

(d) *Germans generally like beer* is equivalent to the non-standard form *Most Germans like beer.* (See 25B10).

25B2 Simple Synonyms for Standard Quantifiers.

(a) *All of the S are P*   becomes *All S are P.*

(b) *Every S is P*   becomes *All S are P.*

(c) *Each S is P*   becomes *All S are P.*

(d) *None of the S is P*   becomes *No S are P.*

(e) *Some of the S are P*   becomes *Some S are P.*

25B3 Articles as Quantifiers. The article "a" or "an" beginning a sentence is interpreted as "all" or "some" according to the context.

(a) *A lion is a feline* is standardized as *All lions are felines.*

(b) *A bird is sitting on a branch* is standardized as *Some birds are sitting on a branch.*

Definitions in this book are usually written in the style:

(c) **Def. 2.** A **proposition** is a complete declarative sentence taken with a certain meaning. [1A def. 2, 2 def. 1] or

(d) **Def. 6.** A **valid** argument is an argument whose conclusion follows necessarily from its premisses. [1B def. 6]

Similarly, in geometry one may define thus:

(e) A **triangle** is a three-sided polygon.

Put abstractly, these are of the forms:

(f) An S is a P (for c and e)

or

(g) An SX is a PX (for d).

No standard categorical form conveys the full meaning of these forms of definition. However, an equivalential definition[1] of form (f), such as (c) or (e)—or an equivalential definition[1] of form (g) such as (d)—entails "All S are P and all P are S" (or "All SX are PX and all PX are SX"). The definition therefore justifies use of either or both of the **A** propositions it entails as premiss in a chain argument.

Thus definition (e) above justifies use of either or both of the propositions "All triangles are three-sided polygons" and "All three-sided polygons are triangles" as premiss.

When the article "the" initiates a sentence, sometimes it can be interpreted as "all"; but sometimes it cannot be standardized so easily.

(h) *The horse is a mammal* is standardized as *All horses are mammals.*

(i) *The horses in this corral are stallions* is standardized as *All horses in this corral are stallions.*

(j) *The horse is found in most countries* is not standardized as *All horses are found in most countries* (which is nonsense). It may be expressed as a nonstandard categorical: *Most countries are places where horses are found.*

---

[1] An *equivalential definition* of a term is a definition that asserts or implies that the term defined can replace or be replaced by the defining term without changing the truth value. (Cf. def. 11 in 5B1, and reference note thereto.)

(k) *The horses in this corral are varied in color* is not standardized as *All the horses in this corral are varied in color.*

The latter sentence is not nonsense, but does not express what the former is more likely to mean. It would probably mean that different horses often (or at least sometimes) differ in color. If so, it is best regarded as having a plural discrete subject term (4B2), neither singular (i.e., individual) nor general.

25B4 Exclusive Quantifiers.

(a) *Only S are P*   becomes *All P are S* (or *No P are non-S*).

(b) *Only S are not P*   becomes *All non-P are S* (or *All non-S are P*).

(c) *The S alone are P*   becomes *All P are S.*

(d) *The S alone are not P*   becomes *All non-P are S* (or *All non-S are P*).

(e) *The only S are P*   becomes *All S are P.*

(f) *The only S is [P]*   becomes *All S are P.*

(g) *Only some S are P*   becomes *Some are P and Some S are not P.*

The difference between (e) and (f) is that in the former the predicate is a general term and in the latter [P] is a singular term. An example of (f) is:

(f′) *The only person in the room is Susan,*

which is standardized as:

(f″) *All persons in this room are Susan.*

It should be noted that in (f″) above both subject and predicate are distributed, since the predicate is a singular term.

25B5 Exceptive Quantifiers.

(a) *All but S are P*   becomes *All non-S are P.*

(b) *All except S are P*   becomes *All non-S are P.*

(c) *None but S are P*   becomes *No non-S are P* (or *All P are S*).

(d) *None except S are P*   becomes *No non-S are P* (or *All P are S*).

Note: "None but" and "none except" are equivalent to "only" when they occur as the initial quantifiers in a proposition. (Cf. 25B4, (a).)

25B6 Negated Quantifiers.

(a) *Not all S are P*   becomes *Some S are not P.*

(b) *Not every S is P*   becomes *Some S are not P.*

(c) *Not any S is P*   becomes *Some S are not P.*

(d) *All S are not P*   becomes (usually) *Some S are not P* and (rarely) *No S are P.*

(e) *Not one S is P*   becomes *No S are P.*

(f) *Not an S is P*   becomes *No S are P.*

(g) *Not only S are P*   becomes *Some P are not S.*

Examples:

(a') *Not all women are mothers*   becomes *Some women are not mothers.*

(b') *Not every man is brave*   becomes *Some men are not brave* (persons).

(c') *Not any flower is beautiful*   becomes *Some flowers are not beautiful* (things).

(d') *All canines are not dogs*   becomes *Some canines are not dogs.*

(e') *Not one person is immortal*   becomes *No persons are immortals.*

(f') *Not a student is late*   becomes *No students are late* (persons).

(g') *Not only dogs are mammals*   becomes *Some mammals are not dogs.*

The form "All S are not P" is deceptive, as it is often mistaken for a form of some **A** propositions. It is not a standard form, and as indicated in (d) above, it usually means the same as "Not all S are P", but may be ambiguous.

Another deceptive form is "No S are not P", which cannot be accepted as being in standard form. It is rare in ordinary language, and we have no actual examples to offer. Of course, "No S are non-P" is acceptable, being the obverse of the **A** form.

In contrast, "Not all S are P" is clearly contradictory to "All S are P". As compared to "Some S are not P", the standard contradictory of the **A**, "Not all S are P" has the advantage that it can be distinguished from the **O** without having to read beyond the subject.

25B7 Adjectival Quantifiers.

(a) *All that is B is C* — becomes *All B things are C (things)*.

(b) *Everything B is C* — becomes *All B things are C (things)*.

(c) *Anything B is C* — becomes *All B things are C (things)*.

(d) *What's B is C* — becomes *All B things are C (things)*.

(e) *All who are B are C* — becomes *All B persons are C (persons)*.

(f) *Nothing is both B and C* — becomes *No B things are C (things)*.

(g) *No one is both B and C* — becomes *No B persons are C (persons)*.

(h) *Something is both B and C* — becomes *Some B things are C (things)*.

(i) *Something is both B and not C* — becomes *Some B things are not C (things)*.

The variables "B" and "C" are adjective variables, that is to say their substitution instances are adjectives or adjectival phrases such as "red", "very friendly", "fattening", "sinful beyond compare", and so on. Examples:

(a′) *All that is forbidden is tempting*   becomes *All forbidden things are tempting (things).*

(d′) *What's beautiful is good*   becomes *All beautiful things are good (things).*

(e′) *All who are ungodly are evil*   becomes *All ungodly persons are evil (persons).*

(f′) *Nothing is both safe and interesting*   becomes *No safe things are interesting things.*

(g′) *No one is both stupid and segacious*   becomes *No stupid persons are sagacious (persons).*

(h′) *Something is both cheap and useful*   becomes *Some cheap things are useful (things).*

(i′) *Something is both expensive and not useful*   becomes *Some expensive things are not useful (things).*

25B8 Adverbial Quantifiers.

(a) *S are always P*   becomes *All S are P.*

(b) *S are never P*   becomes *No S are P.*

(c) *S are sometimes P*   becomes *Some S are P.*

(d) *S are not always P*   becomes *Some S are not P.*

Examples:

(a′) *Kings are always insecure*   becomes *All kings are insecure (persons).*

(b′) *Dictators are never satisfied*   becomes *No dictators are satisfied (persons).*

(c′) *Children are sometimes quiet*   becomes *Some children are quiet (persons).*

(d′) *Students are not always attentive*   becomes *Some students are not attentive (persons).*

25B9 Numerical Quantifiers. We divide numerical quantifiers (i.e., quantifiers containing numerals) into two kinds: integral quantifiers and fractional quantifiers. Some integral forms and possible ways to standardize them follow (where "n" is any integer greater than zero):

(a) *At least* n *S are P* is standardized as *Some class of* n *S is a class of P.*

(b) *At most* n *S are P* is standardized as *No class of* n + 1 *S is a class of P.*

(c) *Just* (or *exactly*) n *S are P* is standardized as *Some class of* n *S is a class of P and No class of* n + 1 *S is a class of P.*

The following are fractional forms and possible ways to standardize them (where "n" and "m" are integers greater than zero):

(d) *At least* n/m *of the S are P* is standardized as *Some class of at least* n/m *of the S is a class of P.*

(e) *Less than* n/m *of the S are P* is standardized as *No class of at least* n/m *of the S is a class of P.*

(f) *At most* n/m *of the S are P* is standardized as *No class of more than* n/m *of the S is a class of P.*

(g) *More than* n/m *of the S are P* is standardized as *Some class of more than* n/m *of the S is a class of P.*

(h) *Just* (or *exactly*) n/m *of the S are P* is standardized as *Some class of* n/m *of the S is a class of P and No class of more than* n/m *of the S is a class of P.*

Examples:

(b′) *At most fourteen students in this room are freshmen*   becomes   *No class of fifteen students in this room are freshmen.*

(g′) *More than half of the students in this room are freshmen*   becomes   *Some class of more than half half of the students in this room are freshmen.*

25B10 Indefinite Quantifiers. Many quantifiers of ordinary language—"many", "most", "a few", and so on—are too vague to be given an equivalential definition in terms of such precise concepts as "at least one". For, though "at least one *S* is *P*" is indefinite in the sense that it does not specify a certain number, it is precise in the sense that one knows that it is false in case no S are P, and true in any other case. Even the person uttering a statement of the form "Many S are P" probably cannot say exactly how many S are sufficient and necessary to make the statement true; still less does anyone else know what number the speaker would take as sufficient. Such quantifiers usually have minimal and/or maximal meanings. Thus for "most" there is a minimal meaning of "More than half"; an argument with this quantifier in a premiss is valid if valid for the minimal meaning.

(a) *Most S are P* entails *More than half of the S are P*; often taken as synonymous by logicians.

It should be noted that this form cannot justifiably be standardized as "Some S are P", since the argument form:

More than half of the M are P
More than half of the M are S
∴ Some S and P

is valid, but the argument form:

Some M are P
Some M are S
∴ Some S are P

is invalid.

It is possible to standardize syllogisms that contain the "Most S are P" form both as premiss and as conclusion. For example,

All M are P
Most S are M
∴ Most S are P

becomes:

All classes of M are classes of P
Some class of more than half of the S is a class of M
∴ Some class of more than half the S is a class of P.

(b) *Almost all S are P* means *Not quite all, Very nearly all, S are P*, stronger than *Most S are P*, but entails *Some S are not P*.

There is no adequate standardization of "Almost all *S* are *P*".

(c) *Many S are P* has a minimal interpretation of *At least two S are P.* (See 25B9, [a].)

The quantifier "many" generally means a large, indefinite number, but sometimes it is used to mean "more than one". Therefore, the minimal interpretation of "Many *S* are *P*" will be as stated above or "More than one *S* is *P*".

(d) *A few S are P* has a minimal interpretation of *At least two S are P.* (see 25B9, [a].)

(e) *Few S are P* means *Not many S are P.*

Like the form "Many *S* are *P*", the form "Few *S* are *P*" cannot be adequately standardized.

25C PREDICATE ADJECTIVES

The predicate of a standard categorical may be either a substantive or an adjectival expression. Some logicians insist that every predicate adjective be replaced by a substantive, but this is unnecessary, as long as a given term is always expressed in the same form.

25C1 Changing Predicate Adjectives to Substantives. Sometimes, in order to reduce the number of terms in an argument, it is necessary to transform predicate adjectives into substantives. One way to do this is to add the term "things" to the adjective if the subject of the proposition is nonhuman, or "persons" if the subject is human. (See 11B and Exercise 11B.)

(a) *All roses are beautiful* becomes *All roses are beautiful things.*

(b) *Some men are intelligent* becomes *Some men are intelligent persons.*

In changing a predicate adjective to a noun or other substantive, care must be taken not to change its meaning. Participles are especially likely to make trouble in such cases. For example, it would be misleading to change

(c) *Some young men in the stadium are running* to

(c') *Some young men in the stadium are runners.*

The noun "runners" suggests that the men are training for track, which is not implied by (c). On the other hand, (c) reports a present action, but (c') has lost this connotation. It is much better to standardize (c) as

(c'') *Some young men in the stadium are persons running.*

In general, it is best to avoid changing an adjective to a corresponding noun form with a different ending, as from *beautiful* to *beauties*, from *good* to *goods* or *goodies*. There is often a shift in meaning.

25D NON-STANDARD VERBS

The main verb in a standard categorical must be a form of the verb *to be* ("is" or "are"). All other verbs, such as *sing, run, climb*, are non-standard as copula. Propositions that have a non-standard main verb are not in standard form.

The procedure for standardizing such propositions is to insert "are" or "is" immediately before the non-standard verb, and to change the expression containing the non-standard verb and its object, if any, to a noun or noun phrase. For example:

(a) *Some men climb mountains* is standardized as *Some men are persons who climb mountains.* The given sentence might not mean the same as *Some men are mountain climbers:* compare the discussion of example (c) in 25C.

(b) *No cats bark* is standardized as *No cats are things that bark* or *No cats are barking things.*

(c) *All physical objects have mass* is standardized as *All physical objects are things that have mass.*

25E NON-STANDARD ORDER

There are two kinds of non-standard order in categorical propositions: The quantifier is in a non-standard position, and part of the grammatical subject is in the predicate position.

The two common forms of propositions with the quantifier in the wrong position are:

(a) *S are all P*, standardized as *All S are P*, and

(b) *S are no P*, standardized as *No S are P*.

Examples of the above are:

(a') *Germans are all beer drinkers*, standardized as *All Germans are beer drinkers*.

(b') *FBI men are no fools*, standardized as *No FBI men are fools*.

Examples of propositions where the grammatical subject is split by the grammatical predicate are:

(c) *Nothing is really accomplished that is not accomplished well*, standardized as *No things that are not accomplished well are things really accomplished*. (By obverting the converse this becomes: *All things really accomplished are things that are accomplished well*.)

(d) *All are saved who pray* is equivalent to *All who pray are saved*, which standardizes as *All persons who pray are persons saved*.

25F PARAMETERS

Some propositions that assert a temporal or spatial relation between events or classes of events cannot easily be standardized unless a certain word, such as "times", "places", or "cases" is added to both the subject and predicate. These words are called "parameters".

(a) *Whenever it rains, it pours*, standardized as *All times it is raining are times it is pouring*.

(b) *He gets angry whenever he is contradicted*, standardized as *All times he is contradicted are times he gets angry*.

(c) *Where there is smoke, there is fire* standardized as *All places there are smoke are places there are fire*.

(d) *Life is probable wherever there is water*, standardized as *All places where there is water are places where life is probable*.

(e) *He never goes to the symphony unless they are playing Beethoven*, standardized as *All times he goes to the symphony are times they are playing Beethoven*.

(f) *A man is presumed innocent unless proved guilty* is equivalent to *A man is presumed innocent if not proven guilty*, standardized as *All cases where a man is not proven guilty are cases where he is presumed innocent*.

The parameter cases can generally be replaced by "times" or "places", but there are instances where it seems less awkward than the other parameters.

25G STANDARDIZING NON-STANDARD ARGUMENTS

An argument is testable for validity (and invalidity) by the four rules (Rules Af, Neg, DMid, and DX) only if it is a chain argument (see chapter 22). A chain argument is composed only of standard propositions arranged so that the conclusion is last (or first) and any two successive propositions share one term. A chain argument also must have the same number of distinct terms as it has number of propositions. Hence, if a chain argument has five propositions it must have five terms. Also each term in a chain argument occurs exactly twice, but not in the same proposition.

When an argument is not a chain argument because it contains non-standard propositions, care must be taken in standardizing these propositions so that the resulting argument contains the same number of terms as it contains number of propositions. If this is not the case then it cannot be tested for validity by the four rules.

For example, the following argument:

(a) Every ugly thing is unwanted.
     Some babies are not ugly.
     ∴ Some unwanted things are not babies.

is not a chain argument, since the first premise is not standard and there are five terms: "ugly thing", "unwanted", "babies", "ugly", and "unwanted things". By standardizing the first premise and by changing the adjectival predicates into substantival predicates we have the following chain argument (which is invalid):

(b) All ugly things are unwanted things.
     Some babies are not ugly things.
     ∴ Some unwanted things are not babies.

In the following example none of the propositions are standard.

(c)   No one is both an alcoholic and a jet pilot.
      None but poor insurance risks are accident-prone.
      Only accident-prone persons are alcoholics.
      ∴ It is false that every poor insurance risk is a jet pilot.

If we standardize the proposition taking care that there will be exactly four terms, each term occurring twice, we have the chain argument (which is valid):

(d)   No alcoholics are jet pilots.
      All alcoholics are accident-prone persons.
      All accident-prone persons are poor insurance risks.
      ∴ Some poor insurance risks are not jet pilots.

In the following example parameters are needed to standardize the propositions as categoricals.

(e)   Whenever the moon is red, a storm is coming.
      Every time a storm comes the barometer drops.
      ∴ When the moon is red, the barometer drops.

After the propositions are standardized, we have the valid argument:

(f)   All times when the moon is red are times when a storm is coming.
      All times when a storm is coming are times when the barometer drops.
      ∴ All times when the moon is red are times when the barometer drops.

Exercises for Chapter 25

EX 25B. Standardize the following propositions (parameters should not be used).

1. None but the Gods are happy.
2. Wombats are marsupials.
3. A circle is a plane figure.
4. Not all woodchats are European birds.
5. Native Italians are not people of Celtic origin.
6. It is not the case that some steels do not contain iron.
7. Nothing but God is an infinite being.
8. The French are great lovers.
9. None of my students are nuns.
10. Each living thing is a priceless treasure.
11. Women are physicians.
12. A man is waiting to see you.
13. The Italians alone are great opera singers.
14. Only some birds are hornbills.
15. All except freshmen are eligible candidates.
16. Not only men are ministers.
17. Taoists are never public officials.
18. Nothing is both a quadruped and a bird.
19. Just exactly fourteen logic students are absent.
20. What is not a bird is not a passerine.

EX 25C–25D. Standardize the following propositions. Change all predicate adjectives into predicate nouns.

1. All cats are carnivorous.

2. Some children sing sweetly.
3. Prime numbers are all odd.
4. Logician think a lot.
5. Philosophers are not all thinkers.
6. Mathematic majors study hard.
7. Depressed people are no fun.
8. Some Greek philosophers were iconoclastic.
9. Every act of goodness is rewarded.
10. All are lost who enter here.
11. Some people shall become saints.
12. Some people always suffer.
13. Nothing is gained that is not gained with goodwill.
14. Not all birds sing.
15. Some are the guardians of the truth and the law.

EX 25F. Standardize the following propositions by the use of parameters.

1. He sleeps when he is tired.
2. She never wears lipstick to the office.
3. He never lies but when holly is green.
4. Where there is smoke there is fire.
5. He gets angry when he loses at chess.
6. Where there is poverty there is sickness.
7. The Smiths always serve wine when they have company.
8. Where you find the lion cubs you will find the lioness.
9. Where there is life, there is hope.
10. He who hesitates is lost.
11. He never goes out for a walk without his cane.
12. No news is good news.

13. She blushes whenever she is embarrassed.

14. He who rides the tiger can never dismount.

15. She always order tea with her meals.

EX 25A–F. Standardize the following propositions. Use parameters if necessary.

1. Nothing is of faith that is not in Scripture.
2. No blessing lasts forever.
3. All fish are not caught by flies.
4. Only the actions of the just smell sweet and blossom in the dust.
5. Justifying a fault doubles it.
6. Sailors drink only gin.
7. Only gin drinkers are sailors.
8. Only sailors are gin drinkers.
9. Sailors only are gin drinkers.
10. Only God understands God.
11. Nearest the king, nearest the gallows.
12. None think the great unhappy but the great.
13. Great men are not always wise.
14. History is all party pamphlets.
15. The hog is never good but when he is in the dish.
16. Marriage is the tomb of love.
17. He dwells nowhere who dwells everywhere.
18. Without children there is no real love.
19. It is false that only the gods are immortal.
20. Nothing is both beautiful and evil.
21. Who hath not served cannot command.
22. When in doubt, abstain.
23. Love alone makes life worth living.

24. He conquers who endures.
25. None but a fool is always right.
26. Woman will be the last thing civilized by man.
27. The heart that loves is always young.
28. He is not a lover who does not love forever.
29. All mankind loves a lover.
30. Where there is love there is no sin.
31. Every couple is not a pair.
32. Marry in haste, repent at leisure.
33. What has a beginning has an end.
34. None but the daring can know success.
35. Not everyone present teaches at the college.
36. None except children were frightened.
37. The abode of the spirit is not in this world.
38. It is false that all flies are caught by sugar.
39. A proposition is either true or false.
40. A stitch in time saves nine.

EX 25, I. Standardize the propositions in the following arguments in such a manner that the result is a chain argument. Test each resulting chain argument for validity.

1. It is raining, since everytime we wish to go on a picnic it rains and today we wish to go on a picnic.
2. I will not vote for a man who favors the Desmond Bill; consequently, I will not vote for Senator Wilson, since he favors the Desmond Bill.
3. Nobody with sound moral sense would favor an international policy that leads to war. Hence Congressman Smith favors such an international policy, for he does not have sound moral sense.
4. Only those members who have paid their dues are allowed to vote and none but voting members can hold office in the club. Therefore, only officers in the club have paid their dues.

5. At least one rule in the club's constitution will be challenged and not all of the challenged rules will be amended; so at least one of the rules in the club's constitution will not be amended.

6. I always put off until tomorrow the things that I should have done today. I should have watered the lawn yesterday; hence I put it off until today.

7. It is false that all odd numbers are primes, so, since no odd numbers are evenly divisible by two, some numbers evenly divisible by two are not prime.

8. The truth is written in the Koran. What you have said is not in the Koran; hence it is not truth.

9. John gets excited when he talks about politics and he is excited now; so he must have been talking about politics.

10. It is said that only the brave die young, but if this is true, since a coward is not a brave man, it must follow that old men are cowards.

EX 25, II. By standardizing the proposition in the following arguments change them into standard sorites (i.e., chain arguments). Examples (with some alterations) are from Lewis Carroll's *Symbolic Logic*. Conclusions are added.

1. Babies are illogical;
   Nobody is despised who can manage a crocodile;
   Illogical persons are despised.
   ∴ Babies cannot manage crocodiles.

2. Everyone who is sane can do Logic;
   No insane people are fit to serve on a jury
   None of *your* sons can do Logic.
   ∴ None of your sons are fit to serve on a jury.

3. No one takes in the Times unless he is well educated;
   No hedgehogs can read;
   Those who cannot read are not well educated.
   ∴ No hedgehogs take in the Times.

4. All the Eton men in this college play cricket;
   None but the scholars dine at the higher table;
   None of the cricketers row;
   My friends in this college all come from Eton;
   All the scholars are rowing men.
   ∴ No friends of mine dine at the higher table.

5. When I work a Logic example without grumbling, you may be sure it is one I understand;
These sorites are not arranged in regular order, like the examples I am used to;
I cannot understand examples that are not arrange in regular order, like those I am used to;
I never grumble at a Logic example unless it gives me a headache.
∴ I grumble at these sorites.

26

The Enthymeme

The enthymeme had a different meaning to Aristotle than it has to contemporary logicians.[1] The contemporary meaning—an enthymeme is a categorical syllogism with a suppressed proposition—goes back at least as far as Arnauld's *The Art of Thinking: Port-Royal Logic*, published in 1662.[2]

26A BASIC DEFINITIONS

Def. 1. The **enthymeme** is a set of two propositions offered as an argument, such that the addition of a third proposition results in a categorical syllogism.[3] This third proposition may be the major premiss, the minor premiss, or the conclusion of the resulting syllogism.

Although the definition does not justify it, one may think of an enthymeme as a categorical syllogism that is missing one proposition.[4] An example of an enthymeme is:

(a) *All politicians are corrupt; therefore Green is corrupt.*

Adding the proposition *Green is a politician* to the two above results in a (valid) syllogism.

The orders of the enthymeme are as follows;

Def. 2a. A **first-order enthymeme** is an enthymeme such that by adding a proposition to it, the proposition becomes the *major premiss* of the resulting categorical syllogism.

An example is of a first-order enthymeme is

(b) *Green is a politician; therefore Green is corrupt.*

since when the proposition—*All politicians are corrupt*—is added it becomes the major premiss of the resulting valid syllogism. See below.

(c) Major Premiss: *All politicians are corrupt.*
Minor Premiss: *Green is a politician.*
Conclusion: *Green is corrupt.*

Def. 2b. A **second-order enthymeme** is an enthymeme such that by adding a proposition to it, the proposition becomes the *minor premiss* of the resulting categorical syllogism.

An example of a second-order enthymeme is (a) above.

Def. 2c. A **third-order enthymeme** is an enthymeme such that by adding a proposition to it, the proposition becomes the *conclusion* of the resulting categorical syllogism.

An example is:

(d) *All politicians are corrupt and Green is a politician.*

The inference is clear: *Green is corrupt.* When this proposition is added to the two above, it becomes the conclusion of a valid syllogism.

26B CRITERIA AND PROCEDURE FOR ADDING A PROPOSITION TO AN ENTHYMEME

26B1 Criteria for Selecting the Proposition to be Added to an Enthymeme. If possible, the proposition added to the enthymeme should be true and the resulting syllogism valid. If one or more premisses in the resulting syllogism is false and/or the syllogism invalid, then the syllogism does not prove its conclusion.

Enthymemes fall into three categories.

The first type of enthymeme is one where it is possible to add a true proposition such that the resulting syllogism is valid. An example is the following enthymeme:

No dolphins are fish, since all dolphins are mammals.

The addition of the true proposition *No mammals are fish* results in the following syllogism, which is valid.

No mammals are fish.
All dolphins are mammals.
Therefore, no dolphins are fish.

The second type of enthymeme is one where the addition of a true proposition results in an invalid syllogism, while only the addition of a false proposition would result in a valid syllogism. In such cases it is best to supply both propositions: the one that is false but makes the resulting syllogism valid, and the one that is true but makes the resulting syllogism invalid. The maker of the enthymeme is then in the dilemma of choosing between a false premiss or an invalid argument. An example follows:

Some dolphins are great poets, since some dolphins are females.

Here the addition of a true proposition *Some females are great poets* results in the invalid syllogism (invalid because of an undistributed middle term: see 21A2, R3):

Some dolphins are females.
Some females are great poets.
Therefore, some dolphins are great poets.

The addition of the false proposition *All females are great poets* yields the valid syllogism:

All females are great poets.
Some dolphins are females.
Therefore, some dolphins are great poets.

In the third type, the enthymeme as it stands may be unsound: (a) It may have a false premiss, or (b) it may have such a form that there is no proposition that, when added to it, results in a valid syllogism.

An example of (a) is the enthymeme *Some mathematicians are jazz lovers, since all jazz lovers are men.* The premiss *all jazz lovers are men* is false.

An example of (b) is the enthymeme *Some philosophers are not cigar smokers, since some authors are cigar smokers.* It makes no difference what proposition is added to this enthymeme to make it a syllogism, the resulting syllogism will be invalid. The term *cigar smokers* will be distributed in the conclusion, but not in the premiss in which it occurs (illicit process on the major term: see 21A2, R4).

26B2 Procedure for Adding a Proposition to an Enthymeme.

Step 1. Determine the two terms that will occur in the proposition to be added to the enthymeme. These are the terms that occur only once in the enthymeme. For example, in the enthymeme *No cats are dogs since no cats are canines,* the two terms that occur only once are *dog* and *canines.* These are the terms that will be used to construct the third proposition.

Step 2. Determine the quality of the proposition to be added by using the rules of quality (rule of affirmative conclusion and rule of negative conclusion: see 21A1). For example, in the enthymeme above the conclusion is negative, therefore if the resulting syllogism is to be valid there will be exactly one negative premiss. Since the premiss in the enthymeme is negative, the added proposition (the major premiss) must be affirmative.

Step 3. Determine the quantity of the proposition to be added by using a derived rule of quantity, **DR6:** *If a premiss is particular, so is the conclusion* (See 21D3). DR6 is equivalent to *If the conclusion is universal, then both premisses are universal.* In our example, the conclusion *No cats are dogs* is universal, so the added proposition must be a universal affirmative, that is, an **A** proposition: either *All dogs are canines* or *All canines are dogs.*

Step 4. Unless the added proposition by the above steps turns out to be an **E** or and **I** (in which case which term is the subject or the predicate does not matter) then determine the order of the terms by using rules 3 and 4 (rule of distributed middle and rule of distributed extreme). In our example, we have a choice of *All dogs are canines* or *All canines are dogs.* The conclusion of the enthymeme is *No cats are dogs,* which distributes both terms, so by the rule of distributed extreme, both of these terms should be distributed in the resulting syllogism. By selecting *All dogs are canines,* which has the term *dogs* distributed, the following valid syllogism results:

All dogs are canines.
No cats are canines.
Therefore, no cats are dogs.

This syllogism is valid. It obeys the four rules of the syllogism (21A1): R1, the rule of affirmative conclusion, does not apply. R2 is obeyed; the conclusion is negative, and it has exactly one negative premiss. R3 is satisfied; the middle term *canines* is distributed in the minor premiss. R4, the rule of distributed extreme, is obeyed; the terms *cats* and *dogs*, which are both distributed in the conclusion, are both distributed in the premisses.

26C NON-TRADITIONAL ENTHYMEMES

All sets of propositions that require more than *one* proposition to be added to it to complete the intended argument form, or result in some form of argumentation besides the categorical syllogism when the appropriate proposition(s) are added, we call "non-traditional enthymemes". There are situations in which a single simple proposition may imply an argument, because both the speaker and audience know the propositions that when added to the single stated proposition make an explicit argument. For example, if Mr. Smith says to Mr. Brown, who is a politician, that *all politicians are corrupt*, the two propositions needed to make the argument explicit are understood by both parties, namely that *Mr. Brown is a politician*, and the conclusion that *Mr. Brown is corrupt*.

There is no good reason why an enthymeme should be defined in terms of a categorical syllogism instead of some other valid form of argumentation. For example, the intended argument, *He is either a fool, or he knows something we don't and he is no fool*, becomes a disjunctive syllogism when the proposition (the conclusion), *He knows something we don't*, is added. The argument *This man is not a minister, since if he is a minister he is an expert on the Bible* becomes a complex hypothetical syllogism when the proposition *He is not an expert on the Bible* is added.

Exercise for Chapter 26

For each of the following enthymemes construct a proposition such that when it is added to the enthymeme the result is, if possible, a valid syllogism. Write the proposition on the first line. On the second line write "T" if you think the added proposition is true, "F" if you think it is false. State the order of the enthymeme on the third line (i.e., 1, 2, or 3).

1. All robins are birds, since all robins are flying creatures.
   Added proposition: _____.
   True or False: _____.
   Enthymeme order: _____.

2. Because he is an American Indian, he must be a good tracker.
   Added proposition: _____.
   True or False: _____.
   Enthymeme order: _____.

3. No camelopards are hornbills and this animal is a camelopard.
   Added proposition: _____.
   True or False: _____.
   Enthymeme order: _____.

4. Some women are famous musicians, so some mothers are famous musicians.
   Added proposition: _____.
   True or False: _____.
   Enthymeme order: _____.

5. All those who know that they know nothing are wise men; therefore Socrates is a wise man.
   Added proposition: _____.
   True or False: _____.
   Enthymeme order: _____.

6. Some snakes are not pythons, so some snakes are not cobras.
   Added proposition: _____.
   True or False: _____.
   Enthymeme order: _____.

7. Caruso was a great opera singer, since Caruso was Italian.
   Added proposition: _____.

Exercises/Chapter 26 365

True or False: _____.
Enthymeme order: _____.

8. Some integers are not primes, so no even integers over two are primes.
   Added proposition: _____.
   True or False: _____.
   Enthymeme order: _____.

9. No mathematicians are Dutch belly dancers and some physicists are mathematicians.
   Added proposition: _____.
   True or False: _____.
   Enthymeme order: _____.

10. All woodpeckers are grub eaters, so some birds are not grub eaters.
    Added proposition: _____.
    True or False: _____.
    Enthymeme order: _____.

27

The Antilogism for N-Pair Arguments

In chapter 23B2, a method was given for eliminating pairs of contradictory terms in arguments, resulting in a chain argument. The chain argument could then be tested for validity by the use of the four rules (see 22B1). In this chapter we present an antilogistic test for validity that applies directly to arguments that contain pairs of contradictory terms (n-pair arguments), thus eliminating the need to reduce the number of terms by reversible inferences (see 23B2).

27A BASIC DEFINITIONS

The definition of a chain argument was given in 22A and the definition of an n-pair argument in 23B2, but as a convenience they will be repeated here.

> **Def. 1.** A **chain argument** is a deductive argument consisting of n (where n is two or more) standard categorical propositions, with n distinct terms, each term occurring in just two propositions, with conclusion last (or first), and two successive propositions always sharing a term.

A chain argument is a two-term argument,[1] a standard syllogism, or a standard sorities.

> **Def. 2.** A **n-pair argument** is an argument such that if all occurrences of "non-" as initial prefix of its terms are canceled, the result is a chain argument.

Aristotelian Logic

The following are examples of n-pair argument forms:

(a) Some *B* are non-*C*
∴ Some *B* are *C*

(b) All *S* are *P*
∴ All non-*P* are non-*S*

(c) All non-*M* are *P*
Some *S* are *M*
∴ Some *S* are *P*

(d) No *A* are non-*B*
All *B* are *C*
Some *C* are non-*D*
∴ Some *A* are not *D*

Def. 3. An **extreme premiss** of an n-pair argument is a premiss that contain the subject or predicate term of the conclusion or the contradictory of such a term.

For example, in (a), (b), and (c) above, all of the premisses are extreme premisses, but in (d) only the first and last premisses are extreme.

We now extend our definition of an antilogistic polyad (see 22B4, def. 7)—which applied only to chain argument—to include n-pair arguments.

Def. 4. An **antilogistic polyad** is a set of (two or more) propositions formed from a n-pair argument by taking its premiss(es) together with the contradictory of the conclusion.

Antilogistic Principle: An n-pair argument is valid iffi its antilogistic polyad is inconsistent.

Def. 5. The **extreme proposition(s)** of an antilogistic polyad are the propositions in the polyad that are identical to the extreme premiss(es) in the argument being tested.

For example:

	Argument Form	Antilogistic Polyad
(d)	No *A* are non-*B*	All *A* are non-*B*
	All *B* are *C*	All *B* are *C*
	Some *C* are non-*D*	Some *C* are non-*D*
	∴ Some *A* are not *B*	All *A* are *D*

In antilogistic polyad of (d) above, the extreme propositional forms are the first and third. "No *A* are non-*B*" and "Some *C* are non-*D*".

27B ANTILOGISTIC RULES

An antilogistic polyad for n-pair arguments is inconsistent iffi it satisfies the following rules:

A1 There is just one particular proposition or all the propositions are universal. (Polyads that have just one particular proposition we shall call "Boolean" polyads.)

A2 If there is exactly one particular proposition, then each term that occurs twice is distributed just once, and for each pair of contradictory terms, both terms are distributed or both are undistributed.

A3 If all propositions in the polyad are universal then two Boolean polyads are formed.[2] Each Boolean polyad is formed by replacing one of the extreme propositions in the original polyad by its subaltern. At least one of these Boolean polyads meets rule A1.

Although these rules look rather formidable, in practice they are easy to apply. For example, we form the antilogistic polyad of (a)

	Argument Form	Antilogistic Polyad
(a)	Some B are non-C	Some B are non-C
	∴ Some B are C	No B are C

and we see that it does not meet rule A2, since the term "C" is distributed and "non-C" is undistributed. Terms (or term variables) that are contradictories should be either *both* distributed or *both* undistributed. Therefore, argument form (a) is invalid.

	Argument Form	Antilogistic Polyad
(d)	No A are non-B	No A are non-B
	All B are C	All B are C
	Some C are non-D	Some C are non-D
	∴ Some A are not B	All A are D

The antilogistic polyad of (d) above violates rule A2 twice: "A" is distributed twice and "C" is not distributed at all. The polyad is consistent, hence the argument form (d) is invalid. Each should be distributed exactly once. Nothing is wrong with the contradictories in the polyad, since for each pair of contradictories both are distributed or both are undistributed.

The following argument form is valid

	Argument Form	Antilogistic Polyad
(e)	No A are non-B	No A are non-B
	All B are C	All B are C
	All non-D are non-C	All non-D are non-C
	∴ All A are D	Some A are not D

since its antilogistic polyad contains just one particular proposition and "A" is distributed just once, "B" and "non-B" are both distributed, "C" and "non-C" are both undistributed, and "D" and "non-D" are both distributed.

The following example invokes rule A3.

	Argument Form	Antilogistic Polyad
(f)	No A are non-B	No A are non-B
	All C are A	All C are A
	∴ Some C are B	No C are B

Since the antilogism contains all universals, two Boolean polyads are formed.

First Boolean Polyad	Second Boolean Polyad
Some A are not non-B	No A are non-B
All C are A	Some C are A
No C are B	No C are B

In the first argument form "C" is distributed in both of its occurrences, hence it violates A2, but the second Boolean polyad meets rule A2, hence it, as well as the original polyad from which it was formed, is inconsistent. Thus argument form (f) is valid. Another example:

	Argument Form	Antilogistic Polyad
(g)	All non-D are non-C	All non-D are non-C
	All B are C	All B are C
	No A are non-B	No A are non-B
	∴ Some A are D	No A are D

The polyad contains all universals, so two Boolean polyads must be formed from its extreme propositions:

First Boolean Polyad	Second Boolean Polyad
Some non-D are non-C	All non-D are non-C
All B are C	All B are C
No A are non-B	Some A are not non-B
No A are D	No A are D

The first Boolean polyad has "A" distributed in both of its occurrences, hence it doesn't meet rule A2, but the second Boolean polyad does meet A2 ("A" is distributed just once and the contradictory pairs are either both distributed or both undistributed, hence it and its parent polyad are inconsistent). Thus argument form (g) is valid.

Exercise for Chapter 27

EX 29. Test the following n-pair arguments or argument forms for validity by using the antilogistic rule. Use the following key.

KEY

    a. Invalid. Polyad violates A1.
    b. Invalid. Polyad violates A2.
    c. Invalid. Polyad violates A3.
    d. Valid. All rules A1–A3 satisfied.

_____ 1. All non-canines are non-dogs and no felines are canines; therefore, no felines are dogs.

_____ 2. All S are P, hence some non-S are non-P.

_____ 3.   All hermits are non-chemists.
           All chemists are scientists.
           <u>Some non-women are not non-scientists.</u>
        ∴ Some women are not hermits.

_____ 4.   All non-B are A
           All non-A are C
           No non-C are non-D
           <u>All non-D are E</u>
        ∴ Some B are E

_____ 5. No A are D and some D are C, so no C are A.

28

The Hypothetical Syllogism

The hypothetical syllogism may be pure or mixed. It is pure if all the propositions that compose it are hypotheticals. It is mixed if it has one hypothetical premiss and one categorical premiss.

The hypothetical syllogism was well known by the ancients. Theophrastus, Aristotle's successor as the head of the Lyceum, developed various figures for the pure hypothetical syllogism, and the Stoics set forth rules for evaluating mixed hypothetical syllogisms.

28A THE HYPOTHETICAL PROPOSITION

The following definition of a "hypothetical proposition" was given in chapter 2, definition 8.

Def. 1. A **hypothetical** or **conditional proposition** is a compound proposition formed by connecting two propositions (categorical or compound) by the words "if . . . then ___" or equivalent expressions (e.g., ". . . only if ___"). The "then" clause is asserted to be true on the condition that the "if" clause is true.[1]

Examples of hypothetical propositions are: "If *I pass chemistry*, then *I will graduate*" and "If *the number 113 is prime* then *it is only evenly divisible by 1 and itself*".

Def. 2. The **antecedent** of a hypothetical proposition is the proposition between the "if" and the "then". This proposition may be categorical or compound.

The antecedents in the examples above are: "I pass chemistry" and "the number 113 is prime".

Def. 3. The **consequent** of a hypothetical proposition is the proposition after the "then". This proposition may be categorical or compound.

The consequents in the examples above are: "I will graduate" and "it is only evenly divisible by 1 and itself."

Since the antecedent and the consequent can be compound propositions, it is possible for a hypothetical proposition to have a hypothetical proposition as a consequent. For example: "If Bill is driving drunk then, *if the police stop Bill, he will lose his license*". The following example has for an antecedent a secondary proposition whose predicate contains a hypothetical: "If *it is true that if Bill resigns from the company then the company will fail*, then Harry will not invest in the company.

Every hypothetical proposition contains exactly one antecedent and exactly one consequent, but care must be taken to avoid ambiguous expressions. An example of an ambiguous expression is: "If Bill works for Mike then John will work for Harry or Tom will work for Bill". Abbreviating the propositions in this expression, respectively as "B", "J", and "T" the expression could be interpreted as meaning:

(a) If B then either J or T, or
    If B then (J or T)

or

(b) If B then J, or T.

Proposition (a) is a hypothetical with "B" as antecedent and "J or T" as consequent. Proposition (b) is a disjunction, with disjuncts "If B then J" and "T". They are not equivalent propositions.

28B THE PURE HYPOTHETICAL SYLLOGISM

Def. 4. The **pure hypothetical syllogism**[2] is a valid argument consisting of two hypothetical propositions as premises and one hypothetical proposition as conclusion. The consequent of one premiss (called the *major premiss*) is the antecedent of the other premiss (called the *minor premiss*). The antecedent and consequent of the conclusion is, respectively, the antecedent of the major premiss and the consequent of the minor premiss.

The form of the pure hypothetical syllogism is:[3]

Major premiss: If p then q
Minor premiss: If q then r
Conclusion: If p then r

An example of the pure hypothetical syllogism is:

If the rain will stop in an hour, then the ball game will be played tonight.

If the ball game will be played tonight, then I will be able to watch the ball game.

Therefore, if the rain will stop in an hour, then I will be able to watch the ball game.

28C THE MIXED HYPOTHETICAL SYLLOGISM

Def. 5. The **mixed hypothetical syllogism** is an argument that has two premisses: a conditional (called the *major premiss*) and a categorical proposition (called the *minor premiss*). The minor premiss affirms or denies the antecedent in the major premiss, while the conclusion affirms or denies the consequent; or the minor premiss affirms or denies the consequent, while the conclusion affirms or denies the antecedent.

Two examples of a mixed hypothetical syllogism are below. In (1), which is valid, the minor premiss affirms the antecedent in the major premiss and the conclusion affirms the consequent of the major premiss. In (2), which is invalid, the minor premiss affirms the consequent of the major premiss and the conclusion affirms the antecedent of the major premiss.

(1) *If Sally is William's aunt then Joan is my cousin.*
Sally is William's aunt.
Therefore, Joan is my cousin.

(2) *If 21 is a prime number, then it is an odd number.*
But 21 is an odd number.
Therefore, 21 is a prime number.

28C1 The Figures of the Mixed Hypothetical Syllogism.

Def. 6. Figure 1 of a mixed hypothetical syllogism is a mixed hypothetical syllogism in which the minor premiss affirms or denies the antecedent of the major premiss.

The forms (3) through (6) in table 28.1 below are in figure 1.

Def. 7. Figure 2 of a mixed hypothetical syllogism is a mixed hypothetical syllogism in which the minor premiss affirms or denies the consequent of the major premiss.

The forms (3') through (6') in table 28.1 below are in figure 2.

28C2 Forms of the Mixed Hypothetical Syllogism. The mixed hypothetical syllogism in figures 1 and 2 has eight forms: ("p" and "q" are any propositions).

Table 28.1: Forms of the Mixed Hypothetical Syllogism

	Ponendo[4] *Ponens*	*Tollendo Tollens*	*Ponendo Tollens*	*Tollendo Ponens*
Figure 1	(3) Valid If p then q p $\therefore q$	(4) Invalid If p then q Not p $\therefore$ Not q	(5) Invalid If p then q p $\therefore$ Not q	(6) Invalid If p then q Not p $\therefore q$
Figure 2	(3') Invalid If p then q q $\therefore p$	(4') Valid If p then q Not q $\therefore$ Not p	(5') Invalid If p then q q $\therefore$ Not p	(6') Invalid If p then q Not q $\therefore p$

Only two of these forms are valid; (3) and (4'). Form (3) is commonly called *modus ponens* or "affirming the antecedent". Form (4') is commonly called *modus tollens* or "denying the consequent".

By substituting "not p" for "p" and "not q" for "q" in the above forms (and reducing "not-not p" to "p") other equivalent mixed hypothetical syllogistic forms can be produced. For example, the following three forms are all equivalent to form (3).

(7) If p then not q
 p
 $\therefore$ Not q

(8) If not p then q
 Not p
 $\therefore q$

(9) If not p then not q
 Not p
 $\therefore$ Not q

The Hypothetical Syllogism

28C3 Valid Forms of the Mixed Hypothetical Syllogism. Forms (3) and (4') are the only valid forms of the mixed hypothetical syllogisms. Form (3) is called *modus ponendo ponens*, which means an argument form that affirms in the minor premiss and in the conclusion. For short, it is commonly called *modus ponens* or "affirming the antecedent". Form (4') is called *modus tollendo tollens*, which means an argument form that denies in the minor premiss and in the conclusion. For short, it is commonly called *modus tollens* or "denying the antecedent".

Def. 8. Modus (ponendo) ponens (affirming the antecedent) is a valid form of the mixed hypothetical syllogism where the minor premiss affirms the antecedent of the major premiss and the conclusion affirms the consequent of the major premiss.

All of the following argument forms are examples of *modus ponens:*

(10) If p then (q or r)
p
∴ q or r

(11) If (p or q) then (r and s)
(p or q)
∴ r and s

(12) If not (p and q) then (if r then s)
Not (p and q)
∴ If r then s

Def. 9. Modus (tollendo) tollens (denying the consequent) is a valid form of the mixed hypothetical syllogism where the minor premiss denies the consequent of the major premiss and the conclusion is the denial of the antecedent of the major premiss.

All of the following argument forms are examples of *modus tollens:*

(13) If (p or q) then not r
r
∴ Not (p or q)

(14) If (p and q) then (r or s)
Not (r or s)
∴ Not (p and q)

(15) If not (p and q) then (if r then s)
Not (if r then s)
∴ (p and q)

28C4 Invalid Forms of the Mixed Hypothetical Syllogism. Of the six invalid forms of the mixed hypothetical syllogism the most famous ones are forms (3') and (4) in table 28.1 above. Form (3') is called the "fallacy of affirming the consequent" and form (4) is called the "fallacy of denying the antecedent". An example of the fallacy of affirming the consequent is:

(16) *If Rover is a cocker spaniel then Rover is a dog.*
Rover is a dog.
Therefore, Rover is a cocker spaniel.

This argument is invalid, since it is possible for both premises to be true and the conclusion false. An example of the fallacy of denying the antecedent is:

(17) *If Rover is a cocker spaniel then Rover is a dog.*
Rover is not a cocker spaniel.
Therefore, Rover is not a dog.

Rover, of course, may not be a cocker spaniel, but may still be a dog. Hence, both premises may be true and the conclusion false. The argument is invalid.

The remaining four invalid forms in Table 28.1—(5), (5'), (6), and (6')—have no claim to distinction as they are so obviously invalid that they are seldom, if ever, mistaken for valid forms.

28D THE INCONSISTENT TRIAD OF THE MIXED HYPOTHETICAL SYLLOGISM

28D1 The Antilogistic Test for Validity. In 22B4 we presented an antilogistic test for chain arguments. We now extend the antilogistic test to cover the mixed hypothetical syllogism. We do not offer such a test for the pure hypothetical syllogism, since it has only one valid form.[5]

Def. 10. A **mixed hypothetical antilogistic triad** is a set of three propositions formed from a mixed hypothetical syllogism by taking its premises together with the contradictory of its conclusion.

Antilogistic Principle: A mixed hypothetical syllogism is valid iffi its mixed hypothetical antilogistic triad is inconsistent.
Antilogistic Rule: A mixed hypothetical antilogistic triad is inconsistent iffi it satisfies the MHA (Mixed Hypothetical Antilogism) rule.
MHA Rule: The triad contains a hypothetical proposition (or propositional form) P, the affirmation of the antecedent of P, and the denial of its consequent.

For example: Let us test the following mixed hypothetical syllogism for validity. *If Joan is a mother, then Joan is female, and Joan is a mother: therefore, Joan is female.*

Argument Form	Antilogistic Triad
If p or q	If p or q
p	p
$\therefore q$	Not q

The triad obeys the rule MHS, since the triad contains a hypothetical propositional form, the affirmation of its antecedent, and the denial of its consequent. The triad is inconsistent, since a hypothetical is false if it has a true antecedent and a false consequent. Hence the last two lines of the triad are inconsistent with the first.

28D2 Formal Counterargument to a Hypothetical. Since any two propositions of an inconsistent triad implies the contradictory of its third; the inconsistent mixed hypothetical antilogistic triad will yield three valid arguments, two of which we are already familiar: *modus ponens* and *modus tollens*. The third argument that is not a mixed hypothetical syllogism has the following form:

p
Not q
$\therefore$ It is false that if p then q.

The premisses collectively express the condition under which the hypothetical "If p then q" is false. An example is: *Fang is a dog and Fang is not a friendly animal; therefore it is false that if Fang is a dog then Fang is a friendly animal.*

28E THE DISTINCTION BETWEEN HYPOTHETICAL AND GENERAL CONDITIONALS

There is a difference of kind between hypothetical propositions such as:

(18) If *patience is a virtue,* then *there are painful virtues.*[6]

(19) If *the earth is immoveable,* then *the sun moves around the earth.*

and hypothetical propositions such as:

(20) If *a number is prime,* then *it is odd.*

(21) If *a child is spoilt, his parents suffer.*

The antecedents and consequents of hypothetical propositions (18) and (19) are propositions. But the antecedents and consequents of (20) and (21) are not propositions. Hypothetical proposition (20) is really a shorthand way of writing: "If 1 is a prime number then it is odd" and "If 2 is a prime number then it is odd", and "If 3 is a prime number, then it is odd", and so on for all numbers. Similarly, hypothetical proposition (21) is a shorthand way of writing "If this child (referring to a specific child) is spoilt then its parents suffer" and 'If that child (referring to a specific child, not the same as the first) is spoilt, then its parents suffer" and so on for each and every spoilt child.

Hypothetical proposition (20) is equivalent to the form "For any x, if x is a prime number, then x is odd". And hypothetical proposition (21) is equivalent to the form "For any x, if x is a child, then x has suffering parents". In these equivalent forms it can be seen that "x is a prime number", "x is odd", "x is a child", and "x has suffering parents" are not propositions.

Hypothetical propositions that do not have propositions as antecedent or consequent are generalized conditionals, and by definition are excluded from the pure and mixed hypothetical syllogism. But these generalized conditionals may so closely parallel hypothetical syllogisms that we will not exclude them from consideration.

For example, the following arguments

(22) If a child is spoilt, its parents suffer.
If its parents suffer, society suffers.
Therefore, if a child is spoilt, society suffers.

(23) If a number is prime, then it is odd.
The number 113 is prime.
Therefore, the number 113 is odd.

are *not* by definition, respectively, the pure hypothetical syllogism and a mixed hypothetical syllogism, since all the propositions in (22) are general conditionals and the first proposition in (23) is a general conditional. But (22) so closely parallels the pure hypothetical syllogism and (23) *modus ponens* that we shall treat such arguments as if they were hypothetical syllogisms.

Exercise for Chapter 28

EX 28. Indicate whether the following mixed hypothetical syllogisms are valid (Val) or invalid (InV). Indicate whether or not the argument is one of the following forms: *modus ponens* (MP), *modus tollens* (MT), affirming the consequent (AC), denying the antecedent (DA).

1. If Wallace resigned, then Bill is president, but Bill is not president, so Wallace did not resign.
   Val or InV   Form: _____.

2. If Wallace did not resign, then Smith did not resign, but Smith did resign, so Wallace did resign.
   Val or InV   Form: _____.

3. The rocket will not reach Mars, because if the rocket is not off its course by more than one degree, then it will reach Mars, but the rocket is off its course by more than one degree.
   Val or InV   Form: _____.

4. If this animal is not a mammal then it is not a wombat and this animal is not a wombat, therefore, it is not a mammal.
   Val or InV   Form: _____.

5. This fish is not a shark but if this fish is a shark then we are in trouble. Hence we are not in trouble.
   Val or InV   Form: _____.

29

The Disjunctive Syllogism

The disjunctive syllogism was probably known to the successors of Aristotle. There is evidence that the early Stoics extensively investigated disjunctive propositions and disjunctive argument forms. However, little of their work survived.

The disjunctive (alternative) syllogism, like the hypothetical syllogism, may be either pure or mixed. The pure disjunctive syllogism, an argument consisting of three disjunctive propositions, is extremely rare and is mentioned in few logic texts.[1] The mixed disjunctive syllogism—called simply the "disjunctive syllogism"—is a very common argument form and is the only one dealt with in this chapter.

29A THE DISJUNCTIVE PROPOSITION

29A1 Basic Definitions.

Def. 1. A **disjunction (alternation)** or **disjunctive proposition** is a compound proposition formed by connecting two propositions (categorical or compound) with the word "or". (See chapter 2, defs. 4a and 7.)

Examples of disjunctive propositions are: "I will have pie for dessert or I will have cake for dessert" and "In five years the United States will find an alternative to oil as a source of energy or its people will have to accept a lower standard of living".

Def. 2. The **disjuncts** of a disjunctive proposition are the propositions in it (categorical or compound) connected by "or".

For example, in the disjunctive proposition "Either John is the murderer or Herman is the murderer or Mary is lying" there are five disjuncts. They are:

(a) John is the murderer.

(b) Herman is the murderer.

(c) Mary is lying.

(d) John is the murderer or Herman is the murderer.

(e) Herman is the murderer or Mary is lying.

In other words, if we let "J", "H", and "M" represent, respectively, the three categoricals in the disjunction, then the disjuncts may be grouped in three different ways:

(f) (J) or (H) or (M). Disjuncts are "(J)", "(H)", and "(M)".

(g) (J or H) or (M). Disjuncts are "(J or H)" and "(M)".

(h) (J) or (H or M). Disjuncts are "(J)" and "(H or M)".

The word "or" is a main operator in a proposition (or propositional form) when the proposition (or form) consists of two disjuncts connected by this "or". For example, in (g) it is the second "or" that is the main operator, while in (h) the main operator is the first "or". The disjuncts in proposition (f) are so grouped that neither "or" is the main operator. Providing that both "or's" are used in the same sense this will cause no trouble.

29A2 The Inclusive Disjunction. The word "or" is used in two different ways in ordinary discourse. It is sometimes used to mean "one or the other but not both" (the exclusive sense) or more commonly it is used to mean "one or the other or both" (the inclusive sense).

>**Def. 3.** An **inclusive "or"** (sometimes called a **non-exclusive "or"**)[2] is an "or" of a disjunction that asserts that at least one disjunct is true.

>**Def. 4.** An **inclusive disjunction (weak disjunction)** is a disjunctive proposition whose main operator(s) is the inclusive "or".

An inclusive proposition is false iffi both disjuncts are false. The disjunction is true if one disjunct or both are true.

In concrete examples the inclusive use of "or" may be detected by the context of the disjunction. For example, the sentence "I will be satisfied if you pay me $10,000 in cash or $10,000 in negotiable bonds" is probably meant as an inclusive disjunction as few people would not be satisfied if they received twice what they asked.

29A3 The Exclusive Disjunction.

Def. 5. An **exclusive "or"** is an "or" of a disjunction that asserts that just one disjunct is true.

Def. 6. An **exclusive disjunction (strong disjunction)** is a disjunctive proposition whose main connective(s) is the exclusive "or".

An exclusive proposition is false if both disjuncts are false or if both disjuncts are true. The disjunction is true iffi one disjunct is true.

In concrete examples it is often possible to recognize an exclusive disjunction by the context of the proposition.[3] For example, the sentence "You may have coffee with your meal or you may have tea with your meal" intends that you may have one or the other but not both. Similarly the sentence "We will go to the movies tonight or we will go to the opera tonight" probably means that tonight just one of these alternatives are to be selected. When evaluating arguments, if there is any doubt as to whether the exclusive or inclusive "or" is intended, assume the minimal interpretation, which is the inclusive "or". For all disjunctive propositions and propositional forms in the remaining sections of this chapter assume the inclusive use of "or" unless otherwise specified.

29B THE DISJUNCTIVE SYLLOGISM

29B1 Definition of Disjunctive Syllogism.

Def. 7. The (mixed) **disjunctive syllogism** is an argument that has two premisses: a disjunction (called the *major premiss* traditionally written first) and a categorical proposition (called the *minor premiss* traditionally written second). The minor premiss denies or affirms one of the disjuncts in the major premiss. The conclusion denies or affirms the remaining disjunct(s) in the major premiss.

Two examples of a disjunctive syllogism are given. In the first, which is valid, the minor premiss denies a disjunct in the major premiss. In the second, which is invalid, the minor premiss affirms a disjunct in the major premiss.

(1) Either Bill will be elected President or Bill will resign.
Bill will not be elected President.
Therefore, Bill will resign.

(2) Either Bill will be elected President or Bill will resign.
Bill will be elected President.
Therefore, Bill will not resign.

29B2 The Figures of the Disjunctive Syllogism. We shall restrict our definition of figure to forms of the disjunctive syllogism in which the variables of the major premiss are grouped into exactly two disjuncts. Examples of such propositions are "*p* or *q*", "*p* or (*q* or *r*)", "(not *p* or *r*) or (*r* and *s*)".

Def. 8. Figure 1 of a disjunctive syllogism is a disjunctive syllogism in which the minor premiss affirms or denies the first disjunct of the major premiss.

The forms (3) to (6) below are in figure 1.

Def. 9. Figure 2 of a disjunctive syllogism is a disjunctive syllogism in which the minor premiss affirms or denies the second disjunct of the major premiss.

Example of disjunctive syllogistic form in figure 2 are in forms (10), (11), and (14) below.

Def. 10. A standard disjunctive syllogism is a disjunctive syllogism in figure 1.

29B3 Forms of the Disjunctive Syllogism. The disjunctive syllogism, in figures 1 and 2, has eight forms ("*p*" and "*q*" are any propositions: categorical or compound).

Table 29.1: Forms of the Disjunctive Syllogism

	Tollendo Ponens	*Ponendo Tollens*	*Tollendo Tollens*	*Ponendo Ponens*
Figure 1	(3) Valid p or q Not p ∴ q	(4) Invalid p or q p ∴ Not q	(5) Invalid p or q Not p ∴ Not q	(6) Invalid p or q p ∴ q
Figure 2	(3′) Valid p or q Not q ∴ p	(4′) Invalid p or q q ∴ Not p	(5′) Invalid p or q Not q ∴ Not p	(6′) Invalid p or q q ∴ p

Only two of these forms, (3) and (3′), *tollendo ponens*, are valid. The remaining six are invalid. Arguments (1) and (2) above are, respectively, in forms (3) and (4).

By substituting "not p" for "p" and "not q" for "q" in the above forms (and reducing "not-not p" and "not-not q", respectively, to "p" and "q") other equivalent disjunctive forms can be produced. For example, the following three forms are all equivalent to form (3).[4]

(7) p or not q
Not p
∴ Not q

(8) Not p or q
p
∴ q

(9) Not p or not q
p
∴ Not q

29B4 Valid Forms of the Disjunctive Syllogism. Forms (3) and (3′) are the only valid forms of the disjunctive syllogism. They are called *modus tollendo ponens*, which means an argument form that denies in the minor premiss and affirms in the conclusion. They may be called *tollendo ponens* for short or "denying a disjunct".

Def. 11. (Modus) tollendo ponens is a valid form of a (mixed) disjunctive syllogism where the minor premiss denies one of the disjuncts in the major premiss and the conclusion affirms the remaining disjunct. (This remaining disjunct may itself be a disjunction.)

All of the following forms are examples of *tollendo ponens*, hence they are all valid.

(10) p or q
   Not q
   $\therefore p$

(11) p or (q or r)
   Not (q or r)
   $\therefore p$

(12) (p or q) or (r and s)
   Not (p or q)
   $\therefore r$ and s

(13) Not (p and q) or r
   (p and q)
   $\therefore r$

(14) Not (p and q) or Not (r and s)
   (r and s)
   $\therefore$ Not (p and q)

The distinction between hypothetical and general conditionals (See chapter 28) is parallel to the distinction between disjunctions whose disjuncts are propositions and those whose disjuncts are not. For example, compare the following:

(i) *Either 5 is an odd number or 5 is an even number.*
(ii) *Either a number is odd or it is even.*

In the first disjunction the disjuncts are propositions; in the second they are not. "A number is odd" is not a proposition, and "it is even" is not a proposition, since "it" refers to any number. Disjunction (ii) may be called a *general disjunction;* its disjuncts are not propositions. It is really a shorthand way of writing a series of propositional disjunctions, for example, "1 is an odd number or it is even, and 2 is an odd number or it is even, and. . . ."

Although arguments that contain a general disjunction are not, by definition, disjunctive syllogisms, some of them so closely parallel the forms of the disjunctive syllogism that it seems arbitrary to exclude them from consideration. For example, the argument

Either a number is odd or even.
4 is not odd.
$\therefore$ 4 is even.

is intuitively valid and is a close parallel to *tollendo ponens* in figure 1. Consequently, we shall treat such general disjunctive syllogisms as if they were (propositional) disjunctive syllogisms.

29B5 Invalid Forms of the Disjunctive Syllogism. Of the six invalid forms of the disjunctive syllogism—forms (4) to (6) and (4') to (6') in table 29.1 above—the most famous ones are forms (4) and (4'). They have a form called *(modus) ponendo tollens* and are the only two of the six invalid forms that become valid if the major premise is interpreted as an exclusive disjunction.

The Disjunctive Syllogism

Def. 12. (Modus) ponendo tollens is an invalid form of a (mixed) disjunctive syllogism where the minor premiss affirms one of the disjuncts in the major premiss and the conclusion denies the remaining disjunct. (The remaining disjunct may itself be a disjunct.)

All of the following argument forms are examples of *ponendo tollens* and are invalid:

(15) p or q
q
∴ Not p

(16) p or not (p or q)
Not (p or q)
∴ Not p

(17) Not p or not q
Not p
∴ q

Some logicians, using a narrower definition of disjunctive syllogism than ours, would not allow the following arguments to be called "disjunctive syllogisms". Form (18) is *ponendo ponens;* form (19) is *tollendo tollens*.

(18) p or q
p
∴ q

(19) p or q
Not p
∴ Not q

29C THE DISJUNCTIVE SYLLOGISM AND THE EXCLUSIVE "OR"

If the major premiss of a (mixed) disjunctive syllogism is an exclusive disjunction then both of the two argument forms allowed by the definition are valid. That is to say a disjunctive syllogism with a strong disjunction as major premiss is valid in both *tollendo ponens* and *ponendo tollens* (forms (3), (3'), (4) and (4') in table 29.1 above). Argument forms (18) and (19) above, even with a strong disjunction as major premiss, remain invalid.

Table 29.2: Forms of the Standard Disjunctive Syllogism

	Tollendo Ponens	*Ponendo Tollens*	*Tollendo Tollens*	*Ponendo Ponens*
Nonexclusive Disjunction	Valid p or q Not p ∴ q	Invalid p or q p ∴ Not q	Invalid p or q Not p ∴ Not q	Invalid p or q p ∴ q
Exclusive Disjunction	Valid p or q Not p ∴ q	Valid p or q p ∴ Not q	Invalid p or q Not p ∴ Not q	Invalid p or q p ∴ q

29E THE INCONSISTENT TRIAD OF THE DISJUNCTIVE SYLLOGISM

29E1 The Antilogistic Test for Validity. As there is only one valid type of (non-exclusive) disjunctive syllogism, *tollendo ponens*, it hardly seems worth the effort to devise an antilogistic test for is validity. However, since the antilogism provides such an easy test for chain arguments (See 22B4) it seems worthwhile to extend it to the disjunctive syllogism (as we have done for the hypothetical syllogism).

Def. 13. A **disjunctive antilogistic triad** is a set of three propositions formed from a disjunctive syllogism by taking its premisses together with the contradictory of its conclusion.

Antilogistic Principle: A disjunctive syllogism is false iffi its disjunctive antilogistic triad is inconsistent.
Antilogistic Rule. A disjunctive antilogistic triad is inconsistent iffi it satisfies the DA (Disjunctive Antilogism) Rule.
DA Rule: The triad contains a disjunctive "premiss" P, the denial of a disjunct of P, and the denial of the remaining disjunct of P. (This remaining disjunct may be a disjunctive proposition.)[5]

For example: Let us test the following disjunctive syllogism for validity: *"Either I will major in chemistry or I will major in physics. I will not major in chemistry; therefore, I will major in physics"*.

Argument Form	Antilogistic Triad
Either p or q	Either p or q
Not p	Not p
∴ q	Not q

The triad obeys rule DA, since the triad contains a disjunctive "premise" (p or q), a denial of one of its disjuncts (Not p), and a denial of its remaining disjuncts (Not q). Hence, the triad is inconsistent and the disjunctive syllogism is valid.[6]

29E2 Formal Counter argument to a Disjunction. Since any two propositions of an inconsistent triad implies the contradictory of its third, the inconsistent disjunctive antilogistic triad will yield three valid arguments, two with which we are already familiar: *tollendo ponens* in figures 1 and 2 (see table 29.1). The third argument that is not a disjunctive syllogism has the following form:

Not *p*
Not *q*
∴ It is false that *p* or *q*.

It should be noted that the premisses collectively express the conditions under which the disjunction is false. An example is: *"I am not for you and I am not against you; therefore, it is false that either I am for you or I am against you"*.

Appendix to Chapter 29A4

29A4 EXHAUSTIVENESS OF DISJUNCTIVE PROPOSITIONS

To assert a disjunctive proposition is to assert that it is exhaustive. For instance, when a chemist asserts that a certain substance is either iodine or bromine he is claiming that these two alternatives exhaust the possibilities for the substance in question. If the turned out to be antimony, then the disjunction would be proved non-exhaustive.

The exhaustiveness of empirical disjunctions—an empirical proposition is a proposition whose terms names actual objects (see 4F1c) or properties of actual objects—is not a matter for the logician, but for the special sciences. Hence, whether or not it is true that the disjunction "This tree is a mountain maple or a striped maple" is exhaustive, is not a question for the logician, but for the dendrologist.

However, there is one kind of disjunction whose exhaustiveness is not a matter of empirical truth—truth known by observation or experiment—but a matter of the kind of logical relation between its disjuncts. This disjunctive proposition has the form "p or not p" (where "p" is any proposition, categorical or compound). When the two disjuncts (related by the main operator "or") are contradictories, then the proposition must be exhaustive; there are no other alternatives. For example, "12 is a prime number or it is false that 12 is a prime number" or "John is six feet tall or John is not six feet tall". Such propositions that are known to be true by virtue of their logical form are called "tautologies".

One form of tautology is the dichotomous proposition. A dichotomous proposition is a disjunction that asserts that a class is divided into two subclasses that are contradictories. Examples: "Birds are either robins or non-robins", "Military officers are either commissioned or noncommissioned", and "The tales of Robin Hood are either fictitious or fact".

Exercise for Chapter 29

EX 29. Evaluate the following disjunctive syllogisms as valid (Val) or invalid (InV). Determine figure.

_____ 1. Either this man is a good actor or he is insane and since he is not a good actor; therefore he is insane.
Val or InV,   Figure 1 or 2.

_____ 2. Either this man is a good actor or he is insane and since he is a good actor; therefore he cannot be insane.
Val or InV,   Figure 1 or 2.

_____ 3. Mr. Green must be the murderer, since he is either the murderer or he is protecting someone and he is not protecting someone.
Val or InV,   Figure 1 or 2.

_____ 4. Mr. Smith cannot be the murderer, since he is either the murderer or Mr. Green is the murderer and Mr. Green is the murderer.
Val or InV,   Figure 1 or 2.

_____ 5. Janet is either in England or in Germany and she is not in Germany, so she is in England.
Val or InV,   Figure 1 or 2.

30

The Dilemma

A "dilemma" (literally "two assumptions") means, in ordinary discourse, "a situation requiring a choice between equally undesirable alternatives". In logic a "dilemma" is the name of a form of argumentation. It may or may not involve undesirable alternatives.

Basically the dilemma is a disjunction of two (mixed) hypothetical syllogisms; consequently, the main purpose for studying it is its practical application. Whenever one must decide between apparently equal alternatives, a knowledge of the dilemma and the ways to refute it will often prove helpful.

30A THE TRADITIONAL DILEMMA

The dilemma has been given various definitions in its long history. Perhaps the most common definition of the dilemma is the following:

Def. 1. A **dilemma** is an argument in which one premiss, the major, is a conjunctive assertion of two hypotheticals; and the second premiss, the minor, is a disjunctive (alternative) proposition. The minor either affirms alternatively the antecedents of the major, or denies alternatively its consequents.[1] The conclusion, respectively, affirms alternatively the consequents of the major, if they differ, or denies alternatively it antecedents, if they differ.

The dilemma form, as defined above, is always valid.

In practice it is far easier to explain a dilemma by presenting its four traditional forms than by understanding the above definition. These forms are listed in 30A1 below.

Some authors, such as Coffey and Keynes, would allow the major premiss of the dilemma to contain more than two hypothetical propositions.[2] Other authors such as Joseph state that "the essence of the dilemma seems to lie in the fact of confronting a man with alternatives at once ineluctable and unpleasant".[3] A more popular viewpoint is expressed by Copi who states that "a dilemma need not have an unpleasant conclusion".[4] The authors accept this latter position and assert that the term "dilemma" describes a certain argument form.

30A1 The Traditional Forms of the Dilemma. The names of the four valid traditional forms are:

(1) Simple constructive dilemma.

(2) Complex constructive dilemma.

(3) Simple destructive dilemma.

(4) Complex destructive dilemma.

Def. 2. A **constructive dilemma** is a dilemma in which the minor premiss alternatively affirms the antecedents in the major. If the constructive dilemma contains a common consequent in the major premiss, it is **simple.** If the consequents differ, it is **complex.**

The form of a simple constructive dilemma is (let "p", "q", "r", and "s" be any propositions):

Major premiss: If p then q, and if r then q
Minor Premiss: Either p or r
Conclusion: Therefore q.

An example:

Major premiss: *If I take physics, I will have a lot of homework, and if I take chemistry, I will have a lot of homework.*

Minor premiss: *Either I take physics or I take chemistry.*

Conclusion: *Therefore, I will have a lot of homework.*

The form of a complex constructive dilemma is:

Major premiss: If *p* then *q*, and if *r* then *s*
Minor Premiss: Either *p* or *r*
Conclusion: Therefore *q* or *s*.

An example:

Major premiss: *If I have Mexican food I will get heartburn, and if I have Chinese food I won't sleep tonight.*

Minor Premiss: *I have my choice of Mexican food or Chinese food.*

Conclusion: *Therefore, I will have heartburn or I won't sleep tonight.*

Def. 3. A **destructive dilemma** is a dilemma in which the minor premiss alternatively denies the consequents in the major. If the destructive dilemma contains a common antecedent in the major premiss, it is **simple.** If the antecedents differ, it is **complex.**

The form of a simple destructive dilemma is:

Major premiss: If *p* then *q*, and if *p* then *r*
Minor Premiss: Either not *q* or not *r*
Conclusion: Therefore not *p*.

An example:

Major premiss: *If Jones is told the truth then Sylvia committed the murder and if Jones told the truth then Brown is lying.*

Minor premiss: *But either Sylvia didn't commit the murder or Brown isn't lying.*

Conclusion: *Therefore, Jones did not tell the truth.*

The form of a complex destructive dilemma is:

Major premiss: If *p* then *q*, and if *r* then *s*
Minor premiss: Either not *q* or not *s*
Conclusion: Therefore not *p* or not *r*

For example:

Major premiss: *If Bill was elected then John resigned, and if Mike was elected then Ralph resigned.*

Minor premiss: *Either John did not resign or Ralph did not resign.*

Conclusion: *Either Bill was not elected or Mike was not elected.*

30A2 The Traditional Dilemmas and the Mixed Hypothetical Syllogism. The relation between the four traditional dilemmatic forms and the two valid forms (*modus ponens* and *modus tollens*) of the mixed hypothetical syllogism becomes obvious when the dilemmatic forms are presented in the following manner:

a *Simple Constructive Dilemma.*

Modus ponens		*Modus ponens*	
If p then q	and	If r then q	
p	or	r	
$\therefore q$	or	$\therefore q$	(q or q) = q

b *Complex Constructive Dilemma.*

Modus ponens		*Modus ponens*
If p then q	and	If r then s
p	or	r
$\therefore q$	or	$\therefore s$

c *Simple Destructive Dilemma.*

Modus tollens		*Modus tollens*	
If p then q	and	If p then s	
Not q	or	Not s	
$\therefore$ not p		$\therefore$ not p	
		(not p or not p) = not p	

d *Complex Constructive Dilemma.*

Modus tollens		*Modus tollens*
If p then q	and	If r then s
Not q	or	Not s
$\therefore$ not p	or	$\therefore$ not r

30A3 Variant Forms of the Traditional Dilemma. The propositions in the minor premiss of a constructive dilemma do not have to be affirmative in order to affirm the antecedents in the major premiss. For example

If p then q, and if not r then s
Either p or not r
Therefore q or s

is a constructive dilemma and so is the form below.

If not p then q, and if not r then s
Either not p or not r
Therefore q or s

It should be observed that the propositions in the consequents of the above examples could just as well have been negative. This would mean that these propositions would also be negative when they occured in the conclusion.

The propositions in the minor premiss of a destructive dilemma do not have to be negative in order to deny the consequence in the major premiss. Example (1) is a form of a simple destructive dilemma. Example (2) is a form of a complex destructive dilemma.

(1) If p then not q, and if p then not s
Either q or s
Therefore not p

(2) If not p then q, and if r then not s
Either not q or s
Therefore p or not r

The simple constructive dilemma is logically equivalent to the form:

If either p or q, then r
Either p or q
Therefore r

By definition this form is not a dilemma. It is a form of a mixed hypothetical syllogism, *modus ponens.*

The simple destructive dilemma is logically equivalent to the form:

If p then, q and r
Either not q or not r
Therefore not p

By definition this form is not a dilemma. It is the form of a mixed hypothetical syllogism, *modus tollens.* (Note that the negation of "q and r" is "not q or not r".)

30A4 The Traditional Dilemma in Enthymematic Form: The Virtual Dilemma.
Many dilemmas have contradictory disjuncts in its minor premiss such that the minor has the form of "*p* or not *p*". For example: "If he lies, he will be condemned, and if he does not lie, he will be condemned. *He lies or he does not lie.* Therefore he will be condemned".

All disjunctive propositions of the form "*p* or not *p*" or "not *p* or *p*" must be true. Consequently, when the minor premiss of a dilemma is in either of these forms it is often omitted and the dilemma is stated enthymematically. Examples are:

(1) If he lies, he will be condemned, and if he does not lie, he will be condemned. Therefore, he will be condemned.

(2) If John is elected he will be overworked, and if John is not elected he will be unhappy. Hence, he will be overworked or unhappy.

30B A NEW TREATMENT OF THE DILEMMA

Since there are invalid syllogistic forms and invalid sorites forms, as well as invalid forms of the disjunctive syllogism and mixed hypothetical syllogisms, it seems perfectly reasonable to allow invalid dilemmatic forms. Consequently, the authors think that the traditional definition of the dilemma, which limits the dilemmas to only valid forms, is too restrictive.

Basically the dilemma is a combination of two hypothetical syllogisms (*modus ponens* and *modus tollens*), therefore, since a mixed hypothetical syllogism may be formally invalid, one might well expect that the dilemma would be defined to allow invalid forms.[5]

30B1 A New Definition of the Dilemma.
In order to allow invalid forms of the dilemma, its traditional definition may be modified as follow:

Def. 4. A **dilemma** is an argument in which one premiss, the major, is a conjunction of two hypotheticals, and the second premiss, the minor, is a disjunction that affirms or denies alternatively the antecedents or consequents in the major premiss. The conclusion of the dilemma respectively affirms or denies the consequents or antecedents of the major premiss.[6]

It is undoubtedly easier to explain by examples the new forms allowed by this definition than it is to understand the definition. This new definition allows the four valid traditional forms of the dilemmas and also includes the four following invalid forms:

Invalid Simple Dilemmas
(1) If p then q, and if p then r
Either q or r
Therefore p

(2) If p then q, and if r then q
Either not p or not r
Therefore not q

Invalid Complex Dilemmas
(3) If p then q, and if r then s
Either q or s
Therefore p or r

(4) If p then q, and if r then s
Either not p or not r
Therefore not q or not s

Dilemmatic forms (1) and (3) commit the fallacy of affirming the consequent. Dilemmatic forms (2) and (4) commit the fallacy of denying the antecedent.

30C METHODS OF REFUTING A DILEMMA

Since dilemmas are often used in debates wherein one party tries to force on his opponent either of two alternatives, the refutation of dilemmas is of some practical importance.

The four ways of refuting a dilemma are:

(1) To challenge the formal validity of the dilemma.

(2) To attack the truth of the major premiss.

(3) To attack the truth of the minor premiss.

(4) To rebut the dilemma by a counter dilemma.

30C1 Challenging the Formal Validity of the Dilemma. A dilemma is successfully refuted if it is shown to be formally invalid. The invalidity of a dilemma is established if either alternative in the minor premiss either affirms a consequent or denies an antecedent in the major premiss (see the four invalid forms in section 30B1). Also arguments in dilemmatic form should be carefully checked in order to ensure that the conclusion, if the alternatives in the minor affirm the antecedents in the major, contain the consequent(s); or, if the alternatives deny the consequents in the major, contain the denial (contradictories) of the antecedent(s). For example, the following are patently invalid argument forms:

(1) If p then q, and if r then s
Either p or r
Therefore either not q or not s

(2) If p then q, and if r then s
Either not q or not s
Therefore either p or r

30C2 Attacking the Truth of the Major Premiss. *(Grappling with the horns of the dilemma)*[7] Even though a dilemma is formally valid it still may be shown to be unsound if one or both of the hypothetical propositions in the major premiss is shown to be false. For example:

If Jones is logical, then he is unemotional; and if Jones is illogical, then he is irrational. Jones is either logical or illogical. Therefore Jones is either unemotional or irrational.

The above dilemmas, though formally valid, can still be challenged by attacking the truth of either or both hypotheticals in the major premiss. If evidence can be produced to show that being logical does not lead to being unemotional or that being illogical has nothing to do with being irrational, then the dilemma is refuted on factual grounds.

30C3 Attacking the Truth of the Minor Premiss. *(Escaping between the horns of the dilemma).* A formally valid dilemma may be attacked by showing that the alternatives in the minor premiss are not exhaustive. In other words, a dilemma is refuted if it can be shown that there is a possible alternative, not stated in the minor premiss, that, if accepted, would not lead to the consequent(s) stated in the major premiss. For example:

If Jones tells the truth, he will reveal his guilt; and if Jones lies, he will be charged with perjury. Either Jones tells the truth or he lies. Hence, Jones will reveal his guilt or be charged with perjury.

This dilemma is formally valid, but if evidence can be produced to show that there is a third alternative, such as remaining silent, and that this alternative would not lead to the unpleasant consequences stated in the major premiss, then this dilemma stands refuted and Jones has "escaped between the horns".

30C4 Rebutting the Dilemmas by a Counter Dilemma. The last way of attacking a dilemma is by using a second dilemma that demonstrates the contradictory of the conclusion of the first dilemma. Dilemmas may be successfully rebutted only if they have a false conclusion or are invalid, since if the dilemma is sound (i.e., has true premisses and is valid) then its conclusion *is* true and its contradictory cannot be demonstrated.

Many so-called "counter dilemmas" are really pseudorebuttals, since they establish only an apparent contradiction. It is quite common to find that both the original and the counter dilemma are defective. Examples of true counter dilemmas are so rare as to be practically non-existent.

Pseudo counter dilemmas may be formed in two ways:

First, the counter dilemma may be formed of entirely new premisses. For example:

Original Dilemma

If I take calculus, I will fail; and if I take physics, I will fail. Either I take calculus or physics. Hence, I will fail.

Counter Dilemma

If I take French, I will pass; and if I take Spanish, I will pass. Either I take French or I take Spanish. Hence I will pass.

The conclusions in the above dilemmas are compatible. The conclusion in the original dilemma, if stated in full, is: "I will fail calculus or I will fail physics". The conclusion of the counter dilemma stated in full is: "I will pass French or I will pass Spanish". Neither conclusion contradicts the other.

Second, what is traditionally called the "counter dilemma" is a pseudorebuttal formed by transposing and denying the consequent(s) in a constructive dilemma, or the antecedent(s) in a destructive one. For example:

Original Dilemma
(Complex constructive)

If p then q, and if r then s
Either p or r
Therefore, either q or s

Counter Dilemma
(Complex Constructive)

If p then not s and if r then not q
Either p or r
Therefore, either not s or not q

A famous example of a dilemma and this type of counter dilemma is the argument given by an Athenian mother to her son in an attempt to persuade him not to enter into politics:

If you say what is just, men will hate you; and if you say what is unjust the gods will hate you. But you must say either one or the other. Therefore you will be hated.

The son replied with the following pseudorebuttal:

If I say what is just, the gods will love me; and if I say what is unjust, men will love me. But I must say one or the other. Therefore I shall be loved.

Both of the above dilemmas are complex constructives and their conclusions are consistent with one another. The full conclusion of the first dilemmas is, "Either you will be hated by men for saying what is just or hated by the gods for saying what is unjust". The second conclusion is, "Either I will be loved by the gods for saying what is just or I will be loved by men for saying what is unjust". As has been said, these two conclusions do not contradict one another.

Exercises for Chapter 30

EX 30, I. Place the correct letter in each blank.

_____ 1. The major premiss of a dilemma is: (a) a disjunctive proposition. (b) a hypothetical proposition. (c) a categorical proposition. (d) a conjunction of two hypotheticals.

_____ 2. The minor premiss of a dilemma is: (a) a disjunctive proposition. (b) a hypothetical proposition. (c) a categorical proposition. (d) a conjunction of two hypotheticals.

_____ 3. A constructive dilemma always has: (a) a minor premiss that affirms the antecedents of the hypotheticals in the major premiss. (b) the same consequents in the major premiss. (c) the same antecedents in the major premiss. (d) a minor premiss that denies both consequents in the major premiss.

_____ 4. A destructive dilemma always has: (a) a minor premiss that affirms the antecedents of the hypotheticals in the major premiss. (b) the same consequents in the major premiss. (c) the same antecedents in the major premiss. (d) a minor premiss that denies both consequents in the major premiss.

_____ 5. A simple constructive dilemma always has: (a) a conjunctive minor premiss. (b) the same consequents in the major premiss. (c) the same antecedents in the major premiss. (d) a minor premiss that denies both consequents in the major premiss.

EX 30, II. Determine the validity (Val) or invalidity (InV) of the following dilemmas. If valid determine the form of the dilemma.

KEY

Simple constructive	(sc)
Simple destructive	(sd)
Complex constructive	(cc)
Complex destructive	(cd)

1. If you don't take logic you will miss a great course, and if you do take logic you will have an eight o'clock class. You either will take logic or

you won't. Therefore, you will either miss a great course or you will have an eight o'clock class.
Val or InV   Form:_____

2. If I marry Sally then I will have to live with her mother, and if I become a priest then I will miss the pleasures of marriage. Either I marry Sally or I become a priest, so I will either live with her mother or miss the pleasures of marriage.
Val or InV   Form:_____

3. If x is a prime number over 2 then it is an odd number and if x is a prime number over 2 then it is divisible only by one and itself. Either x is not an odd number or it is not evenly divisible only by one and itself. Hence x is not a prime number over 2.
Val or InV   Form:_____

4. You will not be able to afford college tuition, since you will go either to Harvard or Yale. If you go to Harvard you will not be able to afford the tuition and if you go to Yale you will not be able to afford the tuition.
Val or InV   Form:_____

5. If he is a mathematician, then he knows about Fibonnaci numbers and if he is a mathematician then he knows differential calculus. But he either doesn't know about Fibonnaci numbers or he doesn't know differential calculus. Hence, he is not a mathematician.
Val or InV   Form:_____

V

Informal Fallacies

31

Proof and Fallacies

31A DEFINITIONS AND CRITERIA OF PROOF

An argument is normally intended to establish or prove a conclusion to a given audience. If it succeeds, it constitutes a proof. If it fails to do so, there is some kind of mistake in it. The error, if in any way "logical" in character—in a fairly broad sense—is called a fallacy.

One way in which you may fail to prove your point is to use an invalid argument. Another way is to use premisses that are not acceptable, perhaps because they are believed to be false, perhaps because you cannot give any adequate justification for them. A logical way to classify fallacies is in accordance with the ways in which they prevent an argument from proving what it claims to prove. Hence we begin our study of fallacies by considering the nature and criteria of proof.

31A1 Definitions.

Def. 1. The **thesis** (of an argument or sequence of arguments)[1] is the proposition to be proved or established. More specifically, it is either a proposition advanced by a person who is prepared to prove it by argumentation, or a proposition whose proof is required by the situation and which the argument implicitly purports to prove.[2]

Within the context of arguments, we use "prove" and "establish" as synonyms.

The thesis may or may not be the explicit conclusion of the argument advanced to prove it. An example in which the thesis is not the conclusion is the case of a prosecuting attorney who proves (the conclusion) that the defendant had an opportunity and motive to commit the crime he is accused of, but does not prove (the thesis required for conviction) that he is guilty of this crime. The thesis that the proponent should be proving may be identical with the conclusion of his argument (the ideal case), may clearly follow from his conclusion (which is sufficient for proof), or may not follow clearly enough from the conclusion to be a satisfactory proof. (The third alternative includes the case where the conclusion clearly does not follow at all.)

> **Def. 2.** A **proof** or **sound argument** or (for emphasis) a **sound proof** is an argument by which its proponent proves a conclusion or a thesis to a given audience.

This definition is not intended to be an analysis of the concept of proof. Such an analysis is given in 31A2. Definition 2 displays the fact that to prove is a tetradic relation, that is, a relation that connects four things. The term defined, *proof,* falls within the genus *argument.* The person presenting the proof is its *proponent.* What is proved is the *conclusion or thesis* of the argument. Those to whom it is proved are the *audience* of the argument, that is, the person or persons to whom the argument is addressed. It must be understood that every proof is a proof *to* some persons or persons.

> **Def. 3.** An **intended** (or **supposed**) **proof** or a 'proof' (in scarequotes) of a thesis is an intended argument that claims to prove the thesis.
>
> **Def. 4.** An **unsound argument** (or **pseudoproof**) is an argument that claims to prove its thesis, but in fact does not.

There are different kinds of proof, but we shall limit our treatment to proofs that occur within the context of deductive logic.

> **Def. 5.** A **categorical proof of a conclusion** to an audience is an argument that draws that conclusion from premises acceptable to that audience in such a way that the audience can see clearly that the argument is valid. Such an argument **categorically proves** its conclusion.
>
> **Def. 5a.** A **categorical proof of a thesis** to an audience is an argument that categorically proves its conclusion to that audience, which can also see that the thesis is the conclusion or follows clearly from the conclusion (or its proof). This is also called **proof in context.**

Def. 6. A **hypothetical proof** of a conclusion is a recognizably valid argument with that conclusion.

A and B both know the traditional syllogistic logic. A asks B, "Is it true that some prime numbers are not evenly divisible by 2?"

B says, "Yes, I can prove it as follows: All prime numbers greater than 2 are odd numbers; no odd numbers are evenly divisible by 2; therefore, no prime numbers greater than 2 are evenly divisible by 2".

A accepts this argument as answering his question.

Here the thesis to be proved was that some prime numbers are not evenly divisible by 2. B does not explicitly state this thesis as conclusion of his argument, but gives a proof with a conclusion from which the thesis follows immediately. A accepts the premisses and sees that the standard categorical syllogism is valid, because it satisfies the rules the validity of such arguments. So the argument is a proof of its conclusion to the audience A. A also sees that the thesis follows from the conclusion; so the argument is also a proof of its thesis to its audience.

In some proofs, one is not making any claim as to the truth of the premisses or conclusion and—though one speaks of "proving a conclusion"—is merely proving it hypothetically. That is, the thesis that is really proved to be true that the conclusion follows logically from the premisses. Such a proof we call a *merely hypothetical proof.* (Also, a hypothetical proof falsely claimed to be categorical is a merely hypothetical proof.)

In a formal deductive system, theorems are said to be proved. But one may make no claim as to the truth of the assumptions of the system, and then the proofs are merely hypothetical proofs. The theorems are proved by showing how they can be validly deduced from the assumptions and previously proved theorems of the system.

Even in a merely hypothetical proof it is not sufficient to state premisses from which the conclusion logically follows. If a conclusion can be derived from the assumptions of a system of geometry by means of a chain of thirty-seven theorems, it does not constitute a proof of theorem thirty-seven—abbreviated "If A then B"—to state the assumptions, then conclude: "Therefore, if A then B".

31A2 Criteria of Proof.[3] For an intended argument to be a proof of its thesis, it must satisfy the following five criteria.

(1) *An Intelligible Argument.* The intended argument must be an argument, intelligible to the audience to whom it is addressed. This means, first, that the intended argument must really be an argument in the strict sense, that is, all of its sentences must be declarative sentences expressing

propositions (not commands, questions, exclamations, or nonsense); and second, the sentences in the argument must be understood by the audience.

If the intended argument contains a sentence that is not a proposition, then it is a pseudoargument and consequently is not a proof of anything. On the other hand, if the intended argument is an argument to the proponent, but its wording is not understood by the audience, then we have a fallacy of unintelligible argument, which is a failure of communication. Of course, an argument that is unintelligible to a person is not a proof *to that person*.

(2) *Validity Recognizable.*[4] The validity of the argument must be recognizable by its intended audience. This means that the argument must be valid; and the audience can recognize that the argument is valid. Of course an invalid argument may be judged to be valid by a person, but it cannot be recognized as valid. (We might say that such an argument is objectively invalid, but "valid to this person".)

This criterion may be violated in two ways: First, the argument may be invalid because it commits a formal fallacy such as illicit process or undistributed middle term, or because it plays upon the ambiguity of a sentence or a term expression, or for some other reason; second, the validity of the argument may not be recognized readily enough because it takes too big a logical step, or in some way demands too much of its audience. In this case, we may say the argument lacks sufficient logical justification, or better, recognizability of validity. If an argument is not recognizable as valid by a person, then this argument, even if valid, is not a *proof* to that person.

(3) *Premisses Acceptable.* The premisses of the argument must be acceptable, that is to say, either they are such as to merit immediate acceptance by the intended audience, or it should be possible to give adequate justification for their assertion. This "acceptability" (or "adequacy") is not an absolute matter, but depends upon the situation: For what purpose the proof is designed, whom it is supposed to convince, and what body of knowledge we have from which we may legitimately draw premisses.

In a formal system, such as a system of Euclidean geometry, the acceptable premisses are strictly limited. They consist of: the first principles, that is, the definitions, postulates (e.g., specifically geometric assumptions), and certain axioms of mathematical or logical reasoning; and the theorems already proved, in sequence, so that everything goes back ultimately to the first principles. In such a system we have failed to prove a theorem if we introduce a premiss in the proof merely on the grounds that it seems self-evident, or can be seen to be true from our diagrams; or use a proposition as a premiss that can be proved in the system, but has not been proved before the theorem in question. In other words, in a formal system, no proposition is admissible as a premiss at a certain step unless it is one of the first principles of the system or a theorem proved before the step.

In less formal reasoning, the limits of acceptability of premisses are not so clearly defined; but there are reasonable standards that apply to most cases. If two people are having a private discussion, each trying to convince the other or hoping to arrive at agreement, it is reasonable for one to put forward as premiss any proposition that he believes the other will accept, or can be brought to accept without too much difficulty. What he shows to follow from premisses accepted by his opponent he has proved to his opponent, though he has not proved it in an absolute sense, and perhaps not even to himself. But he may find he was mistaken in believing his opponent would accept a certain premiss, and that it is after all unacceptable, and cannot be used to prove something to this opponent. For example, a Christian cannot prove the divinity of Jesus from the New Testament to a Moslem, for the Moslem does not accept this as authority; "but it would be a valid *argumentum ad hominem* [argument to the man] to prove to him from the Koran the prophetic mission of Jesus, for the authority of the Koran he acknowledges".[5]

(4) *Conclusion Entails Thesis.* For an argument to be a proof of the thesis to is audience, the latter must recognize that the conclusion of the argument entails the thesis, either being identical with it or sufficient in the context to establish the thesis conclusively. If the conclusion of the argument is irrelevant to the thesis or, though relevant, is insufficient to establish the thesis, then this argument—even if valid and with acceptable premisses—is not a proof of the thesis in question; there is a logical gap between the conclusion and the thesis. We may say the argument is either "beside the point" or "falls short". Such an argument was called *Ignoratio elenchi* (ignorance of the refutation). We call it a *conclusion-thesis gap*. Two examples of conclusion-thesis gap (the argument for the conclusion being omitted) are:

(a) If it is claimed (explicitly or implicitly) that the thesis, *Mr. Smith murdered Mr. Green*, is established because an argument has been given that proves the truth of the conclusion that *the murder of Mr. Green (of which Mr. Smith is accused) was a horrible crime*, then this argument is not a proof of the thesis; it is beside the point.

(b) If the claim is made (explicitly or implicitly) that the thesis, *All Germans are beer drinkers*, is established on the grounds that an argument has been given proving the conclusion *Many Germans are beer drinkers*, then, since the conclusion does not entail the thesis, the argument is not a proof of the thesis; it has some relevance, but falls short of the goal.

(5) *Constant Frame of Reference.* The last criterion is that the frame of reference of an argument remains constant throughout, and the argument is not claimed to be a proof beyond its frame of reference. Every argument has three possible frames of reference: the thought-world of the *proponent* (including presuppositions, prejudices, knowledge, etc.); the thought-world

of the *audience;* and the argument's *domain* or realm of discourse. Sometimes a person is arguing to prove something to himself. Otherwise, the proponent and the audience are different, but their thought-worlds overlap—in a common language, for example.

31A3 Kinds of Audience an Argument May Be Addressed To. An argument may be addressed to the first, second, or third person (of English grammar). First person argument:

(a) To oneself *(ad seipsum).*

Second-person argument, of which we distinguish two varieties:

(b) *Ad hominem,* that is, to a second person or definite group of people, where meaningful dialogue is possible.

(c) To an audience appealed to personally, where no meaningful dialogue is possible (but there may be some feedback); for example, argument *ad populum* (to the people) or appeal to the gallery, appeal to the jury, and so on (one-way personal appeal).

Third-person argument:

(d) To a remote, impersonal audience; for example, argument *ad omnes* (to everyone) or to all rational beings; to posterity; to the experts; etc.

Often contrasted with argument *ad hominem* is argument *ad rem* (to the thing, i.e., to the matter at hand) or argument *ad veritatem* (to truth): "third-person argument" in the most impersonal sense. Thought of as completely objective, this is at least argument to oneself, that is, to one's own reason. It is also likely to be considered third-person argument in the sense of argument to the experts; possibly argument to omniscience.

An argument is a binding proof only to those who accept the argument's premises and acknowledge the argument to be valid. Hence, no argument, just because some group of people accept it as proof, should be claimed to be a proof to some other group of people or to all people. For example, if only one man has accepted the premises and validity of a particular argument, then the conclusion of this argument is proved only to this man. And it would be fallacious to claim on this evidence alone that the argument is a proof to any other man.

The domain of an argument is its subject area, the realm of learning it draws on. Hence the domain of an argument may be physics, sociology, history, mythology, and son on. Generally the domain of an argument is quite a specific area, such as thermodynamics, solid-state physics, history of Athens in the third century B.C., and so on.

31B DEFINITION AND CLASSIFICATION OF FALLACIES

31B1 Definition. Various definitions of "fallacy" are found in contemporary logic texts. There are two distinct genera in logical usage: argument, and type of argument or error. Thus Joseph says: "A fallacy is an argument which appears to be conclusive when it is not". But Copi says "A fallacy . . . is a type of incorrect argument". They both have the idea that a fallacy "*seems* to be correct", which introduces a subjective or psychological standard. For what seems to be correct to one person might seem to another person to be obviously incorrect. We offer the following definition of fallacy, which is to be interpreted in terms of the criteria for proof.

Def. 7. A **fallacy** (i.e., a deductive fallacy) is a type of logical or methodological error[6] in an intended argument that prevents it from proving the thesis it claims or purports to prove.[7]

Every argument that is presented as a proof claims, at the very least, to be valid. The majority of "proofs" not only claim validity, but claim to establish the truth of the thesis. If the intended proof does not meet all of the five criteria listed above, it fails to be a proof and commits a fallacy. Since we distinguish five major ways in which an intended proof can fail, we have five corresponding classes of fallacies (which we shall list shortly).

Since a fallacy is a type of error in an intended argument, it follows that if no argument is intended, then there is no fallacy. In other words, only intended proofs can strictly be said to be fallacious. However, errors in a process auxiliary to proof, such as definition or classification, are commonly called fallacies.

31B2 Classification of Fallacies. The traditional classification of fallacies follows one given by Aristotle in the *Sophistical Refutations*.[8] He divided them into two groups: Fallacies in Language *(in dictione)*, which we call Linguistic Fallacies, and Fallacies not in the Language *(extra dictionem)*. Under the first heading Aristotle listed six fallacies and under the second, seven. All but two of these fallacies are treated by the majority of textbooks in traditional logic, and there is growing recognition of the importance of one of the neglected fallacies, Form of Expression. This has recently reappeared under the name of Fallacies of Grammatical Analogy.[9]

A satisfactory classification of fallacies is notoriously difficult. De Morgan stated: "There *is* no such thing as a classification of the ways in which men may arrive at an error: it is much to be doubted whether there ever *can be*".[10] If this passage is interpreted to mean that no serviceable classifications of fallacies are possible, then it is false. But De Morgan was undoubtedly correct if he meant that no one adequate classification of all possible fallacies can be constructed. E. A. Burtt points out that three different principles for classifying or dividing fallacies have been used in the history of logic, and that the names of some fallacies as well as the fallacies themselves belong to certain classifications and not to others. The fallacy of cross division, Burtt notes, is often committed by logic textbooks because they try to bring together classifications based on these three distinct principles into one grand classification.[11] The three principles of division that have been used to classify fallacies, Burtt states, are:

(i) *Logical form*, defects that make the argument invalid;

(ii) *Rhetorical approach*, from the standpoint of someone disputing with an opponent or appealing to an audience;

(iii) *Psychological approach*, the psychological basis of a fallacious appeal.

A division by defects in logical form may be taken in a narrow sense, giving only the formal fallacies; or in a broader sense, including linguistic ambiguities and confusions, the clarification of which reveals a formal defect. In either case, a classification on this principle can hardly be exhaustive, but is usually fitted into a broader classification.

Aristotle's classifications of fallacies in *Topica* (book 8) and (better known) in the *Sophistical Refutations* are based on a rhetorical or, in his terminology, dialectical approach. Of the same character is the principle of division in the classification we give below, based on the criteria of proof.

A psychological classification is used in Eaton's *General Logic*. For example, formal fallacies appear as fallacies due to inattention to logical form.

Many common species of argument—such as argument *ad verecundiam* (appeal to reverence or to authority) and argument *ad misericordiam* (appeal to pity)—are types of psychological appeal. These are commonly fitted under some rubric belonging to a rhetorical classification such as Irrelevant Conclusion or *Ignoratio Elenchi* (ignorance of the refutation) or, in our terminology, Conclusion-Thesis Gap. Such appeals are not necessarily fallacious; but even where they are, they are not necessarily cases of Conclusion-Thesis Gap. Instead of fitting them into a Procrustean bed, we treat such cases separately in a chapter on "Illicit Appeals" (ch. 34). Such an appeal is commonly an "illicit emotive appeal", that is, an appeal to emotive persuasion in a context where rational persuasion is called for. These appeals belong to a psychological classification, which we have not attempted to complete.

THE CRITERIA OF PROOF	FALLACIES IN PROOF
A. Criterion of Argument	A. In Wrong Genus, i.e.
(1) Intelligible Argument	No Intelligible Argument (Linguistic Fallacy) (i)
B. Criterion of Validity	B. Fallacies of Validity (Logical Fallacies)
(2) Recognizable Validity	Argument *invalid* or validity *unrecognizable*
a. Validity Formal Validity Semantic Validity	a. Argument Invalid Formal Fallacies Linguistic Fallacies ii, iii ii Ambiguity iii Form of Expression
b. Recognizability of Validity	b. Validity Unrecognizable
C. Criteria of Proof-in-Context (Categorical Proof)	C. Contextual Fallacies (argument *may be valid*)
(3) Premisses Acceptable	Unacceptable Premisses
(4) Conclusion Entails Thesis	Conclusion-Thesis Gap
(5) Constant Frame of Reference	Illicit Metabasis (i.e., Shifting Frame of Reference)

We shall now define some of the headings in this classification of fallacies.

Def. 8. A **fallacy of validity** (or **logical fallacy**) is a logical error in an argument that prevents it from being recognizably valid, (i.e., an error that prevents it from being a hypothetical proof).

We distinguish three main kinds of fallacies of validity: formal fallacies, linguistic fallacies (of ambiguity or form of expression), and validity unrecognizable.

We have encountered formal fallacies earlier in this book. For example, a standard categorical syllogism commits a formal fallacy when it violates a rule of distribution or quality (see 21B). Together with the account of each traditional form of argument, we have given an account of the corresponding formal fallacies. However, we have not yet given a general definition of a formal fallacy.

Def. 9. A **formal fallacy** is a fallacy of validity that can be detected in a pure argument form.

That is, a formal fallacy is a fallacy that prevents an argument from being valid, and can be recognized on the basis of a knowledge of the meaning of the form words and the pattern of expressions, without knowing the meaning of the term expressions or the context of the argument.

Def. 10. A **linguistic fallacy** is a fallacy arising from a lack of clear or consistent meaning of expressions, or from faulty interpretation of linguistic similarities or analogies (see ch. 32).

Def. 11. A **contextual fallacy** (or **material fallacy**) is a fallacy rooted in the relation of the argument to its context that prevents the argument, even if valid, from being a proof of its thesis[12] (see ch. 33).

One might also explain a "contextual fallacy" as an error in a hypothetical proof that prevents it from being a categorical proof.

It should be noted that the most natural division of fallacies from the point of view of the formal logician is the dichotomy of Formal and Informal. The informal fallacies might then be divided into linguistic and contextual fallacies. In essence, we have made the first dichotomy by treating only the informal fallacies in chapters 32 through 34. The second division is effected by treating the linguistic fallacies in chapter 32 and the contextual fallacies in chapter 33.

Exercises for Chapter 31

EX 31A, I. Place "T" in the blank if the proposition is true, "F" if it is false.

_____ 1. Every valid argument is a proof of its conclusion to its audience.

_____ 2. If an argument is invalid, its conclusion must be false.

_____ 3. The conclusion of an argument is always its thesis.

_____ 4. If an argument proves its conclusion, it also proves its thesis.

_____ 5. If an argument proves its thesis, it must also prove its conclusion.

_____ 6. An intended argument, in order to be a proof, must meet five criteria, (according to chapter 31).

_____ 7. An argument with a false premiss is called a pseudoargument.

_____ 8. A premiss is acceptable if and only if it is true.

_____ 9. In Euclidean geometry, any theorem that can be proved is always an acceptable premiss.

_____ 10. If the conclusion that is proved does not clearly entail the thesis to be proved, we say there is a conclusion-thesis gap.

EX 31A, II. Briefly explain each of the five criteria for a proof. Give an example for each of a concrete case in which the criterion is violated.

EX 31A, III. Answer the following questions. Give reasons for each answer.

1. Is the conclusion of an argument always the same as the thesis? Is it ever the same?
2. Can an intended proof be an unsound argument? What else can it be?
3. What is the difference between a hypothetical proof and a categorical proof? Is every categorical proof a hypothetical proof?
4. In a merely hypothetical proof, what is the thesis that is really proved? What criteria must a merely hypothetical proof meet?

5. What do the last four criteria of proof have in common that they do not share with the first?

6. What is the significance of putting the word "proof" in *single* quotes? In general, what significance does the text attach to putting an expression in single quotes that are not within double quotes?

7. Is it possible for the conclusion of an argument to be relevant to the thesis, but still insufficient to establish it?

8. Why is it important for the sentences in an intended argument to be propositions?

9. If an argument commits a formal fallacy, what criterion or criteria of proof does it violate?

10. Is it appropriate to define a proof as a valid argument with true premises?

EX 31B. Answer the following questions, giving reasons for your answer (in 1 through 4).

1. Divide fallacies into three major classes, relating them to the five criteria of proof.

2. Is it true that if there is no intended argument there can be no fallacy?

3. What is wrong with the following definition of a fallacy? "A fallacy is an error in an argument that prevents it from being valid".

4. Burtt states that three different principles of classifying fallacies have been used in the history of logic. What are the three principles? What difficulties may be created by using all three? What is the advantage of using more than one?

5. Define the following: fallacy of validity, formal fallacy, linguistic fallacy, contextual fallacy.

EX 31A–B, I. Indicate whether the following statements are true or false.

_____ 1. An argument can contain a fallacy and still be valid.

_____ 2. If an argument contains a fallacy, its conclusion must be false.

_____ 3. An invalid argument must contain a fallacy.

_____ 4. Strictly speaking, if there is no argument intended, there is no fallacy.

_____ 5. A fallacy always contains a false statement.

_____ 6. If an argument contains exactly two fallacies, they may cancel each other out, making the argument sound.

_____ 7. No argument can contain more than one fallacy.

_____ 8. A fallacy is an error that prevents an intended proof from being a satisfactory proof.

_____ 9. A valid argument may have all true premisses and a true conclusion and yet contain a fallacy.

_____ 10. An argument can have all true premisses and a false conclusion, and yet contain no fallacy.

_____ 11. An invalid argument never proves a true conclusion.

_____ 12. No valid arguments commit contextual fallacies.

_____ 13. If an argument proves its conclusion, it can commit no fallacy.

_____ 14. The conclusion of a valid argument is the same as or implies its thesis.

_____ 15. A simple proposition, by itself, may be a fallacy.

32

Linguistic Fallacies

32A DEFINITION AND DIVISION OF LINGUISTIC FALLACIES

Aristotle called linguistic fallacies "fallacies in language" (or, as the medievals translated, fallacies *in dictione*). We define a linguistic fallacy in such a way that it either prevents an intended argument from being an argument or from being valid.

> **Def. 1.** A **linguistic fallacy** is a fallacy arising from a lack of clear or consistent meaning of expressions, or from faulty interpretation of linguistic similarities or analogies (from 31B2).

We divide linguistic fallacies into three principal kinds: No Intelligible Argument, Fallacies of Ambiguity, and Fallacies of Form of Expression (or Grammatical Analogy).

32B LACK OF INTELLIGIBLE ARGUMENT

32B1 Pseudoargument. An intended argument may fail to be an argument by containing a sentence that has no definite propositional meaning. This would make the intended argument a pseudoargument, since an argument, by definition, contains only propositions (and connecting form words).

> **Def. 2.** A **pseudoargument** is an intended argument that is not an argument because a sentence fails to be a proposition, either because it lacks sufficiently definite meaning or because it has a definite non-propositional meaning (e.g., a command).

Figure 32.1: Linguistic Fallacies

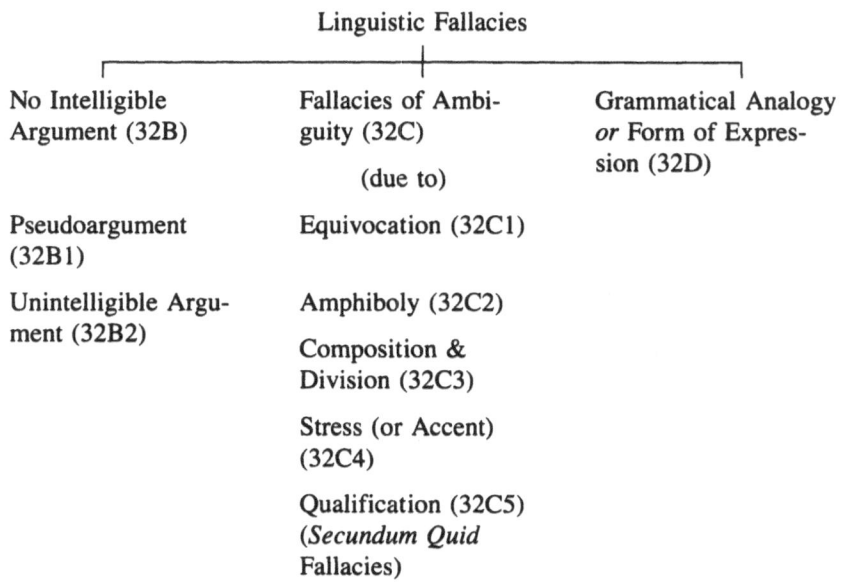

Pseudoarguments result mainly from vagueness or nonsense (lack of sufficiently definite meaning). When examining an intended argument we should heed Montaigne, who said, "No one is exempt from talking nonsense: the misfortune is to do it solemnly". An example of a pseudoargument lacking sufficiently definite meaning is:

(a) *The Incandescent Absolute involutedly evolves with ontological gyrations: therefore all mankind is condemned to the eternal now of groundless freedom.*

An example of a pseudoargument with a sentence (in this case a question) that is not a proposition is:

(b) *You haven't said anything sensible yet; so why don't you shut up?*

32B2 Unintelligible Argument.

Def. 3. An **unintelligible argument** to a given audience is an intended argument that, although intelligible to its proponent, is unintelligible to the audience.

Linguistic Fallacies 425

An unintelligible argument indicates a failure of communication. Unintelligible arguments are generally caused by the proponent using a technical vocabulary that is not understood by the audience (including foreign words) or using a sentence structure more complex than the audience can readily grasp (as is common when adults present arguments to young children). An example of an argument concerning astronomical objects called "black holes" that would be unintelligible to most people is:

> *If two or more black holes collide then the total area of the one-way membranes after the collision cannot be less than that before the collision. Therefore, if two black holes coalesce then the sum of the areas of their separate event horizons is not greater than the area of the final one-way membrane around the object formed by the coalescence.*

The above is an intelligible argument to those who understand the technical expressions. However, to most people this argument would be unintelligible and might even be thought to be a pseudoargument.

32C FALLACIES OF AMBIGUITY

An expression (i.e., word, term expression, phrase, or sentence) is ambiguous if it has at least two definite meanings. But an expression is used ambiguously only if the expression may be interpreted in two different ways in the same context.

Def. 4. A **fallacy of ambiguity** is a logical fallacy in an argument arising from different interpretations of an expression.

Since fallacies of ambiguity are logical fallacies, by the definition of the latter term (ch. 31, def. 8), arguments committing fallacies of ambiguity are invalid, if the interpretation of the ambiguous expression is essential to the argument.

We will now treat the five traditional fallacies of ambiguity.

32C1 The Fallacy of Equivocation. A practical semantical rule that facilitates precise communication is as follows: Each expression, in a given context, should be used in the same sense in every occurrence (see 21C3). If a term expression violates this rule, then (in the given context) it is equivocal; if it obeys the rule, then (in the given context) it is univocal.

Def. 5. A term expression is **equivocal** (or is **equivocated upon**) when it is used in two or more senses in a given context.

Def. 5a. A term expression is **univocal** when it is used in only one sense in a given context.

When an equivocation occurs in an argument, a fallacy results.

Def. 5b. The **fallacy of equivocation** is the logical fallacy in an argument arising from interpretation of an equivocal term expression in two different ways.

An example of the fallacy of equivocation is:

(a) *All criminal actions are illegal acts.*
 All prosecutions for theft are criminal actions.
 ∴ *All prosecutions for theft are illegal acts.*

There is no single consistent interpretation of "criminal actions" that makes both premisses plausible. If the reader is so interpreting the premisses that both are plausible, he must be equivocating upon "criminal actions"; then the argument has no middle term and is not formally valid.

If, on the other hand, "criminal actions" is given a single consistent interpretation throughout the argument, there is no equivocation, and the argument is formally valid (AAA, fig. 1). However, one of the premisses is false.

In "syllogisms" it is generally the middle term expression that is equivocated upon. The fallacy of equivocation may also occur in immediate inferences, as in the following pseudo-obversion:

(b) *Some Nazis were inhuman; therefore some Nazis were not human.*

The premiss is true if the word "inhuman" is regarded as meaning *brutal* or *unfeeling,* but the conclusion is drawn from a second meaning of the word, namely "non-human".

32C2 The Fallacy of Amphiboly.

Def. 6. An **amphibolous sentence** (whether in an argument or not) is a sentence with multiple meanings due to faulty grammatical construction of the sentence or ambiguity of its form words.

Such faulty grammatical construction may be due to incorrect punctuation, incorrect word order, or to the lack of some qualifying phrase that would eliminate the ambiguity.

An example of an amphibolous sentence is:

(a) *I see Croesus the Persians defeating.*

In this example, the word order is at fault, leaving it in doubt as to who is defeating whom. However, not all sentences that leave one in doubt are amphibolous. The following sentence

(b) *If Croesus goes to war with the Persians, a mighty kingdom will be destroyed.*

is not an amphiboly. It was (as Herodotus says) an evasive answer, because it did not say which kingdom would be destroyed. But there is nothing wrong with the grammatical construction of the sentence.

Def. 6a. The **fallacy of amphiboly** is the logical fallacy in an argument arising from different interpretations of an amphibolous sentence.

An example of the fallacy of amphiboly is:

(c) *On campus last night, Professor Merkin gave a factual report on students' sexual activity in the library; therefore we may assume that not all student activity in the library is intellectual in nature.*

In the above argument the amphibolous sentence is the premiss. The plausible interpretation of the premiss is that the professor's report was given in the library, but from this interpretation the conclusion does not follow. The conclusion is deduced from the second interpretation, namely, that the professor's report was about the sexual activity taking place in the library.

An example of a fallacy of amphiboly based on the ambiguity of a form word, in this case "all", is:

(d) *All the angles of this triangle are 180 degrees.*
    Angle A is an angle of this triangle.
    ∴ *Angle A is 180 degrees.*

The first premiss is plausible only if "all" means "all together", but the argument is valid only if "all" means "each and every angle".

32C3 The Fallacy of Composition and the Fallacy of Division (Collective-Divisive Analysis). Aristotle's treatment of these fallacies differs greatly from modern presentations and is no longer regarded as the conventional explanation of these fallacies.

There are two modern versions of these fallacies: the collective-divisive analysis and the part-whole analysis. We treat the first in this section since it is a fallacy of ambiguity. The second is usually a different kind of fallacy, and will not be discussed in this chapter.

a *Collective-Divisive Analysis of the Fallacies of Composition and Division.* Most contemporary logicians treat the fallacies of composition and division as fallacies of ambiguity caused, respectively, by a shift from the divisive use to the collective use of a term and conversely. The definitions of divisive and collective use of a term are given in 4C, definitions 14 and 11.

Definitions 7 and 8 are based on Eaton's.

Def. 7. The **fallacy of composition** (collective-divisive analysis) is a logical fallacy occurring in an argument when the same term is used divisively in a premiss and collectively in the conclusion.

The following argument is an example of the fallacy of composition as just defined, since the term "albino spaniels" is used divisively in the minor premiss and collectively in the conclusion:

(e) *Dogs are common.*
     Albino spaniels are dogs.
     ∴ *Albino spaniels are common.*

We note also that "dogs" is used collectively in the major and divisively in the minor.

Argument (e) cannot be standardized by prefixing the quantifier "all" to each proposition, so as to make it AAA in the first figure. If we try to do this we obtain (e'):

(e') *All dogs are common.* [?]
      All albino spaniels are dogs.
      ∴ *All albino spaniels are common.* [?]

Argument (e) can be translated into an argument with quantifiers, though not all standard quantifiers. Note first that "Dogs are common" is elliptical. There is an implicit reference to some specific area. Let us say it means "Dogs are common in area B". Then argument (e) can be translated as follows:

(e'')   *Many places in area B are places with dogs.*
All albino spaniels are dogs.
∴ *Many places in area B are places with albino spaniels.*

This is not a standard syllogism, but we can see that it is clearly invalid. If "area B" stands for Buffalo, New York, for example, the premisses of (e'') are true and the conclusion false.

Def. 8. The **fallacy of division** (collective-divisive analysis) is a logical fallacy occurring in an argument when either: (i) the same term is used collectively in the premisses and used divisively in the conclusion; or (ii) a term is predicated of a class taken collectively in the premisses, and in the conclusion is predicated of something said to be a member of this class.

Examples of the fallacy of division (def. 8, i) are (f) and (g):

(f)   *All the angles of this triangle are 180°.*
This angle ABC is not 180°.
∴ *This angle ABC is not an angle of this triangle.*

"Angles of this triangle" is used collectively in the major premiss and is used divisively in the conclusion. Thus the fallacy of division occurs even though the angle ABC may not be one of the angles of the triangle in question.

(g)   *Cows are numerous.*
White cats are not numerous.
∴ *White cats are not cows.*

The above argument has a form that, if standardized mechanically (and incorrectly) as "All cows are numerous", would be the valid form AEE figure 2; but it commits the fallacy of division. "Cows" in the premiss is used collectively, while in the conclusion it is used divisively. Consequently, its logical form is invalid.

Leaving the form of (g) as it is, we could get a counterexample by substituting "Albino cows" for "White cats".

An example of the fallacy of division (def. 8, ii):

(h) *The French are a great nation.*
  Charles de Gaulle is French.
  ∴ *Charles de Gaulle is a great nation.*

In this argument, "a great nation" is predicated of the class of the French taken collectively in the premises, and is predicated of Charles de Gaulle (who is stated in the minor to be a member of the class) in the conclusion. It is incorrect to argue that what is true of a class must be true of a member of this class; hence, this argument is invalid.

Another example of the fallacy of division (def. 8, ii):

(i) *Cockroaches existed before men.*
  This insect is a cockroach.
  ∴ *This insect existed before men.*

This argument is invalid, because what is true of cockroaches as a class is not necessarily true of any member of that class. In certain cases the confusion between a term expression used collectively and used divisively may be thought of as an amphiboly caused by the ambiguity of "all". See example (d) under Amphiboly (32C2).

32C4 The Fallacy of Stress (or Accent). By *stress* or *accent* in speech we mean here the giving of prominence to a syllable, word, or phrase in a sentence by pitch or loudness. In print, stress may be indicated by large or heavy type, italics, exclamation marks, and other punctuation marks. Stress may also be conveyed by gestures or facial grimaces.

By stressing a word in a sentence that was not originally stressed or by omitting to stress one that was, the meaning of the sentence may be changed considerably. For example, the sentence

(a) He drinks only distilled water.

does not have the same meaning as the sentence

(b) He drinks only *distilled* water.

Sentence (a), taken literally, means that he drinks nothing but distilled water. He does not drink milk, fruit juice, beer, or anything else. Sentence (b) means that if he drinks water, then it is distilled. He might drink milk, but the only kind of water he drinks is distilled water.

Def. 9. The **fallacy of stress** (or accent) is a logical fallacy occurring when a change of stress on a syllable, word, or phrase changes the meaning of a sentence in an argument.

For example, De Morgan points out that the biblical commandment

(c) Thou shall not bear false witness against thy neighbor.

can be used as a premiss for the following conclusions by respectively italicizing in the commandment the words "bear", "witness", "against", and "neighbor":

(d) It is permissible to *suborn* false witness against thy neighbor.

(e) It is permissible to speak falsely about your neighbor as long as you are *not a witness* against him.

(f) It is permissible to bear false witness *for* your neighbor.

(g) It is permissible to bear false witness against anyone *except* your neighbor.

An example given by Jevons is from the First Book of Kings, verse 27. Italics were used to indicate words supplied by the translators. However, if italics are taken as indicating stress, then a deplorable conclusion about the prophet may be drawn from the following passage.

(h) And he (the prophet) spake to his sons, saying Saddle me the ass. And they saddled *him*.

32C5 Fallacies of Qualification (Secundum Quid Fallacies). There has been much confusion regarding the names and explanations of these fallacies. What we call the fallacies of introducing qualification and eliminating qualification, many logicians call, respectively, the fallacies of accident and converse accident. Yet others call them, respectively, the fallacies of *a dicto simpliciter ad dictum secundum quid* (inference from simple term to term as qualified) and *a dicto secundum quid ad dictum simpliciter*. (For history of these fallacies, see Appendix 32C5.)

a *Fallacy of Introducing Qualification*. In its simplest form this fallacy occurs in one or the other of the following patterns:

(1) *S* is *P*, therefore *S* as qualified is *P*.

(2) *S* is *P*, therefore *S* is *P* as qualified.

Examples of patterns 1 and 2, respectively:

(a) *Men are capable of communicating; therefore men who have died are capable of communicating.*

(b) *Men are rational; therefore men are rational in all matters.*

Def. 10. The **fallacy of introducing qualification** is a logical fallacy involving inference from unqualified use of a term to its use as qualified.

Additional examples of this fallacy are:

(c) *Every man has a right to dispose of his property, hence a man who is legally insane has a right to dispose of his property.*

(d) *Gold is malleable; therefore gold is malleable at absolute zero.*

Examples of the fallacy of introducing qualification that are not strictly cases of patterns 1 and 2 are:

(e) *Every man has a right to his property, hence an insane man has a right to his gun.*

(f) *What you bought yesterday you eat today. Therefore, since you bought raw meat yesterday, you will eat raw meat today.*

(g) *Of course I'm promiscuous, Jesus said we should love our neighbor.*

Example (e) is of a third pattern:

(3) *S* is *P*, therefore *S* qualified as *S'* is *P* qualified as *P'*.

b *Fallacy of Eliminating Qualification*. This fallacy, the converse of the preceding one, occurs in its simplest form when an argument is based on either of the two following patterns:

(4) *S* as qualified is *P*; therefore *S* is *P*.

(5) *S* is *P* as qualified; therefore *S* is *P*.

Examples of patterns 4 and 5, respectively:

(h) *Gold at minus 270° C is brittle; therefore gold is brittle.*

(i) *All men are satisfied with success, therefore all men are satisfied.*

Def. 11. The **fallacy of eliminating qualification** is a logical fallacy involving an inference from qualified use of a term to its use as unqualified.

Further examples of this fallacy are:

(j) *Steel in the form of penpoints is not a good heavy construction material, hence steel is not a good heavy construction material.*

(k) *You are a perfect specimen of a foolish philosopher; therefore you are a perfect specimen of a philosopher.*

Example of a fallacy of eliminating qualification that is not formally a case of patterns 4 and 5:

(l) *There's nothing improper in kissing one's own wife; therefore there's nothing improper in kissing a wife.*

This can be put into pattern 4: take "Kissing a wife" as S, "not improper" as P, etc.

32D FALLACIES OF GRAMMATICAL ANALOGY OR FORM OF EXPRESSION

These fallacies, of which the one-word case is Aristotle's *Form of Expression,* have for the most part been omitted from contemporary logic textbooks. They are, however, starting to reappear and to enjoy a new popularity. Undoubtedly a main cause for this renewed interest in such fallacies is the fascination that linguistic analysis holds for so many modern philosophers.

Unhappily, Aristotle's *Form of Expression* has been called by many scholars *Figure of Speech (figura dictionis).* "Figure of Speech" is now misleading, since it applies to metaphors, similes, personifications, and so on, which have little or nothing to do with Aristotle's fallacy of form of expression. A better name is "fallacy of grammatical analogy", a term used by Wittgenstein and his followers:

Def. 12. A **fallacy of grammatical analogy** occurs when it is argued that words, sentences, or arguments that are grammatically similar (i.e., similar in verbal inflection, in belonging to the same class of words, in having sentences of the same form, etc.) must be semantically or logically similar.

An example of the fallacy of grammatical analogy is:

(a) *The mind cannot be a process or activity, since "mind" is a noun, not a verb.*

A fallacy of grammatical analogy is committed if one argues that a word denotes an action because it has an "-ing" suffix as many verbal nouns do. Aristotle says:

> For it is possible to use an expression to denote what does not belong to the class of actions at all as though it did so belong. Thus (e.g.) "flourishing" is a word which in the form of its expression is like "cutting" or "building" [as in building a house] yet the one denotes a certain quality—i.e., a certain condition—while the other denotes a certain action. (166b15)

Also included under the heading of fallacies of grammatical analogy is the error of judging an argument to be valid because it has the same pattern of form words and term expressions as a valid argument.

It is interesting to note that a version of the famed "category-mistake" of the twentieth century is mentioned by Aristotle as one of the fallacies of form of expression in *Sophistical Refutations* (166b15). Aristotle describes it as the erroneous belief that two expressions denote things in the same category because they have the same ending (grammatical form). By "category" Aristotle is referring to the ten categories—Substance, Quantity, Quality, Relation, and so on—listed in the *Topica* (103b20).

Appendix to Chapter 32A1

32A ARISTOTLE'S CLASSIFICATION OF FALLACIES IN THE SOPHISTICAL REFUTATION

Aristotle recognized and defined four types of arguments in dialogue form: Didactic, Dialectical, Examination arguments, and Contentious arguments (165a39). The subject of the *Sophistical Refutations* is contentious arguments, which is the style of argument used in competitions and contests (165b11). The participators in these contests are not interested in truth, but only in refuting their opponents; or rather, by the use of fallacious arguments, in giving the appearance of refuting their opponents.

Most textbooks fail to mention that Aristotle's dichotomous classification of fallacies, given in the *Sophistical Refutations*, is a classification of unsound refutations.[1] It is important to mention this since Aristotle gives a more complete scheme of classifying fallacies in the *Topica* (162b). Essentially, it is this classification, *not* the one below, that we adopted in this text (see 31B2).

Table 32.1: Aristotle's Classification of Fallacies in the Sophistical Refutations

In the Language (*in dictone*)
1. Equivocation
2. Amphiboly
3. Composition
4. Division
5. Accent
6. Form of Expression

Not in the Language (*extra dictone*)
1. Accident
2. *Secundum Quid* (No English name)
3. *Ignoratio Elenchi* (called Conclusion-Thesis Gap in this book)
4. *Petitio Principii* (begging the question)
5. *Non causa pro causa* (false cause)
6. Consequent
7. Many Questions (Complex Question)

We shall not attempt to present a full account of Aristotle's treatment of these fallacies but shall limit our discussion to those fallacies that modern logicians treat differently.

a Fallacies in the Language. These are fallacies that are caused by ambiguities in the language or by being mislead by linguistic construction or linguistic categories.

(i) *Equivocation.* To Aristotle this fallacy meant what it does to modern logicians, namely, the ambiguous use of a term expression or phrase in an argument such that the argument is invalid.

(ii) *Amphiboly.* Aristotle's examples of this fallacy makes it clear that he regarded it, as do modern logicians, as a fallacy of ambiguity caused by the faulty grammatical construction of a sentence in an argument such that the sentence has a double meaning. An example of an amphibolous sentence given by Aristotle is "I wish that you the enemy may capture" (166a7).

(iii) *Composition.* Aristotle called this fallacy "combination" and meant by it something quite different than what modern logicians call "composition". To Aristotle the fallacy of combination is a fallacy of ambiguity caused by the improper combination of words. An example, not Aristotle's, is *Some of Professor Brown's students are bisexual, since he stated that he has both males and females in his class.* In this argument the words *males* and *females* are being erroneously combined into a word *males-and-females.*

(iv) *Division.* Unlike its modern explanation the fallacy of division meant to Aristotle the improper division of words. An example of this fallacy is: *5 is 2 and 3; therefore 5 is 2 and 5 is 3.* The fallacy occurs because the properly combined expression "2 and 3" in the premise is improperly divided in the conclusion.

(v) *Accent.* In Greek there are many cases where the meaning of a word is changed by a change in accent (and in Latin by a change in quantity of a vowel). Hence, to Aristotle the fallacy of accent occurred when a word is used ambiguously in an argument, the ambiguity being due to changing the stress on a syllable in the word. Since words that have the same spelling and are pronounced differently are extremely rare in the English language, "accent" to modern English logicians means stress or emphasis on a particular word or phrase.

(iv) *Form of Expression.* Misleadingly called by some logicians "Figure of Speech", this fallacy, ignored by most modern logicians, is now staging a comeback. A full discussion of this fallacy, which we call "grammatical analogy", is given in 32D.

b Fallacies Not in the Language. These fallacies have no common bond, except the negative one of not being caused by the ambiguities of a word or phrase, or by the similarity of linguistic construction or categories.

(i) *Accident.* The confused history of this fallacy and the fallacy of *Secundum Quid* is briefly outlined in Appendix 32C5.

(ii) *Secundum Quid.* See above.

(iii) *Ignoratio Elenchi* (Literally "ignorance of the refutation". Called in this book "Conclusion-Thesis Gap"). To Aristotle this fallacy is caused by ignorance of what a refutation is. To refute a thesis one must prove its contrary or contradiction and no other statement. Hence, if one proves a statement that is not a refutation, then the fallacy of *ignoratio elenchi* occurs. Modern logicians treat this fallacy in much the same way as Aristotle did. They describe it as the fallacy of claiming to have proved the thesis, when all that has been proved is a conclusion that does not establish the thesis. (See 33B, Conclusion-Thesis Gap.)

(iv) *Petitio Principii* (begging the question). Aristotle defined this fallacy in the same way as do modern logicians, that is, assuming in the premisses what needs to be proved. Aristotle described in the *Topica* (bk. 13) five ways of committing this fallacy. A full classification of the various ways of begging the question is given in Appendix 33A1.

(v) *Non causa pro causa* (false cause). This fallacy is not discussed in this text, because the way many logicians describe it, it is an inductive fallacy. The way Aristotle described it, it is a contextual fallacy, but one that is rather uncommon in contemporary argumentation. To Aristotle the fallacy of false cause—"cause" in the sense of reason—is the claim that a proof is unsound because it contains as a premiss a proposition proved false by *reductio ad absurdum,* when in fact this proposition is irrelevant to the proof.

Many modern logicians define the fallacy of false cause as the error of mistaking for the cause of an event something that is not its cause. Some logicians also include under this heading the fallacy of *post hoc, ergo propter hoc* (after it, therefore because of it). An example of the latter is: After I wore Aunt Maud's tie I received an "A" on the physics exam, therefore its a lucky tie (i.e., wearing the tie caused the "A" on my physics exam).

(vi) *Consequent.* Aristotle's name for this formal fallacy is seldom mentioned by modern logicians; perhaps because other names are used, such as, "illicit converse", "affirming the consequent", and others. To Aristotle this fallacy was a false conversion, for example, *If a feverish man is hot, then a hot man must be feverish.* Another version of this fallacy is, according to Aristotle, *If B is the consequent of A, then non-B is the consequent of non-A.* This immediate inference is an inference from a proposition to its inverse form. It is, of course, invalid.

(vii) *Many Questions.* According to Aristotle this fallacy occurs when two or more questions are asked as one. An example given by Joseph is *The execution of Mary Queen of Scots was brutal and sacrilegious—was it, or was it not?* This fallacy is regarded by modern logicians as covering assumptive questions such as *Have you stopped beating your mother?, Do you know the explanation of telepathy?,* and *Why must all democracies be corrupt?*

Appendix to Chapter 32C5

32C5 A BRIEF HISTORY OF THE FALLACIES OF ACCIDENT AND *SECUNDUM QUID*

What are now usually called the "fallacy of accident" and the "converse fallacy of accident" were called by the scholastics *a dicto simpliciter ad dictum secundum quid* and *a dicto secundum quid ad dictum simpliciter*. Both of these fallacies will be referred to as "*secundum quid*" fallacies. Peter of Spain followed Aristotle in distinguishing the fallacy of accident from the *secundum quid* fallacies. Modern logicians, with some few exceptions, have used the name "fallacy of accident" and "converse fallacy of accident" for the *secundum quid* fallacies. Aristotle's explanation of accident has been generally found confusing; hence his explanation of the fallacy of accident has been dropped and the name "accident" substituted for the more clumsy expression *a dicto simpliciter ad dictum secundum quid*. The name "converse accident" was substituted for *a dicto secundum quid ad dictum simpliciter*.

The authors agree with Joseph that Aristotle's explanation of accident is inadequate, but they disagree with Joseph's contention that the *secundum quid* fallacies cannot be distinguished from one another. However, it is incorrect to identify the converse fallacy of accident (or *a dicto secundum quid ad dictum simpliciter*) with "erroneous generalization" (Joseph) or "hasty generalization" (Copi). This is shown by the example "Mr. Smith is a deceased banker; therefore Mr. Smith is a banker". This is not an erroneous (or hasty) generalization (since it is not a generalization), though it is a converse fallacy of accident.

Exercise for Chapter 32

Ex 32. Identify the principal fallacy or fault in each of the following.

KEY

NIA	No intelligible argument	S	Stress (or Accent)
Eq	Equivocation (Underline equivocal expression)	IQ	Introducing qualification
Am	Amphiboly	Eli	Eliminating qualification
C	Composition	SQ	Switching qualification (Eli & IQ)
D	Division	FE	Form of Expression
C&D	Composition and Division	GA	Grammatical Analogy (other than Form of Expression)

<u>SQ,(GA)</u>) 1. The argument "A citizen has constitutional rights; therefore a black citizen has constitutional rights", is valid; so then is the argument "A citizen has constitutional rights; therefore a dead citizen has constitutional rights".

_____ 2. Aspirin and cough medicine are drugs taken by people who have colds, so there is nothing wrong with people taking drugs.

_____ 3. Improbable events happen almost every day, but what happens almost every day is a very probable event; therefore improbable events are very probable events. (Jevons)

_____ 4. Color can be perceived directly. A color is light waves of a certain frequency. Therefore, light waves of a certain frequency can be perceived directly.

_____ 5. Wood is a good material for carving. Matchsticks are made of wood. Hence, matchsticks are good materials for carving.

_____ 6. Airplane accidents are increasing. Collisions between Flying Jennies are airplane accidents. Therefore, collisions between Flying Jennies are increasing.

_____ 7. All laws should be respected. The formula "Force = mass times acceleration" is a law. Therefore this formula should be respected.

_____ 8. The impossibility of an affluently charged sublibido prohibits the formation of ego-rationalization. And since such rationalization is directed toward the fractionalization of the lower id, it follows that no tridivision of the psychic energies on the aesthetic plane may be expected.

_____ 9. A man is entitled to his own property. Consequently, you have no right to snatch an insane man's revolver away from him.

_____ 10. If abortions are legalized, then any kind of killing will be legalized.

_____ 11. A newspaper headline: "Atomic War!" Then underneath in small print, "Unlikely, says Senator".

_____ 12. The end of life is death and happiness is the end of life; hence, happiness is death.

_____ 13. In a valid standard syllogistic argument every term distributed in the conclusion must be distributed in the premises, hence in every valid argument every term distributed in the conclusion must be distributed in the premises.

_____ 14. The Northeastern University Students' Political Society is very radical. Mr. Bragg is a member of this society. Therefore, he is very radical.

_____ 15. There is strong evidence for life after death, because I heard that indian chiefs in Oklahoma were complaining about their graves being moved.

_____ 16. The argument "A dog is an animal, hence a three-legged dog is a three-legged animal" is valid; therefore, the argument "A mouse is an animal, hence a big mouse is a big animal" is valid.

_____ 17. Stalin was a Russian, and the Russians are Slavs; therefore, Stalin was a Slav.

_____ 18. The members of the college are students, teachers, and administrative officers. The members of the football team are members of the college; hence the members of the football team are students, teachers, and administrative officers.

_____ 19. Dry bread is better than T-bone steak, since dry bread is better than no food and no food is better than T-bone steak.

_____ 20. Since the words "imperturbable" and "impenitent" signify negative concepts, so then must the word "important" signify a negative concept.

_____ 21. The Germans are a nation. Bismark, Stein, Kant, and Hegel were Germans, and hence must have been a nation. (Hyslop)

_____ 22. Tools are artifacts. Man's hands are tools. Hence, man's hands are artifacts.

_____ 23. If man is a rational animal and if idiots are men, then are not idiots rational animals?

_____ 24. Soldiers are numerous. Five-star generals are soldiers; therefore, five-star generals are numerous.

_____ 25. Husband: I am *not* having an affair with my secretary.
Wife: You said that you are not having an affair with your *secretary*. Therefore you have admitted that you are having an affair with someone.

_____ 26. The moon must be feminine, because its Latin name, *luna,* is feminine.

_____ 27. Alloys of gold are malleable, since gold is malleable.

_____ 28. The parts of this machine weigh over ten pounds. This object is a part of this machine. Hence this object weighs over ten pounds.

_____ 29. I heard that a professors's wife was murdered while cooking her husband's breakfast in a horrible manner. She may have been a bad cook, but I don't think she should have been murdered for that reason.

_____ 30. I have lit the black candles, said the proper invocations; therefore, Lucifer, I command you to appear.

_____ 31. Water is necessary for human life. Ice is water; hence ice is necessary for human life.

_____ 32. Human life will at some time disappear from the earth, for every man must die.

_____ 33. Smoking can cause small babies; therefore, unmarried women should not smoke.

_____ 34. Your auto will not start, because the knooten valve is broken. This follows from the fact that if the knooten valve was working the thing-um-bob on the what-you-call-it would still be so-so, but it isn't.

_____ 35. The police are well trained today and can do just about anything, for I read in the New York Times that "Police Repair Man Killed by Car".

33

Contextual Fallacies

In this chapter we discuss contextual fallacies. These fallacies do not prevent an argument from being valid—an argument that contains a contextual fallacy may or may not be valid—but they do prevent an argument from proving its thesis.

Contextual fallacies, as their name implies, are not caused by errors in the form or matter (words and terms) of an argument, but are caused by errors in relation to the context. The three important aspects of an argument's context are: the justification of its premises, the relation between its conclusion and the thesis, and its frames of reference (the people to whom the argument is supposed to be a proof, and the argument's domain or universe of discourse). An error in one of these aspects causes (respectively) a fallacy of unacceptable premiss, conclusion-thesis gap, or illicit metabasis.

Def. 1. A **contextual fallacy** (or **material fallacy**) is a fallacy rooted in the relation of the argument to its context that prevents the argument, even if valid, from being a proof of its thesis (def. 11 of ch. 31).

A classification of the contextual fallacies is given in the following table, which also includes (in parentheses) the nonfallacious alternatives to conclusion-thesis gap:

Table 33.1: Contextual Fallacies (argument may be valid)

Unacceptable Premiss (33A)	Conclusion-Thesis Gap (33B)	Illicit Metabasis (33C)
1. Begging the Question	1. Kinds of (Sufficient* and) Insufficient Conclusions	1. Illicit Metabasis of Audience, in:
a Argument in a Circle	(a Ideal Conclusion)*	a Argument to Oneself[†]
b Special Cases of Begging the Question	(b Extended Conclusion)*	b Argument to the Man[†]
2. Unsupported Premiss	c Weak Conclusion	c Argument to the People[†]
a Premiss Believed False	d Overlapping Conclusion	
b Premiss Without Evidence	e Irrelevant Conclusion	d Argument to Everyone[†]
c Premiss Insufficiently Supported	* not fallacious	2 Illicit Metabasis of Argument's Domain
		[†] not necessarily fallacious

33A FALLACIES OF UNACCEPTABLE PREMISS

Under the heading of "Unacceptable Premiss", we include any case of a premiss asserted without justification adequate for the purpose of a given argument (see 31A2, (3). A more formal definition of a fallacy of unacceptable premiss is:

Def. 2. A **fallacy of unacceptable premiss** is a fallacy committed by an argument in which some premiss is asserted or presupposed without adequate justification, hence preventing the argument from being a categorical proof.

We subdivide unacceptable premiss into two classes (after Whately, *Elements of Logic*): begging the question, and unsupported premiss.

33A1 Begging the Question. (Or *petitio principii*, pe-tish-ē-ō prin-sip-ē-ī, literally, begging the principle or beginning).[1] In ancient Athens, philosophical discussions were frequently conducted by one man asking questions related to some question in dispute, and the other, the respondent, answering them. Then the questioner, like Socrates, would try to prove a point from the admissions of the respondent. But the questioner should not expect to get the question at issue admitted by asking for its concession directly, or something tantamount to it; this would be "begging the question". More generally, whether question-and-answer method is used or not, Aristotle holds that one is begging the question if one "begs" (demands concession of) or assumes the original point at issue, directly or indirectly. Modern usage of the expression does not usually have in mind the context of a question-and-answer game, but retains the general idea of an attempt to prove something to someone who questions it.

Def. 3. Begging the question (or **question-begging** or *petitio principii*) is assuming or presupposing a point at issue.[2]

In the context of an argument, begging the question involves a premiss or presupposition unacceptable to the second person of the argument. It is then a contextual fallacy of unacceptable premiss; but it is perhaps more often a valid than an invalid argument. (By a *presupposition,* we mean here a proposition that is required for the cogency of the reasoning, but is taken for granted without being made explicit at the given point in the argument.)

a *Argument in a Circle.* Question-begging takes a variety of forms. In the most clear-cut cases, a certain proposition P is explicitly used as premiss, (generally with other premisses, explicit or tacit,) to prove a proposition Q; but in the course of reasoning Q is used or presupposed (perhaps with other propositions) to prove P. Thus the argument makes a full circle. An example of arguing in a circle is:

(a) *God exists, because this fact is testified to in the Bible. And we can have absolute trust in the Bible, because it is of divine origin.*

Note that the statement, "it (the Bible) is of divine origin", given as reason for a reason for the conclusion (i.e., premiss of a premiss), means something like "the Bible was produced with the aid of God", which *presupposes* the conclusion (and thesis) of the argument that God exists. One could not rationally believe the premisses of the argument without already believing the conclusion.

Begging the question is sometimes done by the sophisticated device of a *question-begging criterion* or a *question-begging definition.* Here one introduces into a discussion a criterion or definition that will save the day, thus trying to prove an empirical fact by a priori means, that is, by smuggling the point at issue into the meaning of the terms involved.

An example of a question-begging criterion is given in Charles Darwin's *Origin of Species.* Discussing individual differences within a species, he writes:

(b) Authors sometimes argue in a circle when they state that important organs never vary; for these same authors practically rank those parts as important (as some few naturalists have honestly confessed) which do not vary; and, under this point of view, no instance will ever be found of an important part varying; but under any other point of view many instances assuredly can be given.[3]

Darwin is saying that the naturalists in question have adopted (most of them tacitly) invariance as the criterion of "importance" of an organ; hence it is a priori impossible—not empirically false—that the "important" organs vary.

The introduction *ad hoc* of a question-begging definition or criterion at a nonscientific level is illustrated by the following example:

(c) Mr. Burns states: "*All Bostonians are gentlemen*" (the thesis). Mr. Kelly denies this, asserting: "*Boston Blackie, who was born and raised in Boston, was certainly no gentleman, being wanted by the police for beating and criminally assulting numerous women*". Mr. Burns then replies: "*Boston Blackie is not really a Bostonian*" (implying that a Bostonian is a gentleman by definition).

Sometimes begging the question occurs, not as the "clear-cut" case described in the first paragraph of 33A1a, an argument making a "full circle", but simply as a one-premiss argument (which we shall think of as a "short circle"). We distinguish three cases: (i) The two propositions are logically equivalent; (ii) the premiss logically implies the conclusion but not conversely; (iii) the premiss doesn't logically imply the conclusion, but has some logical connection with it. In the first two cases, the argument is valid, but considered as a proof; it is a fallacy of begging the question if the premiss is no more acceptable than the conclusion in the given context.

The propositions may be equivalent by use of synonymous expressions, by conversion, by relational conversion, and so on. For example,

(d) *He ought to get a raise, because he should have a higher salary.*

In typical contexts, the two component sentences are synonymous, and the argument is valid. But considered as a proof, the argument begs the question, since the premiss is no more—and no less—acceptable than the conclusion.

An example of case (ii), where the premiss implies the conclusion but not conversely, is:

(e) *I wonder if my girlfriend is fickle. All women are fickle, so she must be fickle.*

Considered as a deductive proof, this begs the question by assuming a premiss that is more general than the conclusion and presupposes the conclusion; for the premiss could not be known to be true if the conclusion were not already known. (The premiss is of the type we shall call in 34A a "stereotyped charge".)

In case (iii), the argument is invalid as well as question-begging. For example,

(f) *The Bible is the word of God; therefore God exists and I am going to heaven.*

The premiss presupposes that God exists, but does not imply that the speaker is going to heaven.

We turn now to special cases of begging the question, which we shall *not* call "arguing in a circle", where the question is begged in a fragment of discourse less than a complete explicit argument—perhaps less than a complete proposition, simply a term or a question.

b *Special Cases of Begging the Question:* Question-begging terms, and Question-begging questions.

(i) *Question-begging terms* (or question-begging epithets). According to Jeremy Bentham, the way to beg the question "with the greatest effect, and least risk of detection", is to use a single-worded question-begging term. Such terms (called "question-begging appellatives" in the 1824 edition of *The Book of Fallacies*, and "question-begging epithets" in the recent American edition) prejudge the issue by their eulogistic or disparaging connotations.[4] For example, the disparaging names "massacre", "butchery", and "murder" may be assigned to acts of killing that we disapprove, while eulogistic names such as "auto-da-fé" ("act of the faith"), "execution", and "liquidation" are assigned to ones that we approve. Such emotionally toned words beg the question in argumentation if they prejudge the issue in question and thus assume what is to be proved. Schopenhauer describes the function of question-begging terms from the viewpoint of the user. When a general term plays a key role in a discussion, he points out, you may choose a term with connotations favorable to your point of view. We replace his political example by one drawn from British politics. The opponents of the Conservative call the latter "Tories". This term was first used in the seventeenth century for certain dispossessed Irish outlaws, later for English Royalists or Cavaliers, and is now used by opponents of the Conservative party to identify it "with the bigotry and opposition to reform and progress charged upon earlier Toryism".[5] In return, opponents of the Labour Party call adherents (or proposals) of this party "socialist", whether or not the label is appropriate in the sense of believing in (or leading toward) collective ownership of the means of production.

Schopenhauer also cites a religious example. The names "Protestants" and "Evangelicals", as he says, were self-chosen; "but the Catholics call them *heretics*". He might have added that Protestants have often called Roman Catholics "Papists", alluding to a feature of their church of which these Protestants do not approve. He continues:

> Similarly, in regard to the names of things which admit of a more exact and definite meaning: for example, if your opponent proposes an *alteration,* you can call it an *innovation* as this is an invidious word. If you yourself make the proposal, it will be the converse. In the first case, you can call the antagonistic principle "the existing order," in the second, "antiquated prejudice." What an impartial man with no further purpose to serve would call "public worship" or a "system of religion," is described by an adherent as "piety," "godliness"; and by an opponent as "bigotry," "superstition." This is, at bottom, a subtle *petitio principii.* What is sought to be proved is, first of all, inserted in the definition, whence it is then taken by mere analysis. What one man calls "placing in safe custody," another calls "throwing into prison." A speaker often betrays his purpose beforehand by the names which he gives to things. One man talks of "the clergy"; another, of "the priests."[6]

(ii) *Question-begging questions* (usually called "Complex question" or "Many questions"). All questions are assumptive. If you ask a man for his wife's maiden name, you have assumed, by your question, that he is married. A question-begging question assumes what is to be proved by either directly assuming the point at issue or by assuming a question-begging premiss of the kinds illustrated in 33A1a.

For example, if two people are debating the existence of extrasensory perception and the person who is defending its existence asks his opponent, "Do you know the explanation of telepathy?" then a fallacy has been committed. The question assumes what is to be proved, namely, the existence of telepathy, which is an extrasensory power.

Another type of question-begging question is the compound question (two or more questions asked as one so that a "single answer involves more than one admission".)[7] For example, the question "Do you think that God is benevolent and just—yes or no?" is so stated that either answer involves two admissions. Such questions are question-begging when they are used to trick one's opponent into admitting the thesis or into admitting a proposition (that upon reflection he would not admit) that will lead to the thesis. Such crude ploys as the compound question are met by answering each part of the question separately.

33A2 Unsupported Premiss. Some writers call any case of unacceptable premiss "begging the question". It seems better, however, to explain the latter term in an Aristotelian way, as we have done, and to separate from begging the question all other ways in which a premiss can be unacceptable, calling any such, in Whately's term, an unsupported premiss, that is, one which is not sufficiently supported (and not supported by its conclusion).

Def. 4. The **fallacy of unsupported premiss** is the fallacy committed by an argument in which a premiss, without question-begging, is not sufficiently supported to prove the thesis.

We divide unsupported premisses into three classes: premiss believed false, premiss without evidence (or premiss ex nihilo), and premiss insufficiently supported.

a *Premiss Believed False.* An argument fails completely to prove its point to someone who believes or knows any of its premisses to be false. I can prove something to myself by premisses I believe to be true; and I can think of such an argument as an argument *ad veritatem*, an appeal to the truth. But it appeals only to those who also accept my premisses. If I wish to convince some specific persons, I cannot expect them to be convinced if they reject the premisses advanced any more than if they see the reasoning is invalid.

Of course I may start out innocently, not knowing what another person accepts. But if a premiss is challenged, I can maintain my point only by supporting the premiss, or trying another line of argument.

A specially important case of "premiss believed false" is that of Inconsistent Premisses, or Self-Inconsistent Premiss. A set of inconsistent premisses is known to be jointly false with logical certainty. It is said by most contemporary logicians to "imply" anything; but of course cannot be used to prove anything.[8]

Whately has been rightly criticized for making "false premiss" a material *fallacy*. To have a false premiss is (generally) a fault in an argument but not a fallacy. We have no infallible criterion to decide between truth and falsity; hence no care in reasoning can prevent us from believing some false propositions to be true. But careful reasoning can prevent or detect fallacies. We can, therefore, refrain from using—or withdraw—a premiss believed to be false.

b *Premiss Without Evidence* (or Premiss *ex nihilo*). An arbitrary premiss may be used for which no justification is or can be given. This is all too common, though we may not know that the justification cannot be given unless we ask for it.

c *Premiss Insufficiently Supported.* A premiss may be used for which some justification can be given, but not sufficient for the purpose at hand. The justification may be defective in (i) quantity or (ii) kind.

(i) The premisses may be less known or just as unknown as the conclusion. But the conclusion cannot be any more certain than the weakest link in the chain of reasoning leading to it; so the conclusion is already as well known as the argument could make it.

(ii) The premiss may be of a kind that is inacceptable. For instance, one may appeal to an authority not accepted by one's audience, as in appealing to the New Testament with a Moslem.

33B CONCLUSION-THESIS GAP (OR INSUFFICIENT CONCLUSION)

(Usually called Irrelevant Conclusion or *Ignoratio Elenchi*.)⁹ If a marksman is supposed to hit a certain target and either by deliberation or accident hits another, he can, instead of admitting that he missed, pretend that he hit the right target. Due to the inattention of the judge or the other contestants, he might be believed. The conclusion-thesis gap is analogous to the stratagem of this marksman. It is a case of arguing beside the point. (However, arguing beside the point may also occur as a gap between premisses and conclusion, i.e., as case of invalidity.)

Def. 5. Conclusion-thesis gap (or **Insufficient Conclusion**) is a fallacy committed when an argument purports to have proved its thesis, but has proved at most a conclusion insufficient to establish the thesis.

A diagram illustrating the general form of conclusion-thesis gap in case there is no other fallacy follows:

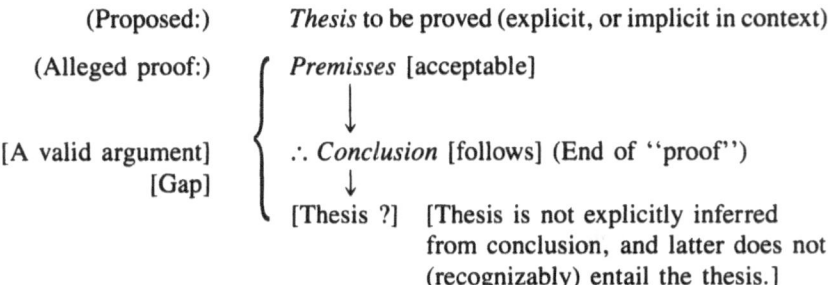

(Expressions in square brackets are commentaries on the 'proof', not parts of it.)

The following is an example of conclusion-thesis gap: The city administration claims that it must impose an additional sales tax to cover its expenditures. It argues for this by showing convincingly that it needs more money to meet its minimum needs, and that the necessary amount can be raised by the proposed tax. However, it fails to show that this tax is better than other possible ways of raising the money. Thus there is a gap between the conclusions actually demonstrated and the thesis to be proved. For other examples, see 31A2, (4).

33C ILLICIT METABASIS[10]

Every argument occurs in a context that has two aspects: the audience to whom the argument is directed and the argument's domain, that is, the subject area of the argument. An argument that is a proof in a given context is not necessarily a proof in a different context; hence it is a fallacy to claim that a proof binding upon a specific group of people is therefore a proof binding upon all people (or a different group of people). It is equally fallacious to claim that a principle proved in the context of a specific science such as biology is hence an established principle in a different science such as sociology. For example, the claim that evolution holds for social institutions because the theory of evolution has been established in biology is a fallacious argument.

> **Def. 6.** The **fallacy of illicit metabasis** (mə-TAB-ə-sis) is a fallacy committed by an argument that is a proof of its conclusion in the context in which it is given, but is claimed, without further justification, to be a proof in a wider or in a different context.

One may think of an illicit metabasis as an illicit shift of the frame of reference (the context) of an argument.

> **33C1 Illicit Metabasis of Audience.** An argument is always directed toward an audience. As indicated in 31A3, there are different kinds of audience it may be directed to: to oneself; to another person or group of people where dialogue is possible (*ad hominem*); to an audience where no meaningful dialogue is possible (e.g., *ad populum*, to a public gathering, etc.); to everyone (*ad omnes*); or to all rational beings. An argument proves nothing to an audience unless the latter accepts the premises and judges the argument valid. But it is illicit metabasis of audience to hold that what one accepts, another will accept.

a *Argument to Oneself (ad seipsum).* It is not fallacious to construct an argument that proves the conclusion to oneself. If you accept the premisses of your own argument and see that the conclusion follows from them, then the conclusion has been proved *to you.* It is, however, a fallacy to claim that a conclusion, because it is proved to oneself, is therefore proved to others. To alter an old proverb: Premisses that are meat for one man are poison for another.

b *Argument to the Man (argument ad hominem).* Literally, argument to the man, that is, an argument aimed to appeal specifically to the person one is addressing: An argument intended "to press a man with consequences (i) drawn from his own principles or concessions" as he has admitted them,[11] or (ii) inferred from his previous utterances, or (iii) drawn from his real or presumed interests, prejudices, circumstances, or associations. Usually, the argument involves pointing out a contradiction between the present view or a certain point of a man to be persuaded and his views or principles—known or inferred—taken to be more permanent.

The argument *ad hominem* is distinguished as subjective and limited from an objective or universal appeal (argument *ad rem*—to the matter at hand; or argument *ad omnes*—to everyone.) The argument *ad hominem* should also be clearly distinguished from Adverse Personalities (argument *ad personam,* i.e., *adversus personam,* a personal attack on the opponnt), which—if not merely expressing hostility—aims to persuade a third party of the defects of one's opponent (see 34A).

The fallacious argument *ad hominem:* It is not a fallacy to press a person with consequences drawn from the person's own principles, inferred from previous utterances, and so on. Indeed, it is difficult to see how an argument or debate could have any persuasive force without dialectical use being made of the principles or concessions of the participants. A well recognized way in which argument *ad hominem* becomes a fallacy is by claiming that what has been proved to the person has been proved to another audience or to everyone. This fallacy we call an illicit metabasis. Schopenhauer warns against this fallacious use of argument *ad hominem*:

> He has, that is to say, either taken up some position once and for all as a prejudice, or hastily admitted it in the course of the dispute, and on this I ground my proof. In that case, it is a proof valid only for this particular man, *ad hominem.* I compel my opponent to grant my proposition, but I fail to establish it as a truth of universal validity. My proof avails for my opponent alone, but for no one else.[12]

It is perfectly permissible to point out inconsistencies in your opponent's admissions. It is also permissible to use the opponent's admissions as premisses from which to infer your thesis (the point you are trying to prove), but anything that is proved in this manner is a proof only to your opponent. It is not a proof to those who do not accept the concessions granted by your opponent. For example, if I wish to prove something to a follower of Aristotle, I may deduce my thesis from certain basic principles of Aristotelian philosophy, but this proof is only *ad hominem*. It may not be a proof to those who are not Aristotelians. Any attempt to claim that this proof is binding on others besides my opponent (and other followers of Aristotle) would be an illicit metabasis. In the same way it would be an illicit metabasis to claim to have proved a proposition universally because you have proved it to a devout Christian by deducing it from certain basic Christian tenets.

In general, an illicit metabasis is committed if it is assumed that an argument that is valid to one man must be valid to all men. Before an argument is a proof to any audience, that audience must accept both the truth of that argument's premisses and its validity.

c *Argument to the People.* The audience, in this case, is a group of people with whom no meaningful dialogue is possible. Examples of such audiences are those who are listening to a lecture or debate on radio or television, or who are being addressed by a public speaker. Also such an audience would be the readers of an argument presented in print.

An appeal to the public is an argument or series of arguments designed to appeal to the kind of audience described above. It is—or is intended to be—based on premisses that the audience will readily accept, and constructed in such a manner that the audience will accept it as valid. An illicit metabasis occurs when it is claimed that an argument that is a proof to such an audience is a proof binding upon a different audience or upon all people.

For example, a speaker addressing members of the Ku Klux Klan might "prove" the inferiority of the black race to his prejudiced audience by basing his argument on certain beliefs held in common by the Klan members and constructing an argument that these members accept as valid. But if the speaker then claimed that he had proved in a universal or absolute sense the inferiority of the black race, he would be committing an illicit metabasis in an argument to the public. In the case of this audience, it would be appropriate to use a common label, *argument(um) ad populum* (argument to the people), which seems always to be used in a sense derogatory to the audience, and often with an aristocratic or elitist assumption of the inferiority of "the people", that is, "ordinary" or lower-class people.

33C2 Illicit Metabasis of Argument's Domain. The domain of an argument is its specific subject area (see 31A2, (5)). It is the region of knowledge from which the evidence for its premisses is drawn. The domain of an argument may be physics, thermodynamics, chemistry, dendrology, mythology, and so on. Illicit metabasis of an argument's domain may occur in two ways.

a *Illicit Generalization of Domain.* An argument is a proof of its conclusion only in its domain. A statement is not proved universally (i.e., in all domains) by an argument, unless its premises are acceptable in every context, which is rarely if ever possible.

An illicit generalization of an argument's domain occurs when it is claimed (or assumed) that because the argument proves its conclusion in its domain, it proves its conclusion in a larger domain or an overlapping domain. For example, if a law of physics has been proved in the domain of mechanics for the macroscopic realm, and with no additional evidence it is claimed that this law has been proved for all domains in physics—the microscopic, the subatomic, and so on—then an illicit generalization has occurred.

b *Illicit Transfer of Arguments Domain.* This fallacy occurs when an argument in a certain domain is claimed or assumed to be, without further justification, a proof of its conclusion in some other distinct domain. For example, to claim or assume that the law *For every action there is an equal and opposite reaction,* which has been proved in mechanics, is therefore proved in the domain of sociology is fallacious. Evidence that demonstrates that mechanical actions have equal mechanical reactions is not evidence that social actions have equal social reactions.

It should be noted that it is often extremely fruitful to use the demonstrated laws in one domain or their analogies as hypotheses in other domains. This constitutes no fallacy, since a hypothesis is a statement that is to be verified; consequently, proof is sought, not assumed.

Appendix to Chapter 33A1

33A1 WAYS OF BEGGING THE QUESTION

OUTLINE OF WAYS OF BEGGING THE QUESTION
a *Begging an Equivalent Premise*
  (i) Begging by the use of the same words.
  (ii) Begging by the use of a synonymous expression.
  (iii) Begging an equivalent by conversion, etc.
  (iv) Begging piecemeal.
b *Begging a Non-Equivalent Premiss*
  (i) Begging a superaltern.
    (a) Begging a universal to prove a subordinate universal or instance.
    (b) Begging an a priori truth to prove an empirical truth.
  (ii) Begging a subaltern.
  (iii) Begging an independent premiss, that is, the premiss is neither by itself, superaltern nor subaltern of the conclusion, by itself.

It should be noted that any of the above can be arguments in a circle. Begging an independent premiss is always circular.

a Begging an Equivalent Premiss. A premiss (or set of premisses) having the same meaning as the conclusion is assumed without warrant. This type of begging the question will be called "begging an equivalent". Begging an equivalent may be done in different ways.

(i) *Begging by the use of the same words.* This form of begging the question is rare. Very common, however, is a practice that might be confused with this type of fallacy, but is not a fallacy of any kind. When an assertion has been proved it may be repeated after an interval on the grounds of its previous assertion in order to use it in a proof.[1]

(ii) *Begging by the use of synonymous expression.* The question may be begged by a premiss that is obtained by simply replacing some expression in the conclusion by a synonymous expression. For example, the following is a question begging explanation: "Opium induces sleep, because it is a soporific".[2]

(iii) *Begging an equivalent to the conclusion.* The question may be begged by a premiss that is equivalent to the conclusion by immediate inference (conversion, relational conversion, etc.). Aristotle said that a man would beg the question if he were to beg one of two things which necessarily follows one another, for example, that the side [of a square] is incommensurable with the diagonal when he has to show that the diagonal is incommensurable with the side. (*Topica*, 163a11, The Loeb Classical Library)

Another example would be to assume as a premiss that Boston is north of New York City, when one has to prove that New York City is south of Boston. These propositions are equivalent by relational conversion.

(iv) *Begging piecemeal.* Another way to beg the question, says Aristotle, occurs "when he divides the proposition up and begs its separate parts; for example, if, when he has to show that medicine is the science of the healthy and of the diseased, he were to claim the two points separately" (*Topica*, 163a9, the Loeb Classical Library). In argument form this would look like:

Medicine is the science of the healthy.
Medicine is the science of the disease.
Therefore, medicine is the science of the healthy and of the diseased.

Begging the question piecemeal could be a variation on any of the three forms of begging an equivalent listed above.

b Begging a Non-Equivalent to the Question. Begging a nonequivalent to the question occurs when a premiss is assumed (in one of the following ways) not equivalent to the conclusion.

(i) *Begging a Superaltern.*

(a) Begging a universal to prove a subordinate universal or instance. This occurs when one begs a premiss that is a superaltern to the conclusion, that is, a premiss that implies the conclusion but is not implied by it.
Aristotle says concerning this fallacy that

when a man begs something universally when he ought to show it in a particular case; for example, if, when he is endeavoring to show that there is one science of contraries, he were to claim that there is in general one science of opposites; for then he is regarded as begging, among several other things, what he should have shown by itself. (*Topica*, 163a11, The Loeb Classical Library)

In order to understand Aristotle's example it should be noted that contraries are one kind of opposites.

Another example of begging a superaltern occurs when one assumes that all metals are conductors of electricity in order to prove that all ferrous metals are conductors of electricity.[3]

(b) Begging an *a priori* truth to prove an empirical (*a posteriori*) truth. This happens when one, claiming to establish an empirical truth, begs a premiss that in effect asserts the conclusion as a necessary truth.[4] This is usually done by a *question-begging definition* or a *question-begging criterion*. An example of a question-begging definition would occur in Mr. Bigot's attempt to prove that Mr. Smith is not a Christian, drawing this conclusion from the fact that Mr. Smith doesn't go to church on Sunday. Challenged, Mr. Bigot supported his argument by the question-begging definition "A Christian is a person who regularly attends a Christian church".

(ii) *Begging the subaltern(s)*. This occurs when one begs a premiss or premisses that are subalterns to the conclusion. These premisses are then used in conjunction with other propositions to prove the conclusion. Aristotle states that one commits this fallacy

> when it is proposed to show something universally and he begs it in a particular case; if, for example, when it is proposed to show that the science of contraries is always one, he begs it of a particular pair of contraries; for he is also regarded as begging separately and by itself something which he ought to have shown in conjunction with a number of other cases. (*Topica*, 163a5, The Loeb Classical Library)

Another example of begging a subaltern would be to assume that all ferrous metals are conductors of electricity and then to use this proposition in conjunction with other to prove that all metals are conductors of electricity.

(iii) *Begging an independent premiss*. This occurs when one begs a premiss that is neither (by itself) a superaltern or a subaltern of the conclusion (by itself). In short, the premiss begged does not imply the conclusion or is implied by the conclusion. A fallacy occurs only if the begged premiss is in fact proved with the help of the conclusion or cannot be proved without assuming the conclusion. For example, in an axiomatic system, theorem 12 may be used to prove theorem 10. This is a fallacy, if theorem 10 has to be proved in order to prove theorem 12. (If the proof of theorem 12 does not depend upon theorem 10, the theorems should be renumbered.) This type of begging the question is an *argument in a circle*, for each proposition (the begged premiss and the conclusion) constitutes part of the evidence for the other.

Exercises for Chapter 33

EX33, I. Answer "T" if the statement is true, "F" if it is false.

_____ 1. A contextual fallacy in an argument prevents the argument from being valid.

_____ 2. A contextual fallacy in an argument prevents the argument from being a proof of its thesis.

_____ 3. Fallacies of unacceptable premiss are divided into two classes: begging the question and unsupported premiss.

_____ 4. By "begging the question", Aristotle meant: demanding concession of the original point at issue.

_____ 5. The premiss must be equivalent to the conclusion in order to beg the question.

_____ 6. A question-begging definition assumes an empirical truth in order to prove an a priori truth.

_____ 7. All circular arguments, if they are intended to be categorical proofs, beg the question.

_____ 8. A question-begging term is a single-worded term that prejudges the issue by its disparaging or eulogistic connotation.

_____ 9. All questions are assumptive.

_____ 10. A question-begging question assumes what is to be proved either by directly assuming the point at issue or by assuming a question-begging premiss.

_____ 11. The fallacy of unsupported premiss is divided into three classes: premiss believed false, premiss without evidence, and premiss insufficiently supported.

_____ 12. Inconsistent premisses or self-inconsistent premiss is an important case of premiss without evidence.

_____ 13. A false premiss in an argument commits the fallacy of premiss *ex nihilo*, that is, premiss without evidence.

_____ 14. The fallacy of Conclusion-Thesis Gap is a case of arguing beside the point.

Exercises/Chapter 33   459

_____ 15. If the fallacy of insufficient conclusion occurs in an argument then the argument is invalid.

_____ 16. One may think of an illicit metabasis as an illicit shift of the frame of reference of an argument.

_____ 17. An argument *ad seipsum* is an argument directed to everyone.

_____ 18. A proof binding upon a specific group of people is a proof binding upon all people.

_____ 19. It is always a fallacy to press a man with consequences drawn from his own premisses or inferred from his previous statements.

_____ 20. Argument *ad hominem* becomes a fallacy when it is claimed that what has been proved "to the man" has been proved to another audience or to everyone.

EX 33, II. Each of the following numbered paragraphs reports or commits one of the fallacies listed in the key below, except that one or two are most plausibly interpreted as not fallacious. Identify the fallacy by choosing the appropriate label.

KEY

AC	Argument in a circle	CTG	Conclusion-thesis gap
QBT	Question-begging term	IM:A	Illicit metabasis of audience
QBQ	Question-begging question	IM:D	Illicit metabasis of domain
UP	Unsupported premiss	NO	No fallacy (or none of these)

_____ 1. I don't know why you won't accept my argument as a proof, since you admit that it is valid and since all of my friends think that it is absolutely convincing.

_____ 2. I was once staying with a man who told me indignantly that he had heard a sermon in which the preacher had said that in Russia the workingman was esteemed more highly than in any other country. I said, "Well, that is quite likely to be true, isn't it?" "True!" my host exclaimed, "it's a pack of lies! Do you know that during the last few years in Russia over twenty thousand people have been killed simply because they were Christians?"

_____ 3. Senator Gafton is thickheaded. How do I justify that charge? It follows from the fact that he is stupid, dense, and obtuse.

_____ 4. The speaker said that he would demonstrate that everything in the universe is subject to the law of evolution, but in fact all he showed was that certain characteristics of fruit flies are explainable by evolutionary laws.

_____ 5. The speaker drew his conclusion logically from propositions basic to the Kabbalah. His audience, all of whom accepted these basic propositions (as did the speaker himself), found the argument convincing. Finally, the speaker declared that his argument was a proof to all rational people.

_____ 6. Mr. X: "Any man who would marry such a woman must have something wrong with him".
Mr. Y: "Why, what is the matter with his wife"?
Mr. X: "It is matter enough to be willing to marry such a man as he is".

_____ 7. You said that you would tell me why you won't marry me, instead you argue against the institution of marriage.

_____ 8. Aristotle is the most famous philosopher in Western civilization, because his philosophy (with modifications) became the official philosophy of the Catholic Church. This came about because Aquinas and others based their philosophies on Aristotle's philosophy. They did this because Aristotle was the most famous philosopher in Western civilization.

_____ 9. No man can will himself to move, unless the will is a force external to the body, since Newton's First Law of Motion—a body remains at rest unless acted upon by an external force—has been conclusively proved.

_____ 10. He is an anarchist, since he doesn't believe in any form of authoritarian government.

_____ 11. The argument that I just gave you seems perfectly conclusive to me: I believe the premises to be true, the argument to be valid, and so on. Therefore, you should admit that this argument is a proof of its conclusion.

_____ 12. Thomas Jefferson was an architect and became the second president of the United States. Therefore, the second president of the United States was an architect.

_____ 13. I will prove that the defendant is guilty of murder. The victim was an elderly man whom the murderer knew was blind.

While the victim was helplessly tied to a chair the murderer shot the victim eight times. I conclude that this vicious murder was the work of a sick, deranged mind.

_____ 14. All radical students are neurotics; therefore, this radical student is neurotic.

_____ 15. A proof is a proof, so what is a proof to one man is a proof to all men.

34

Illicit Appeals

One important function of language is persuasion, which is the use of words to urge or convince someone to act or believe in a certain way (or to refrain from acting or believing in a certain way). Examples of the use of persuasive language are easy to come by. The commercials on television urge the audience to buy certain products, politicians urge their constituents to vote for them, governments try to convince their citizens that preventive wars are necessary, children plead with their parents for later bedtime hours, and students try to convince their instructors that they give an unfair amount of homework.

Every attempt at persuasion is based on an appeal to some authority, principle, or psychological faculty that the persuader thinks will prove effective. The appeal could be to anything: emotions, reason, mysticism, experts in some given speciality, and so on. Some examples: A recruiting sergeant tries to urge young men to join the army by appealing to their patriotism. An elderly mother tries to prevent her daughter from marrying by appealing to pity: "You wouldn't leave your old mother alone in the world". A physicist tries to convince his colleagues that his theory is correct by appealing to empirical evidence and mathematical calculations based on and supported by this evidence. A dictator tries to convince his people that there should be war by appealing to their frustrations, prejudices, and fears.

It is obvious that not all appeals are legitimate, and what is a legitimate appeal in one set of circumstances may not be in another. The purpose of this chapter is to discuss some common illicit appeals that occur in the persuasive use of language. No attempt will be made to impose a formal structure on these illicit appeals, as their variety and nature does not lend itself to a rigorous classification. Nor will any attempt be made to provide an exhaustive list of illicit appeals; such a list would be impossible.

The need for a second classification of fallacies (mostly psychological in nature) based on types of appeal is demonstrated by the difficulty that most logicians encounter in trying to force fallacies viewed as illicit appeals into place in a classification made on different principles. In the previous chapters fallacies were classified by the criterion of proof they violated (31B2). In this chapter the principle of classification is the type of appeal involved. Consequently, we have two distinct classifications for fallacies, which cut across one another. For example, fallacies classified in this chapter as an Illicit Appeal to Pity would by the previous classification be either fallacies of Conclusion-Thesis Gap or Logical Fallacies. Authors who use a single classification usually force such a heading as Appeal to Pity (argument *ad misericordiam*) under a single grouping such as Irrelevant Conclusion, whereas many appeals to pity are rather Logical Fallacies.

An illicit appeal does not have to be a fallacy, for appeals (illicit or not) do not have to occur in the context of an argument. It is illicit and fallacious to appeal primarily to emotions when the situation makes it reasonable to expect an appeal to reason; instances would be a scientific meeting, a formal debate, or any time when one is trying to convince another of the truth of a proposition. It would also be an illicit appeal, but not necessarily a fallacy, to attempt to persuade another to do something by appealing to a standard (such as an institutional authority—see 34B) that is known to the persuader to be less reliable than another available standard.

The types of appeal covered in this chapter are outlined below.

Table 34.1: Types of Appeal

A Appeal to Adverse Personalities
  1. Charge of Inconsistency
  2. Charge of Bad Design
  3. Charge of Bad Motive
  4. Charge of Personal Defect
  5. Charge of Similar Defect (or "*Tu Quoque*")
  6. Charge of Suspicious Connections
  7. Stereotyped Charges
B Appeal to Authority
  1. Appeal to Irrelevant Knowledge
  2. Appeal to Biased Opinion
  3. Defective Transmission
  4. Overestimated Authority
C Appeal to Ignorance
D Appeal to Pity
E Appeal to Force

As we have mentioned, language may be used to persuade people to act or to believe. We shall not concern ourselves with the ethical problems raised by the question of standards for influencing human action, but shall limit our discussion of appeals to illicit attempts to influence a person to believe in the truth of some proposition (34E is an exception).

34A APPEAL TO ADVERSE PERSONALITIES

This appeal—often confused with *argumentum ad hominem* (see Appendix 34A4)—has had a variety of names. It was called *argumentum ad personam* by Schopenhauer and "Vituperative Personalities" by Bentham, who also labeled it *augumentum ad odium*. The appeal to (or expression of) emotion is usually conspicuous. Its persuasive force is based on the false principle that *if you discredit the man, you discredit the man's argument or position*. Bentham states:

> Ignorance and indolence, friendship and enmity, concurring and conflicting interest, servility and dependence—all these conspire to give personalities the ascendancy they so happily maintain. The more we lie under the influence of our own passions, the more we rely on others being affected in a similar degree.

The following list of illicit appeals to personalities is based on Bentham's division of Vituperative Personalities.[1]

34A1 Charge of Inconsistency. It is perfectly legitimate to criticize a person's argument by showing that it contains inconsistent premisses (see 33A2a), and it is also legitimate, if your opponent defends two inconsistent statements in the same discussion, to point out that at least one of them has to be false; but one does not rationally refute a person's argument by demonstrating that he defended an opposing position in the past. Nor does one show the falsity of a person's beliefs by showing that they are inconsistent with his or her behavior. People may fail to practice what they preach and yet preach the truth. A person who is often inconsistent in his or her beliefs and argues first on one side of a position and then the other does express a character trait that most people find undesirable; but people with undesirable character traits can give sound arguments.

34A2 Charge of Bad Design. This error consists of arguing that a person's proposal should be rejected, not because there is anything wrong with the proposal or with their motive for presenting it, but because this person has the design of presenting a bad proposal at some future time. As Bentham points out, anyone who argues in the above manner ought to prove the following: (1) That the person *intends* to present a bad proposal in the future, (2) That such a proposal *will* in fact be presented, (3) that the proposal will prove to be a *bad* one, and (4) That we *can* prevent the acceptance of the supposed bad proposal by rejecting the present proposal. The charge of bad design is no error if these four conditions can be proved, but so seldom is this the case that it is safe to consider it an error barring strong evidence to the contrary.

34A3 Charge of Bad Motive. The relation between a person's argument and his or her motive for presenting it is a causal, not a logical, one; hence it is incorrect to reason that if the person has an improper motive for presenting an argument, the argument should be rejected. As Bentham says, "If the measure is beneficial, it would be absurd to reject it on account of the motives of its author". Therefore it would be fallacious to argue, for example, that *Senator Jones has a personal (or selfish) motive for supporting the Diamond Bill, therefore the Diamond Bill should be defeated.* It would, however, be prudent in the light of Senator Jones's vested interest in the bill to examine it with more than usual care.

34A4 Charge of Personal Defect. By "personal defect" we mean such things as bad character, alcoholism, physical or mental illness, ugliness, stuttering, eccentric mannerisms, poverty, and so on. This device (called by some authors "abusive type of *argumentum ad hominem*") consists of abusing your opponent personally instead of criticizing the person's argument. The user of this appeal, of course, wishes the audience to think that if the person has a defect, then so must his or her position. Examples are numerous: *Professor Lush, the physicist, is an alcoholic; hence his new theory is nonsense.* Or, *The Civil Rights movement cannot be a worthy cause if Mr. Green defends it; he has been in jail five times.*

Of course, when it is a question of testimony and not of soundness of argument, then a person's character may well be relevant to the issue. For example, a witness's unsupported testimony in a court of law would be doubted if it is established that he or she is a psychopathic liar. Charges of bad character or illness are also relevant if the question is whether a person should be elected to office.

34A5 Charge of Similar Defect. (Also called *"Tu Quoque"*, meaning "you too".) This is a variety of the charge of personal defect, namely, the case in which a person accused of improper behavior or some personal defect tries to minimize or cancel the charge by charging the accuser with a similar defect. The rationale behind this ploy may be the principle (often sound) that *the best defense is a good offense* or it may be the false principle *If everyone is guilty, then no one is guilty.* An example of the *"Tu quoque"* charge would be an employee's fallacious argument to his fellow worker, "You can't object to my stealing from you, because I know you steal plenty from the company".

34A6 Charge of Suspicious Connections. In modern times this error is called "guilt by association". This error casts doubt on a person's argument or position by the charge that he or she associates with people of bad character. Of course, knowledge of a person's friends and associates may provide some evidence as to a person's character, but it is no evidence for the soundness or unsoundness of a person's argument or the correctness or incorrectness of his or her position. And furthermore, Bentham points out, the very charge of a suspicious connection rests upon proving the following three points: (1) the badness of character of the alleged associate, (2) the existence of a social connection between the person and the supposed associate; and (3) that the influence exercised on the mind of the person in question is such that in consequence thereof he or she will be induced to introduce and support mischievous measures that otherwise he or she would not have introduced or supported. (*Handbook*, p 88f.).

34A7 Stereotyped Charges. The mechanism in this error is stereotyping. An example would be: *He's all right for a Japanese, but you can't really trust him, you know. Look what they did to us at Pearl Harbor.* A fallacy occurs when the stereotyping is used to impugn the man's character with the purpose of discrediting his argument or opinion. An example is, *Her argument can't be sound. Women aren't as logical as men.*

Most stereotypes are false; for instance, it is not true that women are less logical than men, that Irish are happy-go-lucky people compared with other nationalities, that Jews are only concerned with making money, and so on. Even if a stereotype is generally true, it does not follow that everyone belonging to the class in question has the peculiarities of that class.

34B APPEAL TO AUTHORITY

Not all appeals to authority *(argumentum ad verecundiam)*[2] are fallacies or error, but this appeal is so often abused that the expression "appeal to authority" (or "argument from authority") has the connotation of being incorrect. Part of this appeal's bad reputation is caused by the failure to distinguish between institutional and expert authority. As we shall see, an appeal to an institutional authority, as such, on cognitive issues is always erroneous.

34B1 Expert Authority and Institutional Authority. We live in an age where the advance of knowledge has created experts in every conceivable area of specialization. The layman's knowledge of these specialities is small compared to that of the expert. Consequently, it seems obvious that we must rely on the authority of experts for the information needed to solve the variety of problems we encounter in our lives.

We speak also of the authority of Congress to pass laws or the authority of a clergyman or mayor to perform a marriage. This is a different sense of the word *authority*. We shall call this "institutional authority".

We have mentioned two kinds of authority: expert and institutional. It is important to distinguish between them, since their nature and function are quite distinct.

The authority of the expert is based upon his or her competence, which consists of demonstrable knowledge (or skill) in a certain area of specialization. Hence the authority of the expert is limited to his or her area of competence and is a function of demonstrable ability within this area. One might think of the expert as a *cognitive* authority, that is, one who possesses far more than average knowledge in a certain area.

Institutional authority is a recognized right and power that certain people or agencies have to give orders or to perform certain official or customary functions, such as the making or enforcing of laws and commands or the settling of disputes. This authority may be legal (i.e., legally empowered) or merely customary. Examples of institutional authorities are police, law courts, Congress, city dogcatcher, county coroner, church, business corporations, college trustees. Institutional authority also exists in the family; parents have authority over their children, though they are not always able and willing to exercise it.

Even though expert knowledge may be a prerequisite for an institutional office, the authority of the office still has its sanction in law (or custom), not in knowledge. For example, a person must be a physician in order to be appointed county coroner, but the authority as coroner is not derived from medical knowledge but from the appointment.

The distinction between expert and institutional authority can be brought out by contrasting the ability to do something with the legal right to do it. An expert had the ability (knowledge or skill) to perform well within his or her area of competence, but this does not mean that he or she is legally empowered to do so. For example, a teacher might be highly competent and yet lose the job because of his or her activity as a citizen. On the other hand, no person is competent to perform a task simply by virtue of legal authority to do so. For example, a man may by due process become the president of the United States and be vested with great power, but by no means do great power and great leadership of a nation always go together.

The truth of a proposition is established by appealing to knowledge, not be appealing to legal or political power (or to any other kind of non-cognitive influence).³ Consequently the distinction between expert and institutional authority is important, because the opinion of an expert may serve as evidence for the truth of a proposition, while the opinion of an institutional authority, as such, has no cognitive weight.

The appeal to expert authority, however, is not without its pitfalls. Under certain conditions it is justifiable, under other conditions it is not.

34B2 The Presupposition of Legitimate Appeal to Authority. The legitimate appeal to expert opinion presupposes that the knowledge supporting this opinion is to some extent not comprehensible (or not known) to the concerned parties. If the matter can be resolved by a direct appeal to the evidence and this evidence can be understood and evaluated by the parties involved, then no appeal to expert authority is needed and none should be made.⁴

Once a cognitive need for the appeal to expert opinion has been established, the next task is to show that the alleged expert opinion is acceptable as good and relevant evidence. This is done by showing that the opinion satisfies certain criteria.

34B3 The Criteria for Acceptance of Expert Opinion.⁵ Opinion adduced as authority may be accepted as expert evidence to the extent that the following four criteria are met.⁶

a *Relevant Knowledge.* When a person attempts to support a position by appealing to an opinion of an authority, the person must be prepared to show three kinds of relevancy: The relevance of the opinion to the question at issue; the relevance of the authority's area of competence to the opinion; and the relevance of the authority's training, education, and experience to the claim that he or she is an expert in the area. We shall examine each in turn.

(i) *Relevant Opinion.* The relevance of the opinion is established by showing that it has some bearing on the question at issue. It is not enough that it be an expert's opinion or that the expert be an authority in the field in question. The specific opinion cited must in fact be close enough to the question at hand to be relevant. A passage from Einstein might be cited as authority on a question in mathematical physics although the passage has no real bearing on the specific problem.

(ii) *Relevant Authority.* Not only should the opinion of the authority be relevant to the question at issue, but the person should be an authority in the relevant area of competence. The opinion of an expert baseball player, even though relevant to a question concerning the merits of a breakfast cereal, is not admissible as *relevantly* authoritative, since the player's knowledge of baseball is irrelevant to the question at issue.

(iii) *Expert Authority.* The authority appealed to should be a genuine expert in the claimed field of competence. It is often difficult for a layperson to evaluate the relevancy and the worth of a person's claim to expert authority. In such cases the judgment of reputable experts in the same field of specialization is the value.

The following diagram summarizes the above:

Figure 34.1: Relevant Knowledge for Appeal to Expert Opinion

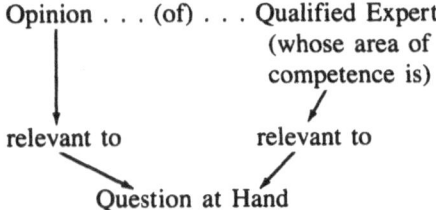

b *Objectivity.* Experts, like other human beings, have a tendency to be influenced by personal interests. Therefore, when it is known that an expert's advice favors personal interest, this advice may justifiably be suspected of bias. The extent to which this suspicion is justified is the extent to which the advice favors his or her own interests and the strength of these interests. For example, little credence should be placed in a researcher's claim that there is no correlation between volume of alcohol consumed and certain liver ailments if it is known that the research was paid for by a whiskey firm.

Bentham mentions the following rule of evidence, which is worth noting: "In a man's own favour his own testimony is the weakest,—in his disfavour, the strongest, evidence".

The impartiality resulting from the absence of the selfish interest is then a favorable factor tending to make the expert's judgment objective and accurate. However, an expert's interest in maintaining a good reputation and self-respect may outweigh other personal interests; if so, he can achieve objectivity of judgment, which is the essential point.

c *Faithful Transmission.* Since experts are seldom present when we appeal to them, we often have to rely on indirect sources such as memory and written materials, both of which are fallible. Therefore, if we appeal to expert opinion at second hand we must be sure that the following criteria are met:

(i) *Accurate Quotation.* Since most appeals to expert opinion are appeals to quotation, care should be taken to ensure accuracy of such quotations.

(ii) *In Context.* When quoting the opinion of an expert authority, care should be taken not to distort the meaning of the original opinion by quoting out of context. All of the context of the quoted passage that is necessary to preserve and convey the meaning of the passage should be given.

Sufficient indication should be given of the source of the reference or quoted materials. The description of the source should be specific enough to allow someone to verify the reference that is offered as evidence.

d *Probable Accuracy.* One's estimation of an expert opinion should be in proportion to its probably accuracy. Hence, the amount of weight to give an expert opinion should be determined by the answers to the following questions: (i) How reliable is the expert, that is, how consistently has his or her judgment been sound? Does the expert have a good "batting average"? (ii) How much confirming evidence is there for the opinion? (iii) To what extent do other experts in the same area of specialization and of equal eminence agree with the opinion in question? Is there a consensus of experts? (iv) How "up to date" is the expert opinion? Has it been repudiated? In other words, the probably accuracy of an expert opinion is a function of (i) Reliability of the expert, (ii) Confirming evidence, (iii) Consensus of experts, and (iv) Recency.

34B4 Illicit Appeals to Expert Authority.[7] We have given four principal criteria for evaluating the extent to which an appeal to expert opinion is legitimate. If any one of these criteria is not met, then the appeal is illicit. The classification of these illicit appeals, as related to the above criteria, follows:

CRITERIA FOR ACCEPTANCE OF EXPERT OPINION	ILLICIT APPEALS TO EXPERT AUTHORITY
a Relevant Knowledge	**a** Appeal to Irrelevant Knowledge
(i) Relevant Opinion	(i) Irrelevant Opinion
(ii) Relevant Authority	(ii) Transferred Authority
(iii) Expert Authority	(iii) Pseudoexpert Authority
b Objectivity	**b** Appeal to Biased Opinion
c Faithful Transmission	**c** Defective Transmission
(i) Accurate Quotation	(i) Misquotation
(ii) In Context	(ii) Out of Context
d Probable Accuracy	**d** Overestimated Authority
(i) Reliability of Expert	(i) Unreliable Authority
(ii) Confirming Evidence	(ii) Unconfirmed Authority
(iii) Consensus of Experts	(iii) Disputed Authority
(iv) Recency	(iv) Repudiated Authority

a *Appeal to Irrelevant Knowledge.*

(i) If the opinion appealed to is not relevant to the question at hand, then, there being no logical connection between the premisses (the opinion) and the conclusion, a non sequitur results. This may be called the fallacy of *irrelevant opinion*.

(ii) The opinion of an expert, even though it may be relevant, is not always an expert opinion, since his opinion may be in an area outside of his specialization. The error of *transferred authority* consists of taking an expert's opinion as good evidence when in fact it is not because his area of specialization is irrelevant to the question at hand.[8] An obvious example of this fallacy would be accepting as expert evidence the political opinion of a man because he is an expert mathematician.

(iii) The error of *pseudoexpert authority* occurs when non-expert authority is offered as reason for accepting an opinion as evidence. There are three common ways in which this fallacy occurs:

The first common mistake is mistaking a non-expert for an expert. This mistake may occur for a variety of reasons, such as being easily impressed by another's knowledge or being deceived by an imposter or a fraud. In such cases it is common for the alleged expert to be neither an expert nor an institutional authority.

The second common mistake is confusing institutional authority with expert authority. It is common to mistake the authority of institutions (legal, political, or customary) for the authority of experts. An example of this confusion is the appeal to tradition as expert authority. Bentham called this the appeal to the "Wisdom of our Ancestors" and refuted it be pointing out that it is an appeal to the wisdom of the cradle of the nation, that is, to inexperience.

The third common mistake is an appeal to absolute authority, or to privileged knowledge. This form of pseudoexpert authority occurs when persons (or an institution) claim that an opinion (their own or another's) is good evidence on the grounds that the originator of the opinion occupies a privileged cognitive position that gives the person a means of knowing things unverifiable and unobtainable by others not sharing this unique position.

An absolute authority will not produce any kind of good evidence for its opinion, and indeed it cannot do so without losing the absolute status of its privileged position. Thus the **paradox of absolute authority:** If the absolute authority does not give good evidence for his opinions, then there are no rational grounds for accepting them; but if the authority does appeal to public evidence (rational or empirical), then he has surrendered his claim to privileged knowledge and has abandoned the absoluteness of his authority.

Appeal to absolute authority is found in mystics who claim that they and they alone have the truth. Mystics generally agree that this truth cannot be communicated, expressed, or confirmed outside of the mystical experience. Also those whose moral decisions are justified solely by the dictates of their conscience are appealing to an absolute authority. To argue that an act is right or wrong simply because one's conscience feels it is right or wrong is to make one's conscience an absolute authority. Such an argument will have no persuasive force for a rational person.

b *Appeal to Biased Opinion.* This fallacy occurs when an opinion offered as evidence can justifiably be suspected of bias. For example, if a psychiatrist accused of murder testified that he was not mentally responsible for his crime, this testimony would not be accepted as expert opinion in a court of law. Also the testimony of lawyers on legal reform may well be suspected of bias due to their professional interest. Bentham calls such a bias "sinister interest"; but this term seems too strong to be always appropriate.

c *Defective Transmission.* It is illicit to appeal to an opinion as evidence when its meaning has changed during its transmission by being altered or quoted out of context; or when the source of the opinion is not given, or given so vaguely that it cannot be located.

(i) *Misquotation.* This error occurs when the sense of a person's opinion is changed by paraphrasing, changing punctuation, or adding words, and this opinion, still attributed to its originator, is offered as evidence.

(ii) *Out of Context.*

The error of "quotation out of context" is like the above, except that the meaning of the opinion is changed by quoting out of context. For example, suppose a critic wrote the following:

> *The Saturday evening performance of "Angels in the Dark" was as exciting as it was unusual. It was unusually bad in both acting and directing, and there was plenty of excitement when the leading man was twice hit in the second act by falling scenery.*

If only the first sentence was quoted, the sense of his opinion would be radically changed.

The context may be a physical situation as well as a linguistic one. For example, if a person tried to establish that Mr. Smith hated Mr. Brown by quoting Smith as saying to Brown, "I'll murder you!", he would be quoting out of context if he failed to mention that this "threat" was uttered at the beginning of a checker game.

The second type of "out of context" errors is "source not indicated". This defect occurs when the reference for a quotation offered as expert opinion is omitted. For quotation from printed material the standard referenceinformation should be given: author, title, publisher or place of publication, date, and page number.

The third error is "empty authority". The appeal to empty authority occurs when a person gives a reference as evidence, but the reference is not a direct quotation and indicates its source in such vague terms that it seems likely that the person giving the reference had no definite source in mind. Empty authority is an extreme case of "source not indicated". Examples of this fallacy are:

> *They say there will be a depression in five years; therefore it will be unwise to invest in real estate.*
>
> *High officials predict a drastic increase in unemployment; hence, we may expect more union activity in the future.*

Other expressions that appeal to empty authority are:

> *Famous Americans have said . . .*
> *Sound morals demand . . .*
> *All decent people agree . . .*
> *Housewives say . . .*
> *People say . . .*
> *Doctors recommend . . .*
> *The experts hold . . .*
> *Everyone knows . . .*
> *The American way of life requires . . .*
> *Government officials agree . . .*

d *Overestimated Authority.* An authority, even if reasonably regarded as an expert, is overestimated when greater confidence is placed in the authority's opinion than is justified. We distinguish four ways—not necessarily independent—in which overestimation may occur.

(i) *Unreliable authority.* An authority's opinion should be weighted, if possible, by the reliability of his judgment, as measured by his success or failure in previous judgments. One would like to know, so to speak, his "batting average". If he can predict no better than a layperson, why consult him? Unfortunately, it is usually difficult for the layperson to obtain accurate information on this matter. For example, a layperson's opinion of a physician he had consulted a few times is "better than nothing", but on the average not much better, and may be completely mistaken. Another physician or medical professional may, however, be able to make a fairly good estimate.

In some areas, inquiry indicates that most of the experts are not very reliable in their judgments on important but difficult questions. We have found this to be the case, for example, in reviewing the opinions of the leading American military experts in the period from the eve of the second World War through the Vietnamese war on such questions as the probable success of American or other forces in a certain operation or in a war as a whole. It seems to us these experts do not look much better on the whole than the French experts who relied on the Maginot line to protect them from German invasion. In contrast, those U.S. Army officers who warned against getting drawn into a land war on the Asiatic continent seem very wise.

The diagnosis and treatment of mental illness is another area where evidence indicates that the reliability of some types of expert opinion is not very high. Some famous experiments in the 1970s, for example, showed that the examiners of persons entering the mental institutions of California were easily deceived, and avoided any later contact with the patients that might have undeceived them.

The authors of this book do not claim to be military or psychiatric experts; and any reader who accepts our undocumented statements on such matters as authoritative has missed the main point of this chapter. We could claim to be experts of a sort on logic textbooks, and could more easily show that logic books usually contain mistakes, logical and non-logical, if we wished to document the limitations of experts. Our intention is to plant a healthy seed of doubt in the minds of our readers. We hope they will be duly on guard, and that some will make their own inquiries in areas that interest them as occasion arises.

(ii) *Unconfirmed authority.* It is always desirable to have evidence confirming the opinion presented by an authority in a given situation, or intelligible arguments supporting the opinion. Where authorities conflict, or the status and reliability of the authority is uncertain, it is especially important that confirmation be available. It is a bad sign if an authority cannot present evidence or reasons for his opinion when asked to do so, and still worse if available evidence points in a different direction.

(iii) *Disrupted authority.* It adds weight to the opinion of an authority if another authority in the field holds the same view, especially if arrived at independently. But if a second authority disagrees with the first, we must weigh one authority against the other, possibly leaving the net weight of authority at zero.

In practical matters (such as whether a certain person is insane), one has to accept the preponderant weight of expert authority. But on theoretical questions, one can scarcely rest content with less than a consensus of experts. The expert, however, and even the novice, may make a tentative judgment on the basis of the preponderance of evidence.

In the physical sciences, one expects to find a consensus of experts in most cases, though there are always disputed frontiers of knowledge. In psychology and the social sciences (such as sociology and anthropology), one does not expect to find a general consensus in the more complicated questions.

Philosophy is something else again. In history of philosophy and in logic, there are wide areas of consensus, though there remain matters of interpretation of certain philosophers, philosophy of logic, and so on, where no definite consensus can be found. In metaphysics, epistemology, ethics, esthetics, and philosophy of religion, diversity of disagreement flourish, with little if any general agreement on methods, criteria of judgment, or results. Within a given philosophic school, such as scholasticism, Anglo-American analytic philosophy, existentialism, and so on, one may find a consensus on some points, but also a wide range of differences on matters of great importance.

If there is no consensus of experts on a certain matter, there may be the alternative of selecting or weighting authorities on the basis of level of expertise—reliability, objectivity, and so on. Such selection almost necessarily presupposes some degree of expertise on the part of the selector. In the absence of a consensus of experts or a justifiable selection, the appeal to authority is of little value except for a person who happens to accept the authority cited. In other words, the appeal to authority in such cases carries weight only to the extent that it is also an appeal to certain beliefs of the person addressed—a special form of argument *ad hominem* in the Lockean sense (33C1).

(iv) *Repudiated authority.* An appeal to repudiated authority occurs when an appeal is made to an opinion that has been repudiated by the very authority appealed to, or in more recent statements by authorities of equal eminence in the same field. In rapidly changing fields—as most of the sciences are at present—it is necessary to make certain that the expert opinions cited are up to date. This is not to say that the most recent opinion is necessarily the most accurate, but it is to say that in many areas of knowledge one is either "up to date" or "out of date". In any case, an appeal to expert opinion should indicate the date of the source, and should not be accepted without such indication.

This concludes our discussion of overestimated authority, the last of the four main types of illicit appeals to expert authority that we have distinguished.

34C APPEAL TO IGNORANCE (*ARGUMENTUM AD IGNORANTIAM*)

The term *argumentum ad ignorantiam* was introduced by John Locke in his *Essay Concerning Human Understanding*. This is sometimes called "appeal to ignorance", but is better called "argument from ignorance", (since it is not primarily an appeal to a feeling or state of mind, as are "appeal to pity" and *"argumentum ad verecundiam"*—i.e., "appeal to reverence for authority"). Locke writes:

> Another way that men ordinarily use to drive others, and force them to submit their judgments, and receive the opinion in debate, is to require the adversary to admit what they allege as a proof, or to assign a better. And this I call *argumentum ad ignorantiam*. . . . It proves not a man to be in the right way, nor that I ought to take the same with him, because I know not a better. . . . I may be ignorant and not be able to produce a better. . . .[9]

In the first sentence quoted, by requiring the adversary "to assign a better", he must mean to require him to produce a better proof to the contrary. In a note to this passage, Fraser quotes Locke's example of argument *ad ignorantiam* in his *Examination of Malebranche*. Locke says that Malebranche, having showed the difficulties of other ways of explaining our ideas, "treats this of 'seeing all things in God' on that account as the true, *because it is impossible to find a better*" P. (411n).

In the *Essay*, Locke presents the argument *ad ignorantiam* as a device of eristics, the art of controversy, in which the proponent of a thesis tries to "drive" an opponent by an argument to this effect:

(a) "You must accept my argument for my thesis, unless you can find a better argument to the contrary".

The argument would be a little less vulnerable if it demanded a little less of the opponent, thus:

(a') "You must accept my argument for my thesis, unless you can find an *equally good* argument to the contrary".

In the Malebranche example, Locke puts the *ad ignoratiam* argument in the form of a stronger, categorical claim:

(b) "You must accept as true my thesis explaining this matter, *because*, as I have shown, *it is impossible to find a better*".

However, one is likely to infer erroneously, from the fact that a better way has not as yet been found, that it is impossible to find a better way.

For an argument of form (a) to "drive" anyone with logical force, one of the two following conditions must be satisfied: (i) There is a presumption in favor of the proponent's thesis, or a burden of proof on the other side, that can only be overcome by *stronger* evidence to the contrary (Cf. Leibniz, *New Essays Concerning Human Understanding*); (ii) There is a practical necessity for an immediate choice one way or the other.

The first condition will be illustrated later. The second would be illustrated by someone who says, during wartime, "I think those are enemy bombers approaching; so, unless you are sure they're not, we had better get into the shelter". This would generally be a reasonable argument (though under special circumstances there might be a stronger argument to the contrary).

As sufficient condition for an argument of form (a') to be a legitimate appeal, we may add to the two conditions above a third: (iii) There is a certain level of support (probability, confirmation, or the like) such that, if a thesis in question attains it, it is reasonable to hold it, and unreasonable to reject it except for a thesis as good or better; and this level has in fact been reached for the thesis in question.

In science, there is generally considered to be a presumption in favor of a scientific theory that is supported by good evidence and sound reasoning, and has come to be accepted by a consensus of expert opinion. For example, the theory that living creatures have evolved has attained this status among European and American biologists. It satisfies condition (i) above, hence justifying an argument of form (a), to the effect that an opponent of biological evolution must present better evidence or arguments against evolution than are to be found in the literature in order to receive serious attention from scientists. On the other hand, many theories as to specific factors involved (such as mutations) and their relative importance have not attained such a strong consensus, and are at the level of condition (iii) or lower.

In law, there is a *presumption of innocence* or a person accused of a crime, and a burden of proof on the prosecution to show guilt, not merely with probability, but "beyond reasonable doubt". This presumption is not based on such a doubtful principle as that an accused person is more likely to be innocent than guilty. It is based rather on a political-ethical principle, that it is less unjust to acquit many guilty persons than to condemn one innocent person. The presumption of innocence justifies a form of argument *ad ignorantiam:* the defendant's plea of "not guilty" must become the verdict if it is not proven beyond reasonable doubt that he is guilty of the crime that is charged. As an American law dictionary reports,

> It is not sufficient to establish a probability, though a strong one, . . . that the fact charged is more likely to be true than the contrary; but the evidence must establish the truth of the fact to a reasonable and moral certainty,—a certainty that convinces and directs the understanding and satisfies the reason and judgment of those who are bound to act conscientiously upon it. This is proof beyond reasonable doubt. . . .[10]

But *absolute* certainty is not required; it is not necessary—and indeed scarcely conceivable—that the occurrence of certain events in the past follows with deductive certainty from the occurrence of certain other events at a later date in the courtroom.

34D APPEAL TO PITY (*ARGUMENTUM AD MISERICORDIAM*)

Some modern textbooks speak of the *argumentum ad misericordiam*—appeal to pity (or appeal for mercy). As a fallacy, this is usually classed as *ignoratio elenchi* or fallacy of relevance. An appeal to pity is of course often simply a request without any argument intended, in which case there can be no fallacy, strictly speaking. Simply as a request, an appeal may or may not be justified, but that is not a question of logic. However, as part of an argument, an appeal to pity may be properly judged as relevant or irrelevant to the question at hand.

Important examples of appeal to pity are found in criminal trials. Insofar as the question is whether the defendant is guilty as charged, an appeal to pity is legally and logically irrelevant, and may be called an illicit appeal.[11] But belief that strict application of the law would result in excessive harshness or other injustice in the given case is likely to influence the juror's judgment on the verdict, and it is not clear that this is necessarily unreasonable. From the legal point of view, however, appeal to mercy is generally relevant only with regard to the sentence passed if the defendant is found guilty.

34E APPEAL TO FORCE (*ARGUMENTUM AD BACULUM*)

A British logician included under the heading "*Ignoratio Elenchi* or *Irrelevant Argument*" the following:

Argumentum ad baculum consists in using the big stick against an opponent, or putting the pistol to his head, instead of reasoning with him. This kind of "argument" is greatly favoured by dictators and gangsters.[12]

The word *"argumentum"* or "argument" is evidently being used ironically here. *"Baculum"* is Latin for "stick"; this is being used as a figure of speech—one kind of synecdoche—consisting of putting species for genus. The Latin name is rendered "appeal to force", meaning originally "use or threat of physical force". This is illustrated by the robber's ultimatum: "Your money or your life". There is no argument and hence no fallacy. It is clearly an illicit appeal from a legal or ethical point of view. But note that the robber, if he had the time and talent, might have expressed his message as a valid argument, with premisses doubtless true and accepted (reluctantly) by his victim; for example, thus: "If you wish to live, you will give me your money. You wish to live; so you will give me your money". This is practically, legally, and ethically equivalent to the short ultimatum; but, in most cases, would be a sound argument. The moral may be drawn, if one wishes, that one cannot live by logic alone.

The scope of the appeal to force is often extended to economic or political force. For example: "If you sell those grapes, we'll boycott your store"; "If you don't support this bill, we'll campaign against you in the next election". In such cases, there is more chance that the appeal to force may occur in the context of a genuine argument intended to produce belief. We see no objection to this extension of the term "appeal to force".[13] (The term *"ad baculum"* would seems less appropriate here—unless one thinks of a stick carrying a placard.) The legitimacy of these appeals is not a logical question.

* * * * * *

Many other appeals—illicit or likely to be illicit—are named in the literature. Hamblin's *Fallacies* (41) lists twenty-four Latin tags with *ad* he has found (including one for each of the five principal appeals of this chapter). The most widely used and misused label is *"argumentum ad hominem"*, to which we have referred in chapters 31, 33, and 34A. Since we make no claim to completeness here, we may be excused from dealing with any of the others.

Appendix to Chapter 34A4

34A4 A BRIEF HISTORY OF *ARGUMENTUM AD HOMINEM*

The history of the expression "argument *ad hominem*" (or *"argumentum ad hominem"*) shows that it has been used in three senses. It has been used to mean:

(i) An argument against one's opponent based on his own principles and concessions.

(ii) Charging one's opponent with inconsistency between his current views upon which his argument is based and his previous views or conduct, with the implication that this inconsistency weakens his argument.

(iii) Charging one's opponent with a personal defect, with the implication that if he as a person is defective, then so is his argument.

Sense (i) of argument *ad hominem* "to press a man with consequences drawn from his own principles and concessions", is quoted from Locke's *Essay Concerning Human Understanding*. This is the earliest definition of this term we have found, although Locke says it is already known by this name. Leibniz follows this definition in his *New Essays Concerning Understanding* and an equivalent definition is current in the Italian *Encyclopedia Filesofica* (Venice & Rome, 1957). In this sense specifically, it is also called argument *ex consessis* (from concessions).

In Schopenhauer's *Art of Controversy* and Whatley's *Elements of Logic*, the argument *as hominem* has been extended to senses (ii) and (iii), that is, it covers the inferred as well as the avowed views of the opponent, but it is still an appeal to the man.

Since the *ad hominem* usually points out an inconsistency between the present views of a man and his previous views or conduct, it is easy to think that, in an argument labeled *ad hominem*, the point is to bring a *charge of inconsistency* against the man, or to recriminate, as in a *tu quoque* argument (*you too* do that for which you blame others for doing). Such a shift can be found in De Morgan's chapter on fallacies, which comments on Whatley. Finally confusion reigned. In current logic books in English, the great majority have switched the meaning of argument *ad hominem* to sense (iii): a charge of personal defect. Max Black is an honorable exception.

We hold that extension from senses (i) to (ii) is acceptable, leaving the argument an appeal to the man; but the switch to sense (iii) has brought confusion and should be abandoned.

Exercises for Chapter 34

EX 34A. Identify the following appeals to adverse personality by placing the appropriate letter from the key in each blank.

KEY

a. Charges of Inconsistency
b. Charges of Bad Motive
c. Charges of Personal Defect
d. Charges of Bad Design
e. Changes of Suspicious Connection
f. Charges of Similar Defect
g. Sterotyped Charges

_____ 1. My professor has a surly personality, his clothes are always rumpled and disarranyed; consequently, I do not believe what he says in his lecturers and never take notes in his classes.

_____ 2. You must be a hypocrite. Here you are an officer in the Army advocating the immorality and wastefulness of war.

_____ 3. I don't care what evidence he can produce to clear himself, former President Nixon must have been involved in the Watergate Affair since so many of his key advisors were involved in Watergate.

_____ 4. I don't care if you are his best friend, your testimony is worthless. He's a jazz musician so he must smoke pot.

_____ 5. In reply to the gentleman's arguments, I need only say that two years ago he advocated the very measure that he now opposes. (Creighton)

_____ 6. Friedrich Nietzsch's philosophical theories are not to be taken seriously, since he died insane, probably of syphilis.

_____ 7. Senator, your argument against the Vietnam war is inconsistent with the position you held six years ago on this subject; therefore, I dismiss your entire argument.

_____ 8. His father and both of his brothers were found guilty of smuggling, so he must be guilty also, even though he gave strong evidence in his own defense.

_____ 9. You argue that your girlfriend is not sexually promiscuous, but of course you are wrong. She is an actress and everyone knows how promiscuous they are.

_____ 10. It's not true that I'm an academically poor student, since you've failed more tests than I have.

_____ 11. This man's character is no good, his manners are no good, his parents were no good, and the section of the town where he lives is no good; therefore, his defense against the crime that he is accused of is no good.

_____ 12. Senator Whatfield's argument for farm subsidies are without value. After all, he owns a farm of several thousand acres and his whole family is engaged extensively in farming operations.

_____ 13. As a Jew who has had many relatives killed by the Nazis it is understandable why you argue that Hitler and many of his followers were mad. But, regardless of the strength of your argument, you must admit that you are personally involved and hence you can understand why I reject your argument.

_____ 14. Do not vote for Senator White's bill, because if it passes he will introduce another bill, which if it passes will harm the economy of this country.

_____ 15. What do you mean I drink a lot! It's true that I drink a quart of whiskey a day, but you drink half again as much, so you should talk.

_____ 16. I do not think that you should agree with this man's opinions, even though I have to admit that they make sense, because I believe that his man will try to get you to agree with other opinions that he has, which I think are perverted and evil.

_____ 17. They say "Birds of a feather flock together"; therefore, since two of his friends were arrested for the possession, he must be involved in drugs too, regardless of what he says.

_____ 18. Your argument for your son's innocence may justly be dismissed, since, as his father, you would naturally be prejudiced in his favor.

_____ 19. Last year you argued for the opposite position to the one you are now defending. Both positions cannot be true, since they are contradictions. Hence, I cannot accept your present position, regardless of what arguments you give to support it.

_____ 20. What do you mean he can't sing? Of course he can, since all Italians can sing.

Ex 34B, I. By placing the appropriate letter in each blank, indicate which of the four criteria for expert opinion each of the following fallacies is most likely to violatle.

Criteria for Expert Opinion

a. Relevant knowledge
b. Impartiality (Objectivity)
c. Faithfulness of transmission
d. Consensus of experts

_____ 1. Appeal to absolute authority.

_____ 2. Empty authority.

_____ 3. Mistaking a non-expert for an expert.

_____ 4. Pseudoexpert authority.

_____ 5. Quotation out of context.

_____ 6. Transferred authority.

_____ 7. Appeal to biased opinion.

_____ 8. Repudiated authority.

_____ 9. Appeal to tradition.

_____ 10. Confusing institutional authority with expert authority.

EX 34B, II. Identify the following fallacies to authority by placing the appropriate letter from the key in each blank.

KEY

a. Irrelevant Opinion
b. Transferred Authority
c. Pseudoexpert Authority
d. Appeal to Biased Opinion
e. Appeal to Absolute Authority
f. Misquoted Text
g. Quotation out of Context
h. Empty Authority
i. Appeal to Repudiated Authority
j. Appeal to Tradition

_____ 1. The manufacturers of white sugar claim that those who say that white sugar is harmful do not know what they are talking about. I think that it is reasonable to accept their opinion, since they must be experts on white sugar. After all they manufacturer it.

Exercises/Chapter 34   485

_____ 2. General Zilch of the U.S. Army, an acknowledged expert of the role of calvary in combat stated that man will never reach the planet Mars. Since General Zilch is an expert, his opinion may be accepted as that of an authority.

_____ 3. Senator Plushbotton, an expert on the social affect of television and a holder of fifty thousand shares of television stock, in the XYZ Network, has stated that the XYZ Network should be granted a new franchise. We should accept his opinion as he is an expert on these matters.

_____ 4. Admiral Seanut of the U.S. Navy is an expert on eighteenth-century naval tactics; therefore, if he says that the Navy needs three billion more dollars for the construction of nuclear submarines we should accept his opinion as that of an expert.

_____ 5. War is justified by the Bible, for the golden rule states: *Do others in before they do you in.*

_____ 6. Original statement of critic: "This play wins first prize for bad acting and directing". When stated in the newspaper it read, "This play wins first prize . . . ."

_____ 7. Of course the Chinese hate Americans. Everyone knows that.

_____ 8. It's true that many scientists believe that atoms contain smaller particles. But I do not believe that this is so, since Lucretius, who was undoubtedly an expert on the atomic theory of matter, wrote that atoms are indivisible.

_____ 9. Former President Nixon has stated that he had no knowledge of the Watergate Affair. Since he was in a position to know we can believe him.

_____ 10. A policeman has more authority than the average citizen; hence, we should regard any policeman as an authority when he states his theories about the cure and causes of crime.

_____ 11. Our country's space program is immoral. After all, didn't Washington favor isolationism?

_____ 12. Hamlet must have believed in Zen for in his famous soliloquy he said: "To be and not to be. There is no question".

_____ 13. For thousands of years women stayed at home and raised the children while their men have provided them with food, shelter, and protection. Therefore, this arrangement should continue, since long-standing tradition should not be violated.

_____ 14. Of course a heavier object will fall faster than a light one (even in a vacuum), since this was reported by Aristotle, who was an expert on physics.

_____ 15. "No, I don't have to give you any reasons for why I believe that the Vietnam War was immoral. It is sufficient that my conscience tells me it was so".

_____ 16. A well-known expert in economics has recently stated that inflation in America will not be a serious problem next year. This is good news, since an expert should know what he is talking about in his own field.

_____ 17. George Washington was an expert on political matters and if he advised that the United States should follow an isolantionist policy, then that is what we should do today.

_____ 18. It was Einstein's opinion that explanatory constructs in science should not be limited to observable entities; therefore Einstein believed that God created the universe.

_____ 19. A person close to the president stated yesterday that the president has a serious heart condition. Such a source cannot be easily doubted, so we may assume that the president is not a well man.

_____ 20. One of the Ten Commandments is "Thou shall commit adultery". This is conclusive evidence that the Bible supports immoral activities.

EX 34C–34D. Identify the following fallacies by placing the appropriate letter from the key in each blank.

KEY

a. Appeal to Ignorance
b. Appeal to Pity
c. Appeal to Force

_____ 1. If you cannot prove an argument form invalid by the use of a logical analogy, then it must be valid.

_____ 2. I would like your company to publically endorse my political candidate. Of course, it's up to you, but I would like you to remember that I own enough stock in your company so that I could make it very difficult for you to retain your seat on the board.

_____ 3. Professor, I deserve an "A" in your course, instead of the "F" you gave me, since I need an "A" to bring my quality point average up, otherwise I will not graduate. If I don't graduate I won't be able to get the job I need to support my new wife.

_____ 4. Kant held that all the proofs for the existence of God were fallacious. He was therefore an atheist. (Jones)

_____ 5. Surely you see that this labor bill represents a poor policy, Mr. Senator. You bear in mind that my organization and its friends can swing a lot of votes in your state.

_____ 6. The defendant is a weak, helpless, woman. She has buried her three children and now her husband is dead. She is alone in the world without either friend or fortune. Therefore, members of the jury, I ask you to find her innocent.

_____ 7. Of course there is a God. Why I would be miserable if there wasn't.

_____ 8. You cannot prove that any other candidate will make a better president of the United States than mine, hence you should admit that my candidate is the best man for the office.

_____ 9. I don't care how many fallacies I've committed. If you don't accept my argument as valid, I'll punch you in the nose.

_____ 10. Mr. Brown must be an innocent man. He was tried for his crime before a jury of his peers and the prosecution was unable to prove him guilty.

VI

Transition to Symbolic Logic

35

From Aristotelian to Symbolic Logic[1]

35A THE ANCIENTS (TO THE SIXTH CENTURY A.D.)

35A1 The Peripatetics (The School of Philosophy Founded by Aristotle at the Lyceum in Ancient Athens).

a *Aristotle.* The greatest name in the history of logic (as well as in philosophy) is Aristotle (384–322 B.C.), who is regarded as the creator of formal logic.

Aristotle constructed the first axiomatic system of term logic (the syllogistic). He also developed, in term logic, a theory of modality. He did not formulate the propositional logic into a system, though he was aware of some of the argument forms and laws of propositional logic.

Bochenski says:

> For the first time in history we find in him [Aristotle]: (a) a clear idea of universally valid logical law, though he never gave a definition to it, (b) the use of variables, (c) sentential forms which besides variables contain only logical constants.[2]

Aristotle's logical treatises, six in number—*Categories, De Interpretatione, Prior Analytics, Posterori Analytics, Topics, On Sophistical Refutations*—are collectively called the *Organon* (the instrument).

b *Theophrastus.* Theophrastus, Aristotle's successor as the head of the Lyceum, made the following contributions to logic: (1) He added five valid moods to the first figure of the syllogism (Aristotle had only three figures and there is some ambiguity as to what he meant by "figure"). Later these five moods were placed under the fourth figure ("figure" now being defined by the position of the middle term in the syllogism). (2) Theophrastus made several significant contributions to the theory of modality. For example, he stated that the conclusion of a modal syllogism must have the same mode as the weaker mode of the two premisses. (3) Finally, Theophrastus developed various forms of the hypothetical syllogism.

35A2 Megarians—Stoic. The Megarians (or "dialectical") school was founded by Euclid of Megara (ca. 400 B.C.), a pupil of Socrates. Zeno of Citum (ca. 300 B.C.), a pupil of Stilpo (a Megarian), was the founder of Stoicism.

The Megarians contributed to logic by their interest in paradoxes, their formulation of theories of modality, and their interest in the analysis of the nature of hypothetical propositions.

Two examples of Megarian paradoxes, both attributed to Eubulides, are:

The Liar: A man says, "I am lying". Is this statement true or false?

The Bald Man or *The Heap:* Is a man with one hair bald? Yes. Is a man with two hairs bald? Yes. Is a man . . . , etc. Then how many hairs must a man have before he is not bald? Where do you draw the line?

These paradoxes were more than mere "party puzzlers" to the Megarians and the Stoics. In attempting to solve them, sophisticated logical distinctions had to be made. A considerable amount of effort was devoted to the analysis of The Liar. Chrysippus, the greatest Stoic logician (second only to Aristotle),[3] is alleged to have written as many as twenty-eight books on the subject.

The Megarians tried to develop a theory of modality in which modes are empirically defined. For example, Diodorus Cronus gave the following definitions (or definitions similar to the following):[4]

1. A proposition p is (now) possible if and only if p is now true or will be true at some future time.

2. A proposition p is (now) impossible if and only if p is not true and never will be true.

3. A proposition p is (now) necessary if and only if p is true and always will be true.

4. A proposition p is (now) not necessary if and only if p is not true or will not be true at some future time.

The debate on the nature of hypothetical statements is supposed to have originated between Diodorus and his student Philo. Philo defined the "hypothetical proposition" as a material implication. Three other popular views were given; one of them defining "true hypotheticals" as strict implication.[5]

The Stoics had a well developed theory of meaning (semantics). They clearly distinguished between use and mention; and between the sentence and its meaning. They also gave an account of natural signs.

The Stoics were interested in compound propositions; conjunctions, disjunctions, and hypotheticals. They developed a system of rules for evaluating hypothetical and disjunctive syllogisms and attempted to axiomatize the propositional logic. This was their greatest achievement.

Bochenski says, "Without exaggeration one can say that the achievements of this period make up antiquity's second basic contribution to formal logic".[6]

35A3 Late Antiquity (Post-Chrysippian to Boethius). After the death of Chrysippus no original contributions to logic were made until the twelfth century A.D., a span of one thousand years. The logicians of late antiquity did little more than systematize and improve (in minor ways) Aristotelian and Stoic logic.

Alexander of Aphrodisias (third century A.D.), a commentator on Aristotelian logic, was one of the best logicians of this period. His major contributions were to make explicit the distinction between the form and matter of arguments and recognized, clearer than his predecessors, the function of variables.

Porphyry of Tyre (third century A.D.), discoverer of the famed "Tree of Porphyry", gave a list of predicables that differed from Aristotle's. Porphyry's major contribution was an extensional view of terms and the recognition of the difference between extension and intension.

Boethius (ca. 480–524 A.D.), though not a great logician, exerted a considerable influence on the scholastics. He gave an explicit and accurate definition of "logical sum", made use of the principle of double negation, and attempted to formulate a rule of substitution for propositional variables. Boethius developed the hypothetical syllogism based on Stoic logic.

35B MEDIEVAL LOGIC (SEVENTH TO FIFTEENTH CENTURIES)

The first logician of note in medieval logic is Peter Abelard. The period from Boethius to Abelard contained no logicians of originality.

Peter Abelard (1079–1142 A.D.) started many of the topics of Medieval logic. His work *Sic et Non* originated the style of argumentation used by the scholastics; a question is stated, all the arguments pro and con are presented, then the distinction and reasoning that resolves the issue are set forth. Abelard also contributed to semantics and the philosophy of logic.

The high point of medieval logic came in the fourteenth century with William of Ockham and his followers, commonly called "nominalists". They were expert technicians, but it is their attempt to explain the universal in terms of the particular that makes their thought appear "modern".

William of Ockham (d. 1349/1350), widely noted for his maxim called "Ockham's razor" (assumptions introduced to explain a thing must not be multiplied beyond necessity), wrote the *Summa Totius Logicae*, which was an attempt to encompass all known logic into one system.

The importance of Ockham and his followers is found in their contribution to the theory of *consequentiae*. Pseudo-Scotus defined "consequence" as:

> a hypothetical proposition composed of an antecedent and consequent by means of a conditional connective or one expressing a reason *(rationalis)* which signifies that if they, viz. the antecedent and consequent, are formed simultaneously, it is impossible that the antecedent be true and the consequent false.[7]

Examples of consequences are:

(1) A man runs, therefore an animal runs.

(2) Socrates exists and Socrates does not exist; therefore Socrates does not exist.

(3) Only a man is an ass, so every ass is a man.

Ockham made a distinction between formal and material consequences that seems to be analogous to the distinction between formal and material implication made by Russell and Whitehead.

In his last chapter on the subject of consequences Ockham gives eleven general rules:[8]

(1) The false never follows from the true.

(2) The true may follow from the false.

(3) If a consequence is valid, the negative of its antecedent follows from the negative of its consequent.

(4) Whatever follows from the consequent follows from the antecedent.

(5) If the antecedent follows from any proposition, the consequent follows from the same.

(6) Whatever is consistent with the antecedent is consistent with the consequent.

(7) Whatever is inconsistent with the antecedent is inconsistent with the consequent.

(8) The contingent does not follow from the necessary.

(9) The impossible does not follow from the possible.

(10) Anything whatsoever follows from the impossible.

(11) The necessary follows from anything whatsoever.

In the fifteenth century, the medievalist's interest in consequences reopened the old debate, started by the Megarians, concerning the meaning of hypothetical propositions (implication).

35C MODERN LOGIC

The philosopher and mathematician Leibniz was a forerunner of modern logic. Leibniz conceived the idea of symbolic logic, a calculus *ratiocinator* (calculus of reasoning), and described its purpose and function. He failed in his attempt to formulate such a system and his influence on succeeding logicians was negligible. Because his logical writings were mostly fragmentary and unpublished, symbolic logic did not develop continuously from his efforts.

The period of modern logic begins in 1847 with the publication of *The Mathematical Analysis of Logic* by George Boole. Boole formulated the first successful algebra of classes and recognized the possibility of a pure calculus that could be given various interpretations. The work begun by Boole was advanced by W. S. Jevons, J. Venn, and E. Schroder.

Augustus De Morgan published a paper in 1859 in which he stated his belief that the syllogism represented only a special case of the logic of relations. The work on the logic of relations was further developed by Charles Sanders Peirce. Peirce was an original thinker and even constructed the beginnings of what we now call "set theory". Unfortunately, he seldom completed the projects he initiated and his work in his own time was not well known.

The German mathematician Gottlob Frege (1848–1925) contributed more to modern logic than any other man. A few of his many contributions are:[9]

(1) Axiomatized the logic of propositions.

(2) Formulated an explicit distinction between constants and variables.

(3) Originated the theory of description.

(4) Made explicit the distinction between rules and laws.

(5) Made explicit the distinction between language and metalanguage.

(6) Developed the predicate calculus.

(7) Made a notable attempt to reduce mathematics to logic.

Bochenski says of Frege, "Various other mathematical logicians at the same time, or even earlier, expounded similar ideas and theories, none of them had the gift of presenting all at once so many, often quite original, innovations in so perfect a form".[10]

Frege's work was continued in the three-volume *Principia Mathematica* (1910–1913) of Alfred Whitehead and Bertrand Russell. Since the publication of the *Principia*, there has been a number of noteworthy logicians: Hilbert, Skolem, Lowenheim, Carnap, and Tarski.

We shall end this brief account of the history of logic by mentioning Kurt Godel, who shook the logical world with his proof (1931) that the attempt to reduce all mathematics to a single axiomatic system was impossible.

Notes

CHAPTER 1

1. Our definition is in the tradition of medieval use of "*propositio*" and of logical use of "proposition" down to the twentieth century. Most contemporary logicians have in mind rather some such definition as: "A *proposition* is the meaning of a declarative sentence." This majority includes some (like Benson Mates in *Elementary Logic*, 1965) who reject or avoid the use of "proposition" in this sense, and speak of sentences or "statements" instead. It also includes some who, after defining a proposition as a meaning, speak of "proposition" as if they were composed of words; for example, they may say that "propositions" are affirmative if they begin with the word "all" and negative if they begin with the word "no". (cf. Copi, *Introduction to Logic*, 5th ed., 170). Since "All S are P" and "No S are non-P" are traditionally equivalent, hence express the same "proposition" in this sense, it is hard to see how one can make the traditional distinction between affirmative and negative categorical propositions if "propositions" are simply meanings.

2. "It is entirely contrary to good English usage to spell premiss, 'premise', and this spelling . . . simply betrays ignorance of the history of logic, and even of such standard authors as Whately [sic], Watts, etc." C. S. Peirce, *Collected Papers*, Vol. 11, 146.

Peirce is referring to Richard Whately, whose *Elements of Logic* (1826) was the most influential logic book in English in its day; and to Isaac Watts, *Logic* (1725). The misspelling of "Whately", which might be a mistake of the editors, is unimportant, but Peirce's attack on the spelling of "premise" is hard to explain. The *Oxford English Dictionary* in the article on *Premise, premiss*, quotes Watts's *Logic* as using "premise", and Whately as using "premises." This article has other information that shows that Peirce's conception of the history of this word is quite mistaken. We suggest that Peirce was mislead by such facts as that Watts spelled "premisses" with double "s" and the singular (rarely used) "premise" with one "s".

Peirce's well-deserved reputation as the first great American logician should not mislead us into thinking that in his unpublished writings he was always historically accurate.

3. For defense of the view that arguments may be neither deductive nor inductive, see the section on "Noninductive Reasoning by Analogy" in Stephen F. Barker's *Elements of Logic* (McGraw-Hill, 1965), chapter 7.

4. Some logicians (e.g., S. F. Barker) use "valid" for any good inductive or deductive argument. Others (who we follow) characterize an argument as valid only if its conclusion follows necessarily from its premises. We take this condition to be sufficient; one might require also that the argument be deductive by intention.

Some logicians explicitly or implicitly limit validity to formal validity. As explained in chapter 3, we do not.

Quine and some other symbolic logicians use "valid" to characterize logical truth (a "tautology") and call an argument "sound" if it is valid in our sense.

5. Some logicians accept also the converse of principle *a*, namely, "If it is logically impossible for the premises in an argument to be true without its conclusion being false, then the argument is valid." These logicians define a valid argument such as (6'): "A valid argument is an argument such that it is logically impossible that the premises be true without the conclusion being true." From this would follow the consequence (drawn by Buridan and Albert of Saxony in the fourteenth century) that any argument with inconsistent premises is valid. For example, this would be valid: "Socrates exists, and Socrates does not exist, therefore a stick stands in the corner". Because of this and other paradoxes, we reject definition 6'.

CHAPTER 2

1. We have not given a definition of form words in any strict sense of "definition". The usual way and probably the best way of making precise what are the form words or formal elements of a given logical system is to list them. All concrete words and most abstract expressions as ordinarily used (e.g., "gravity", "spontaneity", "idealism", etc.) must be excluded from the form words, but a decision that is partly arbitrary must be made as to which abstract expressions are included.

2. Logical subject and logical predicate are distinguished from grammatical subject and grammatical predicate in chapter 7. The terms "subject" and "predicate" may be taken in either sense in this chapter if not specified. We assume that the grammatical meaning is already known.

3. We borrow the terms "primary proposition" and "secondary proposition" from W. E. Johnson, *Logic*, Part I (New York: Dover Publications, Inc., 1964), 50–88. He finds it "unnecessary to give a separate definition of a primary proposition" and apparently attaches meaning to this term only relative to "secondary propositions". We prefer to give "primary propositions" an absolute meaning.

4. This defines *explicit* compounds. There are also exponible propositions—that is, propositions that are analyzed as conjunctions of two or more propositions.

These are implicitly compound; for example, "Jack and Bill are logic students". However, a proposition such as "Jack and Bill are cousins" is not exponible.

5. The scholastic dichotomy into categorical and hypothetical is exhaustive and is the same as ours, because then "hypothetical" meant "compound". Kant's threefold division of propositions—into categoricals, hypotheticals, and disjunctives—is not exhaustive because "hypothetical" to him meant "conditional".

6. Illative propositions ("He is human, therefore he is mortal") are dealt with as arguments. A causal proposition: "He cried because he was hurt". A temporal proposition (from Ockham): "When Socrates runs, Plato disputes".

CHAPTER 3

1. *Symbolic Logic* (New York: Dover Publications, Inc., 1958; Reprint of *Symbolic Logic*, Part I: Elementary, 4th Edition, London, 1897), 118. In the original problem the conclusion is to be determined. The argument is valid (but not formally valid as worded; see 3A2, def. 1).

2. Form words are illustrated in 3A3, after def. 4; and defined in chapter 2, def. 2.

3. Defined, 4A, Def. 3.

4. In the fourth edition (1972) of *Introduction to Logic*, Copi introduces the term "*the specific form* of a given argument", defined as "that argument form from which the argument results by replacing each different statement variable by a difference *simple* statement" (page 229, chapter on Symbolic Logic); in an analogous way, he defines "*the specific form* of a given statement" (page 278). He establishes "the convention that in any argument form p shall be the first statement variable that occurs in it, g shall be the second, and so on" (page 269).

There would be a serious ambiguity in using the name "specific form" for both propositional and term logic, since each argument would have quite different forms according to whether one abstracted from categorical propositions or from terms. To distinguish these forms by such names as "specific propositional-logic form" and "specific term-logic form" would be cumbersome. We shall keep our name "distinctive form" for term logic and shall use Copi's name "specific form" for propositional logic (symbolic or traditional).

We do not define "*the* distinctive form" of a proposition or argument since we find we need two types of distinctive form even for the Aristotelian syllogism: The well-known *SMP* form (21G), and a different form for a Table of Reduction (20D3, 20D4).

5. If we add the premiss "All red objects are colored objects," we obtain the argument form:

(b') All red objects are colored objects and some S are red objects; therefore, some S are colored objects.

Argument form (b') is formally valid.

Some logicians use the term "valid" only for formally valid argument forms (or arguments) such as (b'), and exclude a form such as (b), which we call (semantically) valid.

6. The argument form in 3B1, and the argument form in 3B2, are forms of syllogism—specifically, of *standard categorical syllogism* as defined in 19A. However, the method of counterexample can be applied to invalid argument forms of all types.

CHAPTER 4

1. "Syncategorematic words" and "categorematic words" are synonyms for "form words" and "terms" respectively.

2. Form words occur properly as terms only when they are set off, as by quotes or italics; for example, in the sentence, " 'if' is a two-letter word." In such cases, the word is said to be mentioned but not used (i.e., not used in the normal way). In the sentence quoted, the subject is not the word "if" but a name of the word, formed by putting the word in quotes.

3. "Term" in the general sense of definition 3 could be defined by "term of a proposition", as follows:

> **Def. 3'.** A **term** is any expression—taken with a specific meaning—that *could* be used as a term-of-a-proposition, that is, subject-term or predicate-term.

For example, in the proposition "Socrates was the master of Plato", the name "Plato" does not occur as term-of-a-proposition; but "Plato" is a term in the sense of definition 3', because it *can* be used as subject-predicate of proposition. (But compare note 7 below.)

4. In Peirce's terminology, these terms (*word, sentence,* etc.) will refer to types rather than to tokens.

5. "By the term 'universal' I mean that which is of such a nature as to be predicated of many subjects, by 'individual' that which is not thus predicated. Thus 'man' is a universal, 'Callias' an individual", Aristotle, *De Interpretatione*, chapter 7, Ross edition. Compare J. S. Mill: "A general name is familiarly defined, a name which is capable of being truly affirmed, in the same sense, of each of an indefinite number of things. An individual or singular name is a name which is only capable of being truly affirmed, in the same sense, of one thing". (*System of Logic*, 8th ed., Bk. I, ch. 2. §3)

6. In the most common versions of traditional logic, an expression is not accepted as "meaningful" as subject term or predicate term of a categorical proposition unless there is at least one object of which it can be truly predicated. One way

of carrying out this doctrine would be to take any substantive or adjectival expression as "meaningless" and hence not a term at all if it cannot be truly predicated of anything. A less simple but more adequate way is to exclude empty terms as subject term or predicate term of standard categorical propositions, but admit them elsewhere. Then we could have "believers in unicorn" as a subject term while excluding "unicorns" as subject term. (See chapter 36.) But for what is called the "Boolean interpretation" of categorical propositions—almost universally made by symbolic logicians—empty terms are admitted also as subject term or predicate term.

This note affects the interpretation of the whole chapter 4, beginning with definition 3 and note 3.

7. Johnson (*Logic*, Part I, ch. 7, §1) seems to limit "general names" to substantives. Among "applicatives", which can be significantly prefixed to any general name, he includes "the", "a", "this", "that", "every", "any", and so on. Keynes takes as the criterion of a general name the possibility of prefixing "all" or "some" significantly (*F.L.* §9). But most of these applicatives do not strictly satisfy Johnson's rule, that any applicative can be prefixed to any general name. Most of them cannot be used freely with both grammatically singular and plural forms. "No" and "some", however, may be prefixed to singular and plural forms alike.

Moreover, some of the cited applicatives can be prefixed to a term that is not general. For example, one can say: All Gual is divided into three parts", though "Gaul" (and "All Gaul") is here a singular term. And we can say: "That Jeffrey Terwillinger next door is a handsome fellow".

8. On close scrutiny, one finds a difficulty for the quantifier criterion in such a sentence as "Some beggar is a clever man". For the predicate term, by the usual analysis, is "a clever man"; this would be called a general term, yet we cannot write "Some a clever man . . ."! The trouble is that the indefinite article *a* or *an* is itself an unobtrusive quantifier: a weakened form of "one", interpretable in the present case either as *exactly one* or as *some*, that is, *at least one*. Probably the best solution here is to take the form of the proposition as "Some . . . is a . . .", and take the predicate term as simply "clever man", not "a clever man". This is supported by the fact that if we wished to make a syllogism with the given proposition and give "No clever man is a fool" as premisses, the term common to the two propositions would strictly have to be "clever man".

9. In reply to the question "Are these cats Persians"? it would be meaningful to answer "No, these cats are Siamese". But here the "no" is not quantifying "these cats".

10. We borrow this use of the term "discrete" from the medievals. One of their basic divisions of *suppositio* is into *common* and *discrete* supposition, the former being the usual mode of use of common (or general) terms, the latter the mode of use of singular terms. William of Sherwood and Peter of Spain also speak of "discrete terms", apparently synonymous with "singular terms"; but we see nothing to prevent extending "discrete terms" to include what we call "plural discrete terms", once the need for this last rubric is recognized.

After discovering that such terms as "the Alps" do not fit the usual dichotomy of general and singular terms, we were led by the research of John L. Carafides to Augusta Klein's "A Proposed New Classification of Terms", *Mind*, vol. 23 (1914), 542–549—the only place known to us where this point has been made. She divides terms into general and individual, the latter into proper names and designation, and introduces the grammatical distinction of singular and plural into all kinds of terms. However, she does not use the word "individual" in the same way we use "discrete"; she counts "a poodle" in "*My dog is a poodle*" as an individual term, and excludes abstract terms from individual terms. We prefer to use a word such as "discrete" which, being less familiar in this context, obviously requires explanation. We limit the use of "singular term" to singular discrete terms.

11. It is true that in "*All the Smith brothers are tall*" the predicate applies to the Smith brothers individually, and the subject term is therefore being used as a general term. This can be described by saying that in this example "the Smith brothers" is a general term, or (as we prefer) by saying that the discrete collective term "the Smith brothers" is being used divisively (distributively) in this example.

12. We have no need to distinguish "singular general terms" from "plural general terms", since the grammatical distinction has no logical significance. We can therefore use "singular term" to mean the same as "singular discrete term".

13. Cf. Keynes, §9, page 13 (4th ed.): "Any general name may be transformed into a singular name by means of an individualizing prefix, such as a demonstrative . . . , or by the use of the definite article. . . . Such restriction by means of the definite article may sometimes need to be interpreted by the context, *e.g., the garden, the river*; in other cases some limitation of place or time or circumstance . . . unequivocally defines the individual reference, *e.g., the first man*, . . ."

Leonard speaks of forming a "definite description" by prefixing a "singularizing modifier" to a general term (§18.3). Joseph uses the term "designation" for definite descriptions (ch. 2).

14. As Eaton states (pages 312f):

> The notion of the similarity, or homogeneity, of the things that constitute the whole referred to by a collective term should be emphasized. An army is a collection of *soldiers*, a library, a collection of *books*. . . . Almost any term, "house", "tree", "garden", refers to a whole made up of parts; but we do not think of the parts as a collection (class) of similars. We do not mean by "house" a collection of bricks; or by "garden" a collection of plants, trees, and shrubs. Hence, these terms, though they refer to wholes having parts, are not collective.

15. With Maritian (*F.L.*, page 35), we prefer to speak of *divisive* rather than *distributive* use (or sense), in order to avoid confusion with the concept of the distribution of terms, which is explained in chapter 9.

16. Some logicians treat adjectives as neither concrete nor abstract. They call adjectives *attributive* terms. Eaton argues that instead of distinguishing concrete

(etc.) terms from abstract terms, we should distinguish concrete, abstract, and attributive *uses* of terms.

17. This list of modes of meaning is not exhaustive: It does not include "connotation" as defined in def. 27.

Little standardization of terminology has been achieved in this area of logic. Some logicians use "extension" as a synonym for "denotation", and "connotation" or "comprehension" as synonyms for "intension". Other logicians distinguish these terms. A brief history of the term "connotation" is given by Joseph (p. 156). Our "verbal meaning" was called "connotation" or "linguistic meaning" by C. I. Lewis in *Analysis of Knowledge and Valuation*.

18. The logical terms "inten*s*ion", and "inten*s*ional" are to be distinguished from the psychological terms "inten*t*ion" and "inten*t*ional".

19. An alternative definition by superterms is "An **intension** of a term T is a (property or) set of properties signified by any set of superterms of T". A term does not apply to (or name) the properties in its intensions. It applies to (or names) objects that have these properties. Thus the word "signified", instead of "named", was used in the above definition.

20. A serious attempt to analyze the concept of subjective intension was made by Richard M. Martin in *Intension and Decision* (Prentice-Hall, 1963). Study of this work requires considerable knowledge of contemporary symbolic logic. See review by Richard Montague in *Journal of Symbolic Logic*, vol 31 (1966), 98–102.

If one allows the "group of persons" required for a conventional intension by our definition 23 to have, say, only two members, a subjective intension would become a conventional intension by being accepted by another person. Typically, one has in mind conventions shared by a larger group, such as most speakers of a certain dialect.

21. Analytic intension is called "comprehension" in the *Port-Royal Logic* and in the works of most modern scholastics. The example of "triangle" is from this *Logic*.

The term "brown male dog" formally entails the terms "male dog" and "dog". The term "dog" semantically entails the term "mammal" since the conventional intension of "mammal" is part of (or entailed by) the conventional intension of "dog".

22. The term "objective intension" was used by Keynes, who also suggested using "comprehension" as synonym. Leonard calls this "total contingent intension".

An alternative definition by superterms: the **total objective intension** of a term is the set of all properties each of which is signified by a superterm of the term.

23. John Hospers, *An Introduction to Philosophical Analysis*, 2nd ed., (Prentice-Hall, 1967), 48 n.

Keynes uses "connotation" for conventional intension. However, in literary usage, the term "denotation" means approximately the same as "conventional intension".

24. Most contemporary logicians (Leonard, Copi, etc.) first define the extension of a term, then define intension by extension. To present the modes of meaning of a term in this order seems to us to beg the question, because the conventional intension of a term must ordinarily be known before its extension—which is relative to a given intension—can be determined. "Extension" as we define it (def. 28) is what Keynes (page 30) calls "subjective extension".

25. For some purposes, we may wish to restrict the denotation of a term to some part of it. For example, someone asserting a generalization that *no horses are more than twelve feet high* might not wish to be so definite about the remote past or future, but limit himself to things existing "at present", in the present month or year (or present century). We could say then that he is restricting the term "horses" to its "present denotation", that is, the part of its denotation existing "at present" (made more precise as desired). Of course such restriction may also be placed on extension, or simply *the domain of the term* or *the universe of discourse*. For example, the domain of a term might be Greek mythology, the realm of Dickens's *David Copperfield*, or the possible worlds of Isaac Asimov's fiction.

26. We reserve the expression "null term" for empty terms that are self-inconsistent (e.g., "square circles", "odd numbers evenly divisible by two"). All null terms are empty terms, but not all empty terms are null terms.

27. Cohen and Nagel, *op. cit.*, p. 32. Cf. Keynes, *Formal Logic*, 4th ed., §23.

The law is often stated in simpler forms as follows: "*When a series of terms is arranged in order of subordination, the extension and intension vary inversely*". Cohen and Nagel, who give this formulation also, taking "extension" in the sense of real extension (or denotation), point out that it is not correct. Our examples (b) and (c) are counterexamples to the simple form of the law as relating denotation and intension inversely. The law in any case is not intended to state a numerical precise inverse relationship.

28. Contemporary philosophic usage, unlike ordinary usage, will usually accept a phrase arbitrarily put together and of any length as a synonym. However, again differing from ordinary usage, it usually demands that the synonym be freely interchangeable, at least in "ordinary" contexts.

CHAPTER 5

1. *Topica* 101b 38, trans. E. M. Forster, Loeb Classical Library (Harvard University Press, 1960).

2. Our account of definition is especially indebted to the influential treatise of Richard Robinson, *Definition* (Oxford, 1950), and to Henry S. Leonard's *Principles of Reasoning* (Dover Publications, 1967; a revision of *Principles of Right Reason*, Holt, 1957). Robinson surveys historic and contemporary views and gives his own theory. Leonard has the most complete and systematic theory of definition we have

seen. His Theory of Definition requires 134 pages of exposition, with minimal reference to other writers, basing himself, moreover, on relevant preliminary material, including almost one hundred pages of Theory of Terms and so on.

Two other current textbooks deserve special mention on this topic. The account in Irving M. Copi's *Introduction to Logic* (Macmillan, 1953, 1961, 1968, 1972) has had great influence. James D. Carney and Richard K. Scheer, in *Fundamentals of Logic* (Macmillan, 1964) have a sophisticated treatment, reflecting Wittgenstein's awareness of the inadequacy of conventional doctrine.

3. Compare H. W. B. Joseph, *An Introduction to Logic*, 2nd ed., (Oxford University Press, 1916), 83; Aristotle, *Topica* 139a 28, (2).

4. A. N. Whitehead and Bertrand Russell, *Principia Mathematica*, vol. 1, 1st ed. (1910), 11 (quoted in R. M. Eaton, *General Logic*, 296).

5. That there are exceptions to this is illustrated by a passage in Robinson (*Definition*, 195) in which he speaks of Whitehead and Russell's inconsistency in "implying that the definiendum is an idea" (in a passage a bit after the one referred to in note 4). The use of "definiendum" here is Robinson's rendering of the Whitehead-Russell expression "what is defined".

6. It may be useful to indicate the rules we follow in using boldface type in our numbered definitions. A definition usually has a key word or key phrase, the meaning of which is what the definition is primarily intended to explain. If the 'key word' is a substantive or verb, it alone is printed in boldface. In 1A def. 5, for example, we defined a premiss of an argument. Here "premiss" is the key word, so it alone is in boldface. (See 4F def. 20, for the rare boldfacing of a verb.)

If the key word is an adjective or adverb, both it and the word it modifies are in boldface. Thus in 1B definition 6, defining a valid argument, the key word is "valid", but we boldface "valid argument". (See 4C def. 13, for the rare case where an adverb is the key word.)

Our concept and definition of "key word of a definition" are suggested by Leonard's definition of "the **simple** definiendum of a definition" as "that word or phrase in the definiendum for the sake of explaining which the definition occurs". (*Principles of Reasoning*, §28.5) We might introduce the formal definition:

Def. 4a The **key word** (or **simple definiendum term**) of a definition is either the expression that the definition is primarily intended to define (if it defines a 'word') *or* the expression signifying what the definition is primarily intended to define (if it defines a thing). In a nominal definition, the key word may also be called the **simple definiendum**.

7. For Aristotle, real definitions gave the essential attributes of a species or kind. Modern writers who follow Aristotelian doctrine with modifications generally prefer definition by essential attributes, but may accept merely coextensive attributes. Such writers include Arnauld (in the Port-Royal Logic) and Joseph. Arnauld wrote: "The less exact definition called description is that which gives some

knowledge of a thing by the accidents which are proper [i.e., peculiar] to it and which determine it sufficiently to give an idea which distinguishes it from other things". *L'Art de Penser*, ed. von Freytag Löringhof and Brekle, vol. 1, (F. Fromann, 1965), page 155 of 1662 ed.; our translation. (The reader should beware of the expression "the defined word" in the translation of this chapter (on *définitions des choses*!) by Dickoff and James (1964). Such an expression is not used in the original text, since it is things that are being defined, not words.)

Joseph (*Intro to Logic*, 111f) accepts the second alternative reluctantly, after he finds the distinguishing of essence from property (i.e., *proprium* or coextensive attribute) to be possible and important in geometry, difficulty in physics, and impossible in biology; (ibid., 91–106).

Since we do not require definitions to be equivalential, and recognize incomplete definitions, we do not impose such a restriction on the definiens of a real definition.

8. Robinson does not recognize the category of thing-word definition in this sense, namely, with a thing as definiendum and a word as definiens. He recognizes only a "distinction between the thing-word and word-thing mode of arriving at a nominal definition" according to which we start from; *Definition* 62.

Aristotle's later formulations in the *Posterior Analytics*, Bk. II, which allow different kinds of definition, also indicate that real definitions are thing-word definitions; as when a "definition"—i.e., a definiens—in one sense is "a form of words (*lógos*) which explains *why* a thing exists". (93b38, trans. H. Tredennick, Loeb Classical Library, 1960). But these thing-word definitions at the same time correlate things with things, hence may be regarded as thing-thing definitions. Thus when the thing *thunder*, in Aristotle's example, is defined by the 'word' "Noise due to the extinguishing of fire in the clouds", surely thunder is being correlated with things such as fire and clouds.

9. K. Ajdukiewicz is an exception; see his "Three Concepts of Definition", *Logique et Analyse* (1958), reprinted in *Problems in the Philosophy of Language*, ed. T. M. Olshewsky (Holt, Rinehart & Winston, 1969). As he says, we may define the city of Warsaw (e.g., as "the city which in 1958 A.D. is the capital of Poland"). Opponents of a doctrine of real definition, for example J. S. Mill, commonly interpret it broadly.

10. The dictionary is likely to add some qualification to (a) or (b), such as "about the size of a badger", which helps distinguish the wombat from kangaroos and some other marsupials.

The dictionary might well define in a circle, defining "wombat" by its family *Vombatidae*, and defining the family name in terms of the wombat as the typical member of the family. Dictionaries often avoid a circle by leaving a gap, that is, omitting definitions of the neo-Latin names used in the scientific names of animals.

11. For example, L. S. Stebbing, in *A Modern Introduction to Logic*, revised ed. (Harper Torchbook, 1961), 423f, requires that the defining and defined expressions be asserted to be equivalent. The sentence (a) could indeed be used (injudiciously) to stipulate a new meaning of "wombat", namely, the same meaning as "Australian marsupial". In that case, it would be a definition according to Stebbing.

12. Examples (b) and (c) satisfy Stebbing's other two conditions for a statement to be a definition (see n. 10): It must relate two expressions (i.e., pointing cannot be an essential part of it), and the definiens must contain more words or symbols than the definiendum.

13. If the equivalential definition is a word-word definition (e.g., "The word 'man' means the same as 'rational animal' "), it asserts the equivalence of definiendum and definiens. If it is a word-thing definition, it asserts, for example, that the definiendum "man" is meant to denote rational animals, and it implies the equivalence of definiendum term and defining term. If it is a thing-thing definition, (e.g., "Man is by nature a rational animal"), it asserts that to be a rational animal is the essence of the species Man, and it implies the equivalence of definiendum term and defining term.

An alternative definition of equivalential definition follows.

Def. 6'. An **equivalential definition** is a definition that asserts or implies that the definiendum term has the same intension and extension as the defining term. (Cf. 4F.)

14. Compare Stebbing's restrictions, note 11 above.

If a narrow sense of "definition" is favored, one might restrict our expression "definition statement" (def. 8 below) to this sense, and use "defining statement" (or "definitory statement") in a broad sense.

15. Cf. Mill, *System of Logic*, Bk. I, c. 8, §1: a definition declares "the meaning of a word; namely, either the meaning which it bears in common acceptation, or that which the speaker or writer, for the particular purposes of his discourse, intends to annex to it."

16. Most lists of the functions of language by logicians and philosophers omit the imaginative function; hence, as we see it, they have no proper place for the sentence: "Once upon a time there was a little girl called Goldilocks".

Attention was called to the performative function by J. L. Austin; see *How to Do Things with Words* (Oxford University Press, 1965).

17. James MacKaye in *The Logic of Language* (Hanover, N.H., 1939), 58f, distinguished a *"stipulated definition"*—"a definition adopted independent of custom"—from a *"customary definition"*. The latter is rather our conventional definition (def. 15) than our lexical, though he does not explicitly distinguish these concepts. On his view, stipulated definitions may or may not be customary, but must be explicit (which customary definitions need not be). Max Black's *Critical Thinking* (Prentice-Hall, 1946, 1952) distinguished *stipulated* definition from *reported* definition, "in which a speaker intends to give a definition conforming to some customary or contextual usage" (chapter 11, §3).

R. Robinson (1954) divided word-thing definitions into lexical and stipulative; many subsequent textbooks have used these terms. The distinction applies to word-word definitions as well.

18. Lewis Carroll, *Through the Looking-Glass*, (1871) chapter VI.

19. Our list of five cases is mainly derived from Robinson, 66–71.

20. *Introduction to Logic*, 1st ed., 98f; 4th ed., 121f. However, Copi excludes precising definitions from "stipulative definitions"; he limits the latter to definitions whose definiendum is a new sign, at least in the given context.

21. *Logic of Language*, 59. The definition is introduced by specifying that, when customary definitions fail because of vagueness or ambiguity, "it becomes justifiable to resort to what may be called stipulated definitions".

22. Most contemporary logicians hold stipulative definitions to be simply directive, and deny them any cognitive character. As a consequence, they also deny that stipulative definitions have a truth-value (though they may admit that some element of truth-value is indirectly involved). See Robinson, ch. IV, sec. 2. Leonard is a notable exception; and we are heavily indebted to his account of the cognitive character and truth-value of all definitions, including the stipulative (which he calls "nominal"); *Principles*, unit 27.

MacKaye's view also differed from the current one, inasmuch as he held that "all definitions are true—by definition. . . . A definition, being an identity, cannot be untrue. . . ." (*Logic of Language*, 41).

23. *Ethics and Language* (Yale University Press, 1944), especially ch. IX.

24. The parenthetic alternatives of definition 18—covering transfer of emotive force from defining term to definiendum—do not seem to be explicitly included in Stevenson's account of persuasive definitions. It is appropriate, however, in a general account of definition (which Stevenson was not attempting), to extend the term in this way. Cf. Copi, *Introduction*, ch. 4 §1, (5); §3, (5); some variations in different editions.

25. Aldous Huxley, *Eyeless in Gaza* (Harper & Brothers, 1936), 91. Indications of stuttering have been omitted.

26. American philosophers who are *not* "typical Anglo-American logicians" in the sense intended include Henry B. Veatch, author of *Intentional Logic* (Yale University Press, 1952), Francis H. Parker, coauthor with Veatch of *Logic as a Human Instrument* (Harper, 1959), and Ayn Rand, author of *Introduction to Objectivist Epistemology* (New York: Objectivist, Inc., 1966–67)—though our account is based on none of these.

27. The neo-Thomist Jacques Maritain, in *Formal Logic* (Sheed & Ward, 1946), chap. 1, §2, A, uses "concept" explicitly in both senses. In this book, it may be interpreted in either sense or both, as is appropriate. We generally prefer as objective an interpretation as is reasonable.

28. This definition was suggested by Leonard's definitions of "conceptual definition", pages 295f, §27.5, and page 609. Cf. also C. I. Lewis's "explicative definition", cited by Leonard (page 300n) from *Analysis of Knowledge and Valuation*.

29. This "search for a key" is one of the rational forms of the "search for essence", though Robinson claims to find the latter unintelligible. Cf. below, (v) Conceptual definition as the search for essence.

30. Barker (*Elements of Logic*, 1965, 204f) cites Pater's definition as an example of "revelatory definitions". Such definitions are like the real definitions of the Aristotelian tradition in that they are not intended to "explain words" but "to describe the basic natures of things". However, they are conceived pluralistically: The belief that there is only one correct real definition of a species is rejected. Different definitions may be appropriate for different purposes. Newton's "definition" of force as mass times acceleration, and Einstein's definition of simultaneity, are also cited as examples. (On the former, see 5D1e below.)

31. Robinson, after weighing considerations for and against, judges, "though very tentatively, that we had better give up calling this activity 'definition' or 'real definition' in future, and call it 'analysis' " (178). He omits the tentativeness, however, when he finally concludes that we should drop the term "real definition" in our own philosophizing, and use it only in referring to past literature (190f).

32. See a fuller account of the definitions of the meter in exercises for 5C. These definitions should also be considered in terms of the concept of operational definition: see 5D1d.

33. For a critique of Robinson's critique and an explanation of Aristotle's "essential definition", see David H. DeGrood's "The Status of 'Essential Definition' ", *Darshana International*, vol. 6 (1966), 5–10.

34. *Introduction to Logic*, 1st ed. (1953) 88f, 99f; 4th ed. (1972), 111f, 122f.

35. For the biological use of "Genus", "Species", etc., see 6A, note 4.

36. Joseph, 116.

37. See 5D1, *f*, Contextual Definition; (d) and note 50.

38. Sir William Hamilton's *Lectures on Logic*, ed. Mansel etc. (New York 1880), 343, quotes the German logician W. T. Krug (1819) as dividing all definitions into Nominal, Real, or Genetic, "according as they are conversant with the meaning of a term, with the nature of a thing, or with its rise and production". Augustin Sesmat, in *Logique*, vol. I (Paris, 1950), 95–99, divides the definitions of "constructed concepts" into genetic definitions, static definitions, and those which are both. See also Daniel S. Robinson, *The Principles of Reasoning*, 3rd ed. (Appleton-Century, 1947), 56; A. Wolf, *Textbook of Logic*, 2nd ed. (Allen & Unwin, 1938, repr. 1948), 183.

39. By a "suitable observer" is meant one who has the necessary training and can obtain the equipment required to perform the operations described in the operational definition. Hence an operational definition is not at fault if the operations require equipment or skill not available to the listener. However, if an operation requires equipment that it is not technically possible to build, then the definition is faulty.

40. It is sometimes argued that an operational definition does not give the meaning of its definiendum because its meaning has to be understood prior to

formulating the definiens. This argument is probably based on failure to analyze the process of redefinition described above. It is true that a conventional meaning of the definiendum term in an operational definition must be known prior to formulating the new definiens. But the purpose of an operational definition—which is a conceptual definition—is not to set forth the conventional meaning of its definiendum term, but to provide a precise test for deciding whether or not an object belongs to the extension of the definiendum term.

41. Nobelist Bridgman introduced and explained the term in *The Logic of Modern Physics* (New York: The Macmillan Company, 1927); see also *The Nature of Physical Theory* (Princeton; Dover Publications, 1936). Extension of the concept to psychology is defended by C. C. Pratt in *The Logic of Modern Psychology* (New York, 1939). A good short account of the topic is found in the article "Operationism" by S. S. Stevens in the *Dictionary of Philosophy*, ed. D. D. Runes (Philosophical Library, n.d.,; Littlefield, Adams & Co., 1955).

42. Arthur Pap, in "Theory of Definition," *Philosophy of Science*, vol. 31 (1964), reprinted in *Problems in the Philosophy of Language* (cited note 16 above), 282–88, is the only logician in whom we find quantitative definition as a distinct type. His "quantitative explicit definition" corresponds to our "quantitative equational definition" of definition 29.

43. *Chambers's Etymological Dictionary of the English Language*, ed. A. Findlater (London and Edinburgh, 1899).

44. It might be said that the adjectives "soft" and "high" in definition (b) are quantitative. We may answer, as Aristotle did for the adjectives "much" and "little", "great" and "small", and "these are not quantitative but relative; things are not great or small absolutely, they are so called rather as the result of an act of comparison." *Categoriae* 5b 14–16, trans. Edghill, Ross ed. of *Works*. If one wishes to call such terms "quantitative", they are quite vague in the absence of standards of comparison, and give no quantitative precision.

45. *Categoriae*, 6a 26.

46. The definiendum cannot be expressed as a product, sum, etc. of two distinct variables. An equation of the form "$A \times B = C \div D$" might be said to define each variable in terms of the others, but it is not a form of definition. It can be transformed into an equation that can be taken as a definition, e.g., "$A = C \div (B \times D)$".

47. Our definition of contextual definition is indebted to Leonard's account of contextual versus absolute definition (§28.5), but has added an alternative that seems appropriate.

48. A full critical discussion of the traditional rules is given by Robinson (pp. 140–148).

49. *An Introduction to Logic and Scientific Method* (New York: Harcourt, Brace & World, Inc., 1934), p. 238.

50. After the *Topica* (101b): "A 'definition' is a phrase signifying a thing's essence."

51. This rule holds for all equivalential definitions.

52. One source of this rule is the *Topica* (154a). Here Aristotle says ". . . for the definition put forward must be predicated of everything of which the term is predicated, and must moreover be convertible."

53. The origin of this rule seems to be Aristotle's statement: "Moreover, see if he divides the genus by a negation, as those do who define a line as 'length without breadth': for this means simply that it has not any breadth. the genus will then be found to partake of its own species. . . ." (*Topica* 143a, 11). This, to Aristotle, would be an error, since earlier in the *Topica*, he states "Clearly, therefore, the species partakes of the genera, but the genera of the species . . ." (*Topica*, 120a, 10).

CHAPTER 6

1. Keynes, *Formal Logic*, 4th ed., 446–49.

2. Lynn E. Rose, *Aristotle's Syllogistic*, (Charles C. Thomas, 1968), ch. 1.

3. "Division", *Webster's Third New International Dictionary* (Merriam Co., 1961), 664.

4. If two terms are such that everything named by the first term is also named by the second term, but not vice versa, then the first term is **subaltern** to the second. For example, "cats" is a subaltern term to "mammals". Two alternative ways of stating the same fact are to say that cats are a proper subclass of (the class of) mammals, or that the cat is a species of the genus mammal. The modern biologist, however, uses the terms "species" and "genus" only at certain levels of classification. He says that the domestic cat is a species of the genus *Felis*, typical genus of the cat family *Felidae*, in the order *Carnivora*, in the class *Mammalia* (mammals).

5. Joseph states, "In metaphysical division, we distinguish in a species its genus and differentia, in a substance its different attributes, in a quality its different 'variables' or 'dimensions'; thus we may distinguish in man animality and rationality, in sugar its colour, texture, solubility, taste, and so forth, in a sound its pitch, timbre, and loudness" (*An Introduction to Logic*, 132).

6. Keynes, 4th ed., 443.

7. Many books omit the second requirement, and require only that coordinate classes be jointly exhaustive, not that they be coextensive with the divided class. Probably they presuppose or ignore the second requirement, rather than rejecting it.

8. This division was suggested in Porphyry's *Isagoge* (Introduction). Porphyry (c. 232–304 B.C.) was a disciple of Plotinus. It is assumed that "incorporeal" is equivalent to "noncorporeal", etc.

9. Coffey favors dichotomous division because it can be applied "in a mechanical, mathematical way, within the domain of intellectual concepts, abstracting altogether from the existence or possibility of any objective counterparts for those concepts. This process is known as *Purely Formal Division*" (*Science of Logic*, 116-117).

10. The phrase "Natural Classification", as Mill says, "seems most peculiarly appropriate to such arrangements as correspond . . . to the spontaneous tendencies of the mind, by placing together the objects most similar in their general aspect" (*System of Logic*, Bk IV, ch. 7, §2). It is a strong recommendation of a classification "to the character of a scientific one", he goes on, "that it shall be a natural classification in this sense also. . . . But . . . this circumstance is not a *sine quâ non*; since the most obvious properties of things may be of trifling importance compared with others that are not obvious". Thus "the obsolete division into trees, shrubs, and herbs, . . . though of primary importance with regard to mere general aspect, yet . . . answers to so few differences in the other properties of plants, that a classification founded on it would be as completely artificial and technical as the Linnaean" (in the sense explained in our text).

Our discussion of natural and artificial classification leans heavily on this chapter of Mill. In this and the following chapter, he effectively corrects the superficial view of many modern logicians who fail to make sense of this distinction.

11. Mill points out that "Linnaeus also suggested another and more scientific arrangement".

12. It seems to us a strong confirmation of the objectivity in the concept of natural classification in biology, that the classification arrived at in the nineteenth century prior to the general acceptance of evolution required little basic change after the acceptance of evolution following the work of Charles Darwin and Alfred R. Wallace.

CHAPTER 7

1. Gergonne, "Essai de dialectique rationelle", *Annoles de Math Pures et Appliquees* (Nismes), vol. 7 (1816-17), 189-228.

2. Gergonne, 194f.

3. "The Gergonne Relations", *Journal of Symbolic Logic* vol. 20 (1955), 207-231.

CHAPTER 8

1. "Iffi" means "if and only if".

The term "opposition" here is simply the general name for the relation that any two standard categorical propositions in different form with identical subjects and identical predicates have to one another. We are following scholastic usage. Thus Keynes (following Mansel's edition of Aldrich) defines: "Two propositions are technically said to be *opposed* to each other when they have the same subject and predicate respectively, but differ in quantity or quality or both" (4th ed., 109) Aristotle called contradictories and contraries "genuine opposites"; but said "the particular affirmative is only verbally opposed to the particular negative" (*Prior An.* 63b, Ross ed.).

2. Some logicians, e.g., J. Welton (*Manual of Logic*, vol 1, 2nd ed., 1922) and J. J. Toohey (*Elementary Handbook of Logic*, 3rd ed., 1948)—following E. E. C. Jones—use "education" for "immediate inference". Keynes (126, n. 3) says, "Miss Jones suggests the term *education* as a synonym for *immediate inference*" (*General Logic*, 79).

3. Note that secondary propositions as well as simple propositions are categorical.

We prefer to avoid the problem as to whether a conjunctive proposition counts as one for purposes of definition 2.

4. We might define a "contradictory", a "contrary", a "subcontrary", a "superaltern", a "subaltern" of a proposition in such a way that it may be either opposed to the proposition (as is the contradictory, etc. of 8A) or not opposed. But we do not give the truth-value definitions of these terms now current; cf. 8E.

5. Keynes (page 110) states: "They [a pair of opposed propositions] may be such that whilst both cannot be true, both may be false. This is called *contrary opposition*". By this definition of contraries, followed by most current logic texts, a pair of propositions of the forms "All S are S" and "No S are S" are not contraries. A full discussion of Keynes's definition and its consequences is given in 8E.

6. The scholastics used the term "subaltern", and this tradition is followed by many authors. It conflicts, however, with the use in definition 8a, which is now common.

7. The scholastic term is "superalternant".

8. The scholastic term is "subalternate".

9. Of course it is possible for a pair of contradictory sentences to be both true at different times and to be both false at different times. We are assuming that the members of a pair of contradictory propositions have reference to the same time.

10. Another definition is: "X entails Y" iffi "X therefore Y" is a valid argument.

11. Albert Manne (*Logik und Existenz*, 151) states that the symbol ">—<" is used in the *Mu-Mu-Symbolik* (Munster-Munchen symbolism) to mean, in the logic of propositions, *Kontravalenz*. Hence, "p >—< g" means "p if and only if not g". (He uses this for a truth-function, however, while we use it for a relation based on meaning.)

12. Since **A** entails **I**, and **I** is equivalent to (reversible entails) E^F, it follows that **A** entails E^F. Since **A** entails **I**, and **A** is equivalent to (reversible entails) O^F, it follows that O^F entails **I**. Since **A** entails **I**, and **A** is equivalent to O^F, and **I** is equivalent to E^F, it follows that O^F entails E^F.

13. Another square of opposition could be constructed with impossible affirmative categoricals and necessary negative ones. This could be done by using "non-*S*" as the subject and "*S*" as the predicate. The inference rules would be the same as those given in 8D2.

14. With a priori categoricals, it is possible to have both universals false. For example, "All integers are prime" and "No integers are prime" are both false *a priori* propositions. the opposed **O** and **I** propositions are both true. In this case APR1 holds, but rules APR2 to APR4 all fail: the contraries (**A** and **E**) are both false, the subcontraries (**I** and **O**) are both true, and the alterns (**A**, **I**, **E**, and **O**) have opposite truth-values.

CHAPTER 9

1. Of course to a person who believed in the physical existence of fairies the universe of discourse would be the physical realm.

2. An alternative definition: A universe of discourse is a class that includes all the classes we wish to talk about.

3. See Strawson, 175.

4. An empty term is a term that does not apply to anything in its universe of discourse.

5. In other words neither the subject nor the predicate is an empty term.

6. This argument would hold as well for the particular propositions. If a proposition that has the possibility of being true implies the existence of its subject, then it must presuppose the existence of its subject.

7. Strawson, 173 (Table 3).

CHAPTER 10

1. See Appendix 10A5, Distribution and the Doctrine of *Suppositio*.

2. Notably, John J. Toohey, *Elementary Handbook of Logic*, 3rd ed. (New York & London: Appleton-Century-Crofts, 1948); and Peter T. Geach, "The doctrine of distribution", *Mind* (1956), 67–74, also "Distribution: a Last Word", *Philosophical Review* (1960), 396–398, and *Reference and Generality*, (Cornell University Press, 1962, 1968), see index: "distributed terms", "distribution", "distributive".

3. In this note, for the sake of simplicity, we use "S" and "P" as abbreviations for concrete terms, rather than as variables.

We avoid the usual simple explanation, that the predicate term of "All S are P" (or "Some S are P") is undistributed because the proposition does not imply "All P are S" or perhaps "No P are S". This should lead to the conclusion that the predicate-term of "Some S are not P" is undistributed because this does not imply "No P are S" or "All P are S".

The explanation sometimes given, that the predicate term of "Some S are not P" is distributed because the proposition asserts that part of the class of S's is excluded from the whole of the class of P's, is doubly confusing. It suggests that the terms are to be taken collectively rather than divisively (cf. 4C), which is generally not the case. Also, it leads to the question, doesn't the **A** proposition "All S are P" assert that the whole of the class of S's is included in the whole of the class of P's? (It doesn't assert that S's are included in a proper part of the P's.) Then, according to the "whole" explanation for the **O**, the predicate term of the **A** proposition, it seems, must be distributed!

4. See Appendix 10C.

5. It is tempting to simplify definition 4 and offer something like the following definition in its place:

Def. 4a. A term in a categorical proposition is **distributed in** that proposition iffi every substitution of a non-empty subterm for the term gives a proposition which must be true if the original is true.

But this would be a mistake, because by definition 4a the term "collies" in the proposition *Some collies are dogs* would be distributed. This undesirable result follows because all collies are dogs, by definition.

We give here an equivalent definition of distribution using variables, which the reader may find helpful:

Def. 4b. Where B is subject term or predicate term of a categorical proposition $X(B,C)$, B is **distributed in** $X(B,C)$ iffi, for all terms B', C' such that $X(B', C')$ is true, and all non-empty subterms B_1 of B', $X(B_1, C')$ is true.

6. Definitions 4 to 5b explicitly specify "subject (or predicate) position", or "*subject term* or *predicate term*", since it is possible for a term (in the broad sense) to occur in a categorical proposition, but be neither the subject term nor predicate term. For example, in the proposition *All integers are odd numbers or even numbers*, the term "odd numbers" is in the predicate term, but it is not the predicate term; similarly for the term "even numbers".

7. An equivalent definition of an undistributed term is:

Def. 5b. Where B is subject term or predicate term of a categorical proposition $X(B,C)$, B is **undistributed in** $X(B,C)$ iffi, for some pair of terms B', C' such that $X(B', C')$ is true, there is some non-empty subterm B_1 of B' such that $X(B_1, C)$ is false.

A 'superterm' definition of a distributed term in standard categoricals is possible, and usually much easier to apply to terms that are actually distributed than the subterm test. A *superterm* of a term T is a general term of which T is a subterm. Such a definition is:

Def. 4c. Where B is a subject term or predicate term in a standard categorical proposition $X(B,C)$, B is **distributed in** $X(B,C)$ iffi, for some pair of terms B', C' such that $X(B', C')$ is true, there is some superterm B_1 of B' such that $X(B_1, C')$ is false.

Unfortunately, if definition 4c is extended to non-standard categoricals, undesirable results occur. For example, the subject term of propositions of the form "Most S are P" is undistributed by the subterm test, but the superterm test would say that such terms are distributed; for a true proposition, for example, *Most physicists are college graduates*, can be turned into a false proposition by substituting a superterm for the subject: *Most people are college graduates*. Therefore, in the context of categoricals in general, standard and non-standard, the superterm definition of a distributed term is not equivalent to the subterm definition, and not desirable.

APPENDIX 10A

1. Peter T. Geach, in *Reference and Generality*, (Cornell University Press, 1962), 56, uses "mode of reference" as a synonym for *suppositio*. Maritain, in *Formal Logic*, page 60 says: "The *suppositio* of a term, which we may translate as its 'substitutive value,' is *its function in discourse . . . of taking the place of a thing*".

2. Kneal and Kneal, *The Development of Logic*, (Oxford University Press, 1962), 246.

3. *Summa totius locicae*, I, in *Ockham: Philosophical Writings*, ed. Boehner (Nelson, 1957), 71.

4. As the Kneals say (page 260), the medievals "assigned *suppositio confusa* not only to every term with [explicit or implicit] universal quantification but also to every term which occurred with existential quantification after the universal quantification of another term". The second alternative covers the "merely confused" supposition of the predicate of an **A**: "Every S is (some) P".

5. Work cited, p. 72.

6. Ibid., 73. Ockham further divides confused distributive supposition into *mobile* and *immobile*. The former is illustrated by the distributed terms of the four standard categorical propositions. The latter is illustrated by the subject of *Every man except Socrates is running*. Here the logical descent to a copulative (conjunctive) proposition is made in a more complicated way than in the mobile distribution.

7. The author of some highly competent commentaries on Aristotle's logical writings, formerly attributed to Duns Scotus, is called "Pseudo-Scotus" or "the

Pseudo-Scotus". See Kneal and Kneal, 272–3. He is currently identified with a fourteenth century writer, John of Cornwall (Cornubia). (Cf. Bochenski, *History of Formal Logic*, 149 n.)

APPENDIX 10C

1. Aristotle and most logicians have held that all statements of the form "Every S is every P" are false, or improperly expressed. Sir William Hamilton held that "All triangles are trilaterals" expresses properly the fact that all triangles are trilaterals and all trilaterals are triangles. The present writers follow Ockham and De Morgan, who hold that, e.g., "Every author of *Waverly* is every author of *Ivanhoe*" properly expresses the fact that the only author of *Waverly* is (the same as) the only author of *Ivanhoe*.

If "Only S are P" is taken as equivalent to "All P are S" (as is usual in logic), we have another example of an affirmative proposition with a distributed predicate term.

However, we do not propose to introduce such forms into the elementary Aristotelian doctrine. So, it remains true that the predicate term is undistributed in the standard form of the affirmative propositions.

CHAPTER 11

1. The use of the term *conversion* varies in modern logic, and a clear definition is often lacking. J. N. Keynes in effect limits conversion to valid inferences, though not quite explicitly in his definition (*Formal Logic*, 4th ed., 126f). H. W. B. Joseph's definition (1916) is the one we have followed. Copi's account of conversion followed Keynes's line in the first two editions of his *Introduction to Logic*, then shifted to Joseph's in the third edition (1968).

2. The argument "Some dogs are black; therefore, some black things are dogs" is of course valid; but it is not merely a conversion by our definitions, because a difference in term expressions makes a difference in terms (by our definition of "terms").

CHAPTER 12

1. This definition is analogous to the definition of "contradictory propositions".

2. Some logicians use "not-" for their formal negative prefix.

3. Historically, the use of the expression "complementary term" (instead of, e.g., "contradictory term") derives from the use of "complement" or "complementary class" in talking in terms of classes.

If one starts from classes—as this book does not do—one defines complementary terms by complementary classes. Thus, a complementary term is a term that names a complementary class. For example, the term "non-alligators" is a complementary term (of the term "alligators") in that it names the class of non-alligators, which is the complement of the class of alligators.

CHAPTER 14

1. Aristotle gave examples of contraposition for unquantified categoricals: "for example, 'if man is an animal, non-animal is not-man' " (*Topics*, 113b18). It would be natural and correct to standardize this as contraposition of an **A**.

The word *contrapositive* was used by Boethius (died 524) for the contradictory negative of a term (e.g., non-*S*). What we now call "contraposition", Boethius called *Conversio per contrapositionem terminorum* (conversion by the contraposition of terms). (Keynes, *Formal Logic*, 4th ed., page 134n.)

2. What Keynes (page 135) calls "the partial contrapositive", he called "the contrapositive" in earlier editions. We call it "the obverse converted", and do not count it as a form of contraposition.

CHAPTER 17

1. Since a relation may hold between fictitious entities, or between a real entity and a fictitious one, this argument does not presuppose the existence of the devil.

2. *Categories*, ch. 7, 6b36–7b14.

3. In violation of the established meaning of "non-" in logic, the term "non-transitive" is often used for "mediotransitive". The latter term was proposed by H. M. Sheffer in lectures at Harvard University. "Non-symmetrical" and "non-reflexive" have been similarly misused.

4. Since x and y may be identical in the definitions of 17C, the definition of "asymmetrical" (def. 12) implies that, for any asymmetrical relation R, if $x R x$ then it is false that $x R x$. Hence if R is asymmetrical, it is always false that $x R x$; that is, R is irreflexive.

5. *Summa Logicae*, ed. Boehner, page 245.

CHAPTER 18

1. The arrow "→" between two propositions means that the first proposition entails (or implies) the second, but it does not exclude the possibility of the second entailing the first. Therefore the arrow does not necessarily signify a non-reversible

entailment. The sign "⇋" may be used for a non-reversible entailment. However, we shall ordinarily symbolize non-reversible entailments by a simple arrow: Compare chapter 8.

CHAPTER 19

1. Logic books do not usually consider a categorical syllogism to be "standard" unless the conclusion is stated last. However, if the conclusion comes first, with sufficient indication that it *is* the conclusion—such as being followed immediately by "since"—and the argument is standardized to the extent required by the definition above, then the validity of the argument is readily determined by the usual methods (e.g., the rules given in chapter 21). In 19B1, we define the usual standard order of the propositions in a syllogism, since this is convenient for certain purposes.

2. For those who know the Hebrew alphabet, the pattern of terms in figure 2 is like the letter *beth*, second letter of that alphabet.

Diagrams like ours for the four figures (but not the mnemonic associations with letters) are found in W. A. Sinclair, *Traditional Formal Logic*, 5th 3d. (New York: Dover Publications, 1951; originally published in London by Methuen & Co. under the name of A. Sinclair). The senior author taught these diagrams to his classes before learning they had been published some years earlier.

A mnemonic device that the junior author has used for many years is a numbered grid:

1	2
2	0

The figure is determined by adding the numbers in the corners occupied by the middle term, as shown below:

M	P		P	M		M	P		P	M
S	M		S	M		M	S		M	S

Figure 1   Figure 2   Figure 3   Figure 4
(1 + 0 = 1)   (2 + 0 = 2)   (1 + 2 = 3)   (2 + 2 = 4)

CHAPTER 20

1. There was a clear distinction in Euclid between the common notions (or axioms) on the one hand, and the postulates on the other. The postulates were

assumptions having to do with the specific subject matter at hand, namely geometry. The axioms were more fundamental assumptions of science, having to do with quantity in general; for example, "Things equal to the same thing are equal to each other". The editors of Euclid did not keep his distinction straight, and the sense of it got lost.

2. A rigorous treatment of Aristotle's syllogistic by means of symbolic logic was carried out by J. Łukasiewicz, *Aristotle's Syllogistic from the Standpoint of Modern Formal Logic* (Oxford: Clarendon Press, 1951, 2nd ed. 1957). See also O. Bird, *Syllogistic and its Extensions* (Prentice-Hall, 1964), chapters 1, 2. However, we wish to stay a little closer to Aristotle's system than Łukasiewicz did.

3. Aristotle's use of the term "syllogism" also differed from later use in that he counted only valid arguments as syllogisms. If this were the only difference, his doctrine of syllogisms would be the same as the later doctrine of *valid* syllogisms.

4. The best account of Aristotle's conception of *figure* known to us is that of L. E. Rose, *Aristotle's Syllogistic* (Charles C. Thomas, 1968), chapters 3, 8. Compare Kneale and Kneale, 68–73.

5. Aristotle, *Prior Analytics* I, ch. 7, 29a19–27. Compare Rose, 60.

6. The distinction made in note 1 to 20A1 between axioms and postulates breaks down when logical principles are the subject matter at hand; for they are at the same time fundamental assumptions of science in general. Because of the latter characteristic, and because they lack the arbitrariness commonly associated with postulates, logical principles are called axioms rather than postulates. But the role within Aristotle's logical system of his axiomatic syllogistic forms is more analogous to that of postulates (say, of geometry) than axioms.

7. On what Aristotle meant by "perfect" here, see Rose, Appendix III. (Besides his points 2, 3, and 4, which Rose thinks likely to have influenced Aristotle in calling first-figure forms perfect, we think his points 12, 13, and 16 are also likely to have had influence.)

8. *Prior Analytics* 29b1–25.

Aristotle and his followers also made use of a single *dictum* applicable to both of these syllogisms. It may be stated: "If all *or* no M are P, and all S are M, it follows that all *or* no S respectively are P". Logicians writing in Latin called such a statement a *Dictim de Omni et Nullo* (Dictum concerning All or None), and often thought of it as the single basic principle of the syllogism. We prefer to say that Aristotle took AAA and EAE in figure 1 as axiomatic. Aristotle also considered the forms AII and EIO in figure 1 to be "perfect" syllogisms, that is, syllogisms that need "nothing other than what has been stated to make plain what necessarily follows". They too could be taken as axiomatic. Hence the *dictum* is commonly stated so as to allow the minor premiss to vary in quantity, and to cover four forms (AAA, EAE, AII, EIO) in the first figure. For example: "Whatever is predicated, whether affirmatively or negatively, of a term distributed may be predicated in like manner of everything contained under it" (Keynes, 301). The derivation of the four forms from this is not as obvious as one might wish. In any case, Aristotle's alternative procedure of reducing all the syllogistic forms to two universal forms is more elegant and up to date.

9. Aristotle usually though not always expressed syllogistic forms with *if-then* rather than with *therefore*; that is, as conditionals rather than arguments or argument forms. Łukasiewicz argued that Aristotle's syllogisms were "all implications" and none of them inferences asserting their premisses and conclusions. We agree, however, with A. N. Prior (*Formal Logic*, 116) and L. E. Rose (24–26) that Aristotle used conditional forms as a natural way of talking about syllogisms, but that a syllogism for him was an argument, as it is for the medievals and the moderns.

10. With standard syllogisms, the first two horizontal arrows cannot both stand for non-reversible inferences if argument I is in fact valid. For then both p and q would be particular premisses; but, as we shall see, a valid syllogism cannot have both premisses particular. Also, if a premiss is particular, the conclusion must be particular, and no admissable non-reversible inference can be drawn from it. Hence if one of the premiss arrows stands for a non-reversible inference, the conclusion arrow cannot.

11. Accents for lines 1, 2, and 4 follow O. Bird, *Syllogistic and its Extensions* (Englewood: Prentice-Hall, 1964). But we make lines 3 and 5 hexameters, with due consideration of the vowel quantity as indicated by Keynes (4th ed.). For prose stress, we follow Latin textbook rules. But Bird's stress on second syllable for all but first six names is simpler.

12. When the mnemonic verses first appeared—in William Sherwood and Peter of Spain in the thirteenth century—the fourth figure was not recognized as such, but as the "indirect first", with (what we call) the minor premiss first. The names for this were: Baralipton, Celantes, Dabitis, Fapesmo, Frisesomorum; the first three vowels give the mood. Continental textbooks with names for the fourth figure as such usually give: Bamalip, Calemes, Dimatis, Fesapo, Fresison.

13. The four first-figure forms to which reduction is made will lack k, s, p, and m. But a form in second, third, or fourth figure must have k (or oc), s, or p to indicate reduction. (When we add names for subaltern forms in D2d, they must have x or p.)

14. The names *Camestrop* and *Camenop* have been used occasionally, for example, Prior and by Bird. We introduce *Barbarix*, *Feraxo*, *Cesarox*, which indicate reduction by subalternation (unlike names in the literature such as *Barbari*[1], *Celaront*[1], *Cesaro*[2]). It would be possible, instead of introducing a new letter to stand for subalternation, to use "s" and "p" in combination to indicate subalternation, giving *Barbarips*, *Ferapso*[1], *Cesarops*[2] in place of our x-forms. Subalternation from an **A** proposition may be accomplished by conversion *per accidens* followed by simple conversion: All S are $P \xrightarrow{cpa}$ Some P are $S \xrightarrow{c}$ Some S are P. Subalternation from an **E** may be effected by simple conversion followed by conversion *per accidens*: No S are $P \xrightarrow{c}$ No P are $S \xrightarrow{cpa}$ Some S are not P. But *Barbarix*, *Feraxo*[1], *Cesarox*[2], seem simpler and less *Barbarous* than the forms with "ps" or "sp".

15. For EAO figure 1, regarded as reducible to Celarent, the appropriate name would be *Celarox* instead of *Feraxo*. (It is sometimes called *Celaront*.) We have chosen the names *Feraxo* and *Cesarox* because, for symmetry of the table 20D3, one of these forms should reduce to Celarent, the other to Ferio.

However, EAO figure 2 is also reducible to Ferio; so regarded, the appropriate name would be *Fesaxon* instead of *Cesarox*. So we could use the names *Celarox* and *Fesaxon* in place of *Feraxo* and *Cesarox* respectively. Both names should be changed or neither, to keep the aforementioned symmetry.

16. *Prior Analytics* I, ch. 4, 26a. Aristotle starts actually from the premisses AE in figure 1; his aim is to show that no syllogistic conclusion follows from them.

CHAPTER 21

1. The senior author heard this rule CR1 from the late Paul Henle in the 1940s. W. C. Salmon (1963) attributes it to James T. Culbertson (1958). Rule CR1 is equivalent to CR1':

> CR1' The number of distributed predicates in the premisses equals the number of distributed predicates in the conclusion.

2. It would not be sufficient to say, in place of CR2, that every term is either distributed in a premiss or not distributed in the conclusion. For the middle term (in any non-degenerate syllogism) is not distributed in the conclusion.

Note that the "or" of rule CR2 is, as usual, not exclusive. A term may be distributed in a premiss and undistributed in the conclusion (on the Aristotelian, though not on the Boolean, interpretation).

Rules CR1' and CR2 are due to the authors.

3. The antilogistic method of testing a syllogism for validity was discovered by Mrs. Christine Ladd-Franklin in the late nineteenth century. Generally the antilogism test is used only for the Boolean forms of the syllogism and is represented in the notation of the class logic.

In this section we explain the antilogistic method by the concepts of traditional logic (i.e., distribution, quantity and quality of propositions, etc.) and modify the method so that it may serve as a test for validity for the Aristotelian forms of the syllogism.

4. Some logicians define "antilogism" as an inconsistent triad. This is not equivalent to our definition, as an inconsistent triad is quite different from the assertion that a triad is inconsistent. We favor our definition, not only because it preserves an important distinction, but because it is in keeping with the original meaning of the term.

5. This principle is asserting that a standard syllogism is valid if and only if it is logically impossible for it to have true premises and a false conclusion.

6. This rule can be proved from the two rules of quality: rules Af and Neg. It is easily shown to be equivalent to rule CR1 of §E1.

7. This rule can be proved from the two rules of distribution: rules D Mid and DX. It is seen to be equivalent to rule CR2 of section E1, if we bear in mind that a term is distributed in a standard categorical iffi it is undistributed in the contradictory of the categorical.

8. Rule AR3 is equivalent to the two derived rules of quantity DR5 and DR6 together.

CHAPTER 24

1. In this respect, our treatment resembles that of Aristotle himself. In the *Prior Analytics*, where Aristotle gives his account of the syllogism, examples with singular propositions are hardly ever found. Already in antiquity, however, his followers, the Peripatetics, made more frequent use of them. The Scholastics used them constantly, often in strange forms such as "Socrates is every man".

2. As A. N. Prior points out in *Formal Logic* (page 160), no less an authority than Peter of Spain (12.24) assigns a similar argument to Darii: "Every man is every man; but Socrates is a man; therefore Socrates is every man". Peter's purpose is to show that the odd major premises must be false, because the odd conclusion is false.

3. This kind of translation was proposed by a fourteenth-century writer known as Pseudo-Scotus. Cf. Prior, page 160.

4. The traditional rules give the same results for syllogisms if we standardize the singular negative "s is not P" as a particular negative "Some [s] are not P", while making the singular affirmative a universal as before. Before these rules were established as tests of validity the fourteenth-century scholastics began to assimilate singulars to universals on the basis of certain analogies, especially the analogy between the use (*suppositio*) of singular terms and that of distributed general terms. Thus Ockham points out that singulars can replace universals in a valid syllogism conforming to the dictum concerning all or none, because "just as the subject of a universal actually stands for each thing it denotes, so also the subject of a singular stands for each denotatum, of which it has only one" (*Summa Totius Logicae* III, 1, c. 8; cf. Bochenski, Formal Logic 34.02). Ockham's examples of singulars in this chapter include negatives as well as affirmatives. Ockham attributes "distributive confused supposition" (or the coordinate supposition, "merely confused") only to general terms; but he is preparing the way for the modern doctrine, which applies the concept of distribution also to singular terms.

5. If the reader understands (simple) indirect reduction—explained in chapter 20—and recognizes that "All [s] are P" and "No [s] are P" are contradictory, each entailing the denial of the other, as well as contraries (opposed universals), he

can reduce Camestres with unit term as minor term and Folapton with unit term as middle term to Barbara with unit term as minor term. Similarly, Cesare with unit term as minor and Darapti with unit term as middle reduce to Celarent with unit term as minor term.

6. A and O forms with singular predicate, however, are peculiar. Propositions such as "Every human is Socrates" are fairly common in medieval logic. This is equivalent to "Socrates is every human" (i.e., "Socrates is the only human"). We may write an abbreviated equivalence:

All **H** are {s} ↔ all {s} are all **H**

The form on the right is not standard, however, since its predicate is quantified. Contrary to usual rules, the simple conversion holds:

All **H** are {s} → All {s} are **H**

but not conversely. (The consequent is in fact true and the antecedent false.) All of the quoted or displayed categoricals in this note (except "Socrates is the only human") are of forms extremely rare in ordinary English.

Another odd case is that of the **O**: "Some philosopher is not Socrates". This is equivalent to "No [Socrates] is every philosopher", but not to any traditional standard form with "Socrates" as the subject.

7. "U" was introduced by Archbishop W. Thomson (*An Outline of . . . Laws of Thoughts*), Jevons, and so on, to stand, not only for concrete doubly singulars, but even more for abstract double singulars, such as "Common salt is choloride of sodium", "Rhetoric is the art of persuasive speaking"; and for nonsingulars such as "All the times when the moon comes between the earth and the sun are the sole causes of a solar eclipse". However, we are here excluding from consideration doubly quantified general terms except when they are known to be unit terms.

8. Caution: In standardizing propositions, do not omit the definite article of a definite description; it is needed as a mark of singularity.

9. Leonard says that he chooses "every" as standard sign of quantity rather than "all" "because it gives a standard structure more directly comparable with the standard form for singular statements" (*Principles*, 1957, 1967, §45.3). This is a good reason; but we wish to distinguish an Aristotelian or existential "all" from a Boolean or hypothetical "every". (Leonard's "every" is also hypothetical.) We might have used "each" as an Aristotelian form; it is not only singular, but never collective as "all" often is.

CHAPTER 26

1. See the *Prior Analytics*, 70a10, and *Rhetoric*, especially sections 1356b, 1357a, and 1395b to 1403b. The meaning of the Greek word *enthymeme* is "thought: invention, device, or stratagem". The enthymeme, to Aristotle, was a

rhetorical syllogism whose purpose was to persuade an audience to certain beliefs. The Aristotelian enthymeme was an argument based on proverbs, commonly known maxims, and well known facts. An example of such an enthyeme is "There is none of mankind that is free, for each is a slave to money or chance". The enthymeme, to Aristotel, could have a suppressed proposition (generally a premiss), but this suppressed premiss was one known and accepted by audience: such as a well-known maxim, a proverb, and so on. It should also be noted that the Aristotelian enthymeme need not have the propositions supressed.

2. "An enthymeme, we have already noted, is a syllogism which though complete in the mind is incomplete in expression. In an enthymeme a sentence is left unexpressed, since it can be easily supplied by the author.... Sometimes the supressed sentence is the major premiss; sometimes, the minor; and at times, even the conclusion". Antoine Arnauld, *The Art of Thinking: Port-Royal Logic*, translated by James Dickoff. (New York: The Bobbs-Merrill Company, 1954), 228–29.

3. For every enthymeme there is more than one proposition that, when added to it, will result in a categorical syllogism. For example, the enthymeme *All dogs are canines; therefore all cocker spaniels are canines* becomes a syllogism when any of the following propositions are added to it (as premiss): *All cocker spaniels are dogs, All dogs are cocker spaniels, No cocker spaniels are dogs, No dogs are cocker spaniels, Some cocker spaniels are dogs, Some dogs are cocker spaniels, Some cocker spaniels are not dogs*, and *Some dogs are not cocker spaniels*. Of course only the addition of the first proposition—*all cocker spaniels are dogs*—is true and makes the resulting syllogism valid. See 26B.

4. Although most contemporary logicians follow the *Port-Royal Logic* in defining the enthymeme as a syllogism with a suppressed proposition, we do not. We do not call an argument a syllogism unless it has three explicit propositions. Therefore, we define an enthymeme as an argument such that it is possible for it to become a categorical syllogism by the addition of a proposition.

CHAPTER 27

1. A 2-term argument is a chain argument containing just two propositions. Therefore, the argument contains exactly two terms, each one occuring twice, once in each proposition.

2. A Boolean n-pair argument is an n-pair argument that does not have a particular conclusion and all universal premisses. A Boolean polyad is the antilogistic polyad of a Boolean n-pair argument.

CHAPTER 28

1. The scholastics meant by "hypothetical proposition" "compound proposition".

2. We have restricted our definition of the pure hypothetical syllogism to its conventional form. There are, however, other valid forms of the pure hypothetical syllogism.

The three figures of the pure hypothetical syllogism developed by Theophrastus are:

First figure:
   If A then B If A then B
   If B then C or If B then C
   ∴ If A then C ∴ If not C then not A

Second figure:
   If A then B If A then B
   If not A then C or If not A then C
   ∴ If not B then C ∴ If not C then B

Third figure:
   If A then C If A then C
   If B then not C or If B then not C
   ∴ If A then not B ∴ If B then not A

3. The form of the pure hypothetical syllogism is similar to the standard syllogism in form AAA-1:

All S are M
All M are P
∴ All S are P

4. As used here *ponendo* means that the minor premiss affirms; *tollendo* means that the minor premiss denies; *ponens* means that the conclusion affirms; *tollens* that the conclusion denies.

5. An antilogistic test for the pure hypothetical syllogism can be devised, but the inconsistent triad resulting from its two premisses in conjunction with the denial of its conclusion, namely:

If p then g,
If g then r, and
Not (if p then r)

is not intuitively inconsistent. To see that this triad is inconsistent one must know that the propositional form "Not (if p then r)" is equivalent to "p and not r". Such knowledge belongs to the logic of propositions and is beyond the scope of traditional logic.

6. This example and examples (2) and (4) are from Keynes, *Formal Logic*, 4th ed. (New York: Macmillan, 1906), 249–50.

CHAPTER 29

1. An example of a pure disjunctive syllogism is: "Either he will receive medical treatment or he will not recover from his illness, and Either he will recover from his illness or he will be forced to go on sick leave. Therefore, either he will receive medical treatment or he will be forced to go on sick leave". It should be noted that every valid pure disjunctive syllogism may be changed into a valid pure hypothetical syllogism (and vice versa), since the disjunctive form "p or g" is equivalent to the hypothetical form "if not-p then g"; it is also equivalent to "if not-g then p".

2. Some logicians (Quine, etc.) think that the word "inclusive" is misleading and consequently prefer "nonexclusive".

3. When it is empirically or logically impossible for both disjuncts of a proposition to be true as, respectively, "Maralyn is in Saudi Arabia or Maralyn is in England" or "x is a rational number or x is an irrational number", one might suppose that it is necessary to interpret these propositions to be exclusive disjunctions. However, such a supposition would be incorrect. It is irrelevant whether such disjunctions as these are interpreted exclusively or nonexclusively, since in either case both disjuncts cannot be true. In other words, it makes no difference whether one excludes impossibilities or not. It is superfluous to exclude as a possibility that which is not a possibility, i.e., the impossible.

4. It should be noted that a negative disjunct in the major premiss is denied in the minor premiss by affirmation; see forms (8) and (9).

Maritain (*Formal Logic*, 237) gives four moods for the disjunctive syllogism based on the quality of the disjuncts in the major premiss, that is, first mood, both disjuncts affirmative, as in forms (3) to (6); second mood, first disjunct affirmative, second disjunct negative, as in form (7); third mood, first disjunct negative, second disjunct affirmative, as in form (8); fourth mood, both disjuncts negative, as in form (9). In the authors' opinion Maritain's classification of moods is made primarily on the basis of verbal distinctions and has little use.

5. For example, if the triad consist of a disjunctive form "p or g or r or s" (or "g or r or p or s") and the negation of one of its disjuncts "Not-p", then the remaining form in the triad would be the denial of the remaining disjuncts, expressed as "Not (g or r or s)".

6. This triad is inconsistent since a proposition of the form "Either p or g" is false when both of its disjuncts are false: "Not p" and "Not g".

CHAPTER 30

1. The definition up to this point is from Morris Cohen and Ernest Nagel, *An Introduction to Logic and Scientific Method* (New York: Brace and Company, 1934), 105.

2. Coffey admits, however, that "strictly speaking, where there are *three* hypotheticals and alternants, the argument should be called a *trilemma*; when there are four or more, a *tetralemma* or *polylemma*; but the name dilemma is used generically for all". *The Science of Logic* (New York, Peter Smith, 1938) Vol. 1, 367. The authors suggest that "polylemma" should be the generic name.

3. H. W. B. Joseph, *An Introduction to Logic* (Oxford, 1961) 228.

4. Irving M. Copi, *Introduction to Logic* (New York: The Macmillan Company), 228.

5. There is a precedent for this view in Frye and Levi, *Rational Belief* (New York: Harcourt, Brace & World, Inc., 1941).

6. It is possible to extend the definition of "dilemma" to allow valid forms such as: "If p then g, and if r then s. Either p or not s. Therefore either g or not r". Such forms would be a combination of *modus ponens* and *modus tollens*.

7. The two alternatives expressed in the minor premiss of a dilemmas are likened, when they lead to unpleasant consequences, to the horns of a bull.

CHAPTER 31

1. In discussing fallacies and proof we shall use the term "argument" for any sequence of one or more arguments intended to establish a single final conclusion or thesis, for example, the polysyllogism of traditional logic.

2. Our use of "thesis" is substantially the same as in Alfred Sidgwick, *Fallacies* (1884).

The distinction between "Thesis" and "Conclusion" as the first and fifth steps respectively of the five-membered syllogism of Indian logic corresponds to our distinction (except that we do not require three intermediate steps). See C. L. Hamblin, *Fallacies* (Methuen, 1972), 178–80.

Aristotle has two meanings of "thesis", neither of which coincides with ours: (i) An immediate basic truth that cannot be proved, yet ignorance of which does not completely bar any progress. It is distinguished from an axiom, a basic truth that must be known if anything is to be learned. A thesis is either a hypothesis or a definition (*Analytica Posterior* i, 72a). (ii) A position conflicting with the general opinion, either supposed by an eminent philosopher or supported by a reasoned argument. (*Topica* i, 104b.)

3. Though our terminology differs from Aristotle's, we find the basic concept for each of the criteria 2 through 5 in the "four senses" of fallacious argument in *Topica*, 162 b (Bk VIII, ch. 12). "Contentious reasoning" includes some cases of unacceptable premisses, and also invalid arguments. His second case is our Conclusion-Thesis Gap. The third suggests Illicit Metabasis. The fourth ("false premisses") is another form of unacceptable premisses.

4. The exposition in Hamblin's *Fallacies* of the inadequacy of validity as a criterion of proof led to our revising our earlier account. The inadequacy of truth as a criterion had been recognized in our earliest drafts of this chapter.

5. Sir W. Hamilton, *Lectures on Logic*, Lect. 26.

6. A false premiss as such is an empirical, not a logical or methodological, error; hence a false premiss in an argument does not necessarily make the argument fallacious, although knowledge of its falsity prevents the argument from being a proof for those who know.

7. We might add a definition such as the following:

Def. 7b. An **inductive fallacy** is a type of logical or methodological error in an argument that prevents it from establishing its thesis as sufficiently likely for the purpose at hand.

8. However, Aristotle's famous account in *De Sophisticis Elenchis* is given by him as a classification of "sophistical refutations", not of fallacies in general. His best division of fallacies in general seems to be the fourfold division in *Topica*, 162b, which we have compared to our own division in note 3 above. The dichotomy in *De Sophisticis Elenchis*, however, is elaborated into six species under the first heading and seven under the second, and thus made more concrete and memorable. See Appendix 32A1.

9. See Sec. 32D below. D. B. Terrell, in *Logic* (Holt, Rinehart & Winston, 1967), 159, says: "The expression chosen for this category, 'fallacies of grammatical analogy', is one that has come into favor fairly recently because of the influence of the late Ludwig Wittgenstein and his followers".

10. *Formal Logic*, 237.

11. E. A. Burtt, *Right Thinking, Principles and Problems of Right Thinking*, 3rd ed. (Harper, 1946), 274–279.

For explanation and distinction of classification and division, see our chapter 6.

12. We borrow the term "contextual fallacy" from Professor Neil Gallagher, formerly of SUNY at Buffalo.

APPENDIX 32A1

1. A notable exception is Joseph, who in his text *Introduction to Logic*, 587–589, clearly shows that he recognizes that the classification of fallacies in the *Sophistical Refutations* were formulated in the context of "disputation".

CHAPTER 33

1. Our account of begging the question (*petitio principii*) follows mainly that of Aristotle in *Topica*, Bk VIII, ch. 13, and *De Sophisticis Elenchis*. Aristotle says in

Topica (162b30, presumably a later interpolation) that the account there is "on the level of general opinion", and that "the true account" is given in the Analytics. In *Analytics Prior* 64b36, he says that "whenever a man tries to prove what is not self-evident by means of itself, then he begs the original question." Though the realm of the self-evident is quite restricted for Aristotle, as for most contemporary epistemologists, this later definition unduly restricts the area where begging the question is possible. Most logicians have followed the lead of the *Topica* and *De Sophisticis Elenchis* rather than of the *Analytics Prior* on begging the question.

2. We find much wisdom in the observation of Richard Whately regarding begging the question:

> ... In all correct Reasoning the Premises must, virtually, imply the Conclusion; so that it is not possible to mark precisely the distinction between the Fallacy in question and fair Argument; since that may be correct and fair reasoning to one person, which would be to another, "begging the question"; inasmuch as to one, the Conclusion might be more evident than the Premiss, and to the other, the reverse.
> —*Elements of Logic*, London 1826, 154

Richard Robinson, "Begging the question, 1971", *Analysis*, Mar. 1971, can make little sense of this phrase, because he recognizes only truth and validity as criteria of an argument.

3. *Origin of Species*, 6th ed., ch. 2, section on "Individual Differences".

4. *The Book of Fallacies: From Unfinished Papers of Jeremy Bentham*. By a Friend [Peregrine Bingham]. (London: John and H. L. Hunt, 1824.) See Part 4, ch. 1, *Question-begging Appellatives*. Also *Bentham's Handbook of Political Fallacies*, Revised, edited etc. by Harold A. Larrabee (Johns Hopkins Press, 1952; Harper & Brothers, 1962). For the expression "question-begging appellatives" of Bentham or his English editor, Larrabee puts "question-begging epithets" or sometimes "question-begging names". The only synonym for "appellatives" we find in the 1824 edition is "terms", so we adopt this as the best substitute.

5. *Compact Edition of the Oxford English Dictionary*, (Oxford University Press, 1971), "Tory", A., 1 and 3. This work does not mention the loose use of "socialist".

6. A. Schopenhauer, "The Art of Controversy", Stratagem 12.

7. H. W. B. Joseph, *Introduction to Logic*, 597. Aristotle's examples of "Many questions" are such compound questions.

8. Barker, *Elements of Logic*, (1965), 177–178.

9. It is misleading to call these fallacies, as is often done, fallacies of "irrelevant conclusion", since the conclusion proved may be logically insufficient to establish the conclusion without being irrelevant to it. For example, if the thesis *All Germans are beer drinkers* is claimed to be proven when all that has been estab-

lished is that *Most Germans are beer drinkers*, a fallacy occurs. The conclusion proved is logically insufficient to establish the thesis, but not irrelevant to the thesis, since it addresses itself to the subject at issue and tends to make the thesis more credible. Of course, it is possible for a proved conclusion to be quite irrelevant to the thesis, and we distinguish this as one of three kinds of insufficient conclusion.

We use the term "irrelevant conclusion" only for the case where the conclusion is quite irrelevant to the thesis. "Insufficient conclusion" seems apt; and we have not abandoned this term completely. We find that many students misinterpret it, however; and we prefer our new formula, "Conclusion-Thesis Gap".

10. We find in Aristotle the concepts of metabasis and illicit metabasis, especially what we call "metabasis of domain". The Greek word *metábasis* appears in commentaries on Aristotle's *Posterior Analytics* i, ch. 7: see W. D. Ross, *Aristotle's Prior and Posterior Analytics*, Text, . . . Commentary (Oxford, 1965), 55, 62, 63.

> The first corollary Aristotle deduces from the account just given of the nature of the premisses of scientific reasoning is that there must be no *metábasis ex állou génous*, no proving of propositions in one science by premisses drawn from another science.

The concept but not the term appears in *Topica* 162b (Bk VIII, ch. 12). The third sense of fallacious argument is "(3) when it comes to the proposed conclusion but not according to the mode of inquiry appropriate to the case, as happens when a non-medical argument is taken to be a medical one, or one which is not geometrical for a geometrical argument, or one which is not dialectical for dialectical, . . ."

The view that the argument *ad hominem* is fallacious only insofar as it is an illicit metabasis we find clearly expressed in Whately as well as in the passage from Schopenhauer quoted in 3301. We do not find the term "metabasis" in them or other modern logicians.

11. Locke, *Essay Concerning Human Understanding*, Bk IV, ch. 17.

12. "The Art of Controversy".

APPENDIX 33A1

1. Unless the original assertion was unwarranted, there is no mistake or fallacy here. It would not ordinarily be considered an inference at all, but a repetition, hence not a fallacious inference. Symbolic logicians often formalize this as "*p* therefore *p*". This is as much an inference as any immediate inference. If we take distinct assertions of the same patterns of words or symbols to be distinct statements, we say that one statement is inferred from another just in case the former is asserted on the grounds that the latter has been asserted.

2. If one said "Opium is soporific because it induces sleep" this would be question-begging as an explanation of the properties of opium, but not as an explanation of the meaning of "soporific". For the latter purpose the meaning would be

expressed more exactly thus: "To say that opium is *soporific* means that opium induces sleep".

3. An example of an argument in a circle in the case of begging a superaltern is the attempt to prove that in some cases mercury is a liquid at room temperature from the premiss that in all cases mercury is a liquid at room temperature and then to prove that in all cases mercury is an element at room temperature, because in certain known cases mercury is a liquid at room temperature. This last argument is an induction and is reasonable since mercury is an element and is assumed to have certain fixed properties.

4. There is a distinction between asserting a necessary proposition, for example, "All brothers are males", and asserting the necessity of a proposition, for example, "All brothers are by definition males", or "All brothers are necessarily males". The latter may be called "apodictic". Apodictic propositions need not be true, for example, "A brother is necessarily a friend". This is a false statement. A true apodictic statement may be a necessary statement, for example, "A brother is necessarily a male sibling". This is a true statement. In this fallacy the premiss begged may not be necessary, though necessity is asserted explicitly or implicitly of the premiss.

CHAPTER 34

1. Bentham divides Vituperative Personalities into: (1) imputation of bad design, (2) imputation of bad character, (3) imputation of bad motive, (4) imputation of inconsistency, (5) imputation of suspicious connections, and (6) imputation founded on identity of denomination (i.e., name). Jeremy Bentham, *The Book of Fallacies* (London, 1824) Part 2, 127f. Revised and edited by Harold A. Larabee as *Bentham's Handbook of Political Fallacies* (Baltimore: Johns Hopkins Press, 1952), 83. These imputations are said to be listed in an order such that the conclusion is weaker at each step than in the preceding one. Besides changing "imputation" to "charge", we have generalized "bad character" to "personal defect", added to the list a special case of "personal defect" called "similar defect" or "*tu quoque*" (the latter name is already in the literature), and replaced the clumsy "imputation founded on identity of denomination" by the more up-to-date label "stereotyped charges", which seems to cover the same ground. We have also reordered them according to our estimate of the decreasing likelihood that the charge has merit, but keeping together each pair of similar names (namely, "bad design" with "bad motive", and "personal defect" with "similar defect").

2. The term "*argumentum ad verecundiam*" was introduced in Locke's *Essay Concerning Human Understanding*. "*Verecundia*" does not mean "authority", but "modesty", sometimes "respect" or "reverence". Locke sets forth

> *Four sorts of arguments*, that men, in their reasonings with others, do ordinarily make use of to prevail on their assent; or at least so to awe them as to silence their opposition.

1. The first is, to allege the opinions of men, whose parts, learning, eminency, power, or some other cause has gained a name, and settled their reputation in the common esteem with some kind of authority. When men are established in any kind of dignity, it is thought a breach of modesty for others to derogate any way from it, and question the authority of men who are in possession of it. Whoever backs his tenets with such authorities, thinks he ought thereby to carry the cause, and is ready to style it impudence in any one who shall stand out against them. This I think may be called *argumentum ad verecundiam*.

It argues not another man's opinion to be right, because I, out of respect, or any other consideration but that of conviction, will not contradict him. . . . I may be modest, and therefore not oppose another man's persuasion: . . .

John Locke, *Essay Concerning Human Understanding*, Bk IV, chap. 17, §§19, 22; Fraser's ed. (Oxford University Press; New York: Dover Publications, 1959).

Locke's *argumentum ad verecundiam*, then, is an appeal to modesty in the face of recognized authority, or an appeal to respect for established authority. It clearly covers certain types of illicit appeals to authority in our account, for example, transferred authority, and confusing institutional with expert authority, also typical cases of biased opinion. It does not cover some others, for example, mistaking a nonexpert for an expert nor empty authority.

3. Besides institutional authority (legal or customary power) and expert authority (specialized knowledge or skill), there are people and organizations whose "authority" (i.e. influence) is derived from wealth or popular fame. Such "authorities" as such have no claim to expert knowledge.

4. We may call an unnecessary appeal to authority the **appeal to superfluous authority**. A special case of this error is the converse fallacy of transferred authority, explained in note 8.

5. It is important to note that by "expert opinion" is meant the opinion of an expert in his area of competence. The terms "expert opinion" and "opinion of an expert" (or "expert's opinion") are not equivalent. An instance of the former is always an instance of the latter, but not conversely.

6. The first three criteria are based on those given by Bentham, *The Book of Fallacies*, Part I. We have combined Bentham's first criterion ("the degree of relative and adequate *intelligence*"—"intelligence" in the sense in which we use it in "military intelligence") with his third criterion ("the nearness or remoteness of the relation between the immediate subject of such his opinion and the question in hand"—i.e., the relevance of the opinion) in our first criterion. Our second and third criteria correspond to Bentham's second ("the degree of relative *probity*") and fourth ("the fidelity of the medium" of transmission "[including correctness and completeness]") respectively. Our fourth criterion does not appear in Bentham's list, though he recognizes the importance of such a factor as recency in his discussion of "the wisdom of our ancestors".

7. The authors are indebted to the lectures of Dr. Marvin Farber for most of the special terminology of 34B4, except that which comes or is adapted from Bentham. Some of Dr. Farber's terms are: *fallacy of transferred authority* (and its converse fallacy), *empty authority, repudiated authority, absolute authority*, and *paradox of absolute authority*. The authors have also borrowed heavily from Dr. Farber in their manner of explaining the above terms, but he is of course not responsible for defects in our exposition.

8. The **converse fallacy of transferred authority** occurs when the arguments and evidence a person produces for his opinion are dismissed without consideration, because the person is not an expert in the area of his argument.

An example of the converse fallacy of transferred authority would be an astronomer's refusal to check the celestial coordinates of a garage mechanic to verify his alleged discovery of a new comet, on the grounds that the mechanic is not a professional astronomer.

9. Locke, *Essay Concerning Human Understanding*, Bk IV, chap. 17, sections 20, 22, Fraser edition.

10. John Bouvier, *A New Law Dictionary*, 15th ed., (Philadelphia: J. B. Lippincott Co. 1887), vol. 1, article "Doubt".

11. A famous attack on the appeal to pity in court is attributed to Socrates in Plato's *Apology*.

12. A. Wolf, *Textbook of Logic*, 2nd ed. (London: George Allen & Unwinn Ltd, 1938), p. 364.

13. *In Improving Your Reasoning* (Englewood Cliffs, N.J.: Prentice-Hall, 1970), section 4.1, Alex C. Michalos extends the expressions "appeal to force" and *argumentum ad baculum* still further; e.g., to the argument: "If it's your move I'll quit. [Therefore,] It's my move." The term "force" doesn't seem apt here, and *ad baculum* is even less appropriate. If a name is wanted that covers this and typical appeals to force, we might use *argument by ultimatum*, or, when it is not really an argument *'argument' by ultimatum* (with single quotes as scare-quotes).

CHAPTER 36

1. The information in this chapter is from Bochenski and Kneal and Kneal. For a very readable twenty-six-page chapter on the history of logic the reader should consult Bates.

2. Bochenski, *A History of Formal Logic*, tran. I. Thomas (Notre Dame, Indiana), 98.

3. Undoubtedly some of the ancients respected the logical ability of Chrysippus more than that of Aristotle. Since the works of Chrysippus have not survived, a comparison is not possible.

4. Bochenski, 115.

5. Kneal and Kneal, 128 "Even the very crows on the roofs caw about the nature of conditionals". Stated by Callimachus. Source is *Sextus Empiricus*, Adv. Math. i. 309.

6. Bochenski, 145.

7. Bochenski, 145.

8. Kneal and Kneal, *The Development of Logic* (Oxford University Press, 1962), 291.

9. Bochenski, 268.

10. Bochenski, 268.

Index

Abelard, Peter, 493–94
Ad hominem,
  as kind of audience argument is addressed to, 414
  fallacy of, 452, 480
  history of, 481
Ad omnes, as kind of audience argument is addressed to, 452
Ad populum,
  as kind of audience argument is addressed to, 414
Ad rem, 414
Ad seipsum, 414
Ad verecundiam, 532–33n.2
Ad veritatem, 414
Ajdukiewicz, K., 506n.9
Albert of Saxony, 498n.5
Alexander of Aphrodisias, 493
Alternation, 27
Altern, 158
Alterns, 157
Antecedent, 26, 373–74
Antilogism for N-pair arguments, chapter 27, 367–71
  rules for the, 369
Antilogistic polyad, 368
  extreme propositions in an, 368
Argument(s),
  2-term, 310, 367, 525n.1
  chain. *See* Chain arguments
  deductive, 11
  definition, 4
  domain, 414–15

  distinguished from causal explanation, 8–9
  form of. *See* Argument form
  inductive, 10–13
  intelligible, 411, 417, 423–25
  invalid, 10–13
  n-pair, 23–4, 367–68
  pseudo-argument, 423–24
  unintelligible argument, 424–25
  unsound, 410
  valid, 10
Argument form, 41
  invalid, 43–44
  pure, 42
  valid, 43–44
Aristotelian antilogism, 297–99
Aristotle, 3, 271nn.2–9, 415, 416, 456, 491, 500n.5, 504n.1, 505nn.3, 7, 506n.8, 510nn.44, 45, 512n.1, 517n.1, 518n.1, 518nn.2, 5, 522n.16, 523n.1, 524n.1, 528nn.2, 3, 529n.8, 529–30n.1, 531n.10
Aristotle's classification of fallacies, Appendix to 32A1
Aristotle's deductive system of the standard syllogism. *See* Deductive system of the standard syllogism
Aristotle's six logical treatises, 491
Austin, J. L., 507n.16

Barker, S. F., 498nn.3, 4. 509n.30, 530n.8
Bentham, Jeremy, 530n.4, 532n.1, 532n.6, 533n.6

Bird, O., 521n.11
Black, M., 481, 507n.17
Boethius, 493
Boole, George, 495
Boolean polyad, 525n.2
Bridgman, P. W., 510n.41
Burdian, 498n.5
Burtt, E. A., 416, 529n.11

Carafides, J. L., 501–2n.10
Carroll, Lewis, 507n.18
Chain argument, chapter 22, 309–12
  antilogistic test of a, 311–12
  definition of, 309, 367
  determining the validity of a, 310–12
    rules of distribution, 310
    rules of quality, 310
  extreme term, 309
  major term, 309
  middle term, 309
  minor term, 309
Chrysippus, 492–93
Classification. *See* Division and classification
  artificial, 137–38
  division and, 136–37
  natural, 137–38
  rules of, 138–39
Cohen and Nagel, 504n.27, 527n.1
Coffey, P., 512n.9, 528n.2
Complementary classes, 221
Complementary terms, 220
Conclusion,
  definition of, 6
  identifying, 7–8
Conclusion-thesis gap, 413, 416, 417, 528n.3
Connective, 25
Conditional proposition(s), 25–26, 373
  distinction between hypothetical and general conditionals, 379–380
Consequent, 26, 374
Contradiction, 157
Contradictories, 157
Contradictory terms, 216
  complementary and, 220–21
Contraposition, chapter 14, 233–36
  by limitation, 233
  definition of, 233

Contrapositive, definition of, 233
  valid and invalid, 234
Contrary terms, 216
Contrariety, 157
Contraries, 157
Consequent, 26
Converse, definition of, 205
Converse relation. *See* Relation
Conversion, chapter 11, 205–08
  by limitation, 206
  definition of, 205
  per accidens, 206
  relational, 251–52
  simple, 205
  valid, 206–08
    rule for, 207
    strongest, 207–08
Convertend, definition of, 205
Co-ordinate class, 131
Copi, I. M., 415, 497n.1, 499n.4, 504n.24, 504–5n.2, 508n.20, 508n.24, 528n.4
Correlative expressions, 251
  eliminating correlative expressions in arguments, 324–26
Counterexamples, 44–46
Culbertson, James T., 522n.1

Deductive system of the standard syllogism, chapter 20, 271–289
  Aristotle's deductive system, 271–73
  direct reduction, 274–77
    equivalent direct reduction, 274–76
    non–equivalent direct reduction, 276–77
  indirect reduction, 277–81
    compound, 281
    principle of, 278
    purpose of, 279
    simple, 277–79
  indirect reduction by indirect proof, 278–79
Definiendum, 80–81
  definiendum-term, 84
  simple, 505n.6
Definiens, 81–82
Defining term, 84
Definition, chapter 5, 79–118
  Aristotle's definition of, 80
  Aristotle's method of, 86
  broad and narrow senses of, 87–88

definition of, 89
definition process, 89
definition statement, 89
equivalential, 88
functional types of, 89ff
  conceptual definition, 98–100
  conventional definition, 91
  facetious definition, 97
  lexical definition, 90–91
  persuasive definition, 96–97
  precising definition, 93–94
  real definition, 97–102
  stipulative definition, 91–92
nominal, 83
rules of definition, 61–62
techniques of extensional definition, 113–16
  citational definition, 114
  definition by paradigm example, 114–15
  extensional definition, 113
  limitations of extensional definition, 115–16
  ostensive definition, 114
techniques of intensional definition, 102–13
  contextual definition, 110
  definition by genus and difference, 103–5
  definition by paradigm species, 106
  definition by species, 105
  intensional definition, 102–3
  operational definition, 106–9
  equational definition, 109–10
  synonymous definition, 111–13
techniques of verbal definition, 116–17
  definition of verbal definition, 116
ways of defining, 102–17
Denotation. *See* Term
Diodorus Cronus, 492
Dilemma, chapter 30, 395–404
  definition of, 395
  methods of refuting, 401–04
    attacking the truth of the major premiss (Grappling with the horns), 402
    attacking the truth of the minor premiss (Escaping between the horns), 402–03
    challenging formal validity, 401–02
    rebutting dilemma by counter dilemma, 403–04

  new definition of, 400–01
  new treatement of, 400–401
  traditional forms of, 396–98
    constructive, 396–97
    definition of, 395
    destructive, 397–98
    enthymematic form, 400
    variant forms of, 398–99
Direct reduction. *See* Deductive system of the standard syllogism
Disjunctive syllogism, chapter 29, 383–91
  definition, 385–389
  exclusive "or", 385, 389
  figures of the, 386
  forms of the, 387–88
    modus tollendo ponens, 387
    modus ponendo tollens, 387
    modus tollendo tollens, 387
    modus ponendo ponens, 387
  inconsistent triad of the, 390–91
  invalid forms of the, 388–89
    modus ponendo tollens, 387
Disjuncts, 383–84
Distinctive form, 41–42
Distribution of terms in categorical propositions, chapter 10, 189–195
  definition of distributed term, 190, 193
  definition of undistributed term, 190, 193
  historical introduction to, Appendix to 10A, 196–98
Division and Classification, chapter 6, 129–139. *See* Classification
  cross, 134
  dichotomous, 135–36
  physical, 130
  logical, 129–130
  metaphysical, 130
  rules of, 131–135

Eaton, Ralph M., 502n.14, 416
Enthymeme, chapter 26, 359–63
  criteria and procedure for adding a proposition to, 360–63
  definition of, 359
  first order, 359–60
  non-traditional, 363
    disjunctive syllogism as, 363
  second order, 360
  third order, 360

Escaping between the horns. *See* under Dilemma
Eubulides, 492
Euler diagrams, 150
Exclusive disjunction, 385, 389
Existential import. *See* Existential presuppositions
  problem of, 180-81
Existential interpretations,
  absolute, 184-85
  relative, 184-85
Existential presuppositions, chapter 9, 179-185
  2-pair existential presupposition (2-PEP), 181
  standard propositions, 184
Extension. *See* Term

Fallacy (fallacies), chapters 31-33. *See also* Illicit Appeals
  accident and *secundum quid* (history of), Appendix to 32C5, 438
  classification of, 415-18
  contextual fallacies, chapter 33, 443-54
  contextual fallacy, definition of, 418, 443
    conclusion-thesis gap, 413, 417, 528n.3, 444, 450-51
    illicit-metabasis, 417, 444, 450-54
      audience,
        to everyone, (*ad omnes*), 414, 444, 452-53
        to the man, (*ad hominem*), 414, 444, 451-53, 481
        to oneself (*ad seipsum*), 414, 444, 451-52
        to the people, (*ad populum*), 414, 444, 451, 453
      argument's domain, 444
        illicit generalization of, 454
        illciit transfer of, 454
    unacceptable premiss, 444
      begging the question, 444-48
        argument in a circle, 445
        question begging criterion, 445
        question begging questions, 448
        special cases of
          question begging questions, 448
          question begging terms, 447-48
        ways of begging the question, Appendix 33A1, 455-57
          begging an equivalent premiss, 455-56
            begging an equivalent by conversion, 455-56
            begging piecemeal, 455-56
              by same words, 455
              by use of a synonymous expression, 455
          begging a non-equivalent premiss, 455-57
            begging a superaltern, 456-57
            begging an *a priori* truth, 455, 457
            begging universal to prove an instance, 455-56
            begging a subaltern, 455, 457
            begging an independent premiss, 455, 457
      unsupported premiss, 444, 448-50
        premiss believed false, 444, 449
        premiss without evidence, 449
        premiss insufficiently supported, 449-50
  definition of fallacy, 415
  inductive fallacy, 529n.7
  logical fallacy (fallacy of validity), 417-18
    formal, 418
    linguistic (fallacies), chapter 32, 423-34
      definition of, 418, 423
      fallacies of ambiguity, 424, 425-33
        amphiboly, 424, 426, 427-28
        composition, 424, 428-29
        division, 424, 429-30
        equivocation, 424-26
        qualification (*secudum quid*), 424
          eliminating, 432-33
          introducing, 431-32
        stress (or accent), 424, 430-31
      grammatical analogy (form of expression), 423-24, 433-34
        no intelligible argument, 424
        pseudo-argument, 424-25
        unintelligible argument, 424-25
Farber, Marvin, 534n.7
Frege, G., 495-96
Frye and Levi, 528n.5

Gallagher, Neal, 529n.12

Index 541

Geech, P. T., 514n.2, 516n.1
Godel, Kurt, 496
Grammatical analogy, 424, 433–34
Grappling with the horns. *See* under Dilemma
Gregonne diagrams, 150, 512nn.1–3

Hamblin, C. L., 480, 528n.2, 529n.4
Hamilton, Sir William, 509n.38, 529n.5
Henle, Paul, 422n.1
History of logic, chapter 35, 491–496
Hospers, J., 503n.23
Huxley, A., 508n.25
Hypothetical syllogism, chapter 28, 373–80
  antecedent, 373–74
  consequent, 374
  pure, definition of, 374–75
  mixed, 375–78
    antilogistic test for validity, 378–79
    definition of, 375–76
    figures of, 376
    forms of, 376–77
    inconsistent triad of the, 378–79
    invalid forms of, 377–78
    modus ponendo ponens, 376
  pure, 374–75

Identity statements, Appendix 10C
Ignoratio elechi, 416, 450
Illicit appeals, chapter 34, 463–480
  appeal to adverse personalities, 464–467
    charge of bad design, 464–66
    charge of bad motive, 464, 466
    charge of inconsistency, 464–65
    charge of personal defect, 464, 466
    charge of similar defect (*tu quoque*), 464, 466–67
    charge of suspicious connections, 464, 467
    stereotyped charges, 464, 467
  appeal to authority, 464, 467–76
  argument from ignorance (argument *ad ignorantiam*), 464, 477–79
  appeal to force (argument *ad baculum*), 464, 479–80
  appeal to pity (argument *ad misericordiam*), 464, 479

  expert authority and institutional authority, 467–69
  illicit appeal to expert authority, 471–476
    appeal to irrelevant knowledge
      irrelevant opinion, 472
      pseudo-expert authority, 472
        appeal to absolute authority, 473
        paradox of absolute authority, 472
      confusing institutional authority with expert authority, 472
      mistaking a non-expert for an expert, 472
    appeal to biased opinion, 473
    defective transmission, 473–74
      misquotation, 473
      out of context, 473–74
        empty authority, 474
        overestimated authority, 474–76
        disputed authority, 475–76
        unconfirmed authority, 475
        unreliable authority, 474–75
      quotation out of context, 471, 473–74
      source not indicated, 474
    transferred authority, 472
      converse fallacy of transferred authority, 534n.8
  presuppositions of legitimate appeal to authority, 469
Immediate inference, 155
  table of, chapter 16, 245–248
Inclusive disjunction, 384–85
Indirect reduction. *See* Deductive system of the standard syllogism
Inference(s), (Reversible and non-reversible inferences, chapter 18), 261–62
  definition of, 6
  non-reversible, 262
  reversible, 261
Infimae species, 131
Intension. *See* under Term
Inverse, 239
Inversion, chapter 15, 239–44
  by limitation, 239
  definition of, 239
  partial, 241–42
    by limitation, 241
    simple, 241
    the partial inverse, 242

Jevons, W. S., 495
Johnson, W. E., 498n.3, 501n.7
Jones, E. E. C., 513n.2
Joseph, H. W. B., 501n.7, 505n.3, 505–06n.7, 509n.36 511n.5, 528n.3, 529n.1, 530n.7

Keynes, J. N., 502n.13, 503n.22, 503n.23, 504n.27, 511nn.1, 6, 513n.5, 517n.1, 518nn.1, 2, 526n.6
Klein, A., 501–02n.10
Krug, W. T., 5092n.38

L'Art de Penser, 505–06n.7
Ladd-Franklin, Christine, 522n.3
Leibniz, G., 478, 495
Leonard, Henry S., 502n.13, 504n.24, 504n.2, 508n.28, 524n.9
Lewis, C. I., 503n.17, 508n.28
Locke, John, 477, 481, 531n.11, 532–33n.2, 534n.9
Logic
  definition, 4
  deductive, 10–13
Logical form (and counterexamples), chapter 3, 37–44
  instance (example), 40–41
    degenerate, 45
Lukasiewicz, J., 520n.2, 521n.9

MacKaye, J., 507n.17, 508n.22
Manne, Albert, 513n.11
Martin, R. M., 503n.20
Maritian, J., 502n.15, 5; 70n.30, 527n.4
Mates, B., 497n.1
Megarians, 492–93
Mill, J. S., 500n.5, 506n.9, 507n.15, 512n.11
Modalities
  of assertion, Appendix 2B, 30–31
  Aristotelian modality, 27–29
    adjectives, 28
      improper modal, 29
      improper modal nouns, 29
Montague, R., 503n.20
Morgan, Augustus de, 495

Negative prefixes, 221

Negative term(s), chapter 12, 215–223
  explicit, 215
  privative, 216
N-pair argument, 322, 367–68
Not and Non, difference, 220

Objects, 60–61
  actual, 61
  non-actual, 51
  possible, 60–61
  real, 60–61
Obvertend, definition of, 227
Obverse, definition of, 227
Obversion, chapter 13, 227–29
  definition of, 227
  valid, 227
    rule for, 227
Ockham. *See* William of Ockham

Pap, A., 510n.42
Peirce, C. S., 497n.2, 500n.4, 495
Peter of Spain, 521n.12
Plato, 534n.11
Porphyry of Tyre, 493
Port-Royal Logic, 503n.21, 505–06n.7, 525nn.2,4
Positive term
  explicit, 215
Process-product ambiguity, 88–89
Prior, A. N., 521n.9, 523nn.2,3
Proponent, 410, 413
Proof (and Fallacies), chapter 31, 409–418
  categorical, 410
  criteria of, 411–14
    conclusion-thesis gap, 413, 416, 417, 444, 450–51
    constant frame of reference, 413, 417
    intelligible argument, 411, 417, 423–25
    premisses (un)acceptable, 412, 417, 444–50
    validity recognizable, 412, 417
  definition, 410
  hypothetical, 411
    merely hypothetical proof, 411
  intended, 410
  pseudo-proof, 410
Proposition(s), chapter 2, 23–29
  apodictic, 30, 523n.4
  assertoric, 30

biconditional, 26
categorical, 24
  standard, 145, chapter 7, 145–151
    code-letter notation, 147
    copula, 146
    diagrams of, 149–51
    existential presuppositions of, 148–49, chapter 9
    opposed, 155
    opposition of. *See* Square of opposition
    predicate-term, 147
    quantifiers of, 145–46
    quantity and quality of, 147–48
    standardizing. *See* Standardizing categorical propositions
    subject-term, 146
    2-PEP, 181, 184
compound, 25
  explicit, 498–99n.4
  conjunctive (conjunction), 27
contingent, 28–29
definition, 4
disjunctive (disjunction), 27, 383
  exclusive, 385
  exhaustiveness of, Appendix to 29A4, 392
  inclusive, 384–85
empirical, 28–29
existential, 180
extreme, 368
form of, 41
hypothetical. *See* Conditional proposition.
hypothetical, scholastics' definition of, 525n.1
identifying, 4–5
illiative, 499n.6
impossible, 28
modal, 20
necessary, 28
possible, 28
primary, 24
problematic, 30
secondary, 25
simple, 6
singular. *See* Singular propositions
synthetic, 28–29

Quine, 498n.4, 527n.2

Rand, Ayn, 508n.26
Reducing the number of terms in arguments, chapter 23, 319–326
  eliminating correlative expressions in arguments, 324–26
  eliminating equivalent terms in arguments, 320–21
  eliminating pairs of contradictory terms in arguments, 321–24
  reducing the number of term in nonstandard sorites, 324
Relational conversion, definition of, 251
  with adjectives; 252–53
  with nouns, 253
  with prepositions, 253–54
  with verbs, 252
Relations, chapter 17, 249–56
  converse, 252–54, 325
  definition of, 249
  degree of a, 250
  properties of, 254–56
    reflexiveness, 256
    symmetry, 255–56
    transitivity, 254–55
Replacement rules, 42
Robinson, Daniel S., 509n.38
Robinson, Richard, 504n.2, 506n.8, 507n.17, 509n.31, 509n.33, 530n.2
Rose, L., 511n.2, 520nn.4, 5, 7, 521n.9
Ross, W. D., 531n.10
Russell, B., 505n.4, 505n.5, 496

Salmon, W. C., 522n.1
Schopenhauer, A., 452, 530n.6, 531n.10, 481
Schroder, E., 495
Scotus, Don, 516n.7
Sesmat, Augustin, 509n.38
Sigwick, Alfred, 528n.2
Sinclair, W. A., 519n.2
Singular propositions, chapter 24, 329–35
  negative, 332
  standardizing, 330–34
Sorites, standard sorites, 309–10
Square of opposition, chapter 8, 155–169
  a priori categoricals, 168–69
  inference rules, 159–66
  scholastic vs. modern doctrine of, Appendix 8E, 170–73

Standard (categorical) syllogism, chapter 19, 265–68
   antilogism. *See* Aristotelian antilogism
   counter-examples to syllogistic forms, 287–89
   definition of, 265
   deductive system of the. *See* Deductive system of the standard syllogism
   extreme terms of a, 265
   figures of a, 267–68
     number grid, 519n.2
   formal fallacies of the, 292–93
     affirmative from negative, 292
     illicit process, 293
     inequality of negatives, 292–93
     undistributed middle, 293
   major premiss of a, 266
   major term of a, 265
   middle term of a, 265
   minor premiss of a, 266
   minor term of a, 265
   moods of a, 267
   rules of the, chapter 21, 291–300
     rules of distribution, 291–92, 293
     rules of quality, 291, 292–93
     alternative set of, 295–96
     concise, 296
     derived, 294–95
     formal, 291–92
   standard order of a, 266
   syllogistic form of a, 268
   testing validity of the, 293–94
   24 valid syllogistic forms of a, 282–87
Standardizing categorical propositions, chapter 25, 339–52
   no quantifiers and non-standard quantifiers, 340–48
     adjectival quantifiers, 344–45
     adverbal quantifiers, 345
     articles as quantifiers, 340–41
     exceptive quantifiers, 342–43
     exclusive quantifiers, 342
     indefinite quantifiers, 346–48
     negated quantifiers, 343–44
     no quantifier, 340
     numerical quantifiers, 346
     simple synonyms for standard quantifiers, 340
     standardizing non-standard arguments, 351–52
     non-standard order, 349–50
     non-standard verbs, 349
     parameters, 350–51
     predicate adjectives, 348–49
   standardizing, definition of, 339
Stebbing, L. S., 506n.11, 507n.14
Stoics, 493
Strawson, P. F., 514nn.3, 7
Strong disjunction. *See* Exclusive disjunction
Subalternant, 513n.8
Subaltern genera, 131
Subclass, 58
   proper, 59
Subcontrariety, 158
Subcontraries, 157
Subordinate class, 131
Substantive, 51
Subterm, 58, 192
   Subterm substitution, 192–95
Summun genus, 131
Superaltern, 158
Superalternant, 513n.7
Superalternation, 158
Superordinate class, 131
Superterm, 58, 515–16n.7
Syllogism. *See* Standard syllogism

Term(s). *See* chapter 4, 51–67
   abstract, 59
   collective, 56
   complementary, 220
   complex, 218–19
   concrete, 59
   connotation, 63
   denotation, 64–65
   discrete, 55–56
     singular, 55–56
     plural, 56
   distributed and undistributed, 190–91
   distribution of terms, chapter 10, 189–195
   distinct, 52
   empty, 65
   equivalent, 52
     reducing the number of, 320–21
   extension, 64
     real. *See* Denotation
   general, 53–54
   homograph, 52
   inconsistent, 216

intension, 62
  analytic, 63
  conventional, 62–63
  subjective intension, 63
  negating a, 217
  negative. *See* Negative term(s)
  nominatum, 64
  of subject-predicate proposition, 39
  positive. *See* Positive term
  singular, 54–55, 329
    as predicates, 332–34
    definition of, 55
  subterm. *See* Subterm
  superterm. *See* Superterm
  total objective intension, 63
  unit, 331
  verbal meaning, 66–67
Term expression, 51
Terrell, D. B., 529n.9
Theophrastus, 491–92, 526n.2
Thesis, 409–10, 528n.2
Thomson, Archbishop W., 524n.7

Toohey, J. J., 513n.2, 514n.2
Truth-value, 14

Unit term. *See* under Term
Universe of discourse, 179, 219–20

Validity, 10–15, 37–39,
  of argument forms, 43–44
  formal, 43–44
  semantic, 39
Veatch, H. B., 508n.26
Venn, J., 495

Watts, 497n.2
Welton, J., 513n.2
Whately, Bishop, 497n.2, 530n.2, 531n.10
William of Ockham, 494, 516n.6, 523n.4
William of Sherwood, 521n.12
Whitehead, A. N., 496, 505n.4, 505n.5
Wolf, A., 509n.38
Word-thing distinction, 89

www.ingramcontent.com/pod-product-compliance
Lightning Source LLC
Chambersburg PA
CBHW030102010526
44116CB00005B/61